Revealing Masks

CALIFORNIA STUDIES IN 20TH-CENTURY MUSIC

Richard Taruskin, General Editor

1. *Revealing Masks: Exotic Influences and Ritualized Performance in Modernist Music Theater,* by W. Anthony Sheppard

Revealing Masks

Exotic Influences and Ritualized Performance in Modernist Music Theater

W. ANTHONY SHEPPARD

University of California Press

BERKELEY   LOS ANGELES   LONDON

University of California Press
Berkeley and Los Angeles, California

University of California Press, Ltd.
London, England

© 2001 by the Regents of the University of California

Library of Congress Cataloging-in-Publication Data

Sheppard, William Anthony.
    Revealing masks : exotic influences and ritualized performance
in modernist music theater / W. Anthony Sheppard.
        p. cm.—(California studies in 20th century music ; 1)
    Includes bibliographical references and index.
    ISBN 0-520-22302-0 (cloth : alk . paper)
    1. Music—20th century—History and criticism.   2. Music in
theater.   3. Music theater—History and criticism.   4. Music—
Performance.   I. Title.   II. Series.

ML197 .S552   2001
782.1—dc21   00-034350

Manufactured in the United States of America

09   08   07   06   05   04   03   02   01

10   9   8   7   6   5   4   3   2   1

The paper used in this publication meets the minimum requirements
of ANSI / NISO Z39 0.48-1984 (R 1997) (Permanence of Paper).♾

To Lara

Contents

Illustrations

Preface

Still, you may ask me, if its results are to be the ground of our
final spiritual estimate of a religious phenomenon, why threaten
us at all with so much existential study of its conditions? Why
not simply leave pathological questions out?

   To this I reply in two ways: First, I say, irrepressible curiosity
imperiously leads one on; and I say, secondly, that it always leads
to a better understanding of a thing's significance to consider its
exaggerations and perversions, its equivalents and substitutes
and nearest relatives elsewhere.

   William James, *The Varieties of Religious Experience* (1901–2)

This book offers an interpretive survey of a neglected genre or phenomenon in the history of Euro-American modernist music and theater. I start
with the premise that eccentric works can often reveal elements central to
our understanding of a given period. In the twentieth century, many innovative works arose from a desire to create new forms of music theater. "Music theater" is a loosely defined designation for a genre of staged works developed in opposition to the styles, structures, and social functions of
nineteenth-century opera. In studying these diverse works, I soon discovered that modernist music theater was very often inspired by exotic models valued for integrating the arts in forms of total theater, for their disciplined and detached performance style, and for their ritual status and
function. I argue that the term "exotic" can indicate both temporal and geographical distance and that the three most prominent exotic models for the
development of modernist music theater were Japanese Noh, medieval
Christian drama, and ancient Greek theater. Indeed, a good number of modernist works were based on some combination of these models. Each of them
was understood or imagined imperfectly—a fact that I find to have in-
tensified their appeal.

   Many aspects of these music theater pieces—their musical and dramatic
structure, the form and style of their texts, the relationship between their
performance and the audience space—were shaped by the aspiration to create modern rituals to serve divergent political, didactic, and moralizing purposes. The desire to control human expression on the stage prompted the
use of masks, choreographed symbolic gestures, and stylized or extended
vocal techniques. I argue not only that music theater was a vital modernist
genre, but also that the compositional concerns and cultural themes mani-

fested in these works were fundamental to the history of twentieth-century Euro-American music, drama, and dance.

"Pathological questions" cannot be left out of any study that proposes to examine the intersection of modernism and exoticism. Although such questions are raised throughout the present work, I have tried to save my "final spiritual estimate" for the conclusion. Questions are most urgently provoked by the use of masks and masking techniques in so much modernist music theater. The literal use of masks points directly to the modernist desire to control the human performer and to mark the work as a form of ritual, transcending all mundane forms and purposes of illusionist theater. Masks served to mark the "authenticity" of ritual experience in opposition to the sham of mere entertainment. Such ventures sought to immunize the work from normal modes of critical response and shift the audience's focus from the performer to the creator of the work. In some cases, the desire to escape entertainment values may have been all too successful. The goals of total theatrical unification and ritualization often led away from customary aesthetic considerations. Masks can also be metaphorically evoked. The very act of adopting exotic and ritualistic traits can be a form of masking. We will discover that masking can serve not only as a marker of transcendence but also as a device to obscure pathological interests of various kinds.

The masks of modernist music theater frequently raise specters of misogyny, totalitarianism, and the politics of difference. Potential sites of such concerns are located within three charged relationships: between composer and performer, composer and audience, and composer and the exotic model. The allegation that modernism entailed forms of dehumanization and misogyny in the arts is not new, but it is one that plays out in a very provocative fashion in music theater. The use of masking techniques may reveal an apparently benign attraction to the abstract and anti-naturalistic, a tendency toward megalomania, a device for avoiding the female performer, or a more sinister antihumanist impulse. The masks of exoticism reveal a persistence of nineteenth-century Orientalist views throughout the twentieth century, even within postmodernism. We will find that the exotic continues to be equated with sexual enticement and an erotic paradise. Although cross-cultural musical interaction has created some of the most appealing music of the twentieth century, it remains unclear whether such transactions have entailed, or can ever entail, true "cross-cultural understanding" rather than acts of convenient appropriation.

Music theater is an inherently interdisciplinary genre and my research necessarily includes comparisons with modernist spoken theater and dance as well as studies of the musical and performance aesthetics of the exotic models mentioned above. By focusing on the multiple roles of the performer and the audience and by investigating the intended ritual function of the work, I study aspects of musical performance that have more often concerned ethnomusicologists than music historians. I have allowed "irrepressible curiosity" to lead me on throughout the project, even at the risk of transgressing the apparent boundaries of my subject. My delight in making connections among works, cultures, and disciplines may strike some readers as excessive, but I remain convinced that only a radically inclusive exploration of conditions and contexts can succeed in shedding light on works as marginal, and often downright odd, as those examined here.

In Part I, I investigate the multiple implications of the terms "music theater," "exotic influence," and "ritualized performance." I argue that the creation of new forms of music theater has continued throughout the twentieth century, and I attempt to formulate a conceptual basis for later discussions of exotic influence and ritual performance in this genre. Twentieth-century exoticism has often entailed influence anxiety and has always been an opportunistic, highly selective process. Accordingly, I am more interested in why and how certain exotic models were used in the creation of modernist music theater than I am in pursuing detailed comparisons or assessing authenticity. In the final section of the introduction, I examine the effects of the ritualization process on the relationship between composer, performer, and audience member.

Part II is a cross-disciplinary survey of works created by various modernist composers, choreographers, dramatists, and theater producers. I first discuss the literal and figurative significance of masks in twentieth-century theatrical arts as well as the vital function of masks in world ritual. I then employ the metaphor of masking in discussing the use of extended vocal techniques and nonverbal expression in modernist music theater. I consider the modernist fascination with ancient Greek drama, Japanese Noh plays, and medieval Christian theater and isolate the features that have proved of greatest interest to modernists. Chapters five through seven focus on three pairs of examples. First, I compare the Hellenism of Isadora Duncan with the Greek-style works of Igor Stravinsky and Carl Orff, focusing particularly on the issue of movement versus stasis. Next, W. B. Yeats's political appropriation of Japanese Noh is contrasted with that of Bertolt Brecht and Kurt Weill, with special attention to the tense relationship to music both playwrights exhibited in attempting the creation of a new genre. Part II concludes with an exploration of French medievalist music theater, focusing first on Ida Rubinstein's collaboration with Claude Debussy and Gabriele d'Annunzio and then on her more significant work with Paul Claudel and Arthur Honegger.

In Part III, I discuss works of music theater by British composers, especially in relation to the national revival of the medieval mystery plays and with particular emphasis on the Church Parables of Benjamin Britten. In every case, I explore the role of the audience and the importance of the intended performance venue. Britten exhibited a continued devotion to church performance and to new religious theatrical forms. I examine the elements of Japanese music and theater in Britten's works and unpack their ritualistic features, including his use of stylized vocal effects, his unique approach to the construction of musical time, and the use of an entire repertoire of rehearsed symbolic gestures and movements. I consider issues of appropriation and the relationship between the homosexual and the exotic and argue that Britten sought to "domesticate the exotic" in these works. Later works by Peter Maxwell Davies and Alexander Goehr demonstrate the continued British interest in creating ritualistic music theater and the ever more complex use of masking techniques in an attempt to achieve the numinous.

Part IV considers the use of music theater for purposes of social and religious criticism in the United States. After establishing an early twentieth-century background for exotic influence on American aspirations to total theater, I focus on the provocative works and performance theories of the composer Harry Partch. Partch presents a sustained attempt to create total theater on the basis of Japanese and ancient Greek models. His penchant for political satire leads to a (perhaps surprising) comparison with Leonard Bernstein, underscoring their common use of popular music and ritual structures for purposes of social criticism. Part IV concludes with a consideration of how the same concerns and themes central to American modernist music theater have also appeared in works of popular culture.

In Part V, I first address some of the more problematic aspects of modernist music theater and its creators, including misogynistic tendencies and evident parallels with contemporaneous totalitarian movements. I attempt a balanced assessment of these connections in their historical context, with due acknowledgment of the potentially divergent enticements of the mask. I then consider how exotic influence and the pursuit of ritualized performance and total theater persist in recent "postmodernist" manifestations. I conclude that recent examples reveal a determination to achieve a greater authenticity in relation to the exotic, either through collaboration with the other or by use of sophisticated technology. From this perspective, similarities between recent "postmodern" works and those of the modernists appear to outweigh their differences. The exotic continues to be tapped for the achievement of political and spiritual goals in the theater.

Many people provided crucial support at various stages in this project. For their encouragement, suggestions, and assistance in my research, I thank the following: Daniel Albright, Joe Auner, M. Jennifer Bloxam, Michael Bott at the Reading University Library, Charles Dibble, Patricia B. Fisken at the Dartmouth College Music Library, Don Gillespie, Alexander Goehr, Interlibrary Services at Princeton University, Ione, Peter Jeffery, Phil Karg in the Dance Collection at the New York Public Library for the Performing Arts, Jean McAneny, Susan McClary, Thomas McGeary, Danlee Mitchell, Paula Morgan at the Princeton University Music Collection, Carol Oja, the Pauline Oliveros Foundation, Jann Pasler, Marlys Scarbrough at the University of Illinois Music Library, Gregg Schaufeld at Nonesuch Records, Wayne Shirley at the Music Division of the Library of Congress, Judith Tick, Glenn Watkins, Pam Wheeler at the Britten-Pears Library, Lynne Withey, and Deborah Wong. Financial assistance from the Princeton University Department of Music made possible my research at the Harry Partch Archive, University of Illinois. I am indebted to Suzie Clark, Simon Morrison, and Lara Shore-Sheppard for offering detailed editorial comments and advice on the original draft of this book in 1996. Finally, I am exceedingly grateful to Carolyn Abbate, Philip Brett, Harold Powers, and Richard Taruskin for their important criticisms, which helped to improve this manuscript in myriad ways. Any remaining mistakes or passages lacking in grace or clarity are certainly due to my stubbornness.

Williamstown, Massachusetts
September 1998

Part I

INTRODUCTION: DRAWING
CONNECTIONS IN THE MARGINS

1   Defining Music Theater

[W]e see developing in France, little by little, a theatrical genre
which is not properly speaking ballet, which has no place in the
Opéra, nor at the Opéra-Comique, nor in any of the fashionable
theatres. It is there, in this margin, that the future is being
sketched. . . . This new genre, more consonant with the modern
spirit, remains unexplored land, rich with possibility.

Revolution which flings doors wide open to explorers! The new
generation will continue its experiments in which the fantastic, the
dance, acrobatics, mime, drama, satire, music, and the spoken word
combine to produce a new form; they will present, with very small
means, plays which the official artists will take for studio farces,
and which nonetheless are the plastic expression and embodiment
of poetry itself.[1]

Jean Cocteau (1922)

Although reports of opera's death have been greatly exaggerated, interest
was indeed focused on other genres for much of the twentieth century. These
"other genres," however, did not exclude musical works for the stage. A good
deal of compositional energy that might otherwise have been devoted to
opera was redirected to the quest for new forms of theatrical-musical performance. Several composers who created relatively few operas, or none at
all, composed numerous theatrical works of various sorts—staged works that
fit neither the operatic nor balletic molds. Alternatively, the career of a composer otherwise committed to opera composition might contain a period of
experimentation with new theatrical genres. A higher vantage point is required to appreciate the amount of compositional activity devoted to the theater in the twentieth century. The multitude of works that cannot easily be
labeled "opera," "play," or "ballet" indicates the need for a broader and more
flexible term—thus, "music theater."

As a loose genre designation, "music theater" is not simply a catchphrase
recently concocted by historians of twentieth-century music. Variants of
the term were employed earlier in the century, and the phenomenon was
noted by many. Jean Cocteau was wise to describe the "new form" of theatrical performance through negation or exclusion; attempting to detail exactly what music theater is or what criteria qualify a work for this designation would run counter to the broadly inclusive spirit signaled by the
term. It may be wrong even to think of music theater as a genre, since so
much twentieth-century art has been concerned with genre-blurring. In mu-

sic, the trend began early in the century with, for example, symphonies and string quartets that incorporate the voice (Mahler and Schoenberg continuing where Beethoven left off). The variety of music theater types or sub-genres is vast. The following, a catalogue worthy of Polonius, is but a selection of the terms employed by composers to describe their works of music theater: dance-drama, polytechnic drama, melodrama, monodrama, dramatic oratorio, opera-oratorio, school opera, chamber opera, mini-opera, rock opera, TV opera, radio play, musical play, puppet play, pantomime, dance-pantomime, burlesque, didactic piece, theater piece, and music-theatre. The label "music theater," then, indicates not so much a set of traits signaling a specific new genre as it does a fundamental aspiration toward discovering some novel form of theatrical-musical performance.

Much can be gleaned concerning the early development of music theater from Cocteau's attempts to describe it. Although created in opposition to opera, spoken theater, and ballet, music theater often combined these traditional genres in novel ways, as well as admitting less canonical varieties of performing art. Although works of music theater do tend to employ "small[er] means" than the traditional genres of staged musical performance, they often require a greater variety of performance media. In addition, music theater was perhaps more often radical (in the etymological sense) than revolutionary, in that many prominent works sought to restore theatrical performance to its legendary roots, to a time when all forms were one. Finally, Cocteau's claim for France as the birthplace of this new form is not wide of the mark—although the most prominent composer in Paris at the time happened to be a Russian.[2]

Recent attempts to discuss music theater have tended to follow the route of definition by exemplification, pointing to certain archetypal works. Igor Stravinsky's *Renard* (composed in 1916 and performed in Paris in 1922, the year of Cocteau's remarks) is often cited as an archetype for subsequent explorations in music theater and his *Histoire du soldat* (1918) and *Les Noces* (1917–23) as evidence of a sustained interest in the genre. However, Stravinsky was not alone in creating early examples of music theater: Arnold Schoenberg's *Erwartung* (1909), *Pierrot lunaire* (1912), and *Die glückliche Hand* (1910–13) signaled the range of possibilities. In Germany and Great Britain, initial developments toward music theater were more often led by playwrights and producers than by composers. Later in the century, music theater became a leading interest of composers associated with the British and American avant-garde. Cocteau's prediction of how these theatrical experiments would be received has proven correct for the most part. In music scholarship, works that do not fit into established categories tend to be neglected. Music theater has not received sustained attention by scholars, even though a glance at the work-lists of many twentieth-century composers reveals their eager pursuit of new theatrical forms. It is my contention that these works from the margins constitute the "expression and embodiment" of concerns central to twentieth-century music, modernist art in general, and society at large.

Recently, "music theater" has gained acceptance as a term important to our understanding of twentieth-century music. The most notable indication of this acceptance is the newly expanded presence of the term in the vocabulary of the *Grove* dictionaries. In the *New Grove Dictionary of Opera*, published in 1992, Andrew Clements defines music theater as "a kind of opera and opera production in which spectacle and dramatic impact are emphasized over purely musical factors."[3] Like other recent writers, Clements considers music theater to be a fashion of the 1960s. In the 1986 *New Harvard Dictionary of Music*, Robert Morgan describes music theater as "the combination of elements from music and drama in new forms distinct from traditional opera."[4] Although this definition should also refer to dance, Morgan does give some indication of the broader history and essential "interdisciplinary" nature of music theater in his concise, two-paragraph exposition. Michael Bawtree, a director actively involved with the production and promotion of new music theater, has noted the inherent problems of the term and prefers the phrase "singing theatre."[5] Bawtree is right to point to the possible confusions raised by the words "music theater"—a confusion made evident, for instance, by the fact that in one recent history of twentieth-century music, the index simply collapses references to Broadway musicals with the entry for music theater, as though they were completely synonymous traditions.[6] However, Bawtree's "singing theatre" is no more exact and tends to suggest a type of work that is necessarily sung throughout. Likewise, his designation "singer-actor" for the performer of music theater ignores the larger quest for an ideal "total performer" whose choreographed movement is often equally important to the performance.[7] Finally, Eric Salzman has discussed music theater as a form of mixed media or multimedia, which he defines as "a loosely applied term for theater works or events that involve some merging of arts, forms, techniques, means, and electronic media, all directed at more than one of the senses and generally involving some kind of total surrounding."[8]

For many critics, music theater was primarily a genre of the 1960s and early '70s, one marked by the use of advanced technology and by bold political expression. Paul Griffiths, for example, describes the music theater of this period as involving a "politicization of opera,"[9] and considers the works of the British avant-garde and of such figures as Hans Werner Henze, Luigi Nono, and Luciano Berio as constituting the core examples of the form. Those focusing on British examples tend to employ "music theater" to refer to the presence of theatrical elements in works that are otherwise of concert form. (Bawtree has dubbed this type of work "concert theater.")[10] The tendency to focus on examples from this later period with only occasional reference to the appropriate Stravinskian and Schoenbergian archetypes ignores the great diversity of music theater, its evolving history, and the prominent contributions arising from dramatists and choreographers. Throughout much of the twentieth century, music theater was created for purposes of political expression and frequently employed technological innovations— these are not features limited to works from the 1960s. Attempts to construct generic and temporal boundaries for music theater have consistently fallen short, for music theater is fundamentally about crossing boundaries.

My discussion of music theater as a label for new forms of theatrical performance invites the question: In what ways is music theater distinct from the traditional forms; or, better, why were traditional forms no longer considered sufficient? The rejection of opera by many modernist composers has parallels in the development of modern dance and avant-garde theater in the first decades of this century. One basic motivation for rejecting the traditional forms and "fashionable theaters" had its roots in economic and social concerns. As support for new works waned, and as the operatic canon grew more firmly congealed, the creation of new operas became less feasible. In addition, and as a corollary, many modernists came to disdain traditional performance venues and sought either to bring their theater works directly to "the people" or to reserve their productions for a more select and potentially more appreciative audience. For several works of music theater considered here, the performance location itself was vital—"fashionable theaters" were not deemed suitable. Another basic distinction between opera and music theater involves the intended function of the performance. Modernists looked upon nineteenth-century opera, ballet, and theater as empty entertainment. In contrast, they hoped to create works that would have direct spiritual or political impact in performance. Music theater was often intended as a transformative device that required a receptive audience willing to engage in the performance, rather than a passive audience expecting to be entertained. Of course, Wagner's music dramas had been composed in a similar "modernist" spirit and with similar intentions, but modernists found many excuses for rejecting his example, and many outlets for alleviating their Wagnerian anxieties.

For the modernists, opera had failed in its mission to integrate the arts, barely hinting at the possibilities of "total theater." Wagner had envisioned a grand unification of the arts in the theater, but in the opinion of numerous modernist figures, music predominated in his music dramas, maintaining its autonomy at the expense of the other forms. In music theater, by contrast, the musical component often suffers noticeably when separated from the theatrical production. At the same time, works of music theater tend to allow for a greater range of vocality than employed in traditional opera, both in terms of speech and in extended vocal effects. Finally, although dance had occasionally figured in opera, the genre did not fully integrate physical movement with vocal performance, just as traditional ballet did not include vocalizing performers.

The modernist quest for a form of true "total theater" was pursued along several fronts and in several disciplines.[11] To cite two complementary and classic examples, both Schoenberg and Wassily Kandinsky sought a unified field theory for the coordination of the arts in the theater.[12] This ideal also inspired choreographers and poets and encouraged a great deal of collaborative work and interdisciplinary theorizing. Yet however widespread modernist enthusiasm for "total theater" became, any given creator tended in practice to allow his or her own medium to predominate and to be supported by the others. In addition, we will discover that for some of those involved in the creation of music theater, the "total theater" ideal was too suggestive of Wagner's *Gesamtkunstwerk* and thus offended their anti-Wagnerian sensibilities. Yet even the works of anti-Wagnerians offered a juxtaposition of the several performing arts, including modern forms of technological media, that resulted in genres that were clearly distinct from opera.

Music theater neither simply arose from the remnants of opera at the end of the "great tradition," nor was it developed *ex nihilo*. As composers turned away from nineteenth-century operatic traditions, they turned toward a great variety of models that might serve as catalysts toward the creation of new forms. These potential catalysts included genres as diverse as cabaret and vaudeville, Japanese Noh and Kabuki theater, the *commedia dell'arte*, oratorio and dramatic madrigal, European and East Asian traditions of puppet theater, melodrama, medieval Christian theater, film, and ancient Greek tragedy. Music theater was also influenced by new theories of stage production and acting, the rise of modern dance, the potentials of modern technology for the performing arts, archeological research on ancient performance, and the anthropological and musical study of exotic cultures. Throughout its history, music theater has reflected contemporary social issues to an even greater degree than had been true of nineteenth-century opera. Works of music theater have represented a range of social and religious agendas encompassing communist, nationalist, antiwar, Luddite, feminist, Catholic, anti-Church, and idiosyncratic utopian causes. Catalogues like these are repeatedly inspired by the study of music theater, for music theater is above all a matter of connections.

The impulse to seek correspondences—to cross conventional boundaries—is basic to music theater. Poets, composers, choreographers, producers, painters—all have attempted to create it, often in collaborative efforts. Many works were created in the hope of achieving a connection between the actual performance and some higher state—whether of a religious, political, or a more generally spiritual and moral nature. Finally, music theater was typically based on connections formed (or, perhaps, forced) between exotic, traditional, and contemporary models of theatrical performance. To discuss such multifaceted works, one needs an inclusive historical, analytical, and interpretive approach, in which aspects of production and performance style, for example, can receive attention equal to that accorded musical and textual dimensions. I will be making my own connections and noting correspondences in pursuit of central features and themes. Other possible connections and themes will be left to the reader to draw in the margins of this text. I will be emphasizing contrasting pairs—Britten/Davies, Partch/Bernstein, Duncan/Stravinsky, Brecht and Weill/Yeats, Claudel/d'Annunzio, and Lloyd Webber/Madonna—in the belief that much can be learned through such juxtapositions, and that by considering extreme examples one can discover overt manifestations of elements otherwise central to a given period but implicit. In the words of William James, "it always leads to a better understanding of a thing's significance to consider its exaggerations and perversions, its equivalents and substitutes and nearest relatives elsewhere."[13]

I have repeatedly used "modernist" as a qualifier, but have not yet discussed its signification. The application of "modernism" to twentieth-century music is not of recent coinage—in fact, it was the term of choice for reference to "advanced" or "experimental" twentieth-century music as early as the 1920s.[14] However, as is true for all aesthetic period designations, its meaning proves fairly amorphous when one investigates the various ways in which it has been applied. Although exact definition is impossible, there does exist a set of traits that have been frequently associated with the term. Modernism places a high premium on the generation of new genres of artistic production, on the exploration of the extremes of expression, and on abstraction and formalization. The modernist propensity for radical innovation was initially driven by a self-conscious rejection of nineteenth-century conventions and by the desire to synthesize the arts—not only in the theater. I do not use the term to designate a particular bounded temporal frame. Although "modernism" refers primarily to works created in the first half of the twentieth century, several of the examples of modernist music theater that I discuss were composed in later decades and by figures who might not otherwise be considered modernists. The term has often been employed as an umbrella for the various other "isms" of twentieth-century art. In the conclusion, I will cross over into the realm of recent "postmodernist" music theater in order to investigate what (and whether) connections can be made to the past.

2 The Multiplicity of the Exotic

Looking beyond the borders of one's own culture or discipline, and discovering correspondences and similarities as well as alternatives, can be a satisfying activity, reassuring and enriching. Such interloping ventures, however, have long since lost their glow of innocence. Instead, we are faced with the dilemma of how to encourage the identification of those features that interrelate cultures and—at a more parochial level—academic disciplines, while acknowledging the responsibility to respect difference and expertise. The possibility of reconciling the contending claims and goals of cultural identity and cultural pluralism seems quite remote. It is naive—or at least a product of wishful thinking—to discuss cross-cultural encounters, borrowings, or appropriations without considering the attendant political ramifications and assumptions inherent in such transactions.[1] Cross-cultural influence is never neutral, although to say this is not completely to foreclose the possibility of mutual benefit and respect. The promise and peril of interdisciplinary study directly parallels these broader intercultural border disputes, particularly when interdisciplinary interests lead to the sacrifice of depth in favor of a more superficial breadth.

Works of modernist music theater, and studies that attempt to acknowledge their radical inclusiveness, are both inescapably burdened by this dilemma. In fact, the most common criticism of music theater is that the aspiration to include and to connect produces diluted, rather than transcendent, results.[2] The creation of new forms of music theater was often influenced by encounters with exotic models. This use of the exotic is another clear indication of music theater's penchant for making connections and is its most striking expression of a trait central to twentieth-century music as a whole. At certain points throughout this study, I will interrogate the casual mixing of elements extracted from multiple exotic sources, the transformations of exotic elements without regard to original context, and the specific uses to which the exotic has been put in works of Euro-American music theater. Likewise, I will consider the tensions arising from total-theater aspirations, and will discuss the anxiety of certain playwrights at the interface of music and text and that of certain composers in relation to dance. I want as well to scrutinize statements of authorial intent—statements made at the boundaries between performing art forms and, more pointedly, between cultures.

The "exotic" exists in the mind of the beholder. An "exotic model" of music theater is one that an individual composer, dramatist, or choreographer considers to be beyond the boundaries of his or her culture. Furthermore, exotic features are those that the individual artist happened to notice, admire, and borrow from an exotic model—although "happened" may be the wrong word, since these features were typically sought (or, occasionally, imagined) rather than casually encountered. Thus, the transaction of "influence" is often an active and conscious rather than passive or subliminal experience; it is also a highly selective engagement with the other—one likely to involve a misreading of the exotic model in order to satisfy certain preconceptions or interests. The concept of "influence" itself might seem to be called into question by these works, particularly when the cross-cultural transaction seems to have involved either a form of quotation, or a willful adaptation of the exotic model. I will nevertheless use the phrase "exotic influences" to signal the great multiplicity of ways that the modernists interacted with or reacted to the exotic. My primary focus will be on works that were to some degree informed by the structures, functions, and performance styles of exotic forms of music theater, not on works that merely present exotic locales or adapt exotic plots. As was true for describing "music theater," a brief comparison between nineteenth-century Orientalist opera and modernist music theater's relationship to the exotic will prove revealing.

At first, modernist Euro-American contact with and use of exotic musics appears quite different from the nineteenth-century precedents. Compared to their predecessors, twentieth-century composers experienced a more sustained exposure to music of other cultures, as this music became more readily available through recordings and improved means of travel. Rather than perpetuate the use of arbitrary acoustic signals developed to refer to generic exotic realms, many twentieth-century composers sought to study and to integrate the styles, techniques, and musical details of exotic musics in their compositions. For some, this study was of the armchair variety and relied on ethnomusicological literature and scattered recordings rather than on di-

rect contact. Others sought to immerse themselves in an exotic musical culture and frequently assumed the dual role of composer-ethnomusicologist.
Yet for many, as was common in nineteenth-century European Orientalism, the exotic referent or inspirational source was encountered only slightly
and was primarily a product of the imagination.

The question of relative ethnographic expertise is central to most appreciations of exoticism in twentieth-century music and music theater. However, a difference in level of expertise and encounter does not necessarily result in a difference in the actual use of the exotic. In fact, the exoticism of
modernist music theater differs more in degree than in kind from nineteenth-
century Orientalist opera.[3] Even when studied "in depth," exotic music continued to provide something of a sounding board for Euro-American composers from which to echolocate their own compositional interests. The
exotic, and exotic models of music theater, repeatedly offered conceptual
spaces and specific performance structures for playing out the personal and
political concerns of Euro-American composers. Although increased contact with—or at least interest in—exotic music was one of the most important features of twentieth-century Euro-American composition, detail-
ing elements of influence and determining the significance of specific
intercultural encounters are not straightforward operations. Does a greater
degree of verisimilitude to the exotic source show a greater respect for the
other, or is imitation a sign of cultural arrogance and imperialism? Questions of this nature problematize twentieth-century musical exoticism and
should complicate its interpretation. As a final, somewhat ironic turn to this
topic, some Euro-American composers came to deplore the decreased level
of "purity" in certain exotic musical traditions as global interculturalism
advanced, while others felt overwhelmed by too great a knowledge of exotic musics and either turned away from such influence or stopped composing entirely in order to devote themselves to ethnomusicological pur-
suits. A persistent and complex "anxiety of influence" in relation to exotic
models is found throughout the history of modernist music theater.

The narrative that begins "In 1889, at the Paris International Exposition,
Debussy was entranced by the sounds of the gamelan . . . ," and that ends
with discussions of the current globalization of musical styles, has been told
repeatedly in histories of twentieth-century music.[4] Rather than recite an
overview of the major examples of Euro-American musical exoticism here,
I will provide a general indication of the multiple forms that exotic influence
has taken and the great variety of exotic models acknowledged. To cite an
analogy from modernist art history, a European artist interested in the arts
of sub-Saharan Africa might have created a copy or close equivalent of a

"tribal" mask, or included a representation of the mask in a painting, or perhaps created a work of sculpture that exhibited a more general incorporation of the techniques and aesthetics involved in the construction of the mask. In each case, the dynamics of primitivism are central, and each of the three works of art could have arisen from the same basic impulse. A musical parallel would include works composed for an exotic ensemble and intended to approximate an exotic model, or works that incorporate exotic scales and tunes as found objects or sonic souvenirs, or works that employ and integrate characteristic intervals, styles of ornamentation and rhythm, and concepts of structure derived from analytical study of an exotic music.

Exotic influence in twentieth-century Euro-American music is detectable in such factors as instrumentation, performance technique, intonation system, melodic and rhythmic style, texture, and basic conceptions of what constitutes a musical sound. Interest in exotic musics in the twentieth-century was so prevalent as to include such utterly divergent compositional personalities as Carter and Cage, Bartók and the Beatles. In addition, as the century progressed, exotic influence became increasingly multidirectional and multidimensional. What was treated as "exotic" also varied considerably depending upon the background of the individual composer in question. For some European and American composers, African-American jazz was considered an exotic music. For composers trained in the music of an adopted culture, the traditional music of their native culture could appear exotic. Finally, while some composers concentrated on the music of a specific culture, others attempted to incorporate traits from multiple exotic sources.

In some works of music theater involving exotic influence, the musical component may reveal no stylistic influence at all, or may exhibit influence from an exotic source different from that involved in the genesis of the work's other elements. Exotic influence may be noted in the conception of the work's function, in the demands placed on the audience by the composer, in the relationship of text to music and movement, in the range of vocality, and in such specific factors as the duration and structure of the production. My focus is centered less on a direct and detailed comparison between Euro-American works of music theater and their exotic models than it is on the issue of how exotic models provided collateral justifications for Euro-American composers of music theater, both in terms of the desired function of the work and in relation to the treatment of the human performer. I am concerned less with how a specific exotic model was transformed by a Euro-American artist than with why the model was sought and admired. While modernist composers turned to exotic music theater for a variety of reasons, two features were particularly important. First, modernists found viable models of total theater not in the music dramas of Wagner, but in the performance traditions of East Asia, for example, and in descriptions of ancient Greek theater. In such models, the performer assumed multiple roles, and the several performing art forms appeared fully integrated. Second, the modernists admired exotic models of music theater for their ritual status and function. Euro-Americans repeatedly celebrated, and exaggerated, the devotion and intensity of both performers and audience that they observed in exotic traditions. The creation of forms of stylized performance in emulation of exotic models not only offered the modernists a route toward ritual status for their works but also provided a means for increased authorial control over the production of music theater, and over the individual performer. There is some irony in this appropriation of authority, since in many "exotic" traditions of music theater, the performer is the only living source of the performance. The work is honored for its age, and the performance of canonical works by long dead or anonymous authors is itself part of the ritual.

A major form of exotic influence for the modernists, and one especially significant for the development of music theater, was the exoticism of models that were temporally rather than geographically remote. Such forms as ancient Greek tragedy and medieval Christian theater may appear to be examples of intracultural rather than exotic borrowings, but in practice such influences prove to have been quite similar to the more obviously exotic geographical interactions. That the influence of temporally distant and geographically distant models was interchangeable should not be surprising, for the modernists themselves considered virtually all exotic traditions, living or historical, to be timeless and ancient. A primary feature and goal of modernism was the attempt to recoup some lost past through the creation of modern art. From the modernist perspective, the living music theater of East Asia could provide a window upon ancient forms of ritual performance, including that of the ancient Greeks. As will be noted in part II, the modernists repeatedly pointed to similarities between ancient and contemporary forms of exotic music theater and often created works influenced by a combination of such models. This interest in the archaic coincides with more obvious primitivist conceptions of exotic art and is evidence of the fundamental modernist quest for forms of transcendent and transformative performance.

3 Ritual and Performance

Ritual, in fact, far from being merely formal, or formulaic, is
a symphony in more than music. It can be—and often is—a
symphony or synaesthestic ensemble of expressive cultural
genres, or, a synergy of varied symbolic operations, an opus which
unlike "opera" (also a multiplicity of genres as Wagner repeatedly
emphasized) escapes opera's theatricality, though never life's
inexpungible social drama, by virtue of the seriousness of its
ultimate concerns.[1]

Victor Turner (1982)

This description of ritual, with its (mixed) musical metaphors, is uncannily
suggestive of modernist music theater. Music theater also consists of a
"synaesthestic ensemble of expressive cultural genres," and is a form that
attempts to escape the theatrical trappings of opera in its bid to engage with
"ultimate concerns." The validity of describing music theater as a form of
ritual performance is also supported earlier in the same passage from
Turner: "Ritual is, in its most typical cross-cultural expressions, a synchronization of many performative genres, and is often ordered by *dramatic*
structure, a plot, frequently involving an act of sacrifice or self-sacrifice,
which energizes and gives emotional coloring to the interdependent communicative codes which express in manifold ways the meaning inherent in
the dramatic *leitmotiv*."[2] Turner's repeated analogies between ritual and theater often, as in these two quotations, seem applicable to discussions of music theater. However, multiple definitions of ritual have been offered by
Turner and others, and the examples of music theater considered here do
not fit each proposed set of criteria equally well. Some definitions of ritual
and ritual performance are so inclusive as to prove meaningless for attempts
to describe modernist music theater as a form of performance distinct from
opera. Do all performance genres involve some form of ritual, or is all ritual activity a form of performance? What is the difference between ritual,
ritualized performance, and the theatrical representation of ritual on the
stage? Before determining whether specific works of music theater can be
considered to function as rituals, and before beginning to investigate the creation of ritualized performance in modernist music theater, it is important
to gain some sense of the multiple forms ritual can assume.

   Inspired by the innovative work of Turner, the study of ritual has flour-
ished in the last twenty-five years. In the 1980s, "ritual studies" developed

as a discrete field of research, attracting scholars from multiple disciplines. Anthropology experienced a renewed interest in ritual and became engaged particularly in identifying ritual structures or traits of daily life in "first world" societies. Students of theology have frequently approached ritual studies with the aspiration of reinventing or at least reinvigorating ritual performance in modern worship. Both the practitioners and interpreters of avant-garde theater have explored ritual experience through the study of ritual in other cultures and through experimentation carried out in "performance labs." A major focus, or conceptual framework, of performance studies has involved a new understanding of theatrical performance and actor training as forms of ritual process. It is my contention that experiments in ritual theater and attempts to create new forms of ritualized performance are found in music theater throughout the century, not only in more recent avant-garde theater workshops.

The field of ritual studies has offered multiple definitions of ritual and has been concerned with the classification of distinct forms of ritual performance. In a tree diagram delineating the varieties of ritual, Richard Schechner has divided human ritualization into three large categories: social ritual, religious ritual, and aesthetic ritual.[3] Social ritual, or in Turner's terminology, social drama, consists of the less organized ritualistic activities of humans in everyday society. This category would include the ritualistic behavior of an audience attending an opera or a sporting event—the interactions of an audience both with respect to the performance and within itself, regardless of the performance. Religious ritual covers the rites and celebrations traditionally studied by anthropologists and that initially inspired the quest for basic structures underlying all ritual activity. Schechner's third category, aesthetic ritual, consists of "codified" and "ad hoc" forms and includes ritualistic theater works. Concerning theater, Schechner has referred to two basic types of performance: "entertainment-theater," which corresponds to Turner's concept of "liminoid," and "efficacy ritual," which involves a transformative intent and experience that Turner termed "liminal."[4]

Many works of music theater considered here appear to exist between the religious and the aesthetic modes of ritual performance. These works are most often aesthetic rituals that aspire to or are intended to function as religious rituals, taking "religious" in the broadest sense to include more idiosyncratic forms of spiritual expression and belief. (By way of contrast, the "happenings" of the 1950s and '60s, particularly in their extreme inclusive manifestations, are perhaps best understood as aesthetic rituals that resemble social rituals.) Thus, modernist music theater is a genre created at the margins of several performing art forms, a genre often arising between cultures, and one that repeatedly aspires to the liminal state of ritualistic experience. I am less interested in determining whether a specific work qualifies as a ritual (although this question will resurface repeatedly), than I am in investigating how composers, dramatists, and choreographers set out to create new forms of ritualized performance based on their experience, either direct or imagined, of exotic models of ritual. I will focus on those performative signs borrowed or developed in modernist music theater that indicate ritual intent in order to discover why ritual function and status was so pervasively desired and what social functions these "rituals" were intended to serve.

A crucial question concerning the ritualistic nature of much modernist music theater is whether ritual, properly so called, can be invented by an individual artist or whether it must arise from the processes of cultural tradition. If new forms of ritual are inventible, then perhaps several of the works considered here are not only examples of ritualized performance, but are themselves actual rituals. Two groups have been especially devoted to the invention of ritual performance: theologians or religionists; and persons involved with experimental theater. Building upon Turner's understanding of ritual as a fluid, flexible, and liminal process, rather than a static and conventional structure, Ronald L. Grimes has argued that ritual can be criticized, reformed, and created. Grimes has written: "In most cultures ritualizing is socially anomalous. It happens in the margins, on the thresholds; so it is stigmatized by liturgical classicists and eulogized by ritual romantics."[5] For Grimes, "ritualizing" can be a creative act that does not require the authority of tradition. Grimes is interested particularly in the possibility of reinventing ritual for worship in established religions, but his arguments apply also to more individualistic forms of created ritual. Several contemporary avant-garde directors, most notably Jerzy Grotowski and Richard Schechner, have sought to develop new forms of ritual in experimental theater. Such figures have frequently consulted anthropologists, as is evident in the close association between Schechner and Turner. They have turned to ritual in an attempt to create new forms of theater involving constant experimentation with the performance activity itself, rather than only with the production of a single work.[6] Regarding the possibility of ritual's invention, J. Ndukaku Amankulor has argued for a broader understanding of ritual, one that would recognize the close association of artistic theater and ritual performance throughout the world.[7] Amankulor suggests that some anthropologists and theater critics have been reluctant to acknowledge the theatrical elements of non-Western ritual and the ritualistic aspects of Western theater. These arguments supporting the interpretation of avant-garde Euro-American works of theater as rituals do not address the essential egotism expressed by the individual artist assuming the role of rite-creator. (An extremely healthy ego would seem necessary for those attempting to unify the performing arts in newly invented forms of ritual through the appropriation of elements from multiple exotic traditions.) Although it may be possible to invent forms of ritualized performance resulting in works of ritual function, there is at least one further basic criterion that, for many ritologists, is essential to ritual.

Does ritual require a participating audience? If so, what amount of activity or engagement qualifies for audience participation? As suggested above in reference to Turner's "social dramas," some ritual activity occurs in the audience space in all forms of performance, from the football game to the chamber music concert. In much of the world, theatrical and musical performances are specifically ritual performances, and the division between audience and performer is nonexistent. In ritual performance traditions such as the *mbira dzavadzimu* of the Shona of Zimbabwe, anyone in physical proximity to the performance is to some degree a participant. Perhaps the "audience" as such does not exist in ritual, there being only different degrees of performance responsibility. Turner stressed the importance of inclusive engagement for ritual performance: "Ritual, unlike theatre, does not distinguish between audience and performers. Instead, there is a congregation whose leaders may be priests, party officials, or other religious or secular ritual specialists, but all share formally and substantially the same set of beliefs and accept the same system of practices, the same sets of rituals or liturgical actions."[8]

Of course, much twentieth-century experimental theater blurred divisions between audience and performers. On the other hand, in some forms of music theater commonly discussed as ritual, such as Japanese Noh, there is a division between audience and stage, and the audience can be considered a congregation only in the most general sense. Some rituals are performed for no audience at all—or at least for no earthly audience. Turner's statement does allow for a degree of flexibility regarding audience participation, in that he refers to the audience as a congregation. However, for most examples of invented ritual performance, the inventor could not depend on the audience to behave as though part of the ritual, to "accept the same system of practices, the same sets of rituals or liturgical actions." In fact, the work itself was likely designed to generate a new system of ritual practices and to advocate new beliefs. In some works of modernist music theater, the audience is to function as an engaged congregation, even to the extent of delivering specific lines assigned to it. Other works appear to function primarily as rituals for the performers, rather than for the spectators. The degree of audience participation and engagement, and the mode of ritual performance desired or achieved, will be found to vary greatly in modernist music theater.

Some indications of multiple modes of ritual performance are apparent in traditional operatic production. For instance, Martha Feldman has interpreted *opera seria* as a spectacle whose ritual aspects include interplay between audience and stage and the genre's allegorical relation to broader forms of social ritual.[9] Elements of social ritual are also evident in the production history of nineteenth-century opera. However, a more narrow understanding of ritual as necessarily involving an explicit transformative intent and effect, as achieving liminal states, does not appear to include traditional opera. In many nineteenth-century operas, rituals and religious expression are represented on the stage, but the opera itself is presented as a form of entertainment. Of course, Wagnerian music drama came to inspire, or was intended to inspire, an acceptance of the performance as serving some higher purpose. Even those modernists who vehemently rejected Wagner's model were likely to have been influenced by his conception of theater's transformative possibilities and potential social function.

From a modernist perspective, the performance aesthetics and conventions of opera were altogether too arbitrary, too diva-determined, to function as ritual performance. For many, each aspect of the performance would need to be formalized and regulated by the individual creator, and should be designed for a specific spiritual or political effect. Performance conventions arising from recent tradition were anathema, for the modernists believed fervently in the importance of self-created ritual. To turn this discussion of the ritual function and transformative intent of music theater on its head, we might ask whether the real motivation behind the modernist quest to create ritualized performance on the stage was the desire to suppress the unregulated social ritualizing endemic to the audience space. Moreover, if the author succeeded in convincing an audience that the performance was no mere entertainment, but was rather a form of ritual, then the work would to that extent be immunized from potential criticism. (Conversely, if the audience did not feel engaged in the performance, the "ritualization" of the work might widen the breach between composer and public—only a select group of initiates would appreciate the performance.) Once the audience is conceived of as a congregation and the performers as servants of ritual, then the work has been transformed, as has the role of the author. Rituals are not created by mere composers, dramatists, and choreographers.

Modernist music theater, through the agency of ritualized performance, declares to both performer and audience: "Behold! The Author has been transformed into High Priest." Perhaps this is the unspoken and possibly unconscious transformative intent behind many of the works to be considered here. Perhaps this is the "ultimate concern" of modernist music theater.

How was "ritualized performance" achieved in modernist music theater? The clearest indication of a new performance aesthetic was the radical reconceptualization of the role of the performer. The performer was to function as a devout servant of the performance, no longer as an entertainer expectant of audience adulation. In addition, the basic categories of "actor," "singer," and "dancer" were often no longer applicable—a total, sacred performer was required. For several of these works, preparation for the performance involved far more than simple rehearsals. To serve as initiates, the performers needed to undergo training, a process of education specific to the production of the new genre. The performer was thus both ennobled by the work and made more explicitly subservient to the author than ever before.

The prevailing performance aesthetic in modernist music theater was nonnaturalistic and, to varying degrees, the "fourth wall" was dropped—along with the other three walls of scenic convention. Realism is hardly a requirement of ritual performance. A potential confusion is raised when discussing the acting style prevalent in these works. The performer in modernist music theater most often does not attempt to counterfeit a character. In fact, in didactic or moralistic music theater, the performers inform the audience that they will be assuming certain roles in order to do their ritual work. Yet from another perspective the performers in ritual are presumably transformed into the represented roles in ways not possible in conventional theater. Perhaps a higher embodiment is attained by the performer of ritualistic music theater precisely because common forms of realism are circumvented. A similar conceptual problem is encountered when considering the relationship between plot and performance in modernist music theater. Are the parables and ceremonies of these works reenacted and represented or enacted and experienced on the stage? To some degree, this question can only be answered by the actual performers and audience members involved in specific performances of the work. Although my historical focus is primarily on authorial intentions, we should remember that the realization of even the best prepared intentions remains in the hands of performer and audience during the actual performance.

The audience is often provided with multiple indications of the work's ritual intent in modernist music theater. In many instances the text and plot of the work are appropriated from established religious or ritual sources. Most examples of music theater considered here exhibit a formalized structure and some form of framing device, including processional entrances for the performers. Occasionally, the performance site itself implies a higher purpose for the performance. One particularly prominent indication of ritualized performance in modernist music theater, a characteristic distinct from conventional Euro-American acting styles, was the new insistence upon stylized and symbolic movement. Not only were the movements of the performers in numerous works of music theater carefully choreographed, but these movements were also often drawn from an invented set of symbolic gestures, a set specific to the new genre. As noted above, for the modernists, dance and movement in general needed to be integrated in the performance in order to achieve a total theater ideal and ritual status. For many students of ritual, movement is central. In his study of the potential of ritual for modern society, Tom F. Driver has written: "the ritual mode of performance is characterized by deliberate, disciplined use of the body. In this mode, 'performance' is realized in the most literal way: Specific, finite, identifiable actions are carried out bodily at a definite time and place. Although a ritual includes pretending, the ritual performance itself is no pretense, but an actual, here and now doing." [10] Driver connects ritual performance to primal behavior, and asserts: "In the ritual mode, performance is done bodily and is shown through what we have called display." [11] Movement is a basic concern throughout music theater, although we will discover that this concern occasionally involved a limiting of the performer's mobility rather than the development of a full repertoire of motion.

The creation of ritualistic music theater entailed inventing new symbolic systems, styles, and structures of movement, dramatic text, and music. The "ritualization" of the musical component, or the invention of acoustic indications of ritual, is both the most intriguing and the least generalizable element of modernist music theater. Musical features that are coded for ritual significance vary from composer to composer. However, a penchant for musical extremity is common to most examples of ritualistic music theater. For example, the use of extended vocal techniques, stylized ornamentation, and nonverbal sounds as well as forms of notated speech and chantlike recitation were employed to indicate ritual intent, or at least as signs of spirituality. The musical setting of these works tends toward simplicity and repetition. Musical structure is often constructed with a didactic clarity and can indicate a separation between the realm of the performance and a higher state. For instance, music can play a primary role in the creation of ritualistic temporality by suggesting a static or metatemporal state either through aggressively repeated rhythms or through unmeasured and amorphous musical sections. Finally, in some works the music itself seems to serve as the device of transformation. A major challenge facing the composer of ritualistic music theater was the need to create music that could signal difference—difference in both existential state and in the relationship between the realm of the ritualistic work and daily life. The exotic proved particularly useful for such purposes.

Modernist music theater is a genre of connections, but it is also a genre of masquerades, of transformations realized through cultural cross-dressing and through the assumption of borrowed masks. In the next chapter, I will gather together several of the more widely worn masks of modernist music theater and will examine how they were made to fit. The question of what might ultimately lie behind the use of these masks will be addressed in the conclusion.

Part II

BORROWED MASKS: GREEK,
JAPANESE, AND MEDIEVAL

4 The Masks of Modernism

The Duplicity of Masks

Masks are fundamentally double in function, signification, and experience, serving simultaneously as tools for disguise and as markers of identity. Covering the face renders the individual performer anonymous and neutralizes his or her humanity. At the same time, the performer is defined anew by the mask and is transformed into a deity, demon, or some universal superhuman type, or, conversely, into an exaggerated representation of a subhuman impulse. Beneath the mask, the performer is constrained by the fixed facial expression and at the same time liberated to explore the heightened expressivity of the rest of the body and the voice. The mask enables the performer to enjoy an advantage normally reserved for the audience: freedom to gaze anonymously in a darkened auditorium. The masked performer is allowed to observe from behind a sheltering cover. In modern psychological theater, the masked face may serve to indicate profound duality in a character's personality—a tension between internal and external existence, between a private and a social self. In ritual performance, the masked performer is often regarded as a literal incarnation of the spirit or deity represented by the mask and is allowed to behave as such, free to act without fear of recrimination. Ultimately, a mask is a powerful disembodied signifier that is radically transferrable. Separate from any specific human realization, it functions as a concrete sign of a transcendent identity, regardless of wearer.

The mask serves as an ideal objective correlative for the modernist propensity to transform and transcend the human in the arts. In the context of modernist painting and sculpture, the mask is a sign of a radically new treatment of the human subject. This is evident in the modernist tendency both to disguise the representation of the human in the art work and to find human likeness in inanimate objects and in the movements of machines. The creation and representation of masks by modernist Euro-American artists also points to the widespread general interest in the arts of sub-Saharan Africa, native North America, and Polynesia—a point made most emphatically in the controversial 1984 Museum of Modern Art exhibition entitled "'Primitivism': Affinity of the Tribal and the Modern." The mask is an equally striking artifact of and metaphor for modernist theater and dance. In her *Masks in Modern Drama*, Susan Valeria Harris Smith has provided a thorough documentation of the extensive employment of masks by modernist producers and playwrights.[1] The presence of masks in plays by such figures as Alfred Jarry, W. B. Yeats, Eugene O'Neill, Bertolt Brecht, and Jean Cocteau, attests to two fundamental aspects of modernist spoken theater: the desire to create works of ritual significance and the pervasive influence of exotic models. Modernist playwrights and composers sought to transcend the individuality of the performer and to achieve a universalized drama bypassing the portrayal of realistic human situations and emotions. Masks served their purposes ideally.

Masks in Ritual Performance

> A mask is some alteration of the face—a change of appearance
> for purposes of protection, make-believe, social acceptance, disguise,
> amusement, or religious devotion. A mask is the spirit realized—
> inner urges given shape and form and displayed upon the face. A
> mask is also a medium through which the gods can be invoked. It is
> an invitation to the gods to inhabit an appropriate and available form,
> the mask itself, in order to communicate with the human tribe. A mask
> can attract or repel, reassure or frighten. Masks can be utilitarian or
> decorative or both.[2]

This extremely inclusive definition of masks is based on the premise that any alteration of the face can be understood as masking in the most general or metaphorical sense. In this view, facial expressions themselves are an ever changing series of social masks. The author of the above definition discusses such examples as surgical masks, Ku Klux Klan hoods, protective helmets, sunglasses, and even lipstick. Although it is important to acknowledge the prevalence of masks in daily life, a ritual mask is more than cosmetic. The masks of ritual performance, however, may differ from daily masks more in degree than in kind. Lipstick is but a poor form of masking, while the complex makeup of such Asian theater traditions as South Indian Kathakali dance theater and Chinese opera can be as intricate and distinctive as any mask carved from wood.[3]

To appreciate the power attributed to masks in ritual performance, one must first accept the premise that the human face is the center of personal identity and expression. Four of the five senses are centered on the face and much of both verbal and visual communication emanates from this region of the body. While some cultures employ full-body masks for ritual performance, the facial mask is the essential tool of transformation and transcendence found in numerous parts of the world. By covering the face, the performer is transformed into whatever being is represented by the mask. Masks are often believed to contain a magical spirit and divine quality within them, even when not worn, and are therefore treated as holy objects. In such cases, the mask does not merely represent an extrahuman force but carries that force itself, or is at least honored as a highly charged potential site for the divinity to inhabit. In traditions of ancestor worship, death masks may serve as vessels for the spirit of the deceased and may be consulted by the living as a link to the world beyond. The death mask of the ancestor, or in some cases the very skull itself, is worn to allow that ancestor to live again through the body of the masker. As Mircea Eliade noted, in its manifold forms the mask serves a "dual function: alienation of the personality (ritual and theater masks) and preservation of the personality (death masks and portraits)."[4] Both mask types attest to a basic desire to transcend the realistic present by reactivating a distant past, be it mythical or historical, or by preserving a present reality into the future.

Ritual masks typically present a double assault on realism, covering the human face and replacing it with a face that is fantastic. Rather than counterfeiting the human face, ritual masks offer images not found in daily life, such as the impressive appearance of a god or a demon. Masks are necessary for ritual performance precisely because a human face is not wanted—a superhuman face is required. A ritual mask may suggest the face of an animal or may bear little resemblance to any face at all. E. T. Kirby has noted that "it is the persistent, universal presence of abstraction, most often of geometric abstraction, in these primitive masks which so interested [Western] artists and which so strikingly unites the various styles of works, be they from the Northwest Coast, from New Mexico, the Ivory Coast, or from New Guinea."[5] Kirby argues that in both "primitive" ritual and in modernist theater, abstraction is valued as a direct form of access to the numinous. He suggests that "primitive abstract forms and faces promise or threaten—an order not apparent in nature."[6] Abstraction itself, then, articulates the vast difference between the masked being and the human audience, between the ritual performance and everyday life. As Smith has observed: "The mask signals to the audience that it is present at a ritual, that the natural world has temporarily been made static, heightened, and formalized."[7] Even when a mask is lifelike, its rigidity transcends the face of ordinary man, for only gods and the dead could remain so nobly immobile.

A mask that is relatively naturalistic in appearance often functions as a device for gender reversal—an additional form of concealment and transformation. Ritual performers tend to be male throughout the world, while deities and mythological characters may be of either gender. Thus, masks are employed to enable male performers to portray female beings. Eliade has gone so far as to describe masks as specifically masculine ritual tools. He has stated that while ceremonial nakedness and exposing of the body "increases the magico-religious power of woman" throughout the world, "man, on the contrary, increases his magico-religious possibilities by hiding his face and concealing his body."[8] A mask's power for gender reversal, allowing for male-exclusive performance, was a major feature of world ritual theater adapted by male modernist composers and dramatists. They found it appealing and worthy of emulation; the reasons for its appeal were complicated, and not always benign. The prevalent use of masks for gender disguise in exotic—particularly Asian—theater traditions reinforced Euro-American dreams of the East as a sexually open paradise. The Canadian composer Colin McPhee offers one example of the interrelatedness of masks, the exotic, and sexual desire in twentieth-century Euro-American culture. In his autobiographical account of his years spent studying in Bali, McPhee tells of his purchase of two masks—one of serene disposition, the other, furious. The serene mask reminded him of the beautiful boy dancers that he had enjoyed watching during the previous days: "It grew in mystery the more I looked at it. It had the same sexless calm that I had found so haunting and enigmatic in the faces of the little *légong* dancers I had seen at Saba."[9]

Masked Acting and Edward Gordon Craig

The desire to create works with ritual significance prevalent in modernist drama, dance, and music theater, found an icon in the mask. More than this: it found a device of instantaneous efficacy. Choreographer Erick Hawkins once discussed the mask in this manner:

> For certain ideas you must have the mask. "Little me" is so unimportant. The artist as a priest reminds the audience of the "Big me," and that is what the whole dance is about. With the mask, there is no separation between the "Little me" and the "Big me." They are the

same. It is only when the "Little me" forgets itself and knows that
everything is a part of the "Big me" that there is a common experience.
And, theoretically, that's when you have religion and high art. There
is no reason why theatre art has to be trivial and paltry entertainment.
It can reach as high a spiritual plane as the brains and guts of its
creator.[10]

This urge to realize "Big me" in theater engendered a wide spectrum of
masks in twentieth-century performance practice. Masks are a central component in several plays by Eugene O'Neill, since O'Neill believed that the
mask was the most effective device for expressing "those profound hidden
conflicts of the mind which the probings of psychology continue to disclose
to us."[11] Moreover, he argued that masks are "more subtly, imaginatively,
suggestively dramatic than any actor's face can ever be."[12] (He cited the complex masking of his *The Great God Brown* as especially effective and regretted
that he had not employed masks more extensively in other works.)[13] Smith
has determined that masks were ubiquitous in stagings of musical works from
the first decades of the twentieth century: Sergey Prokofiev's *Love of Three
Oranges* and Stravinsky's *Le Rossignol*, W. T. Benda's productions for Broadway revues, and Fernand Léger's production of Darius Milhaud's *La Créa-
tion du monde* offer a few examples.[14] The proverbial wilderness of the avant-
garde was rife with voices calling for masked performance; modernist
directors demanding the use of masks included Antonin Artaud, Max Reinhardt, Oskar Schlemmer, and V. E. Meyerhold.[15] Of the numerous modernist
figures acclaiming the importance of masks for the creation of a new form
of acting, one of the earliest, most consistent, and emphatic voices was that
of the influential British theater producer Edward Gordon Craig.[16] A survey
of his theories will introduce several central elements of the more general
modernist performance aesthetic.

Craig's theatrical ideal called for an acting style that was depersonalized,
detached, and devoted. In Craig's view, an actor should sublimate his or her
individuality in order to become a restrained, preferably anonymous, servant of the performance, subservient to the director's vision. Theatrical production should be nonrealistic, formalized, and symbolic, and should establish a distance between the plot being enacted and the actual performer
and audience. (This form of dramatic distancing was to receive its most famous exposition under Brecht's rubric *Verfremdungseffekt*, or "alienation
effect.") Rather than attempting to substitute for quotidian reality, acting
should be considered a form of heightened reenactment or ritual process.
For Craig, the mask was the essential tool for achieving this new theatrical

aesthetic and was to be honored as the first emblem of the new acting style. Much of Craig's influential writing on the modern theater appeared between 1908 and 1929 in a journal that he aptly called *The Mask*.

Craig argued that an actor's face could not carry conviction and was therefore not an adequate tool for his ideal theater. He insisted that the actor should not impersonate through facial expression but should represent through symbolic gesture. At a minimum, facial masks were required, because "drama which is not trivial, takes us *beyond reality* and yet asks a human face, the realest of things, to express all that. It is unfair."[17] In Craig's conception, masks would replace an imprecise variety of expression with a profound simplicity and intensity. He concluded that the mask was "the only right medium of portraying the expressions of the soul as shown through the expressions of the face."[18] Irène Eynat-Confino has argued that in addition to the mask's role in revitalizing acting, it "is also closely related to Craig's conception of the ideal art of the theatre as a ceremony in praise of Creation and linked to the restoration of Belief to the world. Its ritualistic, sacred origin and the dualism of life and death embodied in it make it a symbolic means par excellence."[19] The call for masked acting was but the first step in Craig's reform of the human performer.

Craig proclaimed that conventional acting was not a true form of art and offered the following explanation for this assertion: "Art arrives only by design. Therefore in order to make any work of art it is clear we may only work in those materials with which we can calculate. Man is not one of these materials."[20] He believed that the basic human tendency toward freedom and personal expression disqualified the individual actor for the new art of the theater. Masking might not prove sufficient; if so, the actor should be removed entirely from the stage. Clearly inspired by a Nietzschean ideal, Craig eerily christened his new masked performer the "Über-marionette." "The Über-marionette," he wrote, "will not compete with life—rather will it go beyond it. Its ideal will not be the flesh and blood but rather the body in trance—it will aim to clothe itself with a death-like beauty while exhaling a living spirit."[21] Each Über-marionette was to employ multiple masks, reinforcing its symbolic function and further destroying both any sense of the actor's own subjectivity and any suggestion of realism. Eynat-Confino has written that while the reintroduction of the mask as a tool for acting was not considered a threat by contemporary performers, Craig's plan to replace the actor with the Über-marionette caused much consternation.[22] Although Eynat-Confino assumes that Craig intended literally to replace the living actor with an oversized marionette, Craig's use of the term "Über-marionette" is not completely consistent. In light of his several articles on the subject, Craig's general conception of an "Über-marionette" style of acting does not appear limited necessarily to a human-sized puppet; rather, the term seems to have served as a more general metaphor for Craig's vision of a new aesthetic of stylized masked acting.[23] In either case, Craig was to discover an existing tradition of live acting that approximated his vision of the Über-marionette in the performance styles of Asian theater.

Concerning the influence of exotic models on Craig's conception of masked acting, Christopher Innes has written: "Although ancient Greece was his primary inspiration, Craig also found the same 'universal principles' in other theatrical forms, from Indian and Cambodian dance to Javanese puppet plays and Nō drama. He had the opportunity to see a Nō performance in 1900 when a Japanese troupe visited London."[24] Rather than permanently replace the living performer with the marionette, Craig's "real aim was to create a Western equivalent to the highly trained actors of the Nō drama, which in his view exemplified the same intrinsic qualities as the theatre of ancient Greece."[25] Eynat-Confino notes that for models of masks "Craig thought of using heads of Greek terra cotta statuettes and ancient Egyptian figures or some of those from his collection of Japanese, Javanese, and African masks."[26] Although Craig acknowledged the influence of both ancient Greek and Asian performance practice, his relation to the exotic was ambivalent. He warned that there existed a "danger in becoming too early acquainted with a matured foreign development of an art which should be evolved afresh from one's own soil."[27] He also felt that "there is something very depressing in the idea of groping eastwards among ruins for the remains of past centuries" and declared that "it is not the Greek mask which has to be resuscitated; rather is it the world's mask which is going to be created."[28] In other writings, however, Craig indicated that imitating Asian acting techniques was a viable option for the creation of a new theater. In 1921 he wrote: "I have been told (since I wrote of the Über-marionette) of a race of actors that existed (and a few to-day preserve the tradition) who were fitted to be part of the most durable theatre it is possible to conceive. When I heard of this I was astounded, pleasurably astounded. I was told that this race of actors was so noble, sparing themselves no pain and austerely disciplining themselves, that all the weaknesses of the flesh were eradicated, and nothing remained but the perfect man. This race was not English or American, but Indian."[29] Craig concluded that "If the Western actor can become what I am told the Eastern actor was and is, I withdraw all that I have written in my Essay, 'On the Actor and the Über-Marionette.'"[30] The attempt to "become the other" in theatrical performance, to emulate an exotic model, was a primary aim of modernist theater. However, this general enthusiasm for the other was not indiscriminate. We will discover that the modernists tended to find certain exotic models of ritual performance more suitable to their purposes than others.

Masking the Voice and Verbal Expression

One crucial form of masked performance remains to be introduced—a form that can be dubbed "acoustic," "musical," or "vocal" masking. The alteration of a human face by a mask often entails an alteration of the human voice. When the mouth is covered by a mask, vocal sounds acquire a deeper, more resonant tone. The masked voice generally sounds distanced and somewhat larger than life. For example, the over-the-head masks of ancient Greek theater functioned as sound boxes for the performer and allowed the actor's voice to resound with the power of a god or a mythic hero. In Japanese Noh, masks are valued for their subtle aesthetic influence on the voice. The voice projected from behind a Noh mask is intended to sound as though it comes from another world, as do the demons, spirits, and deities in Noh plays. In ritual performance, the invoked deity is understood to be speaking through the mask, through the masked voice of the performer. The mask is required both to disguise the natural voice of the performer and to suggest an extrahuman vocal identity; thus the mask functions doubly in aural perception as it does in the visual dimension.

When the movements of a speaking mouth are covered, the audience is more likely to perceive the vocal performance either as emanating from an ambiguous sounding object (the masked performer), or as arising from somewhere beyond their visual perception in a manner similar to non-diegetic film music. The mask may emphasize the impression that the performer is a mere transmitter of sound and text created by an "authorial other," or it may even suggest that the visible performer is actually mute. In either case, masking the vocal performer tends to displace subjectivity from the individual and transfer it to some implied superhuman voice. Whenever the performer's mouth is not visible, the site of sound is made mysterious. The situation becomes even more complicated when music is present, because the unmasked "singing face" is something of a mask itself. (In his poem *Faces*, Walt Whitman included the "face of the singing of music" in his catalogue of facial types.) The "singing face" differs greatly from both the silent and the speaking faces. The singer's mouth is often dramatically extended, contorted beyond its natural position. Carolyn Abbate has noted that in the nineteenth century operatic composers never attempted to hide this "spectacle of vocal labor" nor to disguise the source of vocal sound. In the twentieth century, to the contrary, composers did indeed make such attempts and frequently sought to disguise the sound of the human voice itself.[31]

The sound quality of an individual's voice is perhaps the ultimate marker of personal identity. Singing itself can be understood as a form of vocal masking, since the singing voice often differs from an individual's speaking voice. However, in the history of European vocal music, the unique sound of a particular singer's voice has been an element not only identifiable but celebrated. In the twentieth century, a wide range of vocal techniques has been developed and employed that conspire to create an abstract voice, masking the performer's individuality. These techniques of abstraction sharply diverge from the European operatic conventions of vocal production or, perhaps, exaggerate certain features of conventional vocality beyond recognition. Such techniques include extremity of register, screams, vocal glides, bestial sounds, extremity in rate of text delivery, explosive accentuation, whispers, exaggerated and affected vocal styles, and singing through objects such as bullhorns (as in David Del Tredici's *Final Alice*). Although elements of extreme vocal technique certainly existed in European music before the twentieth century—the pyrotechnics of the coloratura voice serve as one example—modernism encouraged a much more sustained experimentation in the timbral possibilities of the human voice.[32] An ultimate degree of vocal manipulation and masking was reached through electronic means and computer generation. As early as 1916, the Italian Futurist Filippo Marinetti called for a style of declamation that would "completely dehumanize [the] voice, systematically doing away with every modulation and nuance."[33] Experimental vocal effects may be understood in some cases to provide a new, more powerful means for human emotional expression. Schoenberg's *Sprechstimme* technique is most often considered in this way.[34] In other cases they seem to indicate a nonhuman, or superhuman, voice instead. (This is also true of the highly stylized and intense vocal production employed in Japanese Noh, Kabuki, and Bunraku.) These new vocal effects are so extreme as to signal constantly to the auditor the negation of vocal realism. They can serve as an aural signal of ritual performance—an indication of the presence of the supernatural.

Another technique that has served to neutralize, and thereby mask vocal subjectivity involves a physical separation between the visible representation of a character and that character's audible voice. Several of Stravinsky's works—*The Nightingale* (1914), *Pulcinella* (1920), *Renard* (1922), and *Les Noces* (1923)—in which the singers are relegated to the orchestra pit while the characters are represented by mute dancers, mimes, acrobats, or even props on the stage, are perhaps the best-known examples. Masking through literal separation of vocal sound from representing body became increasingly more complicated throughout the twentieth century. In several works (including another by Stravinsky, *Histoire du soldat,* and Weill and Brecht's *Seven Deadly Sins*), both the singer representing the voice of the character and the dancer representing the body of the character are simultaneously visible. In other works, several performers share elements of one character's split subjectivity throughout the course of the performance.[35] The correspondence established between an individual performer and a specific character may not remain constant. Finally, the possibilities of multiple representation and physical separation in character portrayal increase greatly when film is employed in a work of multimedia theater. Such techniques of separation found a prominent place in the production of modernist music theater.[36]

Of course, the human voice serves not only as a form of identification but also as a primary medium of communication. Vocal sounds are expected to carry meaning. Whether or not one can perceive the meaning of the sung text in opera, performer and audience both behave as though meaningful text is being conveyed. In the twentieth century, the presumption of comprehensible communication in vocal music has not always been maintained. An additional form of vocal masking has involved the disguising of semantic meaning through forms of text setting that seem to ignore textual meaning or that forgo the use of verbal text entirely.[37] Stravinsky's peculiar text-setting style offers an example of this type of vocal masking, as noted below in the discussion of *Oedipus Rex.* One motivation for text setting of this kind was a widespread interest on the part of composers in the sound quality of language rather than in its referential meaning. This impulse is particularly evident in the operas of Gertrude Stein and Virgil Thomson. In a book devoted to issues of text setting, Thomson discussed those aspects of Stein's writing that he, as a composer, found especially appealing: "The whole setup of her writing . . . was to me both exciting and disturbing. Also, as it turned out, valuable. For with meanings jumbled and syntax violated, but with the words themselves all the more shockingly present, I could put those texts to music with a minimum of temptation toward the emotional conventions, spend my whole effort on the rhythm of the language, and its specific Anglo-American sound, adding shape, where that seemed to be needed, and it usually was, from music's own devices."[38]

Thomson found value in having worked with Stein's "text of great obscurity": "It had forced me to hear the sounds that the American language really makes when sung, and to eliminate all those recourses to European emotions that are automatically brought forth when European musicians get involved with dramatic poetry, with the stage."[39] In sections of *Einstein on the Beach*, Philip Glass employed text strictly as material for "music's own devices." He used numbers and *solfège* syllables in extreme repetition to fill musical space and dispensed with the semantic and emotive possibilities of sung text. This form of verbal-vocal masking denies the singer his or her traditional communicative role. In such extreme examples, the vocalist is transformed into an objective sound producer, with no alternative site of subjectivity indicated. The singer is fully masked when no trace of a subjective voice can be heard.

Models of Masked Performance

One of the most prominent expositions of the modernist devotion to exotic theatrical models is found in Antonin Artaud's appreciations of Balinese ritual performance. The following passages are quoted from his celebrated article "On the Balinese Theater."[40]

> The spectacle of the Balinese theater, which draws upon dance, song, pantomime—and a little of the theater as we understand it in the Occident—restores the theater, by means of ceremonies of indubitable age and well-tried efficacy, to its original destiny which it presents as a combination of all these elements fused together in a perspective of hallucination and fear. (53)
>
> . . .
>
> Everything is thus regulated and impersonal; not a movement of the muscles, not the rolling of an eye but seem to belong to a kind of reflective mathematics which controls everything and by means of which everything happens. And the strange thing is that in this systematic depersonalization, in these purely muscular facial expressions, applied to the features like masks, everything produces a significance, everything affords the maximum effect. (58)
>
> . . .
>
> In a spectacle like that of Balinese theater there is something that has nothing to do with entertainment, the notion of useless, artificial amusement, of an evening's pastime which is the characteristic of our theater. The Balinese productions take shape at the very heart of matter, life, reality. There is in them something of the ceremonial

quality of a religious rite, in the sense that they extirpate from the mind of the onlooker all idea of pretense, of cheap imitations of reality. (60)

These statements clearly demonstrate the three central elements that modernist figures found compelling in exotic models: the realization of a form of "total theater"; the intense devotion, control, and calculated precision of obedient performers; and the function of theater as ritual performance. Artaud's fascination with the Balinese tradition stemmed from his perception that "everything in this theater is calculated with an enchanting mathematical meticulousness. Nothing is left to chance or to personal initiative."[41] This desire for a theater of thorough refinement, also expressed repeatedly by Edward Gordon Craig, offers one explanation as to why the older generation of modernists tended to adopt models of Asian ritual performance rather than the more free-form and inclusive styles of much African ritual. (The inclusive approach common to many African ritual performance traditions can be seen as a model for the "happenings" and audience-interactive theater of the later Euro-American avant-garde.) Artaud also admired the degree of integration the several performing arts achieved in the Balinese theater. Commenting on the relationship between music and dance, he wrote: "all these sounds are linked to movements, as if they were the natural consummation of gestures which have the same musical quality, and this with such a sense of musical analogy that the mind finally finds itself doomed to confusion, attributing to the separate gesticulations of the dancers the sonorous properties of the orchestra—and vice versa."[42] Bali was but one exotic locale in which modernists found elements of a performance style to suit their visions of a new theater. As Debussy put it, describing his vision of a "People's Theater,"

> Let us rediscover Tragedy, strengthening its primitive musical setting by means of the infinite resources of the modern orchestra and a chorus of innumerable voices; let us remember at the same time how effective is the combination of pantomime and dance accompanied by the fullest possible development of lighting required for a vast audience. We could glean valuable hints for this from the entertainments arranged by the Javanese princes, where the fascination of speech without words, that is to say of pantomime, almost attains perfection, since it is rendered by action and not by formulas.[43]

Of the numerous exotic models appropriated by modernist composers, playwrights, theater producers, film directors, and choreographers, three performance traditions stand out: ancient Greek drama, Japanese Noh, and medieval Christian theater. The importance of Greek theater to a period of theatrical revolution in the West will come as no surprise, but Noh and the medieval mystery play were no less fundamental. Each of these models had a profound impact on modernist theater in its own right; just as often, however, they exerted their influence in concert. Their compatibility stemmed from several basic features they had in common. Each developed from earlier genres of ritual performance and served originally as a form of religious worship. The performance style of each was antirealistic, highly formalized, and symbolic. Finally, each form represented an integration of music, stylized movement, and text. Not least, they all employed masks.

While the ideal of ancient Greek performance had exerted a formative influence on developments in European theater since the Renaissance, particular elements of Greek performance sparked the interest of modernists. Two of the most influential studies of ancient Greek theater in the early twentieth century were those by A. E. Haigh and Roy C. Flickinger.[44] These two studies can jointly provide a sketch of the modernist conception of ancient Greek performance, for the modernists repeatedly relied on academic scholarship for their encounters with the exotic. Both studies asserted that Greek theater was essentially a form of religious and ritual performance. Haigh devoted his opening pages to the role of religion in Greek theater and drew parallels with medieval mystery plays. He stated that Greek theatrical performances were "regarded as a religious ceremonial, as an act of homage to the god. They never became, as with us, an ordinary amusement of everyday life."[45] Haigh believed that each performance was preceded by a ritual sacrifice. His comments on the status of performer and author would have been especially noted by the modernists: "The poets who wrote the plays, the choregi who paid for them, and the actors and singers who performed them, were all looked upon as ministers of religion, and their persons were sacred and inviolable. The theatre itself possessed all the sanctity attaching to a divine temple."[46] In agreement with Haigh, Flickinger described the theater as a sacred site and the performers as priests.[47] Having stressed the religious aspects of Greek theater, Flickinger added that "everyone in attendance would fully realize that he was present at no secular proceeding."[48] Both writers emphasized the importance of masks in Greek performance. Haigh wrote: "The use of masks is indissolubly connected with the style and character of Greek tragedy."[49] Flickinger listed several functions performed by the Greek mask: the mask served as a means of visual and acoustic amplification in the large Greek amphitheaters, it allowed one performer to assume multiple roles, and a change of masks could effect a major transformation of a character's emotional state.[50] Flickinger warned that the scarcity of masks on the modern stage should not be viewed as a sign of their irrelevance. He then quoted the "respectable authority" Edward Gordon Craig on the power of masked acting.[51] Flickinger also noted the lack of religiosity in the contemporary theater and, by way of contrast, found a significant correspondence between Greek theater and the medieval mystery and miracle plays.[52]

In Noh theater, masks serve several basic functions. They allow male performers to represent female characters, they are the primary device for the dramatic character transformations common in the plays, and they help to create an atmosphere of the supernatural.[53] The Noh mask is regarded as having spiritual power and is treated with a great deal of respect. Benito Ortolani has written that the Noh mask "contains within itself—almost like an independent soul—an active participation in the divine power it received, thus becoming a source of healing and spiritual inspiration both for the actor and the audience. Certain special feelings are therefore considered as generated by the mask itself—as a product of the *kokoro* or 'mind, spirit' of the mask—and not by the actor."[54] Noh plays are often based on the story of an unquiet spirit or demon and frequently require the use of fantastic masks. These plays function as something similar to an act of exorcism, or as a more general means of establishing a bridge between the spiritual and the temporal. Even the nonmasked performers in Noh are intended to perform as though masked. Zeami (1363–1443), the primary theoretician of Noh performance, insisted that the unmasked actor should maintain a neutral face of natural expression.[55] Rather than attempting to develop imitative facial expressions, Zeami called for the actor to rely on body movements for the depiction of a character's emotional state. Noh is an extremely integrated form of theatrical performance, in which neither poetry, nor music, nor dance seems to predominate at the expense of the others. The stylized dance, consisting chiefly of symbolic gesture and restrained movement, is intimately connected to the text and enacts the text's meaning simultaneously with its enunciation in chant. Zeami's secret treatises on Noh performance aesthetics became available to Western scholars only in the early years of the twentieth century, a period that saw some of the first serious and sustained foreign studies of Japanese theater since the 1853 "opening" of Japan.

Japanese Noh and ancient Greek theater have been likened to one another by scholars throughout the twentieth century. Specific similarities have been noted repeatedly, such as the use of masks, a chorus, two or three primary actors, and a restriction to male performers. At the turn of the century, some scholars even suggested that Greek theater had had a distant influence, by way of India and China, on Japanese Noh. Several prominent writers on Japanese theater from the first decades of the century made extensive comparisons with ancient Greek drama. The work of Ernest Fenollosa, compiled by Ezra Pound, provides an example of such comparisons, one that proved especially influential in modernist circles. With reference to Noh, Fenollosa wrote: "A form of drama, as primitive, as intense, and almost as beautiful as the ancient Greek drama at Athens, still exists in the world."[56] He regarded the idea that Noh had been influenced by Greek theater as farfetched, although he did draw the standard connections between the two forms. A writer whose discussion of "things Japanese" was to reach an even wider and more diverse audience than the publications of Fenollosa and Pound was Basil Hall Chamberlain.[57] Chamberlain's low opinion of Japanese music is clear in the following remarks: "Music, if that beautiful word must be allowed to fall so low as to denote the strummings and squealings of Orientals, is supposed to have existed in Japan ever since mythological times"; "Having said that it [Japanese music] may be heard, we hasten to add that it cannot be heard often by ordinary mortals"; "the effect of Japanese music is, not to soothe, but to exasperate beyond all endurance the European breast."[58] Chamberlain expressed his hope that European music would continue to catch on in Japan and that Japanese instruments would be converted into firewood.[59] Finally, he suggested that the Japanese themselves did not enjoy their music and stated that "a Japanese Bayreuth is unthinkable."[60] Given such vehemence, one is surprised to discover Chamberlain's very positive discussion of Noh. He found it "strikingly similar to the old Greek drama," and wrote that the two forms share the "same stately demeanour of the actors, who were often masked" and the "same quasi-religious strain pervading the whole."[61] In spite of himself, Chamberlain felt that in the performance of Noh, the music somehow managed to possess "a certain weird charm."[62]

Medieval European Christian theater included a variety of forms—liturgical dramas, mystery plays, miracle plays, and passion plays—that vary in the degree of their correspondence to the performance styles of Greek tragedy and Japanese Noh. Liturgical dramas, dating from the period 1100 to 1275, were similar to ancient Greek theater and Noh in that they were most often performed in a ritual context, within the church, and by an all-male cast. (The use of masks, however, was restricted to the roles of devils.) Movement and gesture, according to Fletcher Collins, was formalized "much as we find it in the Japanese *nō* dramas and in the vase illustrations of Greek plays."[63] Mystery plays, in contrast, were performed on wagons in the streets and were more communal in their production.[64]

As in Noh theater, the simplicity of stage and setting of the mysteries contrasted with the use of elaborate costumes. Masks appear to have been more common in mystery plays than in liturgical drama. Meg Twycross and Sarah Carpenter have argued that masks were even more prevalent in the mysteries than previously assumed. They suggest that "a mask will provide a physical symbol for a spiritual state, usually a change of state, and must be read symbolically" and that masks served as such moral emblems in the medieval plays.[65] Twycross and Carpenter also assert that (as in Noh and Greek tragedy) masked acting in the mysteries encouraged a greater emphasis on stylized gesture.[66]

A relationship between Noh and European mystery plays has been less commonly suggested than between Noh and Greek tragedy, although there exists specific historical evidence encouraging such a comparison. Japan has been "opened to the West" twice in its history. Before Commodore Perry muscled America's way into Japanese ports in 1853, Saint Francis Xavier had employed other strategies of entry beginning in 1549. Between Xavier's arrival and the expulsion of the last missionaries in 1638, the Jesuits engaged in a variety of schemes to win the souls of the Japanese for the Church. One of these involved a harnessing of the persuasive powers of theater. Thomas Leims has discussed the extensive use of the mystery play by the Jesuits in sixteenth-century Japan.[67] In her history of Japanese music, Eta Harich-Schneider notes that these productions were performed in Japanese, with a mixture of European and Japanese musical idioms and were occasionally staged in the style of Noh.[68] Summarizing our present knowledge of the productions of mysteries in Japan, Benito Ortolani has written: "The resulting picture shows that the Jesuits did show the same eagerness in the use of plays and theatrical illustrations of the Christian truths as a method of educating their students and their faithful in Japan as they did in Europe. As part of their effort of communicating with their converts they became very well versed in the contemporary forms of Japanese theatre, especially the *nō* and *kyōgen*, and adopted in their educational shows some of the indigenous techniques and dances."[69]

Although unaware of the sixteenth-century encounters between Noh and the mystery play, several modernist writers nevertheless drew connections between them. Pound suggested that Noh should be valued for containing elements of religious theater that had not been present in Western theater since the time of the morality and mystery plays.[70] Fenollosa compared the early Buddhist miracle plays, which he described as forerunners to Noh, with the miracle plays of medieval Europe.[71] In 1946, Jacques Copeau made a detailed comparison between the structure and style of Noh performance and the performance of the Catholic Mass.[72] Rather than limit themselves to commenting upon the similarities between Noh and medieval Christian theater, or Noh and ancient Greek theater, numerous twentieth-century producers, composers, and playwrights have attempted to realize these correspondences in their works. Thus, we encounter examples of theatrical performance informed by one of these three models—and, more frequently than one might suppose, works based on some combination of these performance traditions. In the next three chapters, I offer an exploration of the influence of ancient Greek, Japanese Noh, and medieval Christian theater on the works of various modernist figures. The examples considered in each chapter have been chosen to contrast markedly in their appropriation or interpretation of the relevant exotic tradition.

5 Freedom in a Tunic versus Frieze-Dried Classicism: Hellenism in Modernist Performance

Dancing in the Temple of Dionysus: Duncan's Rituals

In 1903, at age twenty-six, Isadora Duncan made a first pilgrimage to Greece with her mother and siblings. The family settled in Athens, established a home on a hill across from the Acropolis, and adopted "ancient Greek" dress for their daily wear. Greece had long been a spiritual mecca for Duncan and was to remain her artistic touchstone throughout much of her career. As a child in San Francisco, she had lived in a home decorated with reproductions of Greek art and had attempted "by instinct to impart to my childish dance what I saw exhibited in the models of art."[1] Her adoption of the tunic held more significance for her than most casual acts of cultural cross-dressing, for it provided a corporeal freedom: "from my early childhood I have considered the freedom of my body essential to the rhythm of movement."[2] Before traveling to Greece, Duncan had studied the postures and implied movement of the figures on Greek vases and in Greek sculpture at the British Museum and the Louvre. Although she later denied attempting to bring the still figures of Greek art to life in her choreography, her artistic imagination was clearly obsessed with the lost art of Greek dance. She considered her previous work in dance to have been "only a prayer" in anticipation of one day living in Greece. Upon arriving in Athens, Duncan enthused: "My idea of dancing is to leave my body free to the sunshine, to feel my sandaled feet on the earth, to be near and to love the olive trees of Greece. . . . Two thousand years ago a people lived here who had perfect sympathy and comprehension of the beautiful in Nature, and this knowledge and sympathy were perfectly expressed in their own forms and movement."[3] She had come to Greece to study its ancient art and architecture and to dance in the sacred theaters and temples. She was to return repeatedly between the years 1904 and 1920, becoming modernism's most famous champion of pseudo-classical culture.

The numerous photographs of Duncan in Greek costume, dancing and posing among the ruins of Athens, testify to the exalted state —a new freedom of physical expression—that she experienced during her sojourns there. Her dances from this period, particularly her *Bacchanale* to the music of Christoph Willibald von Gluck, exhibit an intense delight in traversing space with relatively simple but forceful and athletic movements.[4] Such display of unbounded corporeal energy by a woman was Duncan's most revolutionary move. Duncan consistently celebrated what she imagined to be the "naturalness" of ancient Greek dance. She insisted that her dance resembled that of ancient Greece in its general natural style rather than in its choreographed detail and explained that "dancing naked upon the earth I naturally fall into Greek positions, for Greek positions are only earth positions."[5] Greek dance, as suggested in the artifacts of Greek culture, served as an ideal of human form and movement, an ideal she hoped to achieve in her own work: "if I could find in my dance a few or even one single position that the sculptor could transfer into marble so that it might be preserved, my work would not have been in vain."[6]

Duncan also celebrated the "harmonious unity" of the arts achieved by ancient Greek theater. She believed that the dancing chorus was at the heart of Greek tragedy and that it was necessary to revive its role in order to achieve the powerful impact of ancient performance. "To unite the arts around the Chorus, to give back to the dance its place as the Chorus, that is the ideal. When I have danced I have tried always to be the Chorus."[7] She rejected European opera for having failed to achieve a true unity of the arts and for neglecting the vital role of the dancing chorus. Duncan declared that Claudio Monteverdi had had "no intention of composing operas. 'Opera' is a meaningless word. He intended to accomplish a renaissance of tragedy."[8] Failing to integrate dance, this attempted renaissance proved stillborn. Although she respected Wagner's general artistic program, Duncan felt that he too had failed by not integrating the role of the Greek chorus in his works.[9] Duncan could find no modern example of the "harmonious unity" she sought in the theater, but she claimed to experience this harmony during her own performances in the Theater of Dionysus (see Fig. 1).[10] The unity of Greek theatrical performance was expressed for her in the architectural design of the sacred theater itself.[11]

In the years around 1915, Duncan was dedicated to creating her own "total theater" productions of such Greek tragedies as *Oedipus Rex*, and in April 1915 she presented a month-long "Dionysian season" of Greek theater in

Figure 1.   Isadora Duncan in the Theater of Dionysus. Photograph by Raymond Duncan. (Reproduced with the permission of the Dance Collection, The New York Public Library for the Performing Arts, Astor, Lenox and Tilden Foundations)

New York.[12] As an amateur archeologist of ancient performance, Duncan had sought inspiration in Greek vases and sculpture for her new aesthetic of movement. However, she could only lament the eternal silence of ancient Greek music. Duncan wrote: "to the rhythm of the words of a Greek Chorus one dances easily. Just in hearing them one sees unfolding a frieze of sculpted figures in movement. The music of the Greeks must have accorded with the rhythms of these words. Ah, if it only could be recovered!"[13] Her own attempts to rediscover ancient Greek music among the ruins in Athens are somewhat comical. Of her musical quest, Duncan wrote in 1908: "I have tried adaptations of old Greek music and found it very unsatisfactory. I once had a choir of Byzantine boys sing old Byzantine music for me, but I found that I couldn't dance to it."[14] Cynthia Splatt notes that Duncan had heard these "Byzantine" boys singing "old Greek songs" and decided to employ them as a choir accompanying her dances. She toured with them, before acknowledging the failure of this experiment and resolving to send them back to their families in (modern) Greece.[15] Although Duncan was to dance to the music of a variety of composers, she particularly turned to the music of Gluck for her evocations of the ancient world.[16] She believed that Gluck had partially succeeded where all others had failed and wrote that "Glück better than anyone else understood the Greek Chorus."[17] Duncan assumed that in order for Gluck to have so closely approximated the spirit of ancient theater in his opera productions, he must have studied Greek art as assiduously as she had done.

When in Athens, Duncan often danced in the Theater of Dionysus. For her, this was a sacred site. As early as 1901, she had expressed the desire to build her own temple in which to dance and to teach young "priestesses" of dance, and declared that "dance is a religion and should have its worshippers."[18] These sentiments were expressed again by Duncan in 1903, the year of her first trip to Greece: "My ideal would be to found a temple of ancient art in which, as a sacred priestess, I would devote my life to the worship of the beautiful. I am actively working to promote my idea of the reconstruction of the ancient dances and the ancient dress, and their adoption by as great a number of my sex as possible."[19] She repeatedly insisted that dance be viewed as an elevated form of religious expression rather than as mere entertainment.[20] At one point in her career, she dreamed of creating a ritual dance performance that would include audience participation in gestures of invocation, for she believed that some form of audience movement—similar to that found in modern Catholic and Greek Orthodox churches—occurred in ancient ritual performances.[21] This vision of audience participation was inspired, in part, by her encounter with Alexander Scriabin in 1912. Duncan was entranced by the visionary composer's plans for creating a work of total ritual theater in India and wrote that "His ideas were so in accord with my visions that we confidently looked forward to going to India together and participating in the creation of this temple."[22] Although her dream of constructing a temple to Terpsichore was never realized, Duncan found her own available sites for ritual performance in the ruins at Athens. One of her dances was based on her experience of the Parthenon and was created to "express the feeling of the human body in relation to the Doric column."[23] Concerning the creation of this dance, Duncan wrote that she had come to the Parthenon every day for four months seeking "a dance whose effort was to be worthy of this Temple—or never dance again."[24] She felt "gradually called by the great inner voice of the Temple" but no movement came to her for some time. Only after noticing that the columns were not rigid and straight but that each one was "in flowing movement, never resting"—i.e., that the columns were *alive* rather than *frozen*—did she find her dance, "and it was a Prayer."[25]

In addition to viewing dance as a form of religious expression, Duncan extolled its didactic potential throughout her career. She repeatedly expressed a desire to found a permanent school of dance for children and sought support for such a school in the United States, England, France, Germany, Greece, and the Soviet Union. She spoke of wanting to teach children how to live through dance, and asserted that dance should be employed for the moral and spiritual education of the young: "Before I die, I want to teach hundreds of children how to let their souls fill their growing bodies with music and love. I never taught my pupils any steps. I never taught myself technique. I told them to appeal to their spirit, as I did to mine. Art is nothing else."[26] This desire to employ dance and music for the spiritual education of children harkens back to the ancient Greek ideal of *paideia* and was a goal of several prominent modernist choreographers, dramatists, and composers. Duncan's only sustained opportunity to put into practice her didactic vision was offered in the Soviet Union. In 1921 she was invited by the Soviet government to establish a school in Moscow. In her acceptance letter she wrote: "I want to dance for the masses, for the working people who need my art and have never had the money to come and see me. And I want to dance for them for nothing."[27] Duncan was encouraged by what she sensed to be the spirit of the future in postrevolutionary Russia. Her naive optimism for socialism is proclaimed most lyrically in the following statement: "The spiritual truth of that which passes here I see as a shining vision of the future. The prophesies of Beethoven, of Nietzsche, of Walt Whitman are being realized. All men will be brothers, carried away by the great wave of liberation that has just been born here in Russia."[28] Duncan's trip to Moscow was the second major pilgrimage of her life, and, as with Greece, her dancing style reflected her enthusiasm for a new cultural environment. Her dances of this period were propagandistic, often concerned with such themes as the noble sacrifices of workers and the heroics of war and conveying a sense of committed corporeal power. Despite repeated setbacks and unfulfilled promises by the Soviet government, Duncan wrote that her "three years of Russia, with all its suffering, were worth all the rest of my life put together. There I reached the highest realization of my being. Nothing is impossible in that great weird country."[29] It should come as no surprise that in Russia, Duncan and her students dressed in red tunics.

Although Duncan never succeeded in founding a permanent school for the propagation of her dances and philosophy, her adoption of the Greek tunic and of "natural" movements was widely imitated. Female dance classes in the "Greek style" were widespread in America and England in the early years of this century.[30] (Much of this activity was also derivative of Dalcrozian eurythmics, which owed a good deal to Duncan's model but which Duncan herself scorned as mechanical and inartistic.) A more direct example of Duncan's influence—or at least of parallel interests—is found in the figure of Maud Allan, a Canadian-American dancer who achieved great acclaim in England and who likewise cited the natural movements of the Greeks as her model. Duncan lamented that her style and dances were being imitated in second-rate fashion and that her imitators often received more praise than did she. Although her intense interest in ancient Greece did inspire immediate cultural ramifications, her career served more generally as a catalyst for the birth of modern dance in America. (Walter Terry has pointed to Ted Shawn's quest for a Greek ideal and Martha Graham's use of Greek drama and myth as representing a continuation of Duncan's artistic interests.)[31] Duncan's insistence on freedom of physical expression and of individuality in movement propelled the development of dance throughout the twentieth century.

Duncan's formative artistic and personal encounter with Edward Gordon Craig (the father of her first child) brought her into contact with a theory of performance more radical than her own. She came to employ Craig's theories of stage design and, in turn, influenced his conception of ancient Greek theater. Like Duncan, Craig celebrated Greek theater as a model of ritual performance and declared that "the theatre is not a bar; it is a famous temple."[32] Craig was careful, however, to insist that his ideas and stage designs were not an imitation of ancient Greek models but were only inspired by Greek performance aesthetics. Craig met Duncan shortly after her first trip to Greece and must have heard a great deal of her immediate reactions. Yet their affair ended bitterly, in part because of professional jealousy; Craig's later remarks on the influence of ancient Greece and on the role of women in the theater may be read in light of this failed relationship.

In a 1911 article entitled "The Open Air," Craig derided the contemporary craze for all things Greek and described this fashion as mere "false classicism." He argued that it was vital to discover the performance style of Greek theater but that it was worthless to adopt the outer signs of Greek culture. In veiled reference to Duncan and her imitators, Craig declared that "sandals are not classic, nor is the bare arm or leg a scrap more Greek than Ethiopian" and that "we must avoid sandals, Greek robes, Greek masks, Greek theatres, Greek dancing. . . ."[33] Excluding the reference to masks, this list reads as a direct indictment of Duncan's appropriation of the signs of ancient Greek culture. Craig's misogynistic attitude toward the participation of women in the theater, which inevitably clashed with Duncan's feminism, becomes evident at the end of his essay. He declares that although a woman (in this case, the Italian actress Elenora Duse) may point the way toward a new theater, "there her task ends." In his view—one shared by many modernist figures—the modern theater was to be achieved by men alone.[34]

In terms less combative than Craig's, Duncan maintained that although her work was inspired by Greek art, it was not created in imitation of it. In 1917 she wrote: "It would be wrong to call my art Greek. People have supposed I copied the postures and gestures of Greek statues and Etruscan urns. But it seems to me my art is more universal."[35] This insistence on the originality and universality of her dances, as well as the emphasis placed on modern and futuristic art forms in the following two statements, is in line with the rampant modernist anxiety concerning exotic influence.

> While my dancing owes inspiration to the Greeks, it is not Greek really, but very modern—my own idea.[36]

> From what I have said you might conclude that my intention is to return to the dances of the old Greeks, or that I think that the dance of the future will be a revival of the antique dances or even of those of the primitive tribes. No, the dance of the future will be a new movement, a consequence of the entire evolution which mankind has passed through. To return to the dances of the Greeks would be as impossible as it is unnecessary. We are not Greeks and therefore cannot dance Greek dances.[37]

Duncan asserted on several occasions that she had created an entirely new art of spiritual movement that had little to do with dance. In the 1920s, she denied being a dancer entirely: "All my life I have only 'listened to music.' I have never been a dancer; I do not like any kind of dancing except, perhaps, the Japanese"; and, "I hate dancing. I am an *expressioniste* of beauty. I use my body as my medium, just as the writer uses his words. Do not call me a dancer."[38] Thus did Duncan express her version of that ultimate modernist dream of transcending traditional genres and creating an entirely new form of art.

A Transition: Wagner, the "Greek Theater Movement," and Oedipus

In 1905, at the invitation of Cosima Wagner, Duncan danced in praise of Dionysus in the Bacchanal scene of *Tannhäuser* at Bayreuth. The appearance of Duncan, a disciple of Nietzsche, in the Festspielhaus as a Bacchant was somewhat ironic. However, having just danced among the ruins of Athens, Duncan's performance at the modern Hellenistic mecca of Bayreuth was appropriate. The importance of Greek tragedy to Wagner's conceptions of the theater is well documented, and much of the modernist commentary on ancient Greek performance seems but an echo of sentiments expressed by him decades earlier.[39] In his writings, Wagner repeatedly referred to Greek theater as an ideal, both in contrast to the degraded state of contemporary performance and as a model for the total theater of the future.[40] He particularly celebrated ancient Greek tragedy as a paragon of the theater's potential role in society—a powerful forum for public religious expression.[41] Wagner believed that ancient Greek performers were sacred servants devoted to a ritual celebration and that it was specifically the use of masks that "gave to the performer his weighty character of priest."[42]

Together with Wagner's writings, Bayreuth was itself a focal point in the general turn-of-the-century movement devoted to the revival of ancient Greek performance. This "Greek Theater Movement" derived, in part, from the visions of both Wagner and Nietzsche and from new theories of Greek performance practice based on German archeological work of the 1880s and 1890s.[43] Karen Dorn has noted the direct impact of this archeological and classicist scholarship on modern theater: "Proscenium stages were converted to resemble Greek theatres, and a method of production was developed along the lines suggested by theories of the ritual origin of drama."[44] Wagner's Festspielhaus was cited by several prominent figures associated with the Greek Theater Movement, including W. B. Yeats, as a model approximating the ancient Greek design.[45] Discussions of the Bayreuth auditorium focused on its more inclusive positioning of the audience as manifested in its "democratic" allocation of seats. Several modernist producers attempted to transform conventional theaters in order to approximate this ideal. Dorn has cited Max Reinhardt's 1912 *Oedipus* production in London as being "possibly the most influential production of the Greek theatre movement."[46] The most striking innovation in this performance was a radical alteration of the relationship between performer and audience. Reinhardt placed the chorus facing the stage in the orchestra pit, thus blurring the division between audience space and performance space. Yeats was influenced by Reinhardt's production and attempted to incorporate aspects of the Greek Theater Movement in his own works.[47] Yeats's interest in ancient Greek theater was to culminate in his versions of *King Oedipus* (1926) and *Oedipus at Colonus* (1927).

Oedipus was a subject prevalent in sung as well as spoken theater in the first half of the twentieth century. Stravinsky and Cocteau's *Oedipus Rex*, first performed in 1928, was but the most prominent of several music theater works devoted to this subject. George Enescu set the entire story of Oedipus's life as a four-act opera in 1936, Arthur Honegger wrote incidental music for two productions of the drama, and even Ruggiero Leoncavallo had an *Edipo Re* in the works at the time of his death. Whether as a prolonged reaction to Freud's notorious interpretation of Sophocles, or in response to a particularly strong production such as Reinhardt's, Oedipus formed a prominent part in the general modernist obsession with ancient Greece.[48] Stravinsky's interest in composing an extended work on a Greek subject was sparked by his attendance at a 1922 performance of Cocteau's *Antigonae*, produced with incidental music by Honegger. It has been suggested that his decision to set *Oedipus Rex* may have been influenced by knowledge of Yeats's version[49] or perhaps by memories of the plot that he "had loved most" in his youth.[50] Inspired by Stravinsky's example, Carl Orff composed a massive trilogy of Greek works: *Antigonae* (1949), *Oedipus der Tyrann* (1959), and *Prometheus* (1968).

Although their musical and theatrical treatments differ in many ways, Stravinsky's and Orff's adoption of the classical mask contrasts markedly with Duncan's assumption of the ancient Greek tunic. While Duncan derived vitality and movement from the still figures represented in Greek art, Stravinsky sought the reverse, to transform living performers into immobile classical statues. Duncan was able to imagine dancing figures from a stone frieze while listening to the rhythms of recited Greek, and found freedom and a means for corporeal celebration in the loose-fitting tunic. For Stravinsky, to the contrary, the Greek mask and the frozen statues offered a model for achieving authorial control over the performance. Both Orff and Stravinsky created music of stasis, music in which rhythmic vitality is formalized through brute repetition and in which voices are rigidly sculpted in musical time. Although Orff's musical style derived from Stravinsky's, his obsessive devotion to ancient textual sources resulted in settings approaching pure speech, whereas Stravinsky famously destroyed the sense of his texts by focusing on the musicality of constitutive syllables. While Duncan's Greek-derived dance expressed ecstatic celebration, Stravinsky and Orff employed Greek themes for works of a more codified, stylized, and ceremonial nature. The differences between Duncan's response to ancient Greek theater and those of Stravinsky and Orff appear to be both a matter of sensibility (performerly versus authorial) and one of gender perspective. Duncan was attracted to the bacchic celebration of life in ancient Greek art—the ecstasy and revolt of women dancing freely in the natural world. Stravinsky and Orff were drawn to the hieratic possibilities of a priestly all-male chorus and to the conservative durability of Greek art. The cliché is tempting, and perhaps too obvious: while Duncan danced for Dionysus, Stravinsky and Orff listened for the Delphic, oracular voice of Apollo.

Primitive Classicism:
Orff's Music Theater of Minimal Means

Although it is now most often performed as a concert work, Orff's medievalist *Carmina Burana* was intended as a staged dramatic cantata that would include dance, sets, and costumes. Unlike Stravinsky, and closer to Duncan's interest in ancient Greek ritual performance, Orff was devoted to the total-theater ideal throughout his career. In a 1955 monograph written in close consultation with the composer, Andreas Liess reported that "Orff regards all such theatrical genres as opera and drama as broken and scattered fragments to be collected and reworked into their old organic unity."[51] For many of his works, Orff served as his own librettist, a fact that inspired Liess's rather myopic statement: "The term 'Gesamtkunstwerk' may be relevantly invoked for the first time since Wagner."[52] Orff's two primary models for the creation of his universal "world-theater" of integrated performance were ancient Greek tragedy and the medieval mystery play.[53]

Orff's early theatrical work included adaptations for the stage of the *St. Luke's Passion* (misattributed to Bach) and of a seventeenth-century Munich Jesuit play.[54] Two of his later works are particularly close in style and form to medieval mystery plays: an Easter play entitled *Comoedia de Christi Resurrectione* (1955), and a Christmas play, *Ludus de nato Infante mirificus* (1960). As was true of medieval mystery plays, these works include long sections of spoken text. The music reflects a naive vision of medieval simplicity and transparent symbolism—an aesthetic understanding exhibited in such passages as the rising cadenza presaging Christ's resurrection and in Orff's decision to employ boys for the choir of angels (see Ex. 1). This

Example 1. A musical resurrection symbol: Orff, *Comoedia de Christi Resurrectione* (Schott, 1957)

(continued)

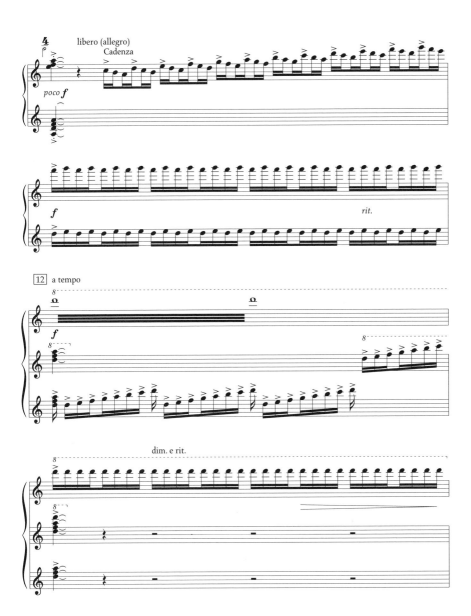

simplicity and transparency was central to Orff's medievalism and is common to other contemporary attempts to compose sacred drama, such as Benjamin Britten's 1957 *Noye's Fludde*. Orff's penchant for employing minimal musical means is even more striking in his text setting. The Greek choral lament for Adonis that begins *Comoedia de Christi Resurrectione* is set as a primarily monotone chant (see Ex. 2).[55] The influence of ancient Greek subjects, ethos, and masked performance on Orff's work is most obvious in the Greek trilogy at the core of his oeuvre.

In both *Antigonae* and *Oedipus der Tyrann,* Orff set Friedrich Hölderlin's translations of the tragedies word for word. In *Prometheus,* he returned to the original Greek—the sound of the authentic text serving as his Delphic voice. For Orff, the ancient words were classical artifacts, durable and potent objects that required only the most minimal of musical settings. Orff's range of text-setting styles in these works included ordinary speech, notated rhythmic speech, *sprechgesang,* recitational singing, and more lyrical singing including isolated melismatic material. The choral sections in both *Antigonae* and in *Oedipus* typify Orff's ritualistic vocal style. In act I of *Antigonae,* just prior to Kreon's entrance, the chorus of Theban Elders delivers a long text beginning "O Blik der Sonne" (see Ex. 3). This primarily syllabic vocal line resembles a stylized patter in which slight variations in duration and pitch give shape to the line without emphasizing textual meaning. The two florid melismas in this excerpt are the only nonsyllabic moments, save one further brief flourish, in the entire fifty-seven measure section. Most of the eighth-note rests in this vocal line are filled by massive punctuations from the percussion orchestra (not shown in Example 3). The chorus continues in the same fashion throughout the passage, with three statements of a twelve-measure explosive instrumental section framing the final two lines. Orff's primitivist percussion music in these Greek works, particularly in such choral sections as "O Blik der Sonne," creates the sound of formalized ritual enactment rather than of free or frenzied bacchic expression.

Orff's determination to set every word of these plays required a form of text setting that actually diminishes the text's importance. Much of the text is set in an undifferentiated style that speeds through time in its sculpted patterns. The vocal line often has a hypnotic affect—adding to its ritualistic subliminal power, but detracting from its specificity of characterization. The minimalist presentation of much of the choral text does, however, serve to set apart the isolated melismatic moments as in Example 3. Slight deviations from the sounding stream of minimal vocality assume a greater importance than possible in a more lyric setting. (Befitting her character, Orff's

Example 2.   A primitivist lament for Adonis: Orff, *Comoedia de Christi Resurrectione*
(Schott, 1957)

(continued)

Example 2. *(continued)*

Antigonae tends to deviate from the vocal norm more strikingly than do the other voices in the work.) In his discussion of Orff's text setting, Liess wrote: "The basic tendency of Orff's music of language, which becomes clearer with each succeeding year and composition, has been characterized by Heidegger as, 'to give voice to the language of language.'"[56] Orff's stylistic evolution from *Antigonae* through *Oedipus* to *Prometheus* validates this statement; he continued to seek the fundamental, the unadorned, and thus, the "classical" elements of ritualistic music. His rhythmic and melodic ostinati, his devotion to percussion, and the monumental affect of his music theater works have much in common with the later style of the so-called Minimalists. As is true of several major Minimalist works, Orff's music theater utilizes minimal musical means in conjunction with a maximal production style, performing forces, and sheer volume. This can result in overwhelmingly expressive moments, although—again as in several Minimalist examples—the significance of this powerful expressivity may ultimately remain obscure.

Orff declared that *Antigonae* was not composed for the conventional opera house, but was designed instead as a ceremonial and cultic work.[57] Even without the guidance of such statements, his settings of the Greek tragedies proclaim their ritualistic intent. Orff sought to reinvent the ancient power of Greek theater by stripping music to its elemental and primal materials; thus his classicism was fundamentally a form of primitivism. His incessant use of repetitive patterns performed by a range of percussion instruments is reminiscent of his *Schulwerk* for children with its didactic goals and methods. Percussion instruments, whether played in the classroom or in the "cul-

Example 3. Ritualistic choral music: Orff, *Antigonae* (Schott, 1949)

tic" theater, serve as tools of transport for Orff, carrying us back to our own elemental existence and our innate musicality. Orff understood Greek theater to be a matter of essentials, a form of ritual performance to which very little should be added at the risk of marring its perfection. Concerning his setting of *Antigonae*, Orff testified: "From the very beginning, I saw that there was nothing to add to Sophocles' text. . . . I consider my work merely as an interpretation of Sophocles' play for our time."[58]

What were Orff's contemporary interpretations of these dramas? What moral lesson was the ritualized performance of ancient Greek tragedy intended to instill in a modern audience? Orff's Greek works do not release

their tension through Dionysian and inclusive celebration; the audience is
to listen to the oracular declarations from their seats. Was *Antigonae*—a
play concerning the burial of the dead following a fratricidal war—created
with the horrors of World War II specifically in mind? If so, was Orff preaching forgiveness to all sides in this work, particularly to the dishonored
brother whose rebellion against the established government had failed so
miserably?[59] Was *Oedipus der Tyrann,* composed more than a decade later,
intended to serve as a reminder of the blindness of rulers and of the need
for purgation? What forbidden fire did *Prometheus* offer to the people in
1968? The tremendous punctuations of Orff's large percussion orchestra,
his insistence on presenting every word of the source text, the persistent
ostinato and recitation of the priestly male choruses—all of these elements
suggest ritual exhortation. Yet neither the text, nor the music, nor the original productions provide an unambiguous message "for our time." Despite
the overwhelming declarative mode of these three works, what is expressed
in their production is a general primitivist impulse toward the ancient magic
of classical performance, rather than an engagement through the theater
with the concerns of modern society.

Stravinsky's Masks of Control and Sculpted Voices

The implications of Stravinsky's earlier ritualistic music theater are equally
murky. Several of his neoclassical works are "classical" in a double sense.
In one standard (although imprecise and narrow) usage of the term, neoclassicism refers to the adoption or adaptation in works of modern music of
"classical" forms or stylistic features derived from the music of such figures
as Bach, "Pergolesi," Mozart, or even Tchaikovsky. Such retrospective references were employed for purposes of "objective" or ironical expression.
Associations made between the musical style of the so-called Classic period
and the aesthetics of ancient Greek art encouraged the use of Greek literary subjects for neoclassical works of ballet, opera, and music theater.
Stravinsky treated Greek mythological subjects in several of his major neoclassical works, including *Oedipus Rex* (1926–27), *Apollon musagète* (1927–
28), *Perséphone* (1933–34), and *Orpheus* (1947). Such works occasionally
received productions based on assumptions concerning the stage design and
function of ancient Greek theatrical performance. Of Stravinsky's works,
Oedipus and *Perséphone* both represent innovations in music theater and
contain explicit elements of ritualistic music and production. In addition,
Stravinsky's ideal for the production of *Oedipus* was based, in part, on his
vision of ancient Greek theater as static and utterly controlled. (The stag-

ing of *Perséphone* was inspired by a less rigid Hellenistic vision.) For Stravinsky, the masks of ancient Greece imparted a ritual dignity to the performance and served as devices of compositional control—control over the totality of the production and over the musical and physical expressivity of the individual performer. But before addressing specific aspects of *Oedipus Rex* and *Perséphone* we need to consider a more basic question.

Can we trust Stravinsky? It has been argued (read: demonstrated) that we cannot. Stravinsky left his critics with an extensive body of autobiographical material, detailed commentaries on his own music, and bold aesthetic pronouncements. On the first page of his 1936 autobiography, Stravinsky promised his readers that he would "take great care not to confuse my present reactions with those experienced at other stages in my life."[60] Little acquaintance with his writings is necessary in order to realize that Stravinsky repeatedly broke this promise throughout his career. Particularly near the end of his life, aided and abetted by Robert Craft, he appeared determined to repackage his career and oeuvre and to offer direction—including suggestions for suitable analytical projects—to future students of his music. However, his retrospective writings have inspired more suspicion than guidance. Most famously, whereas Stravinsky denied having been much influenced by Russian folk music, scholars have demonstrated the opposite. We now tend to approach his writings as though they constituted a modernist mask, one that conceals rather than proclaims central aspects of his life and works. It is even possible to wonder whether Stravinsky's various published statements reflect his own voice or whether they represent the agendas of his associates. This sense of distrust is occasionally heightened by the experience of his music.

From the start of his neoclassical period, Stravinsky was criticized for having abandoned his "true" modernist style and for self-indulgently experimenting with earlier music. His neoclassical swerve was condemned as a willful turnabout rather than a "natural" evolution. Critics concluded that the music was dishonest, that such a facile adoption of past styles indicated both a lack of originality and an artificial impulse. The multiple musical styles discernible in his works were heard as parodistic masks, casually assumed. (Stravinsky's much later turn to twelve-tone composition was likewise received, in some quarters, as a final example of his aesthetic treachery.) Today, Stravinsky's neoclassical music is more likely to be scrutinized for its ideology rather than for its artistic "inauthenticity."[61]

At a more internal level, there exist moments in Stravinsky's music that strike an incongruous, ironic tone—disconcerting moments with unclear implication. These odd passages tend to arise when Stravinsky appropri-

ates a fragment of an unexpected musical style, and are particularly striking in works that are otherwise intense, even ponderous, in affect. Much
of Stravinsky's music exhibits a seriousness worthy of "high" modernism,
but this intensity of purpose itself occasionally sounds like a stylistic mask
that has slipped to reveal an ironic sensibility. These moments of slippage
undermine our trust in Stravinsky's aesthetic commitment and sincerity,
especially within works that signal religious and ceremonial intent. They
have the (perhaps unintended) effect of acoustic winks, traces of Dada buf-
foonery that contradict the composer's late attempts to repackage much
of his music in terms of sincere religious expression and moral commitment. Whereas Orff's Greek works sound committed to the point of
solemnity, Stravinsky's facade of formality is frequently rent by irony. The
issue of Stravinsky's sincerity and its implications for interpretation should
be kept in mind throughout the following discussions of *Oedipus Rex* and
Perséphone.

Much of Stravinsky's oeuvre is purported to be religious or ritualistic.
But there is an important difference between works that depict ritual action
on the stage and those in which the religious or ritualistic intent crosses the
proscenium and affects those seated in the auditorium. *Le Sacre du prin-
temps* and *Les Noces* are depictions of ritual; they do not seem to be intended
to perform spiritual tasks through actual performance. Wilfrid Mellers writes
that in these staged primitivist rituals Stravinsky signaled "we could not
live [the ritual], we could only act it."[62] Mellers described *Oedipus Rex* as
the central work in Stravinsky's career, in part because "the humanist ritual of the opera [*Oedipus*] is linked both with the primitive ritual of earlier
works and with the religious ritual of his later, quasi-liturgical pieces."[63]
Robert Craft has similarly connected *Perséphone* to these earlier works: "Yet
Perséphone, though typologically Christian, is a successor to the *Sacre* in
presenting the rebirth of spring and fertility obtained at the cost of rape."[64]
In comments on *Oedipus Rex* and *Perséphone* made late in his career,
Stravinsky stressed their interconnections with his personal religious experience and identified specific religious stylistic features of their music and
staging. Although Stravinsky had less control over the creation and production of *Perséphone*, and though this later work is less rigorously formal
than *Oedipus*, religious references are more apparent in *Perséphone* and the
implications of its musical style less ambiguous.

Perséphone was commissioned by Ida Rubinstein, a Jewish Russian ex-
patriate dancer, mime, and actress, who through her talent, beauty, and
wealth initiated a new exploration of melodrama as an alternative form of
music theater in the first decades of the twentieth century. Rubinstein's most

famous previous collaboration was with Debussy and Gabriele d'Annunzio on *Le Martyre de Saint Sébastien,* a work to which we will return. Stravinsky had attended its first performance and recognized Rubinstein's general interest in creating religious spectacles for the stage. The commission called for Stravinsky to set André Gide's version of the Persephone myth and stipulated that Rubinstein herself would dance and recite in the title role. Robert Craft has written that the subject of Persephone "must immediately have appealed to Stravinsky as an archetypal resurrection myth. Certainly, as the first audiences recognized, Stravinsky conceived the work as a religious drama."[65] An early letter from Gide to Stravinsky makes clear that the religious aspect of the proposed subject was used to lure the composer's interest. Gide wrote on 8 February 1933: "As you will feel for yourself, the subject itself is halfway between a natural interpretation (the rhythm of the seasons; the corn falling in the soil must die to be resurrected through the sleep of winter) and a mystical interpretation; this way the myth is connected at the same time with both the ancient Egyptian cults and Christian doctrine."[66] Although Gide's letter reveals his awareness that Stravinsky would likely choose to focus on the Christian interpretation of the play, Gide preferred a political reading. As Michael de Cossart observes: "Just before rewriting the poem Gide paid a visit to a coalmine and instantly conceptualized the situation: the miners represented the prisoners in the Underworld, the down-trodden labouring masses. Like Persephone's shades, they too awaited the coming of a humanitarian social system in which all would enjoy an equal share of the light."[67] Obviously, Gide's communist interpretation of Persephone's pity could not stand a snowball's chance in Hades of being supported by Rubinstein or Stravinsky. In the event, Gide participated little in the production of the work and boycotted the final rehearsals and the premiere. He later complained that in transforming his work into a Christian mystery play Stravinsky had distorted it.[68]

Stravinsky's Christianization of the Greek legend was achieved musically. Craft has cited particular "allusions to church music" in *Perséphone,* including a section that Stravinsky himself referred to as a Russian Easter chorus.[69] The performance begins with a prayer by Eumolpe, the priest of Demeter (see Ex. 4). This opening address continues by referring to the audience as an assembled congregation at a ceremonial performance—a moment marked by a trumpet call in the instrumental accompaniment.[70] But the audience had been warned even before this that they were witnessing ritual performance. The very first sound of the piece consists of the archaic bell-like sonority of a struck fifth in the xylophone, harps, piano, and strings. (Perfect fifths, in fact, permeate this opening phrase.) Eumolpe's declamatory

Example 4.   An opening prayer to Demeter: Stravinsky, *Perséphone*
(Boosey & Hawkes, 1949)

(continued)

Cor.

Trb.
Basso

Xil.

2 Arpe

Piano

E.

ter   Qui cou - vres de mois - sons la ter - re

meno *f* e cantabile

non div.

arco

and rounded vocal line contains aspects of word painting. An ornament on each statement of "la terre" is fitting in this address to the earth goddess, as are the musical references to the fundamental theme of resurrection: when Eumolpe mentions Perséphone and her cyclical role as bringer of spring, descending and ascending lines are heard in the string section (see nos. 3–5 and 47–50 in the published score). Much of the music in this work is cyclic and static.[71] Eumolpe's opening prayer motif returns at the end of the work in his benediction (no. 257), thus framing the entire performance. In addition to musical details, several formal traits and narrative conventions in the text mark *Perséphone* as ritualistic, if not an actual ritual performance. Eumolpe, as "celebrant," serves as a narrator standing outside the performance frame. However, he also addresses Perséphone directly and in conjunction with the chorus, offers narrative interruptions, and occasionally provides a character's voice from within the sacred story. When Eumolpe exhorts Perséphone to descend to the Underworld to help her needy subjects, it is as though her ravishment had occurred in the past, as though we were witnessing a ceremonial reenactment devoid of all dramatic action. Finally, Eumolpe sings for Pluton.

Stravinsky's devils speak or dance rather than sing. In *Histoire du soldat*, the role of the devil is shared by an actor and a dancer, while in *The Flood*, Satan speaks. In *Perséphone*, Pluton is represented by a dancer. In his suggestions to Stravinsky, Gide had called for a deep bass voice for the part of Pluton. Stravinsky ignored this request and instead assigned the first sound of "le roi des Enfers" to a bass clarinet (see Ex. 5). Eumolpe then sings what are presumably Pluton's lines. Stravinsky's music for Hades and the enticements of Pluton is somewhat comic throughout (particularly so in the passage at nos. 131–34). Perhaps this less-than-serious music approximates an imagined medieval sensibility, echoing the medieval penchant for representing the Devil on stage as a comic figure, the trickster. Rather than serving as evidence of Stravinsky's ironic detachment, perhaps his musical devils are similar to Orff's ingenuous medievalisms.

As part of Rubinstein's general revival of the melodrama form, *Perséphone* represents an innovation in modern music theater. In a retrospective interview with Craft, Stravinsky regretted that he had not had more control over the creation of this work and noted that "the music was composed and timed to a fixed plan of stage action."[72] It is likely that the staging of *Perséphone* would have been more in the formal and static style of *Oedipus* had it not been for Rubinstein's stipulations for her own dual role as dancer and reciter. Stravinsky might well have preferred to divide the role of Perséphone between a dancer and a speaker—a separation of aural and physical

Example 5.   Pluto's voice: Stravinsky, *Perséphone* (Boosey & Hawkes, 1949)

representations that was central to several of his earlier works, one that offered Stravinsky more control over the individual performer. (Rubinstein was a major celebrity and as usual received a great deal of attention in the press for her representation of Perséphone, something resented by most of the male composers with whom she collaborated.) By so dividing representational responsibility, the composer's own authorial presence is affirmed at the expense of any one performer's authority. In his remarks to Craft, Stravinsky noted that he had preferred the first performance of the work, in which Rubinstein declaimed the text without moving. He had come to believe that "the mime should not speak, the speaker should not mime, and the part should be shared by two performers. . . . I now think it stylistically wrong to grant one stage figure unique powers of speech: the sound of Perséphone's voice is always a shock, for a moment, after a wordless section of mimed or danced movements."[73] This shock arises because the (female) performer, crossing boundaries between media, seems suddenly to usurp the creative role, the ability to achieve total theater. In Stravinsky's ideal production, "the speaker Perséphone should stand at a fixed point antipodal to Eumolpus, and an illusion of motion should be established between them. The chorus should stand apart from and remain outside of the action."[74] (In *Oedipus*, Stravinsky had not allowed for even the "illusion of motion.")

Although Stravinsky had been constrained by the nature of the commission in his allotment of performance responsibilities, he did have a free hand in his treatment of the text. Immediately prior to the premiere, Stravinsky proclaimed his theory of text setting in a published statement. He celebrated the syllable as his musical unit in vocal composition—"in *Perséphone* I wanted only syllables, beautiful, strong syllables"—and stated bluntly that "the word, rather than serving the musician, constitutes a cumbersome intermediary."[75] No wonder that Gide chose to avoid the rehearsals and the first performance. He must have realized that a librettist was not wanted. In an interview with Craft concerning his noncollaboration with Gide, Stravinsky offered an explanation for the poet's dislike of the text setting in *Perséphone*: "the musical accentuation of the text surprised and displeased him, though he had been warned in advance that I would stretch and stress and otherwise 'treat' French as I had Russian, and though he understood my ideal texts to be syllable poems, the *haiku* of Bashō and Busōn, for example, in which the words do not impose strong tonic accentuation of their own."[76] In short, Stravinsky asserts that the provider of syllables had been warned of his limited role prior to the composition. Stravinsky was right—after the composer's treatment of Cocteau's text in

Oedipus Rex, Gide or any other potential collaborator should indeed have been well warned.

Stravinsky's *Oedipus Rex* is the archetypal work of composerly control achieved through masked performance. Stravinsky described the work as a "still life," while others have referred to it as frozen and frigid; clearly Stravinsky's Thebans could not expect the arrival of a dancing Persephone. Early reviews of the work employed similar terms. André Coeuroy summarized the work's affect as "the expression of a force rushing toward the immobile."[77] André Schaeffner, in reference to both *Oedipus* and *Persé-phone,* noted "a fixed, hieratic, mummified quality" and referred to Stravinsky's "recurring tendency toward the static, toward sculptured immobility."[78] *Oedipus* and Stravinsky's provocative statements concerning his intentions continue to inspire a great deal of discussion.[79] The feature that has elicited the most intense response has been the style of Stravinsky's text setting. Stravinsky explained that "in my *Oedipus Rex* the word is pure material, functioning musically like a block of marble or stone in a work of sculpture or architecture"—put simply, words were approached as sounding units without regard for verbal meaning.[80] Stravinsky drastically cut Cocteau's French text and then had the surviving text translated into Latin, an archaic language of ceremony. Finally, he set this text without much regard for verbal comprehensibility. The device of the formal narrator is the last trace of Cocteau's voice and of verbal meaning. Thirty-five years later Stravinsky stated that he hated the role, and would have liked to see it cut.[81] Ridding the work of its narrator/translator would fully erase Cocteau's voice and most of his contribution. It would also fully mask verbal comprehensibility for most audiences. The rigid and masklike qualities of Stravinsky's text setting are also found in his accompanimental music, costume indications, and in the staging desired.

In a discussion of the origins of *Oedipus,* Stravinsky remarked: "I saw the chorus first, seated in a single row across the stage and reaching from end to end of the proscenium rainbow. I thought that the singers should seem to read from scrolls, and that only these scrolls and the outlines of their bearers' cowled heads should be seen. My first and strongest conviction was that the chorus should not have a face."[82] The individuality of the chorus members is masked in Stravinsky's vision; nor do they receive a new face in compensation. Stravinsky's music for the chorus is equally faceless. Example 6 is taken from the beginning of the prayer for relief from the plague. These vocal statues sing in a rigid rhythm throughout much of the work. Rhythm, with Stravinsky often an element of vitality, is instead a means for producing stasis in *Oedipus Rex* and for enforcing musical con-

Example 6.   A priestly chorus: Stravinsky, *Oedipus Rex*
(Boosey & Hawkes, 1949)

trol. "If I have succeeded in freezing the drama in the music," Stravinsky
stated, "that was accomplished largely by rhythmic means."[83] The principal characters in this work are masked musically in another dimension as
well, that of musical stylization. Stravinsky described the plethora of stylistic reference in this work, a major focus of critical condemnation, as forming a *Merzbild*—a nonsensical collage of musical styles.[84] The question remains whether such a Dadaist juxtaposition of styles was truly intended to
further ritual and religious expression.

The echoing of the formal affectations of *opera seria* and oratorio, the
emphasis on stylization in music and staging, and the rigidity of rhythm
reinforce each other in establishing a ceremonial import for the work. In
comparison to *Perséphone*, however, there is little suggestion of Christian
musical reference in the score. Perhaps for this reason, Stravinsky was careful in his retrospective comments to bring the work into the context of his
own religious development. When asked about the religious character of
Oedipus, Stravinsky answered: "In what sense is the music religious? I do
not know how to answer because the word does not correspond in my mind
to states of feeling or sentiment, but to dogmatic beliefs. A Christianized
Oedipus would require the truth-finding process to resemble an *auto-da-
fé*, and I had no interest in attempting that. I can testify, though, that the
music was composed during my strictest and most earnest period of Christian Orthodoxy."[85] He continued by relating how, after having prayed at an
icon, a festering forefinger miraculously healed just as he sat down at the

piano to perform his recent sonata in Venice in 1925. This miracle encouraged him to compose a work based on "the archetypal drama of purification," *Oedipus Rex*, and eventually led to his formal reconversion to the Orthodox faith in April 1926. The decision to set a Latin version of *Oedipus*—to employ a "sacred language"—came to Stravinsky after reading of the "hieratic use of Provençal" by Saint Francis of Assisi.[86] Finally, Stravinsky cited a specific example of religious musical reference in the work: "I was certainly influenced in composing the '*Gloria*' chorus [in praise of Jocaste] by Russian Church ritual: the Holy Trinity is symbolized by the triple repetitions, just as it is in the *Kyrie* of the Mass. But, to begin with, the character of the '*Gloria*' music itself is ecclesiastical."[87]

In addition to the musical and verbal masking in the score of *Oedipus*, Stravinsky explicitly called for masking the physical expression and presence of his performers. The feature that most clearly distinguishes this "opera-oratorio" from both opera and ballet is its aesthetic of movement, or rather, of immobility. Stravinsky stated that the work "may or may not be an opera by virtue of its musical content, but it is not at all operatic in the sense of movement," and that "the stage figures are more dramatically isolated and helpless precisely because they are plastically mute."[88] In the publication of the revised score in 1949, Stravinsky included a production note and a drawing of the stage design by his son (see Fig. 2). Stravinsky's ideal staging "presents the advantage of having no depth"—it is an acoustic frieze composed of immobile performers.[89] The performers are directed to "give the impression of living statues" and are to remain within their "built-up costumes and in their masks."[90] This production aesthetic was inspired by the work's classical subject, and Stravinsky may have had in mind the Hellenistic productions created by Léon Bakst for the Ballets Russes, particularly the style of movement employed by Vaslav Nijinsky and Bakst for *L'Après-midi d'un faune*. Stephen Walsh has suggested that Stravinsky's static ideal had been influenced by Meyerhold's statements on ancient Greek performance. In 1907, Meyerhold asserted that "the Greek classical theatre is the very theatre which modern drama needs . . . it demands statuesque plasticity."[91] Whether or not Stravinsky had Meyerhold's call for a modern "static theater" in mind when composing *Oedipus*, the work itself certainly declares its independence from those who would prefer a theater of dance.

Throughout much of his career, Stravinsky had composed for dancers and was forced to compromise with or even to accede to their production ideas. *Oedipus Rex*, however, was not a commissioned work but was instead Stravinsky's gift to Sergey Diaghilev in honor of the twentieth anniversary of the Ballets Russes. Diaghilev famously considered the work "un cadeau

Figure 2. Igor Stravinsky's ideal stage design for *Oedipus Rex*. Drawing by
Théodore Stravinsky. (Reproduced with the permission of Boosey & Hawkes, Inc.)

très macabre." An opera-oratorio "still life" that so aggressively demanded
the arrest of stage movement was indeed quite a peculiar gift to offer a ballet company. Whereas most modernist figures turned to Greek theater for
inspiration in the creation of integrated ritual performance, Stravinsky
found a model that—with the assistance of a dead language and Baroque
stylization—allowed him to subordinate the roles of both movement and
poetry. What remained were the Apollonian sounds of "pure music."

In 1952, perhaps to reassert his claim on the work, Cocteau revived *Oedipus Rex* at the Théâtre des Champs-Elysées.[92] For this production, Cocteau
again performed the role of the narrator and this time designed the sets and
masks and choreographed a series of *tableaux vivants* himself. (Surprisingly,
Stravinsky later cited the production as being his favorite.) Cocteau's masks
were particularly elaborate and elicited a great deal of comment. His general commitment to the use of visual and acoustic masks in the theater is
made clear by the following statement: "masks and megaphones are better
by far at getting beyond the footlights than ordinary voices and faces."[93]
With this production, Cocteau conjoined an interest in classical performance
with some influence from Japanese Noh. Frank W. D. Ries has written that
although Cocteau "insisted he was not directly influenced by Noh drama
for this revival, he did state that the Japanese had shown him the impor-

tance of the economy of gesture, which could so enhance a pictorial concept."[94] A recent production of *Oedipus Rex* has followed further on
Cocteau's path of unification between Greek and Japanese performance
styles. Julie Taymor's stunning 1992 Saito Kinen Festival production of
Oedipus Rex extended Cocteau's use of masks and employed elements of
Butoh, an avant-garde form of Japanese dance loosely derivative of Noh
movement aesthetics, for both the movements of the chorus and of the
dancer-mime who shares the role of Oedipus with a masked vocalist.[95] The
masking becomes multilayered and powerfully expressive at several points
in this production. (For example, as Oedipus relates that he once killed an
old man at a crossroads, the Oedipus persona is represented by a singer wearing a headdress-mask, the masked dancer, and a masked figurine reenact-
ing the story.) Although aspects of Stravinsky's classical statuesque ideal
remain in these two subsequent productions, both Cocteau and Taymor
clearly felt a need to turn to another exotic tradition of ritual performance
so as to reintroduce movement to the stage.

6 The Uses of Noh

A Nation Masked by Culture

From the violent suppression of the Jesuit missionaries in the early seventeenth century, through 250 years of adamant isolation, to the forced opening by American gunboats in 1853, through a period of accelerated modernization and Westernization, to the surprise result of the 1904 war with Russia, to the bombing of Pearl Harbor and Hiroshima, and through a period of economic ascendancy to the trade disputes of today—the fraught relationship between Japan and the West has been fueled by issues of access and visibility. Before 1854, Japan was one major region that had steadfastly frustrated the West's imperialistic desire to see, know, and control the world. Glimpses of Japan at points of trade only exacerbated this desire. In the Western imagination, Japan was a masked and mysterious nation. In the late nineteenth and early twentieth centuries, Europe and the United States exhibited a tremendous interest in seeing all things Japanese, in discovering that which had been so long concealed. Although Japan became increasingly visible, the image of the "masked Japanese" has never entirely left Western culture. Kenzaburo Oe, the 1994 Nobel laureate for literature, employed the image of the mask when describing contemporary Euro-American perceptions of the Japanese people:

> When I speak of the Japanese as an invisible man, I mean it this
> way: you can see Japanese technology in Europe, you know all about
> Japanese economic power, you know all about the quaint tea ceremony;
> but these are all images, masks of Japanese modesty or technological
> strength. . . . The majority of Japanese images are masks. We followed
> and imitated Western philosophy and literature, but even today, more

than a hundred and twenty-five years after our great modernization, the Meiji Restoration, began and Japan opened to the rest of the world, we are inscrutable in the eyes of Europeans and Americans.[1]

The images and masks of Japan have continued to serve the West as proxies, ensuring that external signifiers, immediately indicative of Japanese culture to the Western eye and ear, would go on being employed by modernist Euro-American painters, composers, and producers to facilitate exploits of creative cross-dressing.

In the late nineteenth century, European and American artists enthusiastically appropriated the surface features of Japanese art without troubling to understand the significance that lay behind the images. Elements of *japonisme* appeared in the work of such artists as James McNeill Whistler, who sometimes dressed his models in Japanese costume just as he imitated certain basic stylistic features of Japanese painting in his work. Literary adaptations of things Japanese came next, in both style and subject matter. (One field of modernist poetry—the Imagism of Ezra Pound and company—was inspired by Japanese poetic style and structure.) Composers of the early twentieth century followed suit by setting Japanese folk tunes. Exposure to the performing arts of Japan lagged behind the intense fascination with Japanese objets d'art. However, the influence of Japanese music theater gradually became widespread, even though much of this influence was based on secondhand description. In the preface to his seminal 1921 collection of Noh plays, Arthur Waley noted that Noh had already begun to influence modern theater in the West and suggested that his project of translation was intended to facilitate such developments: "The theatre of the West is the last stronghold of realism. . . . A few people in America and Europe want to go in the opposite direction. They would like to see a theatre that aimed boldly at stylization and simplification, discarding entirely the pretentious lumber of 19th century stageland. That such a theatre exists and has long existed in Japan has been well-known here for some time."[2]

The list of those figures who, to varying degrees, donned the Noh mask in modernist theater is long. (For example, in French theater, the chain of Noh influence links Claudel, Copeau, Dullin, Barrault, and Cousin.)[3] Having borrowed several of the most obvious elements of Noh, particularly the use of masks, symbolic movement, and ritual dramatic structure, modernist figures tended to re-dress these elements in the fashion of their own cultural costume. Euro-American works and productions based on or inspired by Noh were created throughout the twentieth century to serve a variety of political, religious, and didactic functions. Two archetypal cases of this kind, in which Noh was tailored to fit Western purposes in works of modernist music theater, were the "Plays for Dancers" of W. B. Yeats and the *Lehrstücke* of Bertolt Brecht.

Back to Ancient Ireland via Japan: Nationalistic Noh

Throughout much of his career, Yeats was committed to the theater. The stage offered a powerful platform for the presentation of poetic and nationalistic statements and allowed Yeats to educate his audience in their cultural heritage. His early plays, written before his acquaintance with Noh, were based on Irish legends and were intended to revive the spirit of an idealized bardic and heroic past. The Abbey Theatre, which Yeats helped found in Dublin in 1904 as a home for the Irish National Dramatic Society, was first dedicated to the production of Irish folk drama and aspired to serve as a national theater for Ireland. Although his devotion to Irish legend never ceased, Yeats's theatrical interests soon surpassed the successful folk-style productions of the Abbey Theatre. He sought a more formal, ritualistic style and found a first model when he encountered the production techniques of Edward Gordon Craig.

Yeats first experienced Craig's work in 1901 and was struck by the economy of means and the elegance of Craig's stage production. The two soon established a professional relationship and remained in contact until the poet's death in 1939. In 1910 Yeats acquired a small model stage from Craig which allowed him to experiment with Craig's space-defining blank screens and experimental lighting effects on a manageable scale. The following year, Craig designed a production of Yeats's *The Hour-Glass* for the Abbey Theatre and in 1913 an exhibition of his designs appeared in Dublin with Yeats's enthusiastic support. Yeats repeatedly stated that Craig had opened his eyes to new possibilities for the stage. Through Craig's flexible and subtle stage designs, Yeats was introduced to a new aesthetic of symbolic stage movement and to the power of masks. Finally, although credit for this pivotal introduction is most often accorded to Ezra Pound, Yeats may have first learned of Japanese Noh from Craig's 1910 issue of *The Mask*.[4]

Several critics have argued that when Yeats encountered descriptions of Japanese Noh theater he experienced a "shock of recognition," for his own theatrical aesthetic had been moving toward an approximation of Noh for some time.[5] In truth, Yeats was prepared to appreciate and to adopt only those particular elements of Noh performance that resonated with a theatrical vision already present in his mind. Noh provided a final stimulus encouraging Yeats to embark on a new form of theater. However, Yeats's knowledge of Noh was minimal and twice removed. He never witnessed a Noh performance, nor had Ezra Pound, his primary informant. Pound's own limited understanding of Noh stemmed from his work as editor of the manuscripts of the American scholar Ernest Fenollosa. The transmission of Fenollosa's written descriptions of Noh from Pound to Yeats in 1913–14, and Yeats's subsequent *Four Plays for Dancers* based on his impressions of Noh, constitute a classic topic in modernist literary studies.[6] The best source for determining Yeats's understanding of Noh and how Noh contributed to his theatrical agenda is found in the poet's introduction to the first published Pound-Fenollosa Noh translations, entitled *Certain Noble Plays of Japan.* At the start of this introduction, Yeats states his belief that the Noh plays have "some special value to Ireland" and notes that they "help me to explain a certain possibility of the Irish dramatic movement."[7] He writes that the Noh plots remind him of Irish legends and that Pound's translations have allowed him to invent "a form of drama, distinguished, indirect and symbolic, and having no need of mob or press to pay its way—an aristocratic form."[8] Noh reinforced several aspects of Yeats's developing aesthetic of theatrical performance, including the use of a nonrealistic and simple stage setting, the use of masks for main characters, and the importance of minimal musical accompaniment and intoned text. Noh also proved useful for Yeats's larger agenda.

Although traces of Noh influence have been observed in several of Yeats's late plays, this influence is most directly apparent in his four "plays for dancers," works that constitute a new theatrical genre. These consist of *At the Hawk's Well* (1916), *The Only Jealousy of Emer* (1919), *The Dreaming of the Bones* (1919), and *Calvary* (1920).[9] The first three plays are based in varying degrees on individual Noh plays translated by Pound and Fenollosa.[10] *At the Hawk's Well* and *The Only Jealousy of Emer* form part of Yeats's cycle of plays devoted to the legends of the Irish hero Cuchulain. In *At the Hawk's Well,* set in "the Irish Heroic Age," Cuchulain seeks the well of immortality. He meets an Old Man at the well who warns him of the futility of his quest and the danger of incurring the curse of the Woman of the Sidhe. Cuchulain is transfixed by the hawklike Guardian of the Well and misses his opportunity to drink from the magic water. He then embarks on a battle with the fierce mountain women and thus begins his heroic and tragic destiny. This play is based loosely on the plot of *Yoro* in which a young man seeks an immortal water for the benefit of his Emperor. In *The Only Jealousy of Emer,* Cuchulain's wife and mistress engage in a struggle with the Woman of the Sidhe for the spirit of the dead Cuchulain, whose body has been possessed by an evil being. They triumph, and Cuchulain's spirit returns to his body, although Emer has had to sacrifice her hope of winning back his love. This play corresponds to the Noh play *Aoi no ue,* based on an episode in *The Tale of Genji,* in which Genji's wife, Lady Aoi, is possessed by the spirit of a jealous former wife. As in *The Only Jealousy of Emer,* the plot of *Aoi no ue* involves the exorcism of this evil spirit.

The Dreaming of the Bones is the most political of the four plays and is set in a specific and significant time—1916, following the Irish uprising. A Young Man involved in the rebellion is making his escape in the night when he encounters the spirits of Dermot and Dervorgilla, the legendary medieval lovers whose treachery led to the Norman invasion of Ireland. They lead the Young Man to safety but, upon learning their identities in a climactic dance, he refuses to forgive them and to release them from their purgatory. In this play, Yeats pointedly juxtaposed a tale from Irish legend with current political events. While Yeats's play ends without the resolution of forgiveness, in *Nishikigi*—the Noh model—the spirits of the two lovers who had never been united in life are brought together through the prayers of a priest.[11] For *Calvary,* the last dance play, Yeats turned away from Noh plots and toward Christian scripture for this work of religious criticism. The action takes place on Good Friday, "the day whereon Christ dreams His passion through." The conceit of Christ reexperiencing his march to Calvary in this play is one indication of the influence of Noh theater, in which the principal character is often a spirit reliving a climactic moment from his or her prior earthly existence. On his way to his crucifixion, Christ is faced with the knowledge that his message has been resisted or ignored by many and that his death has not sufficed to save all. Unlike most Noh plays, this reenactment of the tragic tale on stage does not release Christ from his psychological ordeal—he dies feeling forsaken by God.

These four plays contain numerous stylistic elements of ritual performance derived, in part, from Noh theater. Yeats created his own formalized dramatic structure for this new theatrical genre. Each of the plays opens and closes with the ritualistic unfolding of a large cloth by the three Musicians as they sing the opening and closing songs. This framing device both separates the time and place of the performance from the quotidian and allows performers to enter and exit without being seen. *At the Hawk's Well* begins with an invocation, "I call to the eye of the mind . . . ," signaling that, as in Noh, the setting is to be described rather than naturalistically represented and that a spiritual performance of a legendary tale is about to begin. Both the Old Man and the Young Man (Cuchulain) enter through the audience, and thus incorporate the audience space into the ritual performance area. As in many forms of ritual theater, including Noh, the characters and actions of these plays are timeless and generic while also specific to a particular mythic tradition. Yeats's chorus is seated in full view of the audience and describes the setting and actions of the major characters. As in Noh, the sets and props for Yeats's dance plays are stark and symbolic—for example, the well in *At the Hawk's Well* is represented by a square blue cloth. Of the aspects of ritualistic performance that Yeats adopted from Noh for the creation of his new form of total theater, the use of masks, text intonation, and stylized dance proved the most significant and, in the case of dance and music, the most difficult to realize.

The image of the mask is frequently invoked in critical discussions of Yeats and his work. This is due, in part, to the significant appearance of mask imagery in Yeats's poetry and philosophic writings and to the important role of literal masks in several of his plays. Masks are to be worn by several of the major characters in all four of the dance plays. Those performers appearing unmasked are most often directed to wear makeup creating the impression of a masked face. In his introduction to *Certain Noble Plays of Japan*, Yeats discussed the value of masks for his theater in the following terms:

> A mask will enable me to substitute for the face of some common-place player, or for that face repainted to suit his own vulgar fancy, the fine invention of a sculptor, and to bring the audience close enough to the play to hear every inflection of the voice. A mask never seems but a dirty face, and no matter how close you go is still a work of art; nor shall we lose by staying the movement of the features, for deep feeling is expressed by a movement of the whole body. In poetical painting & in sculpture the face seems the nobler for lacking curiosity, alert attention, all that we sum up under the famous word of the realists "vitality." It is even possible that being is only possessed completely by the dead, and that it is some knowledge of this that makes us gaze with so much emotion upon the face of the Sphinx or Buddha.[12]

In this passage Yeats exhibits the modernist fascination for the noble immobility and immutable perfection of the mask as opposed to the living face of the performer. Yeats stops just short of calling for the death of the actor and the substitution of stone sculpture or Craigian marionettes for the human performer. In another context, Yeats celebrates the mask as an "emotional antithesis" to individual subjective expression.[13] In his preface to *Four Plays for Dancers*, Yeats states that "the face of the speaker should be as much a work of art as the lines that he speaks or the costume that he wears, that all may be as artificial as possible."[14] He looks forward to a time when he will be able to write plays inspired by and designed for a set of masks at his constant disposal.[15] In a remark pointing to his exotic models of masked performance, Yeats describes his Cuchulain performer as one "who wearing this noble half-Greek half-Asiatic face will appear perhaps like an image seen in revery by some Orphic worshipper."[16] Yeats was well pleased with the masks designed by Edmund Dulac for *At the Hawk's Well* and boasted in a letter that with the production of this play, masks were "being used for the first time in serious drama in the modern world."[17]

Richard Taylor has written that "like many other dramatists of the period Yeats worked with both antique and exotic forms, and was particularly concerned with the ideal synthesis of the arts that Richard Wagner had originally advocated."[18] The two elements of total theater that proved the most difficult for Yeats to realize satisfactorily in productions of his plays were the dance and the music. Being neither a choreographer nor a musician himself, Yeats had to rely on others. Although he never found the ideal composer to realize his vague musical ideas, for a brief period he did enjoy the services of an inspiring choreographer: the Japanese dancer Michio Ito. Yeats celebrated Ito as the "tragic image that has stirred my imagination" and stated that Ito made *At the Hawk's Well* possible (see Figs. 3 and 4).[19] However, as had been true of Pound, Ito did not bring an authentic understanding of Noh to his collaborations with Yeats. Ito had had some training in Kabuki dance, but his commitment to dance arose only after he witnessed performances by Nijinsky in Paris and Duncan in Berlin. In 1912 he began training in the eurythmic techniques of Émile Jaques-Dalcroze. By the time he reached London and began his professional dancing career, Ito was fully committed to the aesthetics of modern Euro-American dance.[20] Like Ruth St. Denis and Duncan, Ito based his dance style, in part, on his impressions of Egyptian and Grecian gestural movement as depicted in ancient art. Helen Caldwell notes that Ito composed a number of dances in an "avowed ancient Greek style."[21] Ito's choreography was dominated, like Noh and ancient Greek dance forms, by symbolic gesture.[22] His dancing also exhibited something of the modernist and Noh styles of masked performance. Caldwell observes that "in performance Ito kept his face immobile so that personality was further excluded and idea enhanced."[23]

Although Yeats's encounter with Japanese dance was filtered through European modernist influences, his basic understanding of the aesthetics of Noh dance was fairly perceptive. As in Noh, the dramatic climax in each of his "plays for dancers" is marked by a major dance. Travels of great distance within the drama are symbolically depicted by simple circular walks on stage and through the narration of the chorus or a secondary character, as in Noh

Figure 3.   Michio Ito in the mask of the Guardian of the Well in *At the Hawk's Well*. Photographer unknown. (Courtesy of the Reading University Library)

performance. In his introduction to *Certain Noble Plays of Japan*, Yeats wrote that in Noh dance "[t]he interest is not in the human form but in the rhythm to which it moves, and the triumph of their art is to express the rhythm in its intensity. There are few swaying movements of arms or body such as make the beauty of our dancing. They move from the hip, keeping constantly the upper part of their body still, and seem to associate with every gesture or pose some definite thought. They cross the stage with a sliding movement, and one gets the impression not of undulation but of continuous straight lines."[24] When Ito left for New York in 1916, Yeats's vision of dance for his plays left with him. In the 1921 preface to *Four Plays for Dancers*, Yeats wrote that for future productions "the dancing will give me most trouble, for I know but vaguely what I want. I do not want any existing form of stage dancing, but something with a smaller gamut of expres-

Figure 4.   Michio Ito as the Guardian of the Well in *At the Hawk's Well*.
Photographer unknown. (Courtesy of the Reading University Library)

sion, something more reserved, more self-controlled, as befits performers within arm's reach of their audience."[25] Ito went on to perform *At the Hawk's Well* in New York City in 1918, in California in 1929, and in Japan in 1939. The play was then adapted in 1949 and entered the Noh repertory as *Taka no Izumi*, thus completing one of the many circles of cross-cultural encounter in the twentieth century.[26]

Of the several components of Noh performance, Yeats received the least information about the music. However, what he had been told concerning the use of a few instruments for minimal accompaniment and concerning the style of the vocal chanting formed part of his "shock of recognition." Throughout his career, Yeats was both determined to discover a musical form of recitation for his poetry and plays and utterly opposed to most forms of text setting and singing. His own poetic readings were celebrated for their musicality. Yeats sought to revive an ideal bardic style of poetic and dramatic recitation—a prelapsarian style in which speech itself was musical. He claimed, in turn, to be either tone deaf or to be attuned to more ancient forms of music than those available in the modern world. He wrote that "my ears are only comfortable when the singer sings as if mere speech had taken fire, when he appears to have passed into song almost imperceptibly."[27] His ideal form of text delivery was one close enough to singing so as to be notated but also close enough to speech so as to be perfectly understood. The poet's distrust of the musician and his belief in the magical potential of vocalized words are both evident in his notes to *Calvary*: "I have written the little songs of the chorus to please myself, confident that singer and composer, when the time came for performance, would certainly make it impossible for the audience to know what the words were. I used to think that singers should sing a recipe for a good dish, or a list of local trains, or something else they want to get by heart, but I have changed my mind and now I prefer to give him some mystery or secret."[28] Music was a major element of Yeatsian theater, but its presence was carefully circumscribed.

The singing of Irish folktunes in many of Yeats's plays was one expedient solution for the poet's musical misgivings, one that also served as a musical reinforcement of his nationalistic themes. But Yeats was to find a creative solution that appears to have satisfied his ideal for a musical delivery of text. In a 1902 article entitled "Speaking to the Psaltery," Yeats wrote: "Since I was a boy I have always longed to hear poems spoken to a harp, as I imagined Homer to have spoken his."[29] This essay was written immediately following the fulfillment of this long-held wish. Yeats relates that a friend had just performed poetry for him with her voice and with a beautiful stringed instrument and notes that "although she sometimes spoke to a little tune, it was never singing, as we sing today, never anything but speech . . . nor was it reciting, for she spoke to a notation as definite as that of song, using the instrument, which murmured sweetly and faintly, under the spoken sounds, to give her the changing notes."[30] This friend was an actress named Florence Farr, and the instrument was a psaltery designed by Arnold Dolmetsch. Farr shared Yeats's ideals for poetic recitation and dramatic singing. In 1909 she published a collection of writings on her new vocal art, written by critics and herself, which she dedicated to "W. B. Yeats, who suggested to me the notation of speech; also to Arnold Dolmetsch, who invented for me a musical instrument sympathetic to the speaking voice, calling it a psaltery."[31] Farr wrote that "the difference between speech and singing is this—that in speech each word has a melody of its own, which starts from a certain keynote on which it is uttered, while in singing the melody of the separate word is sacrificed to the melody of the phrase."[32] She celebrated the power of spoken words and referred to the "East," where utterances were considered magical.[33] Her book concludes in the grand Yeatsian spirit: "The mystery of sound is made manifest in words and in music. In music we know and feel it; but we are forgetting that it lives also in words, in poetry, and noble prose; we are overwhelmed by the chatter of those who profane it, and the din of the traffic of the restless disturbs the peace of those who are listening for the old magic, and watching till the new creation is heralded by the sound of the new word."[34]

Farr's vocal technique proved inimitable, despite her attempts to notate it, and so Yeats was forced to rely on composers for his musical needs. In his publication of *Four Plays for Dancers,* Yeats included music for two of the plays. In addition to designing the first production of *At the Hawk's Well,* Edmund Dulac had also composed the music. Dulac stressed, in his note to the printed score, the importance of achieving a simplicity in musical style—an aim that his composition indeed meets. The only suggestion of the influence of Noh on Dulac's music is in the minimal instrumentation and in his instructions for the accompaniment to the dialogue. Dulac composed for a bamboo flute, harp, drum, and gong, and noted that the drum and gong should be "oriental" in form. He also wrote that "the drum and the gong must be used at times during the performance to emphasize the spoken word; no definite notation of this can be given, and it is left to the imagination and taste of the musician."[35] Yeats never understood that Noh is chanted throughout. In the dance plays he limited the sung passages to the text of the four instrumentalists. At Pound's instigation, Yeats turned to Walter Morse Rummel, a composition student of Debussy and noted pianist, for *The Dreaming of the Bones.*[36] Rummel's notes on the music for this play indicate that he had acquired a basic understanding of the Farr-Yeats-Pound vocal aesthetic through his brief contact with Yeats in Paris. Rummel wrote: "Music of tone and music of speech are distinct from each other. Here my sole object has been to find some tone formula which will enhance and bring out a music underlying the words."[37] Like Dulac's, Rummel's instrumentation is both small in scale and Orientalist in style. Rummel called for a harp or zither to reinforce the solo voice, a flute, a one-string bowed instrument ("more like a Hindu Sarinda") and a drum of "oriental model."[38] Yeats wrote very little about the music for these plays, but he did indicate that Dulac's music for *At the Hawk's Well* was suitable and that it could serve as a model for the later plays. Although he remained wary of all musical settings of his verse, Yeats consistently acknowledged the important function of music in ritual theatrical performance.

In many cultures, ritual is a democratic and inclusive event for all members of the society, while in others, ritual performance is reserved for a priest caste and is witnessed by an initiated and noble few. As poets, Yeats and Pound particularly admired the poetic subtlety possible in an "aristocratic" form of theater such as Noh. Yeats clearly believed that his "plays for dancers" were a form of ritual that could only be appreciated by an aristocratic or ideal audience. In 1929, Yeats famously wrote: "I always feel my work is not drama but the ritual of a lost faith."[39] For Yeats, ritual theater represented "the most powerful form of drama . . . because everyone who hears it is also a player."[40] For ritual to be achieved through the performance, Yeats believed that it was necessary to limit the audience to those who could engage intellectually and spiritually in the performance. He therefore decided to remove his plays from the public stage and its demands for realism and to offer these works in the privacy of the aristocratic drawing room. This desire to create theater for a select few was expressed by Yeats as early as 1899. "Why should we thrust our works, which we have written with imaginative sincerity and filled with spiritual desire, before those quite excellent people who think that Rossetti's women are 'guys,' that Rodin's women are 'ugly,' and that Ibsen is 'immoral,' and who only want to be left at peace to enjoy the works so many clever men have made especially to suit them? We must make a theatre for ourselves and our friends, and for a few simple people who understand from scholarship and thought."[41] Yeats hoped to create plays that were "remote, spiritual, and ideal" for an audience composed of the "right people."[42] In his note to *The Only Jealousy of Emer,* Yeats rejoices in his "freedom from the stupidity of an ordinary audience."[43] He fused his devotion to Irish myth and legend with the general antirealistic and ritual elements of Noh performance to create an intimate form of sacred theater, a theater not unlike a private seance. Yeats's interest in the occult is a celebrated topic of literary modernism, and these small plays can be understood as an expression of the general modernist fascination for the mystical and spiritual. The "noble plays of Japan" assisted Yeats in his efforts to invent an "aristocratic" and ritualistic theater that could call up the heroic ancestral spirits of ancient Ireland for the benefit of his modern nation.

Noh as Didactic Theater: Communist Noh

Verfremdungseffekt, episches Theater, neue Sachlichkeit, Gebrauchsmusik, Gemeinschaftsmusik, Gestus, Zeitoper, Schuloper, Lehrstück—the sheer density of aesthetic terms and new genre designations employed by Bertolt Brecht and his collaborators bears witness to the intense experimentation prevalent in German theater and music during the Weimar period. The style of acting and theater production signaled by the adjective "Brechtian" was one of the most influential developments of the modernist stage.[44] Like others considered here, Brecht's desire to reform theatrical performance and to reconceive its social function resulted in a large quantity of quasi-theoretical and prescriptive writings. Brecht's essays and productions raise many of the issues that I have identified as central to modernist music theater history. Several of his plays require the use of masks. His celebrated *Verfremdungseffekt* or "alienation effect"—an acting style that emphasizes the difference and separation between performer and character—represents a major departure from naturalistic acting, just as his techniques of "epic" stage production diverge from traditions of naturalistic scenic design. In addition, Brecht's oeuvre exhibits a sustained attempt to incorporate music in theatrical performance and to develop a form of music theater in opposition to traditional opera. His evolving conception of performance was informed by his limited contact with models of Asian theater and several of his works are adaptations of specific Japanese and Chinese plays. Finally, Brecht forcefully preached against the notion of theater as mere entertainment and intended his productions to involve the audience and to serve as a form of social commentary and political enlightenment.

Although Brecht's artistic project appears to fit neatly within the framework of this study, his theories of theatrical performance and his contact with exotic models diverge somewhat from the general pattern of modernist music theater. Brecht's plays are intended to function as transformative works that engage rather than amuse the audience. However, while some have referred to Brecht's theater as a form of secular and communal ritual, the resultant sense of community inspired by successful productions of his plays derives more from a confirmation of shared beliefs displayed in didactic performance than from the spiritual transformations of a ritual ceremony. Brechtian characters represent average and generic types rather than Yeatsian heroic figures, though in certain works they suggest figures of mythic stature arising from within modern society. While Brecht repeatedly discussed the importance of music and scenic design in theater and affirmed their crucial function in his works, he did not seek to create a form of integrated total performance. In fact, Brecht stridently denounced the *Gesamtkunstwerk* ideal as a muddled form that inevitably led to the degradation of each individual element. He called for a radical separation of the performing arts in his epic theater and declared that "words, music and setting must become more independent of one another."[45] The basic elements of total theatrical performance are present in his works, but they appear juxtaposed rather than integrated. In effect, Brecht extended his concept of "alienation" in acting to include the relationship established between the various forms of performance in his presentational theater. Brecht asks his audience to maintain a healthy skepticism, rather than suspend its disbelief, and to remain fully aware of the artificiality of theatrical performance.

Brecht's *Verfremdungseffekt* proved a central concept in modernist act-ing and a prominent expression of the "New Objectivity" in the arts of Weimar Germany. Nevertheless, it represents a performance aesthetic somewhat different from others considered here. While Yeats attempted to transform his performer into a heroic or superhuman being and Stravin-sky seemed primarily concerned with concealing the individuality of his performers, Brecht called upon his actors to remind the audience of their actuality by presenting a detached narration of the character's actions and emotions.[46] By maintaining an identity separate from their characters, Brecht's actors bridge the distance between stage and audience. In Yeats's theater, masked acting—whether involving the literal use of a mask or as a description of the more general performance style—served as a device of magical transformation. In Brechtian performance, the persona of the char-acter was treated as though it were contained in a mask held away from the performer's face, so that the performer's identity was never confused with the performed role.[47] Although the Brechtian aesthetic differs from Yeats's conception, in both cases the new style and theory of acting represents a sustained attack on theatrical illusion. For Brecht, these techniques were meant to promote social transformation through didactic performance. The Brechtian theater functions neither as a bourgeois living room for emotional catharsis nor as an aristocratic temple for secret rituals, but rather as a sem-inar room in which performers present social issues for critical reflection and moral truths for indoctrination in staged parables. The ultimate artis-tic goal was to reform the role of the theater in modern society: "Once the content becomes, technically speaking, an independent component, to which text, music and setting 'adopt attitudes'; once illusion is sacrificed to free discussion, and once the spectator, instead of being enabled to have an ex-perience, is forced as it were to cast his vote; then a change has been launched which goes far beyond formal matters and begins for the first time to affect the theatre's social function."[48]

Brecht's first use of the term *Verfremdungseffekt* is found in his 1936 ar-ticle on Chinese acting. During a trip to Moscow in the previous year, Brecht had witnessed a performance by the acclaimed Chinese opera performer Mei Lanfang and his troupe. Like Yeats upon learning of Noh theater, Brecht was struck by the similarity between this exotic model and his own developing performance aesthetic. The importance of Chinese culture in Brecht's works and artistic imagination was considerable.[49] Several of his plays were either based on Chinese tales or set in China, while others appear to contain as-pects of Chinese performance style, as Brecht understood it. In the 1936 ar-ticle Brecht expressed his admiration for several specific features of Chinese acting. He noted that the Chinese performer does not behave as though unaware of the presence of an audience—the "fourth wall" is entirely absent. Concerning the Chinese performer, Brecht wrote: "The artist's object is to appear strange and even surprising to the audience. He achieves this by looking strangely at himself and his work."[50] Brecht admired the controlled portrayal of human emotion in the Chinese theater and praised the Chinese actor's complete mastery of the *Verfremdungseffekt*: "He limits himself from the start to simply quoting the character played" and to "exhibiting the outer signs of emotion."[51] Brecht speculated on the possibility of adopting certain aspects of Chinese performance in modern European theater and wrote that "It is not entirely easy to realize that the Chinese actor's A-effect [alienation effect] is a transportable piece of technique: a conception that can be prised loose from the Chinese theatre."[52] Having acknowledged the possibility of future influence, he was careful to assert his creative independence from this exotic model: "The experiments conducted by the modern German theatre led to a wholly independent development of the A-effect. So far Asiatic acting has exerted no influence."[53] Brecht never intended to imitate Asian theater. Instead, he was interested in "prising loose" those particular elements of performance style that were congruous with his own developing theories and that provided a model and encouragement for "those who need such a technique for quite definite social purposes."[54] Appropriations from the exotic are highly selective transactions.

The possible impact of Japanese performance aesthetics on Brechtian theater has somewhat less historical support. However, numerous critics have argued that Brecht's theories of performance have much in common with the aesthetics of Noh, and some have suggested that this influence is apparent in the *Lehrstücke* ("learning" or "didactic" plays) produced around 1930. It is possible that Brecht witnessed performances by a Japanese company in October 1930 and January 1931 in Berlin. This troupe did not present authentic Noh or Kabuki productions, but may have performed some scenes in the style of Kabuki.[55] Other critics have suggested that Brecht was influenced by Japanese performance at secondhand through his contact with modernist Russian theater production. Both Sergey Eisenstein and V. E. Meyerhold had a direct impact on Brecht, and both directors in turn readily acknowledged the influence of Japanese theater in their work. Meyerhold, for instance, developed his own form of stylized movement and emulated the Japanese example of the "total performer." Still another possibility is that Brecht had learned of Paul Claudel's experiments with Noh techniques and developed his own ideas from general descriptions of Claudel's productions. Finally, several commentators have assumed that Brecht's pre-

1930 knowledge of Japanese theater was based primarily on published scholarly descriptions.[56]

Asian theater served as but one of several models for the creation of the *Lehrstück*. This genre was a product of the general modernist interest in the potential social functions of art; a concern that assumed specific forms in Weimar Germany, including the *Gebrauchsmusik* ("functional music") and *Gemeinschaftsmusik* ("communal music") movements. The most prominent composers associated with this aesthetic were Paul Hindemith and Kurt Weill, both of whom collaborated with Brecht on the development of the *Lehrstück* genre.[57] Before joining Brecht and Weill on the composition of the first *Lehrstück*, a 1929 interactive radio play entitled *Der Lindberghflug*, Hindemith had already written several works for school performance and had demonstrated a commitment to amateur participation in the theater. Hindemith also collaborated with Brecht on the second example of this genre, a work first entitled simply *Lehrstück*, and later retitled *Das Badener Lehrstück vom Einverständnis*. In his introduction to the score of *Lehrstück*, Hindemith underscored the importance of audience participation and declared that, for him, this was the primary goal of the performance. Brecht and Hindemith differed on this point—Brecht stressing the importance of the *Lehre*, or message, of each work—and their collaborative association quickly ended.[58]

Although Brecht did not fully endorse Hindemith's radically inclusive approach to performance, audience engagement and limited participation were essential components of both the theory and the performance of *Lehrstücke*. An important model for the genre is found in the performances of communist workers' choruses in Berlin and in the mass communal and children's plays prevalent in Soviet Russia. Russian communal performances involved casts of thousands and were often designed to recreate revolutionary events in acts of patriotic celebration. The influence of these models is apparent in Brecht and Hanns Eisler's *Die Maßnahme* (*The Measures Taken*), which was first performed by the Greater Berlin Workers' Chorus. Audience participation is crucial in this play. The audience acts as a jury and delivers a verdict on the case being reenacted; of course, this so-called control chorus is controlled fully by Brecht himself, for it delivers only the lines assigned to it. *Die Maßnahme* is the most overtly didactic of the *Lehrstücke* in its propagation of a communist lesson. Tatlow has argued that "participation in *Die Maßnahme* is a secularized act of ritual; it is a demonstration of faith."[59] Rather than discussing his theater in terms of ritual, Brecht was inclined to draw analogies to the classroom. He intended his audience to learn through both active and intellectual participation in the didactic performance.[60]

A central role in Brechtian theater, including the *Lehrstücke,* was accorded to music. Like Yeats, Brecht both valued music's role in the theater and distrusted its powerful presence. He was wary of composers, and feared a loss of authorial control in their settings of his text.[61] (In an early stage of his career, he evaded this problem by singing his poetry to melodies improvised with the aid of a guitar.) Several of Brecht's most famous plays, including *Die Dreigroschenoper* and *Aufstieg und Fall der Stadt Mahagonny,* owed a great deal of their success to Weill's music. Brecht reacted to the popularity of the musical numbers by either attempting to belittle their importance or, later in his career, by claiming to have dictated the melodies to Weill himself.[62] (Brecht's conflicted approach to music is also evident in the nonsensical term he coined for the type of music he desired for his theater: *Misuk.*) Like Yeats, Brecht railed against the traditional forms of operatic singing and called for an "untrained" vocal style with minimal accompaniment. Brecht described the music of traditional opera as being similar to an intoxicating drug that numbed the minds of the audience, and argued that conventional art music "seduces the listener into an enervating, because unproductive, act of enjoyment."[63] He felt that the need for a new form of music theater was imperative, for traditional opera was nothing more than a "culinary art," completely unsuited to didactic purposes.[64]

In spite of his antagonistic relationship with musicians, Brecht declared that "music plays the chief part in our thesis."[65] To evade the dangers of musically masked text and of the insidious subliminal powers of music, Brecht sought to unmask music by exposing its artifice and emphasizing its separate presence. This separation and distancing was to be achieved through a variety of techniques. Brecht called for "music which takes the text for granted."[66] He noted that the composer should not try to fuse the musical setting with the meaning of the text but rather maintain a cool distance from the text and even compose against its emotional affect.[67] The Brechtian vocalist was called upon to extend the *Verfremdungseffekt* to the act of singing: "the actor must not only sing but show a man singing."[68] The actor should not drop into song subtly but should "clearly mark it off from the rest of the text."[69] Thus, all singing is a form of sung song in Brecht's theater—as an audience, we are never to pretend that singing is a natural form of vocal communication. These divisions between words and music could be emphasized through various production techniques. As an exemplary model, Brecht cited the 1928 production of *Der Dreigroschenoper,* which employed a dramatic change of lighting for each song, displayed the title of each number on a screen, and presented the instrumentalists in full view of the audience.[70] Brecht also sought to defuse the potentially intoxicating effects of music by calling for settings of utmost simplicity and banality. Brecht wrote: "A good way of judging a piece of music with a text is to try out the different attitudes or gests with which the performer ought to deliver the individual sections . . . For this the most suitable gests are as common, vulgar and banal as possible. In this way one can judge the political value of the musical score."[71] Music was valued by Brecht, but only insofar as it served the greater purpose of the performance.

Contrary to the impression formed by his writings, Brecht's musical collaborators were also fully engaged in the creation of a new form of music theater. In addition to claiming that he had whistled melodies for Weill, Brecht asserted that he was responsible for Weill's break with Expressionism and subsequent adoption of a simpler, more popular musical language.[72] (Successful as they were, the Brecht-Weill collaborations were fraught with tension.) Weill himself cited Ferruccio Busoni's formative influence on his developing musical aesthetics, rather than Brecht's, and stressed the value of simplicity throughout his writings: "In the transparent clarity of our emotional life lie the possibilities for the creation of new opera; for precisely from this clarity arises the simplicity of musical language that opera demands."[73] Unlike Brecht, Weill celebrated the "triumph of *Gebrauchsmusik*" and emphasized the importance of a democratic musical style accessible to all.[74] Insisting that the invention of the radio, the medium for the first *Lehrstück*, dictated a new simplicity in music, he wrote: "The content and form of these radio compositions must also be capable of interesting a large number of people of all classes; and the means of musical expression also must not cause any difficulty for the untrained listener."[75] Most pointedly, Weill declared the centrality of the composer for the creation of a new theater: "for the theatrical form that aims at saying something about mankind, music is indispensable."[76]

Weill was fully aware of contemporary developments in music theater and of their historic significance, as is evident in such statements as the following: "Perhaps a later era will term what we are creating only an intermediary genre. . . . one can label neither ballet nor the genre compounded from ballet and opera as an ultimate result. What Stravinsky attempted in his *Soldier's Tale* undoubtedly can be appraised as the intermediary genre with the most certain future. Standing on the boundary between play, pantomime, and opera, this piece still displays such a strong predominance of operatic elements that it perhaps can become the foundation for a certain course of new opera."[77] In addition to his discussions of the style and role of music in the theater, Weill considered the appropriate form and function of theatrical performance itself. During the development of the

Lehrstück, he declared that the new theater *"must be as 'topical' in its means of expression as in its subject matter."*[78] Like Brecht, he was committed to the presentation of moral lessons in the theater. He argued that the *Lehre* of the didactic plays were more forcefully transmitted through music and insisted on a larger purpose for musical performance: "music is not an end in itself, but serves those institutions that need music and for which a new musical production represents something of value."[79] Weill also claimed that the *Lehrstücke* and *Schuloper* were forms of musical education, and that *"the practical value of didactic opera consists precisely in the study,* and as far as the performers are concerned, the performance of such a work is far less important than the training that is linked to it."[80] He offered his *Lehrstück* compositions as models for young composers and producers for the creation of new music theater: "At precisely this time, when it is a matter of positing new foundations for the genre of 'opera' and of redefining the boundaries of this genre, an important task is to create prototypes of this genre, in which the formal and thematic problems of a primarily musical form of theater are examined afresh on the basis of new hypotheses."[81]

The most successful of the *Lehrstücke,* and the only example explicitly based on a Noh model, was Brecht and Weill's 1930 *Der Jasager.* This work particularly calls into question Brecht's authorial claims. *Der Jasager* began as a translation into German by Elisabeth Hauptmann (whose work was often left uncredited by Brecht) of Arthur Waley's English translation of the Noh play *Taniko.* (Brecht's final text for this work is virtually identical to Hauptmann's translation.)[82] In *Taniko,* as reconstructed by Waley, a young boy sets out on a ritual pilgrimage with his teacher in order to pray for his ailing mother. While crossing the holy mountains, he becomes ill and is forced to stop. The other pilgrims resolve to throw him off a cliff in accordance with a religious custom regarding illness during a pilgrimage. The boy agrees to his fate, and the pilgrims sadly hurl him into the valley. Waley had substantially altered the affect of the original play by not translating its final section, in which the boy is brought back to life by a saint. Hauptmann and Brecht further adapted the play by secularizing it as much as possible and by establishing the concept of *Einverständnis,* or consent for the common good, as the *Lehre* of the work.

Der Jasager was intended specifically for student performance and is thus a *Schuloper* as well as a *Lehrstück* (see Fig. 5). The students serve simultaneously as the performers of the work and as the intended recipients of the moral message. (The Teacher is the only role requiring an adult performer— a casting decision that further emphasizes the didactic nature of the per-

Figure 5. *Der Jasager* at New York's Henry Street Settlement, 1933. Photograph by Paul Parker. (Reproduced with the permission of the Yale University Music Library, Kurt Weill and Lotte Lenya Papers)

formance.) In addition to the ritualistic elements of presentational theater retained from their Noh model, Brecht and Weill added a framing chorus that forcefully extols the virtue of *Einverständnis* and clearly proclaims the work's didactic purpose. This Great Chorus declares in full voice: "What we must learn above all is consent" (see Ex. 7). In accordance with the abilities of student performers, Weill's music is in a simplified style throughout, but particularly in this stark chorus. The fugal character of this number imparts an air of solemnity, as do the rigid, plodding quarter notes of the vocal line. These musical traits have led Gottfried Wagner to discuss this chorus in terms of Weill's "musical propaganda."[83]

Did Weill fully support the lesson of *Einverständnis* in this work? In a contemporaneous interview, Weill stated unambiguously that the purpose of *Der Jasager* was to teach the student performers the importance of consent: "That is what students should learn. They should know that a community which one joins demands that one actually bear the consequences. The boy goes the way of the community to the end when he says yes to being tossed into the valley."[84] In spite of Weill's assertions, some critics have heard an undermining of this message in his musical setting. Ian Kemp has suggested that the "demotic rhythms of the foxtrot" heard as the three students decide to abandon the boy and to continue their journey, signal "Weill's bitter comment on the corruption implicit in mass behavior."[85] This might seem a case of wishful hearing, particularly in light of Weill's extensive comments on the potency of "topical" musical styles and in view of his devotion to simple and popular settings. Paul Humphreys argues that

Example 7.   Starting with the moral of the story: Weill, *Der Jasager*
(Universal Edition, 1957)

Weill's music for *Der Jasager* does not undercut the textual affirmation of *Einverständnis*. However, Humphreys attempts to strike a balance on this issue: "For Weill, *Der Jasager* is an expression, rather than an espousal or a rejection of, the act of agreement and its accompanying consequences."[86] He asserts that the music is not propagandistic, for Weill perceives "both the tragedy and the inevitability" of the denouement.[87] Even this interpretation is too eager to disassociate the music from what the writer clearly regards as an unattractive lesson—a gambit that Weill himself rejected. In contrast to Brecht's "alienating" conception of ideal text setting, in which musical and textual affect conflict rather than agree, Weill stressed music's ability to support the *Lehre* of a work.

Der Jasager's brutal lesson of *Einverständnis* is common to several of the other *Lehrstücke*. The communist implications of "acquiescence" are presented explicitly in *Die Maßnahme*, in which an individual agrees to be sacrificed for the greater good of world revolution. John Fuegi has argued that *Die Maßnahme* "is a direct transposition of the religious and mythic core of *He Who Says Yes* [*Der Jasager*] into the contemporary political sphere," and has noted that an early draft of this play was actually entitled *Der Jasager*.[88] The use of masks is highly suggestive in this work. The communist agitators, who reenact their story before the "control chorus," relate how they had adopted masks for protective disguise while in China, thus effacing their individuality for their revolutionary work. When the Young Comrade removed his own mask of communist ideology and exposed his identity, when he responded as a feeling individual rather than in accord with communist doctrine, he was necessarily sacrificed—with his full consent. The agitators note that the Young Comrade's face had changed while under its mask and that they had cast him into a lime pit after killing him in order to burn away all traces of his identity and to protect their revolutionary campaign from exposure. The chorus commends their actions.

The first example of the genre, the 1929 *Lehrstück*, also presents a stark lesson proclaiming the unimportance of the individual. In the final scene, titled "Examination," the chorus methodically leads the protagonist—a crashed airman and capitalist hero—to the inevitable conclusion that when he dies, no one dies, for the individual is of no significance. (In several of the *Lehrstücke*, the omniscient and triumphant chorus is either synonymous with the audience itself or stands in for the proletariat in the theater.) In contrast to the political interpretations suggested here, several critics have argued that the *Lehrstücke* were not works of communist propaganda, and that the genre encouraged critical thinking rather than political indoctrination. Roswitha Mueller, in particular, objects to narrow interpretations of these works and insists that *Lehrstück* should be translated as "learning play" rather than as the more highly charged "didactic play."[89] Mueller claims that the *Lehrstück* "cannot be contained as a kind of dogmatic Marxist-Leninist thesis play" and cites Brecht's use of post-performance questionnaires and his willingness to revise, particularly in the case of *Der Jasager,* as evidence of his ideological flexibility.[90] The production history and revisions of *Der Jasager* provide some support for this contention. At the suggestion of a group of student performers, who had objected to the boy's agreement to die, Brecht decided to revise the work. In the second *Der Jasager,* Brecht maintained the basic structure—although in this version, the boy asks to be thrown from the cliff for fear of being left alone. In addition, Brecht strengthened the rationale for the tragic decision by indicating that the welfare of the entire village depended upon this trip in search of medicine and that to return on account of this boy would cause many to suffer. Brecht then wrote a new work, based on the same Noh play, in which the boy refuses to be sacrificed. In this version, entitled *Der Neinsager,* there is no urgency pervading the trip and no logical reason to sacrifice the boy, only an irrational "Great Custom" that calls for the death of anyone who becomes ill during the mountain crossing. Since Brecht intended to transmit an entirely different *Lehre* with *Der Neinsager,* he revised the work in order to prepare the new lesson from the beginning. The message of this play, a *Lehre* equally useful for revolutionary communism, is that "great customs" should not be obeyed blindly, that bourgeois tradition should not rule over rational action. Brecht intended *Der Jasager* and *Der Neinsager* to be performed together.

Although Brecht and Weill's commitment to a specific *Lehre* in *Der Jasager* may be questioned, I argue that the *Lehrstücke* were intended to provoke a certain kind of directed "critical thinking" in their audience: thinking leading to communist views of society. Brechtian music theater was calculated to encourage social transformation through stage performance, be it primarily didactic, participatory, or dialectic. It remains unclear why the members of the "Brecht workshop" found Japanese Noh to be a suitable model for their new music theater. Yeats and Pound had admired the noble refinement and aristocratic exclusiveness of Noh—features that would seem to lend themselves poorly to the development of a democratic laboratory for social inquiry. Interpreting the *Lehrstücke* as didactic and propagandistic, Andrzej Wirth has argued that Noh provided an ideal model for communist music theater, for it proclaimed "a constant ideological core."[91] Wirth also notes, however, that the Noh-based *Der Jasager* was both embraced by some pro-fascists and condemned by some Leftists.[92] As a final sign of its potential flexibility, *Der Jasager* was adopted by the German Ministry of Education and was produced in schools throughout the country.[93] Thus, a mixed—but predominately communist—message was disseminated to the general public, with the support of the government, through a genre of inclusive performance and in the fashion of an imagined Japanese Noh.

7 Medievalism and the French Modernist Stage

The Sacred Theater of Claudel: Noh *Mystères*

In a mid-1930s discussion of Noh, Paul Claudel wrote: "When Mme. Ida Rubinstein asked me to write a biblical piece, with music by my old friend and faithful collaborator Darius Milhaud, I quite naturally turned my thoughts toward the sacred drama of Japan, which I had watched assiduously and admiringly for five years."[1] One might well wonder why Claudel considered it "natural" to present a Christian subject in the style of Japanese Noh. Claudel—a devout Catholic poet devoted to the creation of religious drama—had served as the French ambassador to Japan from 1921 to 1927, had studied Japanese theater in its several forms, and had written extensively on Noh and on the affinity between Japanese and Christian ritual performance. Significantly, the Noh audience reminded Claudel of a Christian congregation engaged in ceremony. He claimed that in the Noh theater "we do not see a play on one side and an audience on the other, separated by the drama's make-believe as if by a flame-filled chasm."[2] Echoing Artaud's appreciations of Balinese ritual, Claudel noted that in Noh "the actors have the solemnity and reverence of mystics, while the audience brings a disciplined attention, and a mind sharpened and purified by abstinence from every outside distraction."[3] While Yeats and Brecht appropriated aspects of Noh drama for nationalistic and political purposes, Claudel sought to employ Noh in the service of Christianity. However, he was not alone in connecting Noh performance style to Christian subjects and to the medieval mystery play—Yeats's dance-play *Calvary* (1920) had preceded Claudel's Noh-inspired works, and Britten's Church Parables would follow. These figures were retracing the path of the sixteenth-century Jesuit missionaries in Japan, but with an opposite direction of purpose. Rather than joining techniques of Noh performance to Christian doctrine and mystery play for the conversion of exotic "others," the modernists sought to revive religious performance for the edification of their home audiences.

Claudel consistently emphasized two fundamental features of Noh theater that appealed to his theatrical conceptions and that would play a prominent part in his own work. The first characteristic was what he referred to as the "double" function of the Noh chorus, in which category he included both the vocalists and the instrumentalists. On the Noh chorus, Claudel wrote: "First of all it is the listener. It takes a word from the lips of the actor and weaves it into a tapestry of images and sayings. It adapts thought to speech. But both above and below poetry and music, Nō drama adds a third element, which is the exclamation, the cry, the reverberation of the character's emotion until it returns to him again. That is what is called in Japan the *Ah!*"[4] In these comments, Claudel appears to refer to the *kakegoe*, the explosive vocal cries of the Noh drummers, which may function as a form of time keeping, but which are experienced primarily as musical sound. In one essay, he remarked: "The musicians often add prolonged howls on two notes, one deep, the other shrill. This gives a strange dramatic impression of space and remoteness, like the noises of the countryside at night, the formless calls of nature. Or perhaps it is the cry of an animal groping toward speech and always failing to reach it, a despairing effort, painful and vague."[5] The effective use of vocalisms was a primary interest of the poet, an interest that influenced his collaborations with composers on works of religious music theater.

Throughout much of his theatrical career, Claudel was intent on exploring the range of vocal possibility existing between pure speech and song. He once wrote: "Between music and speech there is a whole domain, that of exclamation, which has hitherto not been used, and which offers the most interesting possibilities."[6] Claudel documented his "unique" use of vocalisms by referring to his creation of the sounds of a stormy night in the first act of his *L'Otage*. (Of course, nonverbal vocalism had been explored, to some extent, in nineteenth-century European opera—most often in the form of the wordless chorus as used so effectively, for example, by Verdi in the act III storm of *Rigoletto*.) For Claudel, the chorus was primarily a voice, or group of voices, rather than a visible presence on the stage. Not only did the immobile chorus of Noh theater support his vision, but he also considered the chorus of ancient Greek theater a prototypical congregation, whose vocal function had been continued in the Catholic Mass. We will discover that Claudel's pursuit of the *"Ah!"* expressivity of wordless choruses was central to his attempts to create transcendent voices in the theater.

In addition to the expressive vocalisms of the chorus, Claudel was also fascinated by the movements of the individual performers in Noh. The slowness of gesture in the dancing of the principal character, the *shite* role, was a feature that he repeatedly discussed and sought to incorporate in his productions. Claudel's description of Noh dance is striking: "Like a teacher repeating and explaining, someone is slowly reproducing our past acts before our eyes, so that now we can understand how every one of our poor random gestures was the unconscious imitation of some eternal attitude. It is as though a statue took shape for a moment in front of us."[7] In addition to Japanese theater, Claudel also had a more limited experience of Chinese performance and was similarly entranced by its style of gesture and dance. Like Brecht, Claudel felt particularly fortunate to have witnessed the artistry of the Chinese opera star Mei Lanfang, writing, "His attitudes flow from one to another so deliciously that he does not so much express every feeling and emotion as transport them into the realms of music."[8] The use of gesture, of controlled and limited movement, was central to Claudel's theatrical ideal. Asian theater had taught him the value of statuesque presentation in religious performance.[9]

Prior to his encounter with Noh and his collaborations with Rubinstein, Claudel had already demonstrated an interest in the medieval mystery plays and in creating modern religious works for the stage. One of his most successful plays, the 1912 *L'Annonce faite à Marie*, was inspired by the *mystères* tradition. Rubinstein's commissions encouraged him to focus more intensely on religious drama. *Le Festin de la sagesse* (1934), the "biblical piece" referred to by Claudel in the quotation opening this chapter, was specifically designed as an experiment in the adaptation of Noh performance techniques for a work of Christian theater. This play is based on the parable of the Feast, in which a ruler compels his reluctant subjects to attend the celebration of his son's wedding. It is clear from Claudel's discussions of this work that the influence of Noh was primarily on the style of stage gesture and movement. To satisfy the commission, he had to create a mime role for Rubinstein, but he found no suitable character in the parable itself. He therefore added the allegorical character Wisdom, whose Christian mission he defined as "the calling of the prodigal and recalcitrant to the communion of God."[10] Ironically, the play's success in attracting an audience to the religious performance would depend, to some extent, on the draw of Rubinstein herself. As it turned out, Rubinstein lost interest in the work and chose instead to produce a play whose subject she had specified.[11]

When Rubinstein and Honegger first approached Claudel concerning the possibility of creating a work on the subject of Joan of Arc, Claudel adamantly refused. In a lecture delivered at several performances of *Jeanne d'Arc au bûcher,* the poet discussed his initial reluctance to treat Joan in a dramatic work. He asserted that in creating a play based on a historical figure, the author is constrained by the subject and lacks creative freedom. He had found this to be particularly true of Joan of Arc, for "it is she who does as she likes with us, and simply by being there restricts us to the inglorious role of bystander or impresario. We cannot make Joan speak, we can only let her speak."[12] Although Claudel focuses on his reluctance to be dominated by his historical protagonist, he may also have been responding negatively to the dominance of his patron. Before considering Claudel's solution to his initial concerns, and Honegger's musical setting of the play, let us turn to Rubinstein herself and to her previous works of religious theater in order to discover how she came to commission a mystery play from the devout poet. Claudel's decision to collaborate with her on religious theater works will appear surprising in light of Rubinstein's past public image.

A Spectacle of Religious Androgyny: The Legs of Saint Sebastian

Although her influence on the Parisian stage in the 1910s and '20s rivaled Diaghilev's and her skills as a mime and reciter were widely acclaimed, Ida Rubinstein's most laudable attributes, for many, were her legs. Her initially scandalous public image was based, in part, on her various portrayals of Salome, and on her appearances in *Cléopâtre* and *Schéhérazade* with Diaghilev's Ballets Russes. Her performances as Salome and Cleopatra included moments of nudity, and her portrayal of Zobeïda opposite Nijinsky's Golden Slave in *Schéhérazade* stunned the audience with its sexual violence. Rubinstein's participation in the Salome craze (inspired by the wild success of the 1905 Strauss opera) placed her in the ranks of such dancers as Loie Fuller, Maud Allan, and Ruth St. Denis, as well as with hundreds of American vaudeville performers. In 1908, in St. Petersburg, Rubinstein presented her first incarnation of Salome in her own production of Oscar Wilde's play, with music by Alexander Glazunov, sets by Léon Bakst, and choreography by Mikhail Fokine. This production was censored by the Russian Orthodox Church. In a decision that would radically alter Rubinstein's career, the censors declared that the production could go ahead, as long as Wilde's text was not heard. Rubinstein decided to perform the play in mime. She had begun her performance career with the aspiration of becoming an actress, but with this Russian production of *Salome* and her performances for Diaghilev, she became a mime and quasi-dancer. In her subsequent revival of the melodrama form, she pursued a dual performance role as both speaker and mime.

Eventually, in works such as *Jeanne d'Arc au bûcher*, she would concentrate solely on her role as reciter.[13]

Diaghilev admired Rubinstein's performance in her St. Petersburg *Salome*, and inadvertently supported a rival-to-be when he asked her to assume the title role in his ballet *Cléopâtre* during his first full Parisian season. Even in her performances with the Ballets Russes, Rubinstein primarily struck poses rather than danced. She was nevertheless a tremendous success. Unlike Diaghilev, she was both an impresario and the principal performer in her commissioned productions. Fokine assisted Rubinstein with the production of an uncensored *Salome* in 1912, and eventually abandoned the Ballets Russes in her favor. She contributed directly to the tension between Stravinsky and Diaghilev by commissioning Stravinsky to compose *Le Baiser de la fée* for her in 1928. During this same year, she formed her own ballet company and thus continued to compete with Diaghilev during his final years. In spite of her image as an exotic dancer of androgynous beauty, and the fact that many resented her power as a wealthy patron and her insistence on performing in her commissioned works, Rubinstein had a major impact on the development of music theater in France.

Gabriele d'Annunzio was one for whom Rubinstein's legs were a principal focus of attention. He reportedly exclaimed after having witnessed her performance in *Schéhérazade* that he had finally found "the legs of Saint Sebastian for which I have been searching for years!"[14] Although d'Annunzio's interest was sparked by Rubinstein's striking androgynous appearance as a mute dancer, he created a work that offered her first dual role as both a mime and reciter (see Fig. 6). The resultant 1911 *Le Martyre de Saint Sébastien* of d'Annunzio and Debussy is closer to the decadent atmosphere of Wilde's *Salome* than to the religious dramas of Claudel.[15] In its performance, with stage design and Orientalist costumes by Bakst, *Le Martyre* held more in common with current productions of religious spectacles than with medieval performance. (However, d'Annunzio did consult the Sorbonne scholar Gustave Cohen in the attempt to base his play on medieval performance and referred to the acts of *Le Martyre* as "mansions," the medieval term for the series of raised platforms or booths on which the *mystères* were performed.)[16] D'Annunzio's insistence on having a woman play the title role was at odds with the general trend toward all-male performance in modernist music theater and was more in line with fin-de-siècle interests. This verse play was very much a decadent holdover and an opportunity for its misogynistic author to take morbid delight in seeing Rubinstein shot with arrows on stage. As part of his preparation for the creation of this work, d'Annunzio took up archery himself.[17]

Figure 6.   Ida Rubinstein as Saint Sebastian. Photographer unknown. (Reproduced with the permission of the Dance Collection, The New York Public Library
for the Performing Arts, Astor, Lenox and Tilden Foundations)

D'Annunzio's theme of androgyny and his bold treatment of a religious subject were mirrored by Debussy in his incidental music for this work. Debussy's decision to assign the roles of the young twin brothers, whose martyrdom inspires Sebastian's conversion, to two contralti might not have seemed remarkable in another composition. However, the voice of Sebastian's soul heard in the final section of the work, entitled "Paradise," calls for some comment.[18] As if to remind the audience, or to brazenly emphasize the fact that a woman's voice and body have represented Saint Sebastian throughout the performance, The Soul of Sebastian is represented by a high soprano voice (see Ex. 8). On the terrestrial stage, Sebastian was represented through speech, albeit female speech. In heaven, unexpected gender association is further flaunted through the conventions of celestial song.

Sebastian is associated with both Adonis and Christ in this work. In act III, "The Council of False Gods," Sebastian presents the Passion through dance and by speaking the lines of Christ. His performance includes lamentations for Adonis sung by a female chorus. In an example of musical androgyny, similar to the music for the voice of Sebastian's soul, the woeful lines of Christ/Adonis are given to a soprano. Debussy remarked that in this work, "the cult of Adonis is combined with that of Jesus: a very beautiful notion in my opinion."[19] Robin Holloway has heard connections to Wagner's *Parsifal* in Debussy's setting. Holloway argues that Sebastian is identified with Amfortas in his longing for pain, and with Parsifal in his acting out of Christ's passion.[20] He provides several examples of musical relationships between *Le Martyre* and *Parsifal* but does not pursue a comparison of Debussy's work and Wagner's *Tristan und Isolde*. The beginning of act IV, "The Wounded Laurel," corresponds to the beginning of act III in *Tristan*—both wounded heroes face death. There seems to be a distinct echo of the shepherd's English horn solo from *Tristan*, act III, in Debussy's prelude to act IV of *Le Martyre*. Tristan offers one further dimension to the already multilayered Sebastian/Christ/Adonis persona of d'Annunzio's martyr.

Debussy's sincerity regarding the religious expression of *Le Martyre* has been repeatedly questioned. Scholars have combed through his public and private remarks, and have turned to secondhand reports of his emotional behavior during performances, all to determine Debussy's degree of commitment. Although he seems to have disparaged Rubinstein's commission in his private correspondence, his public remarks (as one would expect) defend the spiritual integrity of the work. In an interview given during the composition of the score, Debussy stated that he believed "in a renaissance of liturgical music."[21] His comments on *Parsifal* are particularly interest-

Example 8.   The voice of Sebastian's soul: Debussy, *Le Martyre de Saint Sébastien* (Durand, 1911)

ing: "Wagner himself called his works 'spectacles.' He knew only too well how to resist the temptations of humility to partake of religion. He adopted poses too dramatic for prayer, and his lofty artificial theories never left him."[22] In another interview, Debussy proclaimed his own sincerity and argued that the music of *Le Martyre* was entirely suitable for the demands of church worship.[23] Debussy identified simplicity and modesty as necessary elements of religious expression, and this opinion is evidenced by his music. However, the work was produced as an elaborate and lengthy spectacle that inspired more boredom than spirituality. In addition, *Le Martyre* had been dealt a forceful blow when the archbishop of Paris forbade all Catholics to attend its performance under penalty of excommunication. Debussy and d'Annunzio issued a declaration protesting their sincerity, but neither the archbishop nor many subsequent critics have taken them at their public word.[24]

It is a bit ironic that the *Martyre* collaborator whose religiosity seems most secure was Rubinstein herself. Rubinstein was to grow even more commit-

ted to religious theater and to the medieval *mystères*, even though she had
twice received strict censure from religious authorities. By the time of *Jeanne
d'Arc*, Rubinstein was converting to the Catholic faith and devoting herself
to acts of charity as a Dominican tertiary sister. Rubinstein's medievalism
was another form of exoticism. She had followed in Duncan's footsteps in
making a pilgrimage to Greece prior to her production of *Antigone,* and had
traveled to Palestine for *Salome. Jeanne d'Arc* required a trip to the Latin
Quarter. In April 1934, Rubinstein witnessed a performance of a *mystère*
at the Sorbonne under the direction of Gustave Cohen and Jacques Chail-
ley.[25] This experience inspired her to commission her own mystery play on
the subject of Saint Joan, and she soon sought Honegger's help in enlisting
Claudel for the project. Michael de Cossart suggests that "What made Ida
turn again and again to Claudel for inspiration was probably not so much
his reputation as France's most eminent poet as his intense spirituality. As
her own interest in mysticism and religion took on almost obsessional proportions, his example meant a great deal to her."[26] With the assistance of
Claudel and Honegger, Rubinstein would shed her exotic/erotic image.

A Medieval Martyr for Modern France

Claudel's solution for retaining authorial control in the face of the dominant historical figure Joan of Arc and his performer/patron Ida Rubinstein,
was based on a gesture—a simple and symbolic movement that suggested
the absence of all other movement. As though in a dream, Claudel envisioned the bound hands of Joan making the sign of the cross at the moment
of her death. This gesture was the "creative power" that "evoked and
sanctified the whole play." "Just as Christ cannot be separated from his cross,
so Joan of Arc must not be separated from the instrument of her passion,
her martyrdom and her sanctification—the stake."[27] Claudel decided that
the entire work would take place at the moment of Joan's martyrdom—she
would remember her triumphant history while firmly bound to the stake,
thus the work's title: *Jeanne d'Arc au bûcher.*

Geoffrey K. Spratt has described the structure of this work as "a suite of
symbolic visions of a dream-like nature seen by Joan during the period in
which she is tied to the stake prior to her ultimate sacrifice."[28] In addition
to Claudel's structural use of the flashback technique, there exist several textual suggestions that the entire work is a contemporary reenactment of
Joan's martyrdom—that Joan has been brought to the modern stage in spirit
to reexperience her crisis. It is as though she had remained in Purgatory for
centuries and that only in the twentieth century and in this work (written

some fifteen years after her canonization) does she experience redemption.[29] Specific lines support this interpretation, such as this from scene ix: "Rouen! you did burn Joan of Arc, but I will triumph over you, and nay, you will not hold me forever!" In answer to the calls (in scene vii) of Saints Margaret and Catherine for her to go forth, Joan says "I will! I will! I go! I go! I am gone," and narrates her escorting of the king. As in Noh drama, dramatic action, travel, and the passage of time are narrated and symbolically presented rather than realistically acted. Throughout the play, Joan pieces together her story with the aid of Brother Dominic, also a speaking role, and through the emotional outbursts of the chorus, which condemns and praises her in turn. Three models of ritual performance—Noh theater, the Catholic Mass, and ancient Greek theater—contributed to Claudel's development of this dramatic form. On the central function of the chorus in this work, Claudel wrote:

> I have always been attracted by the primitive form of drama called
> *dithyramb,* . . . One solitary figure, the only one with a face of his
> own, speaks amid a semicircle of voices which, simply by being there,
> lure and compel him to speech. Every poet has known this auditory
> horizon, this confused murmur of jumbled phrases, echoing and re-
> echoing until at last they give birth to words. The Greek Chorus later
> gave it a liturgical form which has been perpetuated in Church services.
> So when Mme. Ida Rubinstein asked me to make Joan of Arc the
> subject of a dramatic poem supported by vocal and instrumental
> music, I naturally thought at once of a kind of Mass.[30]

To this primitive Greek chorus, Claudel added the supporting role of Brother Dominic, who functions similarly to the *waki* role in Noh, just as the solo figure, Joan, functions as a *shite.*

By tying Joan to the stake, Claudel effectively denied her active agency. Joan is to learn, through this performance, that her previous actions have all been God's will, that she was only acting out a preordained script and that her ultimate significance is her martyrdom. We do not witness Joan's heroic and historic actions; rather, we await her sacrifice throughout the work. As in many Noh plays, the saint has returned to this world to relate her story. However, the *shite* in Noh is allotted a final climactic dance expressing his or her past deeds and emotions. Claudel allows Joan one final gesture: the drama ends as Joan lifts her hands to heaven and her chains fall away. Claudel not only bound his historic protagonist to the stake; he also bound Ida Rubinstein in this religious performance. Rubinstein went to the stake for dancing the Passion of Christ in her role as Saint Sebastian, while in *Jeanne d'Arc* she is tied to the stake from the start. As Claudel stated, the stake is Joan's inescapable symbol—it is her mask, a mask that both marks her as a martyr and limits her to the passive mode of recollection. On the use of masks in Noh theater, Claudel wrote:

> But the mask has the same function throughout Nō drama—to cut the character off from the present time, and to keep the outward form of the passion he expresses, in the age of which he is the symbol and the historic or legendary event which he helped to make. Between him and us, between the *Shite* and the *Waki*, is this hard unalterable mask, the final seal of something that can no longer be changed. . . . The past, or a dream, comes to life for a moment and answers our questions, but does not sever the threads which bind it to the other world, does not take off that face which exists only to hide what is behind it. The actor is hidden, and the more he shows himself, the more he shows the thing that hides him.[31]

The stake allowed Claudel to hide Rubinstein's past as a dancing Salome and to bring Joan to the stage for the benefit of modern France.

In contrast to Rubinstein, Honegger posed no dilemmas for Claudel; in fact, the two proved ideal collaborators. Honegger, a devout Protestant, was equally interested in creating new forms of religious theater and had had great success with such biblical dramas as *Le Roi David* (1921) and *Judith* (1925), both of which he subsequently revised as dramatic oratorios (the genre of *Jeanne d'Arc*.) Honegger's experience with religious theater dated from 1918, when he composed some incidental music for *La Mort de Sainte Alméenne*, a mystery play by Max Jacob. Two works that combined a Swiss patriotism with religious expression were the dramatic oratorio *Nicolas de Flue* (1939) and an incomplete setting of a Passion play (composed 1940–44 and intended for a day-long performance in a Swiss village), fragments of which Honegger assembled as a choral work entitled *Une Cantate de Noël* (1953).

Honegger was also devoted to the ideals of total theater. In 1929, surveying recent developments in music theater, he wrote: "I believe firmly also in the possibility of a regeneration of dramatic music."[32] He declared in 1932 that "opera is finished: its obsolete forms are no longer acceptable nor even accepted" and dreamed of a "collaboration which would succeed in being total."[33] This dream was soon realized in his collaboration with Claudel on *Jeanne d'Arc*. Honegger's interest in achieving productions of total theater during this period was inspired, in part, by his work with Paul Valéry and Rubinstein on *Amphion* in 1929. Valéry had first conceived of the play in the 1890s and had approached Debussy in 1894 with his visions of a work of total theater based on this Greek legend concerning the divine power of music. (Like many others, Valéry intended to realize a form of the *Gesamtkunstwerk* ideal where Wagner had "failed.") In addition to his setting of Valéry's melodrama *Amphion,* Honegger had composed music for several other Rubinstein theater commissions, including *L'Imperatrice aux Rochers: Un Miracle de Notre-Dame* (1925), d'Annunzio's *Phaedre* (1926), and Valéry's ballet-melodrama *Semiramis* (1933). Claudel, Honegger, and Rubinstein had each experimented separately in the creation of religious music theater before joining forces for *Jeanne d'Arc,* which would prove the most successful modernist *mystère.*

Like Claudel, Honegger was interested in exploring the range of vocal possibility that lay between speech and pure song. Many of Honegger's works contain speech in various degrees of fixed notation, with and without musical accompaniment, and serving a variety of dramatic functions.[34] For example, in *La Danse des morts,* an oratorio written with Claudel in 1938, Honegger set God's text as notated choral speech. In composing sung text, Honegger declared that "the word cannot be subordinated to the melody. It is the word, on the contrary, which ought to create the melody, for each word has a melody of its own."[35] It is a small step from an interest in the sound-quality of words to an interest in nonverbal vocal sounds. Both speech and nonverbal vocalisms play central roles in *Jeanne d'Arc.*

Joan of Arc ranks with Saint Cecilia as one of the great listeners in Christian legend. Hearing the voices of Saints Michael, Catherine, and Margaret in the ringing of her village church bells, she was inspired to reunite France. In setting Joan's story, the creation of these heavenly voices is clearly the most vital task facing the composer. Extraordinary means are necessary in order to make audible the inaudible, to achieve spiritual transcendence on stage through sound. Honegger found two ways of representing celestial sound in *Jeanne d'Arc.* Scene i is entitled "The Voices of Heaven." In this scene Honegger appears to have realized Claudel's conception of the vocal expressivity of choral "exclamation," directly transferring Claudel's sonic descriptions into music (see Ex. 9). These choral vocalisms are the only voices heard in this brief scene. They thus constitute Joan's celestial voices in their primal form, later becoming specific in scene vii with the solo motifs of Saints Catherine and Margaret. In this later scene, the voices of the saints are understood to grow out of the sound of bells. In scene ix, when the voices of Catherine and Margaret return, Joan again demonstrates that she hears them, while Brother Dominic claims he cannot. As the scene gathers intensity, the chorus joins with the voices of the saints. Joan hears this music also and says, "It's all mankind united the living and the dead who say: Daughter of God! Joan!"[36]

Example 9.   The Voices of Heaven: Honegger, *Jeanne d'Arc au bûcher*
(Editions Salabert, 1947)

(continued)

To make audible Joan's transcendent voices, Honegger employed a new musical technology, calling upon the exotic sounds of the ondes Martenot, an electronic instrument invented in 1928 and used extensively by several prominent modernist French composers. Although it is heard at various points in the score, even in conjunction with the voices of Joan's accusers, it is most strongly associated with celestial music, and is first heard in scene i as part of the "Voices of Heaven." It is heard again as Joan makes the sign of the cross in scene ii and, most significantly, assists in the creation of the bell sounds in scene vii. The ondes Martenot adds a poignant line to Joan's feeble song in scene x, the only point in the work when Joan sings rather than speaks. Finally, this electronic voice supports the chorus in its praise of Joan as the flames leap ever higher (see Ex. 10). As Joan's chains break and fall away, it is the exotic, electronic voice of the ondes Martenot that assists her ascension with its tremendous two-octave glissando. At the moment of Joan's death, Saint Margaret sings her celestial motive one final time, but now with nonverbal expressivity on vowel sounds.[37]

Saint Joan had received such ardent attention since her canonization in 1920 that Claudel and Honegger's version might have been greeted as a bit passé in 1938–39 had it not been for the threat of war. As it turned out, *Jeanne d'Arc au bûcher* was hugely successful. The exotic performer who had shocked and titillated Paris thirty years earlier had metamorphosed into a patriotic saint whose vehicle was music theater. As Michael de Cossart relates, "The French government realized the patriotic significance of [Rubinstein's] work and, on the strength of it, awarded her the grand cross of

Example 10.   The ondes Martenot in praise of Joan: Honegger, *Jeanne d'Arc au bûcher* (Editions Salabert, 1947)

an *officier* of the Légion d'Honneur on 24 May 1939."[38] As with Duncan's dance in revolutionary Russia and the *Lehrstücke* of Brecht and Weill in Weimar Germany, Rubinstein's music theater had been found worthy of adoption in the name of the nation. *Jeanne d'Arc* received many performances in Vichy France.[39] This reception encouraged Claudel and Honegger to add a prologue to the work in 1944. The prologue combines the opening text of Genesis with references to Joan's creation of France and prepares the performance as a retelling of a historic past that had been echoed by the more recent "great darkness" experienced in the modern nation.[40] We will discover in the following chapter that the French revival of the medieval mystery play was echoed in postwar England as part of another sort of nationalist agenda.

Part III

THE MYSTERIES OF BRITISH MUSIC
THEATER; OR, DRESSING UP FOR CHURCH

8 The Audience as Congregation

Playing without a Proscenium

Through most of the history of opera production, the audience has fulfilled its role as spectator and has had few other responsibilities. At times, it has been left in the dark in order to train its gaze toward the stage. In other periods, its fickle attention had to be more actively wooed as audience members pursued their own interests in the auditorium space. Although Wagner, in particular, built his demands for respect and concentration into the very design of his performance temple, even his audience continued to find comfort in their passive status as spectators.[1] While actively engaged in the social rituals of opera-going, and often more than willing to communicate its reactions to the stage and thus potentially affect the performance directly, the traditional opera audience was not required to participate. Opera took the proscenium for granted.

With the creation of new forms of ritual music theater in twentieth-century Europe and America came a radical reconceptualization of the audience's role and of the performance space itself. A basic trend toward increased audience participation, and away from the notion of performance as commercialized entertainment, reached one extreme in the "happenings" of the 1950s and '60s. These events were based on the premise that everyone present was a participant and that all sound and movement within the performance space constituted the performance. But the move toward audience involvement had begun much earlier. Scriabin's projected masterwork *Mysterium,* partially sketched at the time of his death in 1915, was a forerunner of this radical conceptual shift. As noted above, figures such as Claudel and Artaud envied the engaged and devout audiences of exotic performance traditions. Although Craig quipped that the modern audience "need not fear that we shall ask them to sport a mask,"[2] other modernists did ask the audience members to imagine themselves as, or to become, ritual participants. Yeats wrote for an initiated audience composed of the "right people." In Brecht and Weill's *Der Jasager,* children—the intended audience—were co-opted by the production to serve as the performers. Rather than attempting to dictate certain social values to passive spectators, the *Lehrstück* genre required that the audience do some of the performance work themselves and thus imbibe the moral and political lesson as they enacted it.

Occasions during which some Euro-American audience members would be accustomed to participate significantly include the religious services of Christianity. In the Catholic Mass, for example, there is a clearly defined audience/congregation and performer/celebrant space. However, at various points in the ceremony the audience must participate using vocal responses and a variety of physical movements. At a certain point in the religious performance, the audience members leave their space and approach the main performance area. Of course, the "audience" considers itself a congregation attending a religious service rather than a "performance," but, as anthropologists and performance theorists have argued, the structures of ritual share many features with more obvious forms of performance activity. The status and function of performance as ritual, whether observed in the religious ceremonies of exotic lands or at home in the parish church, became an ideal that many modernist composers and playwrights hoped to realize in their own works for the theater.

Some attempted to bring the church to the stage, while others took their works inside the church. Debussy and d'Annunzio's *Le Martyre de Saint Sébastien* and Honegger and Claudel's *Jeanne d'Arc au bûcher* are but two examples of the much broader interest in staged spiritual performance. Also in France, Henri Ghéon wrote numerous works intended as popular religious dramas, including *Les Trois Miracles de Sainte Cécile* (1924), *Le Triomphe de Saint Thomas d'Aquin* (1924), and *La Vie profonde de Saint François* (1925). In Spain in the mid-1920s, Manuel de Falla was at work on a "scenic cantata," entitled *Atlàntida,* celebrating Christopher Columbus and the Spanish nation. This incomplete work was projected for a church performance and included chant material. The German producer Max Reinhardt, whose work had a major impact in England and America, was particularly devoted to the revival of communal religious theater and to church performance. "The Church," he wrote, "especially the Catholic Church, is the very cradle of our modern theatre."[3] Similar efforts are discovered in modern dance during the first decades of the twentieth century. The American dancer Ted Shawn, for instance, created a complete worship service in dance in 1917.[4] These modernist works can be understood to have developed from an earlier, romantic preoccupation with things medieval.

Benjamin Britten is the most prominent twentieth-century composer to have created works of music theater specifically intended to be performed in church. These works include *Noye's Fludde* (1958), *Curlew River* (1964), *The Burning Fiery Furnace* (1966), and *The Prodigal Son* (1968). (Britten designated each of the last three pieces a "parable for church performance.") In *Noye's Fludde*, the intended audience is required to behave in church as they would on any Sunday morning, and many of their children are likely to be members of the cast. Britten asks the audience to join in the singing of three hymns in the performance and at two points in his score notes that "the congregation stands." In the three Church Parables, the audience members are directly addressed as a congregation, but they are asked only to imagine themselves as such; participation is neither required nor desired.[5]

Robin Holloway asks, in his discussion of the audience's role in Britten's Church Parables, "Do the spectators also dress up, in fancy, to become illiterate peasants receiving a 'sermon in sounds'?"[6] Donald Mitchell offers one answer when he states, "we become the very congregation before which a Mystery is to be enacted, a decisive change in status."[7] "Enacted" is the crucial word in this interpretation. Britten's performers reenact a moral tale known to all in a manner parallel to that involved in the celebration of the Christian communion service. Rather than attempting to "become the character" or to create an illusion of reality, the role of the performer is to present the prescribed symbolic actions and text of the ritual. (A priest is not an actor playing Christ but rather one who speaks the sacred performance.) Yet, for such ritual performances to be considered fully successful, some form of "mystery" must be experienced, not merely presented. When such works are designed for church production, the space itself may force the audience members to imagine themselves differently, to believe that they are worshippers, and to participate in the ritual performance through this act of active imagination. A church is a coercive performance space that does not permit an audience to remain passive during the service. Before turning to a more detailed discussion of Britten's church works, it is important to establish first the context in which *Noye's Fludde* appeared in 1958 and to discover that this was not an isolated experiment in communal religious performance, but rather that it arrived as the crest of a veritable wave of mystery play revivals in mid-century England.

God Off and On the British Stage

God had been banned from the stage for some 350 years when in 1951 the deity was allowed back by the British government. From the thirteenth through sixteenth centuries, the performance of mystery plays served as an extremely successful form of religious expression both on the continent and in England. In the early fourteenth century, mystery plays became central to the Corpus Christi celebration and were performed by local guilds in a narrational procession through the town. These religious plays presented the Christian scriptures from Creation to Redemption.[8] Only five complete English mystery cycles survived to the twentieth century; these include the York and Chester manuscripts that were to form the basis of the modern revival. By the end of the sixteenth century, in the wake of the Reformation, the performance of mystery plays had been suppressed in England and would remain so until the mid-twentieth century.

Prior to the onset of the mystery play revival in the 1950s, prominent examples of religious theater were created by various modernist figures in Great Britain. One eccentric example is George Bernard Shaw's *Saint Joan,* which was produced in 1923, three years after the canonization of Joan of Arc. In 1928, John Masefield and Gustav Holst created *The Coming of Christ* for performance in Canterbury Cathedral, and Frank Bridge completed his children's opera *The Christmas Rose* the following year. The formation of the Religious Drama Society in 1929 further encouraged the development of a new religious theater during the interwar period. The plays of Dorothy Sayers, including a series of radio plays on the Passion produced during World War II and entitled *The Man Born to Be King,* were also based on religious subjects. Of course, the most notable example of this trend is T. S. Eliot's *Murder in the Cathedral,* which was commissioned specifically for performance in Canterbury Cathedral in 1935 and was inspired, in part, by Yeats's experimental plays. In 1937, Eliot wrote: "If we want a living religious drama we must be prepared to accept something less sedative, and perhaps something which may cause us some discomfort and embarrassment in the process of getting used to it."[9] Indeed, Eliot argued that to "simply re-act the medieval plays" was not a worthy aim. He hoped to amend the lack of contemporary religious plays by creating new forms of religious drama, and he was not alone in this endeavor.

Victorian sensibilities had been firmly opposed to the portrayal of religious themes on stage, and nineteenth-century British theatrical censorship strictly reflected this outlook.[10] Around the turn of the century, even such operas as Anton Rubinstein's *Christus* and Camille Saint-Saëns's *Samson et Dalila* were banned by the national censor. Although the revival of religious drama was not fully under way until mid-century, and the cessation of theatrical censorship in England did not occur until 1968, some earlier attempts were made to perform the medieval mystery plays themselves. A 1901 private production of the morality *Everyman* was the first modern performance of a medieval religious play in England. In 1912, Yeats invited a production of three plays from the Wakefield cycle to be performed at the Abbey Theatre. Throughout the 1930s and '40s, parts of the mystery cycles were performed, although always with adaptations to console the censors. A 1930 production of the Chester Flood play, later set by both Britten and Stravinsky, was allowed under the provision that God would not be represented physically on the stage but only by an offstage voice. A physical impersonation of God was deemed blasphemous and raised the taboo against idolatry, while an aural portrayal posed the fascinating challenge of representing the unheard divine voice, particularly in works of modernist music theater. Thus, a disembodied God had to suffice until the levee broke with the 1951 production of the York Festival cycle.[11]

World War II, like World War I, had profoundly unsettled conventional views of society and had drastically damaged England's national psyche, or so the government feared. In 1951, with the goal of instilling "moral capital" into the nation, the British government announced the "Festival of Britain." Every community was called upon to celebrate British culture and history in its own traditional fashion. The town of York chose to revive its famous medieval mystery cycle. The bans were relaxed, and the first production proved extremely successful; performances were repeated every three years thereafter. As John R. Elliott Jr. states in his detailed study of the modern revival, the initial production faced the problem of how to "stage an act of worship that would be entertaining to the skeptical, while at the same time creating an act of theatre that would be palatable to the devout."[12] The producer at York, Martin Browne, announced that "only persons who sincerely believe in Christian doctrine" would be considered as acceptable performers. It was also decided that both the roles of God and Jesus would be performed anonymously and without pay. Especially sensitive scenes such as the nailing to the cross would occur out of the spectators' sight.

With the 1957 production, the York revival reached the height of its success and, with the increased use of older dialect and the addition of a few more plays from the full cycle, came closest to a "textual authenticity." At the same time, critical reactions to the production called for more emphasis on dramatic integrity and entertainment and less on the function of solemn religious service. The simplistic stylization of the acting, another attempt at authenticity, was explicitly criticized.[13] For a period beginning with a 1960 "Brechtian" production at York, modern performance of the mysteries changed radically. The town of Chester had been producing a series of mystery cycles since 1951 and, although its productions were initially even more conservative in style than those of York, by 1973 Chester was offering a rock-style cycle in a circus tent that had "more than a touch of *Godspell*."[14] In a bid for a more communal spirit, the 1976 York production involved giant puppets and was set as a medieval carnival. These innovative productions were exceptions to the prevailing pious British performance aesthetic. The musical mysteries of Benjamin Britten, to which we now turn, remained well within the more conservative mainstream.

"The Congregation Stands"

Britten's *Noye's Fludde* was completed in December 1957 and was first performed on 18 June 1958, one year after the most successful of the York mystery cycle productions. Britten had been commissioned by the education programming division of a commercial television company to compose a setting of one of the highly popular medieval mysteries. Having already intended to compose such a work, he proceeded with *Noye's Fludde* even after the commission fell through.[15] In the context of the general national revival of the mysteries, Britten's work comes late and is traditional. He chose to set one of the least controversial and problematic of the Chester cycle plays: Christ makes no appearance in the tale and God need be presented only as an offstage voice.[16] The text was taken from A. W. Pollard's *English Miracle Plays, Moralities and Interludes* with only occasional cuts and reorderings made by Britten in order to tighten the play. The medieval spellings are retained in the score but modern pronunciation is to be used virtually throughout the performance.[17]

Perhaps the most striking aspect of *Noye's Fludde* is its reliance on child performers. Children assume the roles of Noye's Sons and their Wives, Mrs. Noye's Gossips, the dancing Raven and Dove, the Chorus of Animals, and a majority of the instrumentalists (see Fig. 7). The orchestra includes simple parts for amateur string players, recorder players, and buglers, and such percussion instruments as "slung mugs" and handbells. Only a few professional musicians are required. Britten composed works for children throughout his career and must have been attracted to the mystery play genre by its traditional basis in amateur local production. Simplicity allows for inclusion, and inclusion is fundamental to certain forms of ritual. *Noye's*

Fludde has been one of Britten's most popular works with British audiences, although perhaps it never has had an "audience" in any conventional sense of the word.

At three points in this work, the audience, or "congregation" in Britten's designation, is required to participate in the singing of well-known English hymns. The work begins with a brief orchestral introduction at the end of which the congregation should rise and sing the hymn "Lord Jesus, think on me."[18] Hymn singing is one of the most coercive of musical genres, for it is virtually impossible not to respond to the call of the organ, to rise and at least hum the tune of the hymn: hymns are thus a potent unifying force. British critics of *Noye's Fludde* repeatedly speak of a sense of nostalgia experienced during these moments of participation. And indeed, Britten's intended audience would have been accustomed from an early age to join in at these moments of communal singing.

The line between music theater as a form of entertainment and as a form of ritual is crossed in this work during the singing of these three hymns. The hymn text, "That, when the flood is past, / I may eternal brightness see, / And share thy joy at last," implies, in the context of the performance, that the work itself is designed to bring us toward this spiritual goal. In a nation that had only recently begun to relax its rules concerning the embodiment of religious subjects in a work of theater, this invocation of God in performance, and especially in a church, must be construed either as an act of serious religious expression or as blasphemy. The audience is not merely asked to "dress up, in fancy" but to accept the work as a form of worship. An audience member who does not subscribe to the Christian faith is put in almost the same awkward position as a nonbeliever at any religious service.

During the opening hymn, Noye proceeds to the stage area by walking through the congregation as though he were an amateur arising from its midst. Noye kneels upon reaching the performance area and the voice of God is heard as if in immediate answer to the audience's choral prayer. God's voice is marked "tremendous" and is spoken in quatrains with a free recitation for the first three lines and a rhythmically notated fourth line. The introductory note to the score describes God's voice as highly musical and rich, and indicates that the speaker need not be a professional actor but should speak "with a simple and sincere delivery, without being at all 'stagey.'"[19] As God begins to give Noye instructions on how to build the ship, a significant overlapping of their voices occurs. Noye joins God in a rhythmic declamation of the first few words for three lines of text, allowing God

Figure 7. The cast of *Noye's Fludde*. Photograph by Zoe Dominic. (Reproduced with the permission of Dominic Photography)

Example 11.   God and Noye's duet: Britten, *Noye's Fludde* (Boosey & Hawkes, 1958)

to finish each of these lines, and then delivers God's final line of instructions himself (see Ex. 11). This is the only point in the work at which Noye speaks rather than sings, as though he knows God's text already and is thus able to join in with the recitation and partake in God's vocal idiom.[20] The moment makes explicit the notion that the performance is a ritualistic reenactment of a story known to all, including Noye the character.

At the end of the work, after singing the final hymn, the audience is instructed to remain standing in order to receive God's final lines as a benediction, blessing this work of religious offering. By placing the performance in a church, employing child performers, and calling upon the audience to participate, Britten requires his congregation to behave appropriately for this religious service and seems to immunize the work against criticism: a communal ritual is not subject to the same aesthetic scrutiny as is a work of "mere" entertainment. The musical and dramatic suggestions of ritual performance in *Noye's Fludde* were to become far more formalized and overt in the Church Parables of the mid-1960s. Rather than a communal offering performed by "ordinary people," the Church Parable genre would be derived from a more aristocratic ritual form. With *Curlew River,* Britten integrated his visions of a medieval England with a more recently encountered exotic model—Japanese Noh.[21]

9 Britten's Parables

The Parable of "A Comparable Setting," or, Domesticating the Exotic

The story of Britten's encounter with Japanese Noh is an oft-told tale whose first and most provocative telling was provided by Britten himself in his program notes for the June 1964 production of *Curlew River*. I quote these notes in full:

> It was in Tokyo in January 1956 that I saw a Nō-drama for the first time; and I was lucky enough during my brief stay there to see two different performances of the same play—*Sumidagawa*. The whole occasion made a tremendous impression upon me: the simple, touching story, the economy of style, the intense slowness of the action, the marvellous skill and control of the performers, the beautiful costumes, the mixture of chanting, speech, singing which, with the three instruments, made up the strange music—it all offered a totally new "operatic" experience.
>
> There was no conductor—the instrumentalists sat on the stage, as did the chorus, and the chief characters made their entrance down a long ramp. The lighting was strictly non-theatrical. The cast was all male, the one female character wearing an exquisite mask which made no attempt to hide the male jowl beneath it.
>
> The memory of this play has seldom left my mind in the years since. Was there not something—many things—to be learnt from it? The solemn dedication and skill of the performers were a lesson to any singer or actor of any country and any language. Was it not possible to use just such a story—the simple one of a demented mother seeking her lost child—with an English background (for there was no question in any case of a pastiche from the ancient Japanese)? Surely the Medieval Religious Drama in England would have had a comparable setting—an all-male cast of ecclesiastics—a simple austere staging in a church—a very limited instrumental accompaniment—a moral story? And so we

126

came from Sumidagawa to Curlew River and a Church in the Fens, but
with the same story and similar characters; and whereas in Tokyo the
music was the ancient Japanese music jealously preserved by successive
generations, here I have started the work with that wonderful plain-
song hymn "Te lucis ante terminum", and from it the whole piece
may be said to have grown. There is nothing specifically Japanese left
in the Parable that William Plomer and I have written, but if stage
and audience can achieve half the intensity and concentration of that
original drama I shall be well satisfied.[1]

The crossing from *Sumidagawa* to *Curlew River* was not as straightforward
nor as immediate as Britten suggests.[2] In fact, it was not for a full eight years
after his first experience of the Noh play in Tokyo that Britten completed
this work, and Peter F. Alexander has convincingly shown—in his study of
the correspondence between Britten and his librettist William Plomer—that
the compositional journey was rather tortuous.[3] Standard narratives repeated in several books on Britten's life and music have been based on the
composer's somewhat misleading program notes.

Plomer first served as Britten's librettist for the opera *Gloriana*, which
premiered in 1953, and the two had pledged to collaborate in the future.
The poet spent several years in the late 1920s teaching English language
courses in Japan and wrote several novels and poems inspired by his experiences during this period.[4] As Britten prepared for his own 1956 Asiatic
trip and concert tour—including stops in Bali, Thailand, Japan, and India—
Plomer strongly recommended that he attend a Noh performance while in
Tokyo. Britten traveled with Peter Pears and their friends the Prince and
Princess Ludwig of Hesse and the Rhine. While in Tokyo, he conducted a
broadcast concert that included a performance of his *Sinfonia da requiem*.[5]
Prince Ludwig's travel diary entries of 11 and 18 February 1956 make it
clear that the friends' first impressions of Noh were not favorable. Prince
Ludwig wrote that the "beginning of one of the plays we watch is so strange
and unreal, that one wants to burst out laughing at this deadly serious gibberish. But once one can follow the sense of scene and words through the
translations our friends brought for us, one becomes more and more interested, fascinated, moved by this completely stylized art." We also learn that
they initially found it difficult to appreciate the singing in "strained voices,
like people about to vomit."[6] But Britten's opinion of Noh soon changed
and he became especially attached to this particular play once he understood
the basic story. He made certain to see the same production again before
leaving Tokyo and had a sound recording of *Sumidagawa* made for him.

Upon his return to England, Britten wrote to Plomer about his strong impressions of Japanese Noh and his desire to make a setting of the play. Britten's initial idea was to retain much of the Japanese scenery and poetic imagery; he requested that Plomer make a simple English translation of the play. (Thus, Britten's original conception does seem to have been something of a "pastiche" of the Japanese drama.) However, by April 1959 Britten had decided to transpose the entire story to a Christian context. Plomer referred to this suggestion as "setting fire to your—and indeed my—kimono" but confessed that he also had been concerned by their attempt to transport the Noh play without appropriate modifications.[7] Only after radically changing the context of the work from a Japanese Buddhist to an English Christian setting—after domesticating the exotic and substituting the drab robe of the medieval monk for the colorful kimono of courtly Japan—was Britten able to proceed with the composition.

This phenomenon of domesticating the exotic is common to many examples of cross-cultural appropriation or (more neutrally) of influence in the twentieth century. Modernist Euro-American composers repeatedly discovered what they had been looking for in their exotic models and tended to adopt only those prevalued elements. Such exotic features then took on a special fluid status: having been extracted from their specific native environment they became "exotic" in general and lost their particular meanings. Stripped of their original context, they were routinely cloaked with new meanings, and they were readily combined with traits from other exotic sources.[8] Concomitant with this craving for the unfamiliar, the pursuit of the exotic includes a strong desire to bring it back home. The acquisition of foreign characteristics and techniques is often followed by a process of cross-dressing these traits in aesthetic clothing taken from the wardrobe of one's native culture. In his study of Japanese influence on British and American literature, Earl Miner developed a "three cycle" formulation for Western artistic contact with the exotic—consisting of interest, imitation, and absorption.[9] Miner's "absorption" process is potentially the most interesting and problematic, for it points to the common difficulty in remaining comfortable in the realm of the exotic for long. Only after first being "absorbed," made familiar, or transformed beyond recognition were exotic elements safely dealt with and utilized in modernist works.

As noted in part II, within the writings of those modernist figures who appropriated various exotic sources in their work one discovers many declarations of independence distancing the writer from the source. The initial interest and appeal is celebrated, but much effort is directed toward establishing the degree of difference between the new work and the exotic model.[10] The "absorption" process can be considered part of this larger "anxiety of influence" in relation to the exotic. Yeats, for example, passed quickly through the cycle of interest, imitation, and absorption and employed only the most general attributes of Noh for his own political and artistic projects. Edward Said has argued for the consideration of Yeats as a poet of "decolonization" who, like his "third world" contemporaries, resisted imperialism in his work.[11] But Yeats was also a "colonizer" who blazed the trail that many others, including Britten, would follow in their uses of Japanese Noh. Like Yeats, who had moved from three plays based on Noh models to an entirely Christian context with his final dance play *Calvary*, Britten moved progressively away from his exotic source both in the composition of *Curlew River* and in the evolution of the Church Parables. This departure from the exotic toward the security of a "comparable setting" was of paramount importance to Britten's creation of this genre.

Once Britten thought to transfer *Sumidagawa* to a Christian framework, and after Plomer suggested that the performance itself could be set in medieval England as a mystery performed by monks, the function of *Curlew River* shifted from entertainment to religious ritual. (The work is most similar to a medieval miracle play, since it deals with a saint's—the boy's— miraculous healing of his demented mother through his message of Christian hope.) In his correspondence with Plomer, Britten requested a complete transformation of the original play and wrote that the loss of the Buddhist elements would be fine since "they don't mean much to me."[12] Britten added text to strengthen the Christian imagery and made the distinction between the "heathen" abductor and the saintly child more explicit. This process of Christianization in *Curlew River* resonates with Britten's entire career.

Britten's compositional predilection for Christian themes is perhaps too obvious to require extensive recapitulation here. The 1946 opera *The Rape of Lucretia* involved a transformation (similar to *Curlew River*) of the original text and plot to a Christian moral context. This "heathen" tale is Christianized in the lines of the narrating chorus and in the epilogue. *A Ceremony of Carols* (1942), *Saint Nicolas* (1948), *Canticle II: Abraham and Isaac* (1952), *Noye's Fludde* (1958), and the *War Requiem* (1962), are additional examples of Britten's use of Christian ritual preceding the composition of *Curlew River*. The two latter Church Parables bypassed exotic plot and legend, and instead were based directly on biblical stories. In *The Burning Fiery Furnace*, Britten turned to the Old Testament story from the Book of Daniel of the three young Israelites who refused to worship at the altar of Nebuchadnezzar. In addition to the increasingly remote traces of Noh influence, this Parable contains some conventional Orientalist signs in the music for the Babylonians.[13] Only with *The Prodigal Son* was the process of Christianization completed and an actual Christian parable set. In the context of Britten's entire oeuvre, the transformation from Japanese Noh to Christian miracle play in *Curlew River* appears almost predetermined.

"In Tokyo the Music Was the Ancient Japanese . . . "

Although Britten's statement that there is "nothing specifically Japanese left in the Parable" is correct for the most part, some elements of the composition nevertheless suggest the influence of Japanese music. The small size of the ensemble roughly corresponds to the instrumentation found in Japanese *nohgaku*, the music for Noh. The solo flute is given a significant role, as it is in Noh, and the percussion occasionally is used to punctuate specific moments in time in much the same manner as the three *nohgaku* drums, the shouts or *kakegoe* of the drummers, and the percussive foot stamps of the Noh dancer. Britten's construction of musical time—including the sensation of time suspension, the inexact coordination between individual musical lines, and the overall pace—also corresponds strongly with the *nohgaku* aesthetic.

Curlew River is performed without a conductor and contains sections of free alignment—with different instrumental and vocal parts moving at different tempi—and passages suggestive of heterophony. Britten created a special fermata sign, the "curlew," to indicate that one musical line should pause until joined by the others. At several points, individual lines are marked "freely" and a general "controlled floating" predominates in the work. At the instant when the Madwoman announces that she was the dead child's mother, musical and dramatic time are momentarily suspended, creating, what would be termed in Italian opera, a moment of *stupendi universali* (see Ex. 12). This is an extreme example of the general flexible approach to rhythm and meter that is prevalent in this work. The treatment of musical time in *Curlew River* not only signifies the influence of Japanese music but also resembles the flexibility of time and rhythm experienced in a Christian service and in congregational hymn singing. Although in many cultures ritual music is highly rhythmic and tightly synchronized, especially when used to inspire a state of trance, in Japanese *nohgaku* as well as in much Christian choral singing, there is a freer approach to rhythm and a greater emphasis on arrival at certain temporal moments.[14]

Britten conflated his aural memory of *nohgaku* with concerts of *gagaku*, the ancient court music of Japan, which he also attended while in Tokyo. In

Example 12.   Realization of the Madwoman's identity: Britten,
Curlew River (Faber & Faber, 1965)

(continued)

Example 12. *(continued)*

(continued)

an article devoted to Britten's interest in the Japanese *sho,* a *gagaku* instrument, Mervyn Cooke establishes its influence on the organ part in *Curlew River,* an influence he finds "disconcertingly authentic."[15] Not only do the arpeggiated and held chords of Britten's chamber organ sound similar to the *sho,* but, as Cooke demonstrates, these chords are nearly an exact transcription of the same pitch collections. William Malm points to other musical similarities while also mentioning several fundamental differences in basic musical construction between Britten's music and *nohgaku.* Britten's use of characteristic motifs, a balanced musical structure, and the importance of closure in *Curlew River* are distinctly Western musical concerns.[16] To my ear, the music of *Curlew River* often sounds equally influenced by the Balinese gamelan, particularly in the orchestral fantasy section during the ceremonial robing. Rather than pursue a detailed comparison between *nohgaku* and Britten's music, I will instead consider those specific musical and dramatic elements that Britten adopted and created in his effort to raise his work to the level of religious expression.

The Madwoman's Musical Mask

Many elements of ritual structure and characterization are inherent in the Noh form itself and were retained in Plomer's libretto. With the addition of the framing ceremonial entrance and final recession of the monks, *Curlew River* is clearly marked as a ritual performance. A rigorous three-fold frame begins and ends the work; this musical and dramatic structure consists of the chant procession, the address of the Abbot, and the orchestral fantasy on the chant melody. In addition to its ritual structure, which becomes somewhat routine in the later Parables, *Curlew River* is emphatically non-naturalistic throughout. The Abbot instructs the audience to "attend to our mystery," thus transgressing any assumed boundary of dramatic realism. Similar to the *shite*'s entrance in Noh, each major character enters with a formalized introduction. Britten bluntly emphasizes this character-

Example 13. The Madwoman's entrance: Britten, *Curlew River*
(Faber & Faber, 1965)

(continued)

istic by musically introducing each character with his or her corresponding instrument and motif. The Ferryman, for example, announces his occupation and identity after first being announced by his ever-present horn theme. The use of these motifs remains clear throughout the work, clarity being a basic characteristic of most didactic rituals. Britten derives much of the melodic material of the piece, which is of limited variety, from the framing chant, as though tapping into the religious powers of an established ritual

music. Robin Holloway has described Britten's Church Parable musical construction as non-developmental and as built instead upon repetition and ostinato in clear blocks of melodic material.[17]

The music for the individual characters is also highly formalized and stylized. The vocal style of the Madwoman alternates, for the most part, between a static monotone recitation and wild glissandi. These glissandi, followed by rapid triplet figures, are the strongest musical sign of her madness.[18] They are heard and later imitated mockingly by the Ferryman and chorus. Immediately before her entrance, we hear the flutter-tongued flute that serves as her instrumental marker (see Ex. 13). The Ferryman and Traveller hear this sound as well and associate it with the Madwoman's voice.

Example 14.   The Madwoman's transformation: Britten, *Curlew River*
(Faber & Faber, 1965)

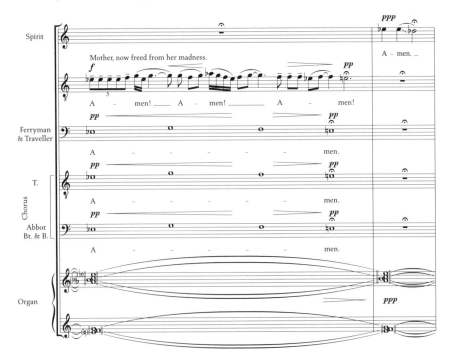

After the flute plays and before the Madwoman sings, the Ferryman asks the Traveller, "But first may I ask you / what is that strange noise / up the highway there?" and again, after hearing the Madwoman sing, "May I ask, did you see / who it is that is singing?" Not only do they hear her approach, but they perceive it as singing; it is this singing that indicates her madness. The chorus also hears her and says, "We wish to hear her singing. / We will laugh at her crazily singing."

Using a specific instrument to refer to or signal the presence of a specific character is hardly novel, yet the degree to which Britten establishes this marker and continues to use it in the work calls for comment. The Madwoman's flute line serves as a mask—one that she is unable to shed until the final scene of redemption and healing.[19] At the end of her first vocal entrance, the flute, which has shadowed her singing, spirals off, extending her vocal line and thus her voice after she has physically stopped producing sound. At a later point in the score, Britten marks the flute line to be played "like the voice"—as though this had not been the case since the Madwoman's first entrance. After being led to the tomb of her child, her semi-tonal oscillations of mourning are also echoed by the flute. The flute maintains its role as a marker for the Madwoman up until the passage when the voice of the boy's spirit is heard joining in the prayer. At this point she hears the flute as the sound of "voices, / Like souls abandoned," and then vocally shadows the flute's Curlew bird cries. As the spirit appears, the flute is exchanged for a piccolo, and when the Madwoman sees the image of her son and asks, "Is it you, my child?" the piccolo answers while the boy circles his mother. The use of flute and piccolo is meant, of course, to establish musically the familial ties, but the gradual removal of the flute from its close association with the Madwoman also suggests the abatement of her madness. By the end of the child's redemptive message and benediction, the Madwoman has recovered her sanity and sings a melismatic "Amen" that is in sharp contrast to her earlier music. She has been cured through the Christian message of redemption and now sings free of her mask of madness—the flute (see Ex. 14).

"The Solemn Dedication and Skill of the Performers"

In *Curlew River,* as in much ritualistic and didactic theater, the characters are universalized, nonspecific types. The performers representing the Madwoman, Ferryman, and Traveller all wear masks that cover their eyes, forehead, and nose. Britten initially was not in favor of using masks in this work: in his letter to Plomer suggesting the adoption of a Christian background for the play, he mentioned the "colossal problem" of using masks as in Noh. He also had criticized Stravinsky's use of masks in *Oedipus Rex* for their part in what he felt to be a work of "impersonal comment."[20] However, by the time he finished composing *Curlew River* he had come to appreciate the potential of masks in ritual theater. He realized that a mask could override issues of gender, for the mask makes the character and remakes the performer. Similarly, one need only hear the instrumental and vocal markers in order to identify the character being presented. The performers of Britten's Church Parables are doubly covered, first as "monks" and then in the robes and masks of whatever characters they are to represent.

Another form of masking and stylization is apparent in the choreographed movements for this work. Britten was clearly most impressed by the "marvelous skill and control of the performers" in his experience of Noh. Noh is fundamentally a form of dance theater in which movements are precise and are of symbolic significance. The physical control and intensity required for Noh are the features that most often impress foreign observers.

In *Curlew River,* all movements are carefully described in the production notes included at the end of the published score. These notes were written by Colin Graham, producer and director of *Noye's Fludde,* the three Church Parables, and several of Britten's operas, including *Death in Venice.* Britten and Graham worked out all of the movements for the performance of *Curlew River* while Britten composed the score in Venice, closely coordinating movement with music.[21]

Several of the modernist ideals for physical movement in ritual theater are expressed by Graham in his production notes. He writes: "The action of the story itself should be as formalized as a ritual: unlike naturalistic acting, emotion should never be expressed by the face or eyes but always by a rehearsed ritualistic movement of the hands, head, or body."[22] He insists that movement "should be as spare and economical as possible" and that "every movement of the hand or tilt of the head should assume immense meaning." He continues by warning that these movements require "enormous concentration on the part of the actor, an almost Yoga-like muscular, as well as physical, control" and relates that the original cast "underwent a strenuous course of movement instruction and physical education before rehearsals began and this training was maintained throughout the engagement." These guidelines for future productions suggest that performers would need to train specifically for this piece. The work is no conventional form of entertainment, but instead requires the services of initiates who will subordinate their individuality to the purposes of the ritual. As Eric Walter White has noted, "The effect of this stylization was to isolate the players within their parts."[23] The new high-intensity performance aesthetic demanded by *Curlew River* is perhaps its most radical feature.

"A Totally New 'Operatic' Experience"

The act of genre creation often entails collaboration and the establishment of a performance ensemble trained for the new form. In composing *Curlew River,* Britten sought a "new 'operatic' experience" and therefore assembled a production team and cast dedicated to the performance of his "parables for church performance." Plomer wrote the librettos and Graham directed and produced all three works. The same costume designer and movement director were retained for each production, and the principal members of the initiated cast remained fairly constant, as did the instrumentalists. Many of the techniques of movement and characteristics of the musical structure of the Parables even influenced Britten's final two operas. For instance, Eric Roseberry has suggested that the "ritualistic spareness of gesture in *Death in* Venice . . . springs directly from *Curlew River* and the Noh play conventions."[24]

Most of the basic elements of *Curlew River* were carried over to the two later Parables. The same stage, set, and performance location, and even the same venue—the annual Aldeburgh Festival at the Orford Church in Suffolk—were common to all three. The musical and dramatic structure, the core instrumental ensemble, and the fundamental performance aesthetic were also constant. Having established the basic outlines of the genre with *Curlew River,* Britten was able to make modifications in *The Burning Fiery Furnace* and *The Prodigal Son* while continuing to employ similar ritualistic and masking techniques. One constant and prominent feature of these works was the "all male cast of ecclesiastics." Male roles dominate Britten's oeuvre, and in the Church Parables Britten was able to utilize the male voice exclusively.[25] The gender limitation on the performers of Japanese Noh and of medieval liturgical drama, at least in Britten's vision of it, was clearly a very desirable trait—a justification the composer had been searching for.

The Man Behind the Mask

On 11 February 1956 in Tokyo, Britten had admired the "exquisite mask" of the female character that "made no attempt to hide the male jowl beneath it." What was the audience at Orford Church on 13 June 1964 to see, hear, and admire when Peter Pears entered beneath his mask as a monk playing the role of the Madwoman in *Curlew River*? Plomer was concerned that an English audience might consider it odd for the role of the mother to be played by a man, but Britten and Pears had settled on the use of a dress-role from the start and argued that the conceit of a medieval setting with a performance by monks would account for this innovative casting decision. The alterations made by Britten to the final climactic scene of the work indicate that he also found the question problematic, despite his assurances to Plomer.

Although the libretto for *Curlew River* remains quite close to the original Noh play, the highly dramatic encounter between the mother and the spirit of her son is different. In *Sumidagawa,* the mother "chases" the boy in a poignant attempt to grasp his hand, but he disappears and she is left weeping. The British composer and conductor Oliver Knussen has studied an earlier version of this scene in *Curlew River* and has remarked that it was "very strange indeed—a man dressed as a woman groping for a small boy."[26] After watching the scene in rehearsal, Britten also must have feared that it would appear "very strange." (In this case dramatic action resonated too suggestively with life.) Britten's final version, in which the mother is quietly and

Figure 8. The Madwoman and the spirit of her son in *Curlew River*. Photograph by Zoe Dominic. (Reproduced with the permission of Dominic Photography)

slowly "transformed" and healed as the spirit of her child solemnly circles around her once without physical contact and then sings his lines of Christian comfort and hope (see Fig. 8), was composed late in the rehearsal period.[27] Considerations of sexual suggestion were central to many of the alterations made by Britten in his literary sources on the way to the completed work.

Britten's sexuality and its significance for our understanding of his music have been much discussed subjects in recent scholarship. During his adult life, although he openly lived with his lover Peter Pears and made little attempt to hide his attraction to adolescent boys, Britten wore something of a half-mask, hiding his sexuality by choice and by law. During the years of the Church Parables' gestation, the late 1950s to mid-1960s, legal issues concerning the rights of homosexuals were a matter of intense public debate in England. In the early 1950s, with strong encouragement from the United States CIA, the British government viewed homosexuals as a Cold War security risk and pursued a policy of harassment.[28] Until the late 1960s, repressive British law required homosexuals to hide their sexual orientation and relations or face prosecution that could lead to life imprisonment. The Sexual Offenses Act of 1967 legalized private adult homosexual acts but retained many restrictions.[29]

In his biography of Britten, Humphrey Carpenter relates that Britten's sexuality was a much-discussed topic among the performers and staff associated with his work and that the composer's attraction to adolescent boys was a source of both controversy and tension throughout his professional career. Critics have had little trouble in making connections between Britten's sexuality and his operas and works of music theater. A cursory glance at Britten's oeuvre reveals a prominent dedication to the adolescent male voice, a strong tendency to set texts written by homosexual authors, and subjects that repeatedly signal male homosexual love, desire, and persecution. Although considerations of Britten's sexuality have offered many important critical insights in discussions of his operas, this scholarly approach has recently become somewhat routine.

Rummaging in an Exotic Closet

Britten scholarship was first brought "out of the closet" to a significant degree by Philip Brett's 1977 article on *Peter Grimes*.[30] Brett convincingly viewed the opera as an allegory on the homosexual condition and an act of catharsis for Britten's hidden feelings of persecution as a homosexual and pacifist in an intolerant society. Brett also suggested that Britten's self-imposed "exile" in the United States during World War II, the period immediately preceding the premiere of *Peter Grimes,* was prompted by a similar fear of persecution. Britten's sexuality became a focal point in studies of his operas throughout the 1980s and into the next decade. Writers such as Arnold Whittall, who to this point habitually avoided the subject (pointing instead to Britten's pacifism), also began to focus on questions of sexuality in the operas by the early 1990s.[31]

Although such discussions have usually centered on the more conspicuous examples such as *The Turn of the Screw, Billy Budd,* and *Death in Venice,* considerations of Britten's sexuality have been brought to bear on his entire operatic oeuvre. Clifford Hindley has progressed through Britten's operas, creating readings suggesting that Britten often encoded a "gay-affirmative" message in his works. For Hindley, Quint in *The Turn of the Screw* offers the young Miles a positive companionship of homosexual exploration.[32] Hindley offers an equally optimistic reading of *Death in Venice* and suggests that Britten considered Aschenbach's love for Tadzio to be not only a destructive obsession leading to his death but also a "positive possibility of a sublimated love of youthful male beauty."[33] He pursues a similar line of argument in discussions of *Billy Budd, Albert Herring, Peter Grimes,* and *The Burning Fiery Furnace,* managing to pull an affirmative declaration out of every operatic closet.

Brett rightly criticizes this "gay-affirmative" reading as being insensitive to Britten's actual reticence, to his sense of tragedy, and argues that these interpretations are a result of projection and identification on the part of recent scholars. Concerning Hindley's discussion of *The Turn of the Screw,* Brett attempts to reassert the fundamental ambiguity of the opposing readings of Miles's relation to Quint and to the Governess. He argues that Britten would have identified equally well with the reluctant and confused Miles as with Quint, the older male attracted to adolescent boys.[34] Brett has offered his own critical overview of Britten's corpus of operas and its relation to his homosexuality in two prominent collections devoted to musicology and sexuality.[35]

A critical insight was developed by Christopher Palmer in a 1985 article on *The Turn of the Screw.*[36] Palmer pointed to Britten's use of Orientalist passages derived primarily from Balinese gamelan music for the seductive sounds of Quint. Although his melismatic calls to Miles might be heard as only vaguely non-Western, Palmer showed that the sound of Quint's characteristic accompanying music, particularly his celesta motif, derived directly from Britten's experiences of gamelan music. Britten's introduction to this music was through the Canadian composer Colin McPhee in New York, where both lived during World War II. McPhee had lived in Bali, written important studies of its music, and composed works influenced by the gamelan. His years there represented an opportunity not only for him to encounter an exotic music, but also to enjoy homosexual relations with relative freedom and little sense of stigma. (In the first half of the twentieth century, Bali was viewed as a sexual paradise by many Euro-American artists.)[37] Thus, Britten's first impressions of Bali and first exposure to gamelan music were filtered through McPhee's unique descriptions, transcriptions, and experiences. During Britten's own 1956 tour of Asia he encountered Balinese culture and music at firsthand. Mervyn Cooke has written a comprehensive account of this experience and has analyzed the multiple occurrences of gamelan-inspired music in Britten's works.[38]

Britten's 1956 Asiatic tour not only exposed him to exotic musical sounds; it also inspired, or reinforced, an imagined realm of sexual permissiveness that would remain in his Orientalist memory. In his travel diary, Prince Ludwig observed that "in these eastern countries, differences of sex, (among the dancers at least), have become rather indistinct. A kind of bisexual dance-being has emerged."[39] During his stay in Bali, Britten particularly enjoyed watching the performance of the boys' gamelan, a type of ensemble initially formed by McPhee twenty years earlier. This connection between the musical exotic and homosexual opportunity is central to several of Britten's operas and receives its clearest expression in his final opera, *Death in Venice*. In this work, the roles of Quint and Miles from *The Turn of the Screw* are reversed; the middle-aged man, Aschenbach, is drawn to the adolescent boy, Tadzio, who is represented by the gamelan-inspired musical signs of an exotic paradise. Tadzio remains a silent dancer throughout the work and is thus admired by Aschenbach solely for his physical beauty. Aschenbach, in the course of the opera, comes to prove that a mask can reveal as well as conceal. (Oscar Wilde made this point in 1891 when he wrote: "Man is least himself when he talks in his own person. Give him a mask and he will tell you the truth.")[40] Aschenbach's progress toward the acknowledgment of his innermost desires is achieved when he allows himself to be made up as a dandy and sings the Elderly Fop's insinuating tune—when he dons the mask of his desire.

The "Self-Affirming Homosexual" with "God on His Side"?

The metaphor of "the closet" has appeared in many (if not in most) discussions of the relationship between homosexuals and society.[41] The phrase "coming out," explicitly tied to this dominant metaphor, has been employed for a range of political as well as analytical purposes, and has perhaps been overused. The "closet" seems inevitably to suggest both an enclosed, unrepresentable space, and the mysterious activities that might occur in those darkened, cramped quarters. "Closeted" evokes the image of a withdrawn homosexual hiding from society. I believe that the image of the "mask" might better serve such discussions by removing emphasis from a mysterious and enclosed space and by focusing on the daily, complex interactions between homosexuals and a predominantly heterosexual society.[42] In this sense, "masked" homosexuals employ multiple masks as selectively applied devices of concealment for fear of persecution. But the metaphor is adaptable—it could also describe the position of the individual who has "come out." In this sense, a homosexual mask of identification, a fixed, unremovable marker that inescapably defines an individual as gay is locked onto its wearer by society. The advantages of "coming out" are diluted if society insists on narrowly defining and relating to the emerged individual in terms of his or her sexual preference. During Britten's lifetime, his "mask" was clearly a disguise. Yet, in current Britten scholarship, the composer's sexuality is becoming a marker that tends to predetermine our critical readings; it is the face that we have come to look for and the one we continually find.

In his article "Homosexual Self-affirmation and Self-oppression in Two Britten Operas," Clifford Hindley develops a metaphor of the concealing mask for his reading of *The Burning Fiery Furnace,* the second Church Parable. Hindley places a great deal of emphasis on the name transformation scene in which the three young Israelites are given Babylonian names by Nebuchadnezzar and his Astrologer. This moment is given little significance in the Book of Daniel but is highlighted by Plomer in his libretto. The Three state that "Names cannot change us; / what we are we remain," thereby affirming their separate identity when surrounded and confronted by others. Hindley suggests that Plomer stresses this moment in order to expose the underlying concern of this Parable: "the degree of 'masking' or hypocrisy that may cause a person to disguise his true nature in order to fit into society at large."[43] The more common interpretation of this work emphasizes the theme of intolerance of racial and ethnic difference, particularly in light of the Holocaust. In Hindley's view, the "mask of a false name" for the outsider or immigrant is similar to the concealment that homosexuals were forced to practice in Britten and Plomer's England.

Hindley interprets *The Burning Fiery Furnace* as a "parable of the homosexual's experience within an oppressive society," and, as in his multiple discussions of Britten's operas, he finds a positive message in this work. For Hindley, this work "may (and should) be read as a parable about the need for the homosexual not to deny his inner nature when put to the test."[44] This gay-affirmative message involves a paradox since, as Hindley agrees, both Britten and Plomer wore masks of concealment throughout their careers. Hindley attempts to address this problem by claiming that this very work can be heard as an implicit statement of their joint determination to remain true to their sexuality in the midst of a hostile society—a somewhat circular argument. Hindley interprets *The Burning Fiery Furnace* as a reversal of the negative homosexual tale of oppression in *Peter Grimes*. By enlisting the religious form of the Church Parable, Britten is said to demonstrate that "the self-affirming homosexual who acts with integrity now has God on his side."[45] Removing one's masks is an act sanctioned by God.

This optimistic reading, however, runs counter to Britten's reluctance to remove his own mask during his life. Britten was, by all accounts, very reticent regarding his sexuality and was keenly concerned by the possible censure of society. Rather than enjoy the Babylonian celebration and the performance of the dancing boys during the feast (as Britten had done in Bali), the three young Jews refuse to eat and to indulge themselves. The angelic, pure, and wordless boy's voice in the furnace is earned only through self-denial. An alternative reading of *The Burning Fiery Furnace* as a work of cathartic atonement, perhaps as an expression of self-indictment for not having maintained "British standards" of thought or behavior while being entertained in exotic lands, would be mere conjecture. I offer it in order to maintain the dual possibilities first expressed in Brett and Hindley's contrasting readings of *The Turn of the Screw*. Although the possibility of a homosexual message of declaration in this parable of religious faith remains uncertain, a "gay-affirmative" reading of *The Prodigal Son*, the third and final Church Parable, would prove far more problematic. In general, the Church Parables are just as likely to have served as opportunities for Britten to work out, in a religious setting, personal anxiety regarding his own sexuality as to have provided occasions for publicly, if covertly, asserting the moral integrity of the homosexual male in mid-century England.

"What Do These Strange Voices Mean?"

In a genre of such musical and dramatic sparseness, of such formalized structure, slight alterations from the original model can carry great significance. *The Prodigal Son* begins with a processional chant, as do the previous two

Church Parables. In these earlier works, the performer playing the Abbot addressed the congregation before assuming whatever specific role he was to represent. This created a clear separation, without overlap, between the frame of the chanting monks and the mystery to be presented. In *The Prodigal Son*, the Abbot, already in costume as the Tempter, interrupts the chant and thus breaks the structural frame. Rather than introduce the mystery and describe the lesson to be learned from a position outside of its performance, the Tempter instructs the audience to "see how" he will disturb the order of a peaceful family and tells them that "What I bring you is evil." In *The Burning Fiery Furnace*, the Abbot had warned his congregation that he would need to assume the role of a wicked man, but assured them that it was all for the "glory of God."

The Tempter, like many of the male characters of dubious morality in Britten's operas, has a high, often chromatic, vocal line.[46] As he encourages the Younger Son to accept the temptations offered to him in the sinful city, he employs a sinister and sinuous *Sprechstimme* and is accompanied by glissando harmonics on the double bass (see Ex. 15). Christopher Palmer notes that the music for the Tempter's first vocal entrance is the same as the celesta accompanimental motif for Quint in *The Turn of the Screw*.[47] Palmer uses this musical detail to support his reading of Quint as a clearly evil force in the life of young Miles. (Hindley, of course, strongly objects to this interpretation and regards Quint as a symbol of positive homosexual exploration.) With *The Prodigal Son*, Britten created a more explicit situation of a musically seductive Tempter offering such possibilities to a young male. However, this exploration is placed firmly in the context of sin and guilt—a context that even Hindley would be hard pressed to reverse.

An additional musical moment in *The Prodigal Son* complicates Hindley's view of another of Britten's operas. The Parasite chorus welcoming the Younger Son to the city has music similar to that of the Elderly Fop's young male companions in their praise of Venice, another city of sin, in *Death in Venice* (see Ex. 16a and b). This musical connection underscores the similarity between the dangerous offerings of these two male choruses. It is interesting to note that Britten composed much of *Curlew River* and *The Prodigal Son* as well as this final opera while in Venice.[48] Venice seems to have served for Britten, as it has done in the imagination of so many "northern" artists and writers, from Ruskin to Sargent, Hoffman to Mann, as a familiar, yet exotic spot; decaying, touched with sin, a temptation to which they repeatedly return.

The temptations in *The Prodigal Son* are offered not by the Tempter him-

Example 15. The Tempter's voice: Britten, *The Prodigal Son* (Faber Music, 1971)

self but are announced by a chorus of distant boy sopranos (see Ex. 17). These voices are accompanied by glissando harmonics on the viola, a family resemblance to the Tempter's double bass harmonics, and by the alto flute—both instruments of somewhat ambiguous gender association in terms of range. The Younger Son asks "What do these strange voices mean?" and "What are these strange promises?"; the Tempter acts as an interpreter of each temptation, the Parasite chorus coaxes the Younger Son to accept, and

Example 16a.   The Parasites' welcome: Britten, *The Prodigal Son* (Faber Music, 1971)

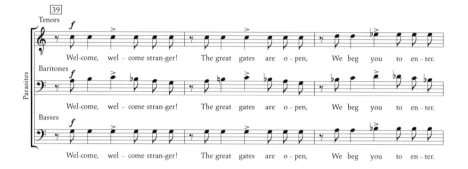

then the Tempter demands payment for the pleasures rendered. This rigid pattern of temptation, acceptance, and payment is maintained for the promises of wine, sexual pleasure, and gold.

I am particularly interested in the second temptation: the "delights of the flesh," the "Nights of ecstasy, / joys of fierce completeness," the "pangs of piercing sweetness." Rather than attempting to determine the meaning of these "strange promises," we should consider the significance of Britten's use of these particular "strange voices." By the mid-twentieth century, the voice of the boy soprano might appear almost as strange to an audience as would the high adult-male voice—or at least in such a suggestive context as this. Of course, the Church Parable is explicitly a genre of male performance, but in no other moment of the Parables is the absence of the female voice more problematic than during this scene. In *Curlew River* the boy soprano voice was used for a message of Christian hope. In *The Burning Fiery Furnace* boys served both for seductive entertainment and for the voice of the redemptive angel in the fiery furnace. In *The Prodigal Son* boys sing the part of whores and of temptation. A sound traditionally associated with the pure strains of heavenly angels is assigned here to the siren calls of sin.

In the temptation of drink, the Parasites offer the wine and become drunk along with the Younger Son. For the temptation of the flesh, the Parasites are instructed to "advance, beckoning." Their text speaks of inversion— "Nights are days, / days are nights, / Come and taste / dark delights"—and their music consists of small reflective and hypnotic figures, constituting their simple, mirror-imaging musical phrase, which in the tenor line, first descends and then ascends, reflecting upon itself (see Ex. 18). Eventually the Younger Son is "hidden from view"—presumably by the Chorus of

Example 16b. The Fop and the Youths: Britten, *Death in Venice* (Faber Music, 1975)

Example 17. The second temptation of the Distant Voices: Britten, *The Prodigal Son* (Faber Music, 1971)

Parasites. As with all physical gesture and movement in the Church Parables, this covering or hiding of the Younger Son can be understood symbolically. Is he removed to that mysterious closeted space from which the distant boy voices beckoned? If so, what takes place there? Underneath the beckoning music of the Parasites beats a constant tattoo on the drum, harp, and double bass. This creates a primitivist setting for the hidden actions occurring in the eleven measures before "the Younger Son reappears, exhausted."[49]

The temptations of the city leave the Younger Son weak and penniless; there is little musical or textual indication that he has enjoyed these experiences. Only the (seemingly celibate) pastoral male world of his father's home in the country offers a positive environment. We are offered comfort in the spiritual rather than physical pleasures of the initiates of the Aldeburgh Festival, the simple "monks" at Orford Church performing these three Parables. Britten may have yearned for the temptations and possibilities of the exotic realms of his imagination, often represented musically by the sounds of the gamelan, but he always returned to the more conventional comforts of home.

Example 18.   The tenor Parasites' lines of inversion: Britten, *The Prodigal Son* (Faber Music, 1971)

"A Moral Story"?

A parable is designed to illustrate moral, spiritual, and religious truths. The word is derived from the Greek *parabolē*, meaning comparison. The literary strategy of constructing a timeless, universal, and simple story in order to suggest a larger truth pertaining to contemporary society is fundamental to the genre. A parable shares something with the riddle—a hidden message is to be derived from the story told. A parable calls for interpretation. What truths did Britten intend to convey in his "parables for church performance"? What are the lessons to be learnt, the interpretations to be formed from the experience of these works? Robin Holloway reduces the potential meanings of each piece to single generic elements of Christian doctrine: *Curlew River* delivers a Christian message of redemptive hope, *The Burning Fiery Furnace* extols the importance of faith, and *The Prodigal Son* preaches love and forgiveness. Holloway's narrow interpretations of the Parables lead him to belittle their messages as being of the "drabbest stoicism."[50] Donald Mitchell draws connections between Britten's conception of the function of his art and Auden's definition of "parable art," an art that would "teach man to unlearn hatred and learn love."[51] We have observed that other critics have read these works and Britten's operas as personal allegories of specific contemporary social issues—whether of homosexual oppression, racial and ethnic intolerance, or of the pacifist's precarious position in a militant, nationalistic society. The potential layers of parable interpretation, of "comparison" and connection between a surface meaning of the presented tale and a hidden moral, are thus multiple in these three works.

The possibility that the inherent Christian message of each Parable, the "surface meaning" in Plomer's libretto, was also one of Britten's primary meanings should not be denigrated. Rather, the larger significance of Britten's strong attachment to Christianity in his life and work should be considered. As mentioned above, Christian themes and subjects were central to Britten's composition throughout his career. For Britten, Christianity seems to have offered a form of protection, a cover that concealed or even atoned for the one aspect of his life that did not correspond to his self-image of a conventional, successful member of the upper middle class. We should also consider Britten's choice of these three specific stories. Both *Curlew River* and *The Burning Fiery Furnace* center on individuals who are persecuted by society, a theme common to many of his operas. In the third Church Parable, a deviant is forgiven and welcomed home. (Perhaps Britten saw himself as something of a prodigal, having left his country during wartime for the United States but being later welcomed back and honored by society.) All three stories, as didactic religious texts, preach compassion, tolerance, and forgiveness for the other—whether one chooses to define this individual as different in political, ethnic, or sexual terms.

While any specific intentional message may remain opaque, Britten's desire to draw upon traditional religious expression in these works is clear. But does Britten succeed in engaging the audience of the Church Parable on a spiritual level? Do the elements of formalized structure, stylized gesture, and religious setting combine to create a work of ritual? Or is this only playing at religion, a mere masquerading in church? Britten moved from an inclusive idiom of community religious performance in *Noye's Fludde* to a refined form performed by a group of trained initiates in the Church Parables. Perhaps only the performers experience these later works as ritual. The audience or "congregation" no longer was called upon to participate in the reenactment of biblical mysteries but instead became the silent recipient of lessons to be learned. The Church Parables may be performed for the moral benefit of all present, but their success depends upon the willingness of the audience to assume the role of a silent congregation. Only if both "stage and audience" are able to "achieve half the intensity and concentration of that original drama," the Japanese Noh and the medieval mystery, could a form of ritual be achieved and would Britten "be well satisfied."

What is the moral of my own parable, the "parable of a comparable setting"? Is Britten's Christianization of the exotic and staging of the Christian ethically problematic? In two important articles Philip Brett has briefly commented on the Church Parables and has addressed this very question. For Brett, *Curlew River* "engages with the music of Asia on terms that are not at all patronizing, because they put so much of Western musical history at risk in an attempt at a genuine relationship that acknowledges and celebrates difference: Britten's grounding of his work musically in Western chant and dramatically in the English mystery play provides the basis for a clear-headed reinterpretation of and homage to Eastern conventions."[52] In another context, Brett has written that by transforming the exotic model into a comparable setting, "Britten opened up conditions in which he was able to pay homage to an Eastern tradition by adapting and imitating some of its musical and dramatic procedures without patronizing it, and without using it as a vehicle for the projection of Western fantasies. It is a project that tries hard to avoid the colonizing impulse, though of course it reflects the romantic utopianism also associated with the phenomenon of Orientalism in the West."[53]

We have yet to develop adequate criteria for a critique of the "post-colonial," or even to determine whether the "post" actually has been achieved or whether the latter decades of the twentieth century witnessed "cultural imperialism" in other forms. In discussions of opera and music theater these issues play out in the domain of Orientalism or in the apparently more neutral study of "influence." I have frequently used the word "influence" in this discussion in order not to foreclose the possibility of Brett's "genuine relationship that acknowledges and celebrates difference." On an analytic level, the relationship between Britten's music and Japanese *nohgaku*, or even more so with Balinese gamelan music, often appears different in degree in comparison to nineteenth-century evocations of the exotic in Orientalist opera. And yet we have seen that, continuing in the grand Orientalist tradition, Britten consistently aligned exotic music with the sexual and the seductive, if less clearly with the evil and the sinful. If recent readings are to be accepted, then Britten not only utilized the exotic as a "vehicle for the projection of Western fantasies" but for more personal fantasies as well.

The argument that gays are exotic within their own culture and are thus to be considered somewhat innocent of Orientalism in their interactions with other cultures has become increasingly common. In a recent interview, Lou Harrison (who has denied the existence of a gay musical aesthetic) suggested that gays share a special affinity for the exotic. Mark Levine reports: "Harrison tells me that in his travels—to Korea, Japan, Indonesia, New Zealand—he was apt to acquire a lover who would guide him through the local culture. 'You've already crossed one major social border, just to be gay,' he says.

'So crossing other boundaries and being open to possibility comes rather naturally. You've already stepped outside.'"[54] This view is problematic. The position of the Euro-American gay male in the twentieth century was clearly one of marginalization and oppression. Yet as a Euro-American male, the gay man retained economic and political power in relation to the exotic other. Privileging sexual difference over broader cultural differences can lead to myopic interpretations.

Although Britten's more intimate knowledge of some of his exotic sources allowed him to "pay homage" without reductively caricaturing them, the uses to which he put the exotic nevertheless fail in evading the "colonizing impulse." Brett's attempt to redeem Britten from charges of Orientalist thinking is misdirected, for the Japanese remained Britten's ultimate exotic. Far from putting "Western musical history at risk" in these works, Britten played it safe by recasting Noh in a Christian musical idiom. In addition, Britten freely appropriated those aspects of Japanese Noh that appealed to him while discarding those Buddhist elements that meant little to him. Once a musical or dramatic element was coded as exotic, it was combined by Britten with other such elements without regard for their divergent initial contexts. Britten's use of a seemingly "native" Christian context and of medieval religious drama can likewise be considered an appropriation or reinterpretation for his own purposes and fantasies. At one level, the Church Parables and *Noye's Fludde* are clearly acts of homage and religious offering. And yet, by performing these rituals of Christian expression in a religious space, employing children and the audience itself for *Noye's Fludde*, deriving the melodic substance of each Parable from Gregorian chant, and basing his new genre on preexistent exotic models, Britten repeatedly enclosed his own meanings and artistic creations in a protective borrowed framework. For Britten, exotic models consistently served as convenient masks. "Influence" and "borrowing" are never neutral transactions, however well intentioned.

10 Later British Mysteries

"Music-Theatre"

Britten did not return to the Church Parable genre after completing *The Prodigal Son*, nor did other composers directly adopt the form. However, some of the features developed in Britten's three Church Parables were to influence British music theater and opera throughout the remaining decades of the century. The three most prominent figures interested in creating works of ritualistic music theater were Peter Maxwell Davies, Alexander Goehr, and Harrison Birtwistle. (All three were fellow students at the Royal Manchester College of Music and are often considered jointly in discussions of postwar British music.) With the 1967 formation of the Pierrot Players by Davies and Birtwistle (an ensemble inspired by Schoenberg's early experiment in music theater and re-formed by Davies in 1970 as the Fires of London), music theater became the central genre or performance ideal of the British musical avant-garde. Music theater soon transgressed the loose generic boundaries established by earlier figures and came to invade all forms of concert music. Davies, in particular, composed numerous examples of "music-theatre" including such works as *Eight Songs for a Mad King* (1969), *Vesali Icones* (1969), *Missa Super l'Homme Armé* (in its 1971 revised form), *Miss Donnithorne's Maggot* (1974), and *The Medium* (1981). Each of these pieces blurs the conventional distinctions between concert and dramatic musical categories to some degree. Davies' interest in experimenting with alternative forms of music theater is also evident in those works that he subtitled "masque," "mini-opera," "children's opera," and "chamber opera."

Ritual has been central to many of the staged works of these three composers and has taken various forms. For example, Birtwistle's *Punch and Judy* (1967), designated by the composer as a "one-act opera," is rigidly and repetitively structured and exhibits features of ritual performance without having associations with an established religion. Stephen Pruslin, Birtwistle's librettist, writes that their aim in this work was to create a "stylized and ritualistic drama for adults" based on the traditional puppet-play for children.[1] The use of a "Choregos" character is but one indication that *Punch and Judy* is intended to be experienced as a ritual on the scale of Greek tragedy rather than as merely an amusing, or shocking, slapstick puppet piece. (Birtwistle had experimented with ancient Greek theatrical forms in *Monodrama*, composed in 1967 but subsequently withdrawn by the composer.) Lacking a referential religious context, the moral of this ritualistic work and the purpose of its performance remain unclear. The traces of Britten's Church Parable influence are more readily apparent in works based on Judeo-Christian subjects such as Davies' *The Martyrdom of St. Magnus* and Goehr's *Naboth's Vineyard* and *Sonata about Jerusalem*.

A Contemporary Martyr

Christianity is as important a factor in Davies' music as it was for Britten's— although Davies' treatment of this subject is far more radical, frequently bordering on the blasphemous. Many of his works involve parodic transformations of models from medieval Christian music and several of his theatrical works are based on Christian themes and imagery. Davies' full-length opera *Taverner*, completed in 1968, dramatizes the religious struggles, conversion, and music of the sixteenth-century English composer and contains a mock passion play staged by Death. *Vesali Icones* is a piece for solo cello, small ensemble, and a nude male dancer whose movements superimpose images from the anatomical drawings of Vesalius onto the fourteen Stations of the Cross. Davies' *Le Jongleur de Notre Dame* (1978), a "masque" for mime, baritone, and instrumental ensemble including children's band, is something of a Christian miracle play performed by monks. In 1976 Davies composed a "chamber opera," *The Martyrdom of St. Magnus*, to his own libretto based on the Orcadian poet George Mackay Brown's 1973 novel *Magnus*. Davies had admired Brown's works for their use of "a language which is almost a ritual language."[2] His interest in the Orcadian figure of Saint Magnus developed after his first visit to the Orkney Islands in 1970, where he was soon to make his home. Saint Magnus was a twelfth-century Viking pacifist whose story is found in the Icelandic *Orkneyinga Saga*. Davies composed a *Hymn to St. Magnus* in 1972, which, like many of his earlier works, involves parody of early religious music. *The Martyrdom of St. Magnus* was created for the first St. Magnus Festival, of which Davies was co-artistic director, and the inaugural performance took place in the St. Magnus Cathedral at Kirkwall.

Davies' "Notes on Performance," printed at the beginning of both the score and libretto, offer an interesting perspective from which to view this "chamber opera" as a work of ritual music theater.[3] The work is performed by only five singers, four male and one female, who together play twenty-six roles. The first production was performed by the Fires of London, Davies own ensemble. This use of a specially trained performance group is very common to works of ritual music theater. In his notes, Davies writes that the piece is "ideally to be played in the round; in a small hall, to an audience of not more than 250, seated on the floor in a circle round the arena. There should be no extraneous light—the hall should be sealed against the intrusion of light and sound." He asks that "both cast and instrumentalists should be in position and totally silent (no tuning!) when the audience is admitted," and that the performance start and the doors close as soon as the audience is seated. Productions of this work should "always be characterized by simplicity." Davies also created a more accessible, less dense musical texture for this work than was typical of his earlier compositions.

The audience for *St. Magnus* is to be virtually locked in—removed from any "intrusion" by the outside world. Programs are to be left in the lobby as an unwanted distraction, a reminder of the external world, and a suggestion that the event is a mere performance. The division between the pre-performance temporal and spatial reality of the lobby and the performance realm of *The Martyrdom of St. Magnus* is to be absolute. Davies' ideal is an intimate, devoted audience brought close to the performance. When not participating in the action, the cast members, wearing modern workday clothes, are instructed to sit on a bench near the performance space—in effect, to become one with the audience. The instrumentalists are asked to wear informal clothes throughout the performance. These details are part of Davies' attempt to make the conventional gulf between performers and audience as small as possible. As in most ritual music theater, symbolic masks and costumes are used and "no attempt should be made to hide the ritual of change of identity or prop"—theatrical illusion and realism are not desired goals.

The work is in one act consisting of nine scenes connected by brief and seamless musical transitions. The performer assuming the role of Blind Mary is to be lying face down on the ground before the audience enters. Blind Mary is a gypsy and fortune-teller; she is also something of a prophetess, who addresses the audience directly and who occasionally serves the function of a critical chorus. As the performance starts, she slowly makes her breathing heard as she comes to life in the performance space. Blind Mary begins to hum, gradually entering the realm of sound. She first sings unaccompanied and is then joined by a solo guitar. As an introductory Wagnerian Norn she sings of the loom of fate on which the web of bloody battle is being woven. The first scene represents the legendary battle between the Norsemen and the Welshmen in which Magnus sang psalms rather than fight and was not harmed by the enemy arrows, thus demonstrating his spirituality. Two Heralds, holding masks and banners, present the entire battle through their boasts and descriptions of the action. The Norse Herald performer assumes a mask in order to become instantly the King of Norway and to announce that the cousins Hakon and Magnus will become joint earls of Orkney upon the death of their fathers.

In the second scene, which takes place in a suspended and ambiguous temporal dimension, Magnus is met first by the Keeper of the Loom, the guardian of his soul which is to be woven on the "loom of the spirit," and is warned that he will undergo five temptations. The Tempter immediately appears. He is announced by the bass drum and is initially accompanied by a trumpet as was Britten's Tempter in *The Prodigal Son.* Although a baritone, he frequently sings in an exaggerated, unnatural falsetto. In his third temptation he offers Magnus the coat of state of the earls of Orkney, which rightly belongs to both Magnus and Hakon, in an extreme falsetto voice (see Ex. 19). Here the ambiguity of the high male voice is once again associated with evil.

Time is an unstable framework in *The Martyrdom of St. Magnus.* The third temptation is offered as Magnus is preparing to become earl upon the death of his father; in the fourth temptation, which immediately follows in musical time, the Tempter refers to five years having passed since Magnus assumed his earldom. Chronological narrative and dramatic continuity are not priorities in this ritualistic reenactment of well-known events from the saint's life. Scene iii is a deft condensation by Davies of several scenes in the novel in which commoners are cruelly treated by soldiers. Blind Mary, serving the function of a Greek chorus and directly addressing the audience, reports one representative atrocity committed by each side in the civil war between the joint earls Hakon and Magnus. She denounces and curses the audience directly and says that "You are evil, you soldiers, whatever side you support." A meeting is arranged in scene iv to discuss conditions for peace. The Bishop of Orkney announces that he will not attend the peace conference for he believes that Orkney needs "something more in the nature of a sacrifice, the true immaculate death of the dove." On the way to the peace conference in scene v, Magnus realizes that he will be treach-

Example 19.   The Tempter's voice: Davies, *The Martyrdom of St. Magnus*
(Boosey & Hawkes, 1987)

erously killed but resolves to go in order to offer himself as a sacrifice for
peace. He experiences a vision of himself "in the mask of a beast, dragged
to a primitive stone." In the sixth scene Hakon resolves to kill Magnus. He
refuses all overtures of compromise in a voice of extreme violence. Davies
had employed violent vocal effects as a mask of madness in *Eight Songs for
a Mad King* and in *Miss Donnithorne's Maggot*. In this scene, a "nasal, military, a hysterical, 'automaton,' shrieking" vocal mask is sounded by Hakon
to exhibit the depths of human brutality.

In some sections of this work, periods of time are instantly traversed
within the brief transition between two scenes or during a single passage of
dialogue. In the pivotal seventh scene the dramatic temporal frame is
rapidly, but systematically, transferred from the twelfth century to the
present. The Reporters deliver a series of news flashes which indicate that
the negotiations are not working. The music gradually advances the action
and setting from the realm of twelfth-century polyphony to the foxtrot of
the twentieth century. Various musical styles are signaled in a condensed
progression through music history.[4] Magnus is thus executed in a "police
cell in any contemporary totalitarian state." The performer is now referred
to generically as The Prisoner. In Brown's novel the sacrifice occurred
specifically in a Nazi concentration camp, but Davies made the setting and
message more universal and thus more applicable to a range of current and
future contexts. Brown's novel places more emphasis on the specific miracle, while the opera, particularly through the use of violent vocal effects,
stresses human brutality.[5] In the final scene, "The Miracle" of this miracle
play, Blind Mary regains her sight while praying at the tomb of Saint Magnus. Monks chant in the background. Blind Mary ends the work by telling

the audience to "carry the peace of Christ into the world," and the chanting monks recess "leaving total darkness except for Mary's candle, and silence." This benedictory end inevitably reminds one of Britten's Church Parables. Davies created a similar example of religious music theater, but made the potential contemporary relevance of his work far more explicit.

Separating the Voice from Its Mask

Goehr's *Triptych* is a "trilogy of music theatre pieces" consisting of *Naboth's Vineyard* (1968), *Shadowplay* (1970), and *Sonata about Jerusalem* (1971). Each piece is approximately twenty minutes in length and requires a similar performance force. Of the three, *Naboth's Vineyard*, a "dramatic madrigal," and *Sonata about Jerusalem*, a "cantata," are thematically and structurally the most related and are particularly relevant to this discussion of religious and ritual music theater. Both are based on religious stories containing aspects of the parable form, have a similar contemporary significance and reference, and share many of the same musical and dramatic techniques of ritual theater. In a discussion of *Naboth's Vineyard*, Goehr denied that its conception was influenced by Britten's Church Parables and instead claimed the dramatic madrigal and Monteverdi's *Combattimento di Tancredi e Clorinda* as models. He also acknowledged the importance of the *Lehrstücke* of Brecht, Weill, and Hindemith for his own concepts of music theater.[6] Goehr's pieces contain elements of stylized structure and performance aesthetic that suggest the influence of exotic models. As Melanie Daiken writes, "Goehr's presentation appears on the surface neutral, ritualized as it is in the style of the Japanese Nō theatre or the Renaissance dramatic madrigal."[7]

In both *Naboth's Vineyard* and *Sonata about Jerusalem*, Goehr created stylized forms of separation between a silent performer physically representing a given character and the sung text associated with that character. The story of *Naboth's Vineyard* is taken from 1 Kings 21. King Achab desired the vineyard of Naboth and offered a favorable trade. Naboth refused on the grounds that God did not permit him to give away his inheritance. Queen Jezebel had Naboth stoned on false charges of blasphemy and Achab assumed ownership of the vineyard. God sent the prophet Elijah to reprimand Achab, and Achab repented and humbled himself before God. God decided not to punish Achab but to bring calamity to his house in the days of his sons. In Goehr's setting of this tale, two mimes represent the various characters through the use of multiple masks and movement while soloists sing the characters' lines. (This is similar to the separation that occurs in certain works of Stravinsky such as *Renard*. Multiple representation of a character was taken even further in Birtwistle's 1986 *The Mask of Orpheus*.) The producer of the premiere performance of this piece, John Cox, notes in the score that "every attempt was made to keep the mimes indistinguishable from one another so that the masks were the only 'characters.'" The masks are to be shared and exchanged at several points, blurring any direct association between an individual performer and a specific character. The miming is not to be coordinated or choreographed with the music, and all of the singers, instrumentalists, and mimes are intended to be visible and of equal visual importance.

Goehr achieves an additional degree of separation and distancing by having the text of the individual characters sung by soloists in Latin—a recurrent masking language in modernist music. The three solo vocalists frequently combine to form a narrating trio or duet, serving a "translation" function in this work similar to the role of the narrator in Stravinsky's *Oedipus Rex*. The speech and actions of certain characters are thus represented in a threefold presentation: the descriptive narration in English, the Latin text of a solo singer, and the mask and movement of a mime. In the passage in which Jezebel writes letters in Achab's name instructing the Elders to form an assembly in order to accuse and denounce Naboth, the visual and musical representational framework becomes highly complex. The tenor and bass first describe Jezebel's letter writing in sung English. The contralto then sings the text of Jezebel's letters in Latin while the tenor and bass, vocally representing the Elders, "read" these letters also in Latin, immediately repeating and overlapping her lines. Meanwhile, the mime wearing Jezebel's mask is also to employ a double mask representing the Elders. This mask is revealed to be two-sided, with the accusers represented on the reverse side, during the enactment of the denunciation of Naboth (see Fig. 9). Naboth's mime is to appear confused as he appeals to the mask of the Elders only to have it rapidly alternate with its reverse side. With such a density of vocal separations and multiple masks, confusion is certainly an understandable response.

By splitting the expressive locus of each character in this manner, Goehr diffuses the possibility of our associating a given character's emotions and personality with an individual performer. No single performer is allowed to "become" a specific character or to assume full responsibility for representing a specific role. Each performer in this work is required to assume multiple functions and to represent multiple characters. For instance, in the brief fifth section of the work, one of the mimes speaks as a narrating voice. As Naboth dies, a mime serves as a percussionist and strikes a tam-tam. Each

Figure 9.   Multiple masks in *Naboth's Vineyard*. Photograph by Laelia Goehr. (Reproduced with the permission of Alexander Goehr)

vocal soloist sings multiple roles throughout the course of the piece. To take one example, the tenor serves multiple functions and vocally represents several characters: a neutral narrating voice as part of a duet or trio, the role of Achab, the chorus of Elders in a duet with the bass, a percussionist playing the tambourine, and the spoken English component of the "voice of the Lord." The audience is not asked to empathize with the plight of a realistic recreation of a character but instead to witness the ritualized presentation of this tale.

A narrator is employed also in *Sonata about Jerusalem*, as are two mimes—in this case representing the Jews of Bagdad rather than individual characters. The text of this work is based on a twelfth-century chronicle relating how the Jews of Bagdad came to believe that the day of the Messiah was at hand and that they would be lifted up and returned to Jerusalem. They climb to their rooftops on the appointed night and wait in high emotion only to be disappointed and ridiculed the next morning. A structurally repeated Latin refrain describing the wrathful "day of the Lord" is taken from the autobiography of Obadiah the Proselyte. A three-part female chorus sings this refrain and is minimally identified as representing the Jewish women of Bagdad by the sets of "little oriental or Indian bells" that they are to play as they sing. The narrator, a bass soloist who loosely "represents the power of the King of Bagdad," informs the audience that the Jewish women were required by the governor of Bagdad to wear little bells around their necks as a sonic signal of their Jewishness. Once again representation is split into three components: the female chorus, marked by a bit of tinkling Orientalism, represents the Jews audibly, the narration of the bass soloist describes the requirements for Jewish visual identification in English, and the mimes dress themselves in the manner prescribed by the narrator and thus assume the role of the Jews through their silent actions.

Daiken remarked that the subjects of *Triptych* are universal and timeless. While this is a basic claim of ritual theater, the themes of *Naboth's Vineyard* and *Sonata about Jerusalem* also have a more pointed contemporary relevance. Goehr himself identified a parallel between the tale of *Naboth's Vineyard* and the "Nazi trial of the aristocrats involved in the July 20 plot against Hitler."[8] The hope of deliverance and the foundation of a new and powerful Jerusalem in *Sonata about Jerusalem* resonate with both the war period in Nazi Germany and the contemporary situation in the Middle East. *Sonata about Jerusalem* was commissioned by the "Testimonium, Jerusalem Foundation" for a celebration of Jewish history and of Jerusalem as the historic center of Jewish spirituality. Goehr's work was one of seven commissioned pieces which were to deal with the subject of Jewish suffering and were to be based on a medieval textual source.[9] The work's contemporary relevance is possible precisely because its subject matter is also both "universal and timeless."

The Voices of God and Experiencing the Mystery

The Messiah never arrives in *Sonata about Jerusalem* but God does make an appearance to Achab, in that contested vineyard once belonging to Naboth, and the Divine has been heard, if not seen, in numerous works in this century. For a monotheistic deity, the Judeo-Christian God has received some surprisingly polyvocal settings in twentieth-century opera and music theater. The most prominent modern setting of the voice of God is found in Schoenberg's *Moses und Aron* as Moses receives his calling from the voice in the burning bush. Faced with the formidable challenge of creating this divine sound, Schoenberg chose to employ a six-part *Sprechstimme* chorus and six solo singing voices. In *The Flood*, Stravinsky created his voice of God

Example 20.   The voice of God: Goehr, *Naboth's Vineyard* (Schott, 1968)

with two stentorian basses while limiting the mortals to the realm of speech. Stravinsky set God's lines in *Babel* in a similar fashion, with a group of male voices; the rest of the text is spoken by a narrator. As we have seen, Britten chose the opposite alternative—in *Noye's Fludde,* God speaks from offstage while the mortal characters sing.

In Goehr's *Naboth's Vineyard,* the representation of God is once again multilayered. In the concluding section of the work, Elijah first speaks for God as a prophet and then "becomes God" himself. The "voice of the Lord" is formed by the contralto and bass singing in Latin while the tenor speaks or intones an English translation (see Ex. 20). Goehr's God both speaks and sings, as does Schoenberg's, and is both multivocal and bilingual. Rather than speaking directly to Achab, God fulfills the role of eternal narrator by speaking about him. The production notes indicate that the mime representing Elijah should be transformed into God, but there is no indication how this is to be achieved.

What might the mask of God look like in this work, and what would the audience see? Throughout the world, a ritual performance is considered successful only if divine presence is realized. Some form of transubstantiation or spiritual possession must occur. Is God's presence or some form of spirituality experienced in these modern mysteries of British ritual music theater? The composers considered here went to great lengths in a common attempt to elevate their works to a level of ritual or religious expression. As we have seen, they turned to a variety of models and devised numerous musical and dramatic techniques for this purpose. The audience was asked to reimagine itself and to relinquish its position as passive spectator. The performers were also required to assume new and multiple roles and to perform with the intensity and dedication of initiates. These experiments in music theater went beyond an attempt to return God to the stage. Basic notions of the social function and significance of the musical work, the role of an audience, and the very location of the performance were fundamentally altered during this period in British music. Similar developments in music theater were taking place in the United States, although along uniquely American lines.

Part IV

THE VARIETIES OF RITUAL EXPRESSION
AND CRITICISM IN AMERICAN
MUSIC THEATER

11   Orientalists and a Crusader

"Salut au Monde!" on Broadway

> O take my hand Walt Whitman!
> Such gliding wonders! such sights and sounds!
> Such join'd unended links, each hook'd to the next,
> Each answering all, each sharing the earth with all.
> . . .
> I see ranks, colors, barbarisms, civilizations, I go among them, I mix
>   indiscriminately,
> And I salute all the inhabitants of the earth.
>
> Walt Whitman, Salut au Monde!, ll. 1–4; 161–62

Walt Whitman's *Salut au Monde!* is a poem of ecstatic celebration, a proclamation of America's unique global position. Americans, thought Whitman, were ideally situated to exercise a transcendental, globe-encompassing imagination—to imagine themselves as citizens of the world. *Salut au Monde!* is the ultimate expression of such a seemingly benevolent imperialist vision. In this poem, Whitman exhibits a boundless enthusiasm for cultural diversity and (in 226 lines) catalogues the peoples and places that he sees and hears in his mind: the desire to encompass within himself and to experience the culture of each nation on earth is insatiable. Whitman appears pregnant with the world: "Within me latitude widens, longitude lengthens" (14). Declaring himself to be a citizen of many nations, he dreams of being accepted as the poet and lover of every land:

> My spirit has pass'd in compassion and determination around the whole
>   earth,
> I have look'd for equals and lovers and found them ready for me in all
>   lands,
> I think some divine rapport has equalized me with them.
>
> (212–14)

This extravagant catalogue aria aspires, through sheer length, to repletion. The nineteenth-century Don Juan of American interculturalism is in love with all inhabitants of the planet, and is eager to know them all.

Although Whitman's visual perceptions in *Salut au Monde!* occupy more than a hundred lines, his aural experience of the voices and music of the world, in answer to the question "What do you hear Walt Whitman?," take up only eighteen. This is hardly surprising. In the mid-nineteenth century, little of the world's music had been heard in America, whereas visual representations and evocative objets d'art were plentiful. In *A Broadway Pageant* (a celebration of the first visit by Japanese dignitaries to New York in 1860), Whitman envisions all of the peoples of Asia arriving in a grand parade to pay their respects and to be renewed by America.[1] This state visit represents nothing less than the fulfillment of America's global destiny: "the answer that waited thousands of years answers" (19); "You [America] shall sit in the middle well-pois'd thousands and thousands of years" (67); "the ring is circled, the journey is done" (71). Significantly, Whitman describes the physical appearances of the parading Asians and smells the sultry perfume of the Orient; yet he hears no song but his own, for "lithe and *silent* [emphasis mine] the Hindoo appears" (35). The generic "singing-girl" of the Orient is also here, but again, she is not heard. Instead the procreative, imperialist chant of Whitman, the American, sounds out loud and clear, drowning out the exotic din on Broadway:

> I am the chanter, I chant aloud over the pageant,
> I chant the world on my Western sea,
> I chant copious the islands beyond, thick as stars in the sky,
> I chant the new empire grander than any before, as in a vision
>   it comes to me,
> I chant America the mistress, I chant a greater supremacy,
> I chant projected a thousand blooming cities yet in time on those
>   groups of sea-islands
>
>   (55–60)

The poet does hear the "thunder-cracking guns" that "arouse me with the proud roar I love" (10). (The threat of hearing these American sounds had "opened" Japan to the West in 1853–54.) His song proclaims his, and America's, "greater supremacy." Now that the Orient has finally obeyed its summons, the poet asks his hot young nation to be considerate and respectful to "venerable Asia, the all-mother" (73). It is time for the young nation to come to know its Oriental elders.

The actual sounds of Asia would not come to Whitman's Manhattan for some decades, but once the music of the East was heard by Americans, several composers responded with an enthusiasm that echoed the ardent interculturalism of the poet. Henry Cowell (1897–1965) rhapsodized about the music of the world a hundred years after Whitman's *Salut* in his oft-quoted 1955 statement "I want to live in the *whole world* of music." Raised in San Francisco, Cowell acquired an early familiarity with East Asian music in particular.[2] He studied comparative musicology with Charles Seeger in California and then with Erich von Hornbostel in Berlin before traveling extensively in the Middle East and East Asia in later life. Dane Rudhyar (1895–1985) declared, in a 1933 article entitled "Oriental Influence on American Music," that "all human music should be close to us."[3] He predicted that "the Gateway to the Orient is through Occidental America. It is therefore natural to assume that it will be through America that the influence of Oriental music will first be felt in the Occident." [4] Another composer, Henry Eichheim (1870–1942), was not content to wait for Asian music to reach America. He became one of the earliest Americans to travel in order to study Asian music (making five trips to Asia starting in 1915) and was the first American composer to employ exotic instruments in his works. As a composer-ethnomusicologist, his lectures extolled the new musical resources available to American composers in Asian music. Although the sounds of Whitman's exotic "singing girl" were eventually heard and appreciated by Americans, the certainty of America's centrality and divine right to global musical absorption—proclaimed in Whitman's chant—resonated throughout the twentieth century.

The idea that the world contained undiscovered "musical resources" waiting to be exploited by the composer through encounters with the exotic was central to much twentieth-century American music. These resources included new scales, orchestral colors, and forms of music theater. The "excavation" by American composers of Asian music and, later, of African music has taken multiple forms. For some composers, experience with exotic cultures provided an entirely new conception of music; others attempted to immerse themselves in a detailed study of a particular musical culture and to create works within that tradition. Cowell's *Persian Set* (1957) and *Homage to Iran* (1957), for instance, sound like sonic imitations; indeed, Cowell once stated that *Persian Set* was "a simple record of musical contagion." Such pieces suggest that Cowell's notion of living in the "whole world of music" involved composing within various exotic styles rather than incorporating elements of exotic musics into one's own style. The idea that an individual composer could produce works within the "whole world of music" involves a certain problematic egotism, as does the belief that one could "go native" at will.

The earliest symptoms of an Orientalist contagion in American music occurred at the level of melodic borrowing. Charles T. Griffes (1884–1920) and Emerson Whithorne (1884–1958), contemporaries and friends, employed Chinese, Japanese, and Javanese melodies (acquired through printed transcriptions) in their compositions of the 1910s and '20s, respectively. While Whithorne studied Asian music in the British Museum, Griffes encountered the exotic nearer to Whitman's Broadway. Of the first wave of American Orientalists, Griffes was the most successful. Although his compositional career lasted barely twelve years, a brief summary is in order here. He was the American Orientalist most influenced by East Asian theater and dance; his knowledge of the exotic derived from research in the New York Public Library, performances in New York City theaters and Chinatown, association with such dancers as Michio Ito, and from transcribed melodies given to him by the soprano Eva Gauthier after her extensive Asiatic concert tours.[5] He attended performances of "Oriental" theater, such as the 1912 production entitled *The Yellow Jacket*, an adaptation of three Chinese plays accompanied by modified Chinese music performed on authentic instruments, and Max Reinhardt's *Sumurun*, an "oriental pantomime."[6] As was true of many American composers, a primary impetus for Griffes's interest in the musical exotic was his work with modern dancers. He became associated with Adolf Bolm, the founder of Ballet-Intime, in 1916, and through Bolm met Michio Ito who had only recently arrived in New York after his collaborations with Yeats.

Through Ito, Griffes came into closer contact with pseudo-Japanese theater. He attended Ito's Noh-style production of the play *Tamura* in the Fenollosa-Pound translation. In addition, Griffes toured as an accompanist with Ito and his company of Japanese dancers and musicians in August of 1918. During this tour the group performed Yeats's *At the Hawk's Well* with music by the Japanese composer Kosçak (Kosaku) Yamada.[7] In 1918 Griffes composed *Sho-Jo*, a "Japanese pantomime," which Ito danced several times. Ito also danced to Griffes's *Sakura-Sakura*, an orchestration of a Japanese folk melody, and to his *The White Peacock*. Donna K. Anderson reports that in one Ballet-Intime program, Griffes's *Sho-Jo*, *Assyrian Dance*, and *Sakura-Sakura* were performed along with Indian vocal music and Asian dance.[8] In her study of Ito, Helen Caldwell suggests on the basis of contemporary reviews that Ito's dances helped create an audience for Griffes's music.[9] Griffes readily acknowledged Ito's influence and encouragement: "Japanese music should not be too largely infused with Western ideas and procedures; yet Michio Ito himself, who understands the music of his native land *au fond*, believes that it will gain breadth of expression, that its beauties will be more widely understood if brought into modified contact with Western influences."[10] Griffes described *Sho-Jo*, a work based on three Japanese folk melodies, as an example of "developed" Japanese music and claimed that his orchestration was "as Japanese as possible." He also noted a general trend in modern music "toward the archaic, especially the archaism of the East," and included the influence of ancient Greek aesthetics within this contemporary movement.

In addition to his association with the Ballet-Intime company and with Ito, Griffes was involved with the experimental theater movement in New York during the 1910s. He served as a pianist for the Neighborhood Playhouse before composing his dance-drama *The Kairn of Koridwen* for performance there. The Playhouse, a radical Off-Broadway theater founded in 1915, was intended as a philanthropic project and initially employed amateur performers.[11] The artistic ideal of the Playhouse was to achieve productions of fully integrated theatrical performance. During its twelve-year existence, in addition to producing plays by modern dramatists, the Playhouse produced a Japanese Noh play, a "Burmese ritual," a medieval French miracle play, and a "Hindu drama."[12] Near the end of his life, Griffes was engaged by the Playhouse to compose a "festival drama" of total-theater proportions and exotic inclinations based on Whitman's *Salut au Monde!*.[13]

Griffes, who actively sought this last commission, must have been inspired by its immense opportunities for musical exoticism. This collaborative project, initiated in 1919, the year of the poet's centenary, divided the poem into three acts. At the time of his death Griffes had only managed to sketch the music for the first act. The second act employed "authentic" ritual music of various world religions, and the third was completed by another musician in time for a 1922 premiere.[14] Thus, six decades after Whitman wrote *Salut au Monde!* an American composer in New York City had experienced Asian music to the point where he might approximate the musical sounds unheard by the poet in a work of total theater that expressed Whitman's vision of America as a "unifying influence for peoples of the world"—an especially inspiring concept in the aftermath of World War I.[15] In this production, music theater, the exotic, and the spirit of Whitman were harnessed for the dissemination of a utopian message of cross-cultural unification and reconciliation.

Although later American composers tended to have a more thorough knowledge of their exotic models, their music theater works remained true to the basic motivations and themes found in examples from the first decades of the century. The most prolific American Orientalist composer of the second generation has been Alan Hovhaness (b. 1911). In addition to the extensive exotic influences evident throughout his massive orchestral oeuvre, Hovhaness has since the late 1950s composed about a dozen works of music theater. As Arnold Rosner indicates, several of these works are in the style of Japanese and Korean theater and in the spirit of the medieval mystery play.[16] Like many of Hovhaness's compositions, these theater pieces were intended to express mystical and religious themes, as well as aspects of the composer's Armenian heritage. Hovhaness's musical exoticism is achieved through characteristic instrumentation, the use of a limited number of pitches in a predominately melodic texture, and a vocal style that includes chantlike passages and extensive sliding between pitches, often within the range of a semitone. His musical structures and textures are generally extremely simple.

Hovhaness's 1962 chamber opera *The Burning House,* based on Armenian mythology, is in performance and musical style somewhat akin to Japanese Noh. Hovhaness composed this work while spending a year studying Japanese music in Japan. As in Noh, the text is based on a mythological tale and is written in a sparse poetic style. In his libretto, Hovhaness evokes an archaic feeling by dropping articles and paring the lines down to a bare verbal minimum.[17] Like Noh, *The Burning House* is accompanied by flute and percussion only. Another Noh-like feature is the use of only two or three main characters and a male chorus. There are two vocal roles, Vahaken and Death, and a silent character—the Demon—played by a dancer.[18] (Vahaken, normally spelled Vahagn, is the ancient Armenian god of war and courage. He was believed to have fire for hair and was celebrated as a dragon slayer.) The chorus comments on the action and occasionally sings the lines of the principal characters, assisting in the enacting of the tale and thus similar in function to the Noh chorus. The work begins with a prologue in which Vahaken announces himself in the darkness with a slow and solemn chant. He endures a confrontation with Death and is triumphant. Vahaken then fights the Demon in a slow, stylized dance that involves no bodily contact.[19] He triumphs again and the Chorus sings his praise. The work ends with Vahaken's transformation into a "burning house," a blazing sun in the universe. With *The Burning House,* Hovhaness created a ritual performance based on the mythology of ancient Armenia and influenced by the style of Japanese religious music theater—a thoroughly intercultural artistic enterprise that might have been appreciated by the founders of the Neighborhood Playhouse.

A "Polytechnic Drama" of Protest

Griffes and Hovhaness offer contrasting examples of American contact with exotic theater. However, neither composer was primarily interested in the quest for a new form of total theater or in its potential social function. Although Griffes's attempts to incorporate exotic elements in his compositions predated his encounters with Gauthier and Ito, his integrated stage works were the result of collaborations with modern dancers and producers. In short, Griffes provided musical backdrops for the theatrical visions and social messages of others. Hovhaness's works of music theater (somewhat like Britten's Church Parables) represent transformations and adaptations from exotic models rather than sustained experiments in total theater.

Interest in just such experimentation is evident in the works of at least one American composer active in the first decades of the twentieth century. John J. Becker (1886–1961) was devoted to creating a unique form of *Gesamtkunstwerk*, which he called "polytechnic drama," and exhibited a suitably Wagnerian utopianism regarding its social function. Becker is the least known member of what Don C. Gillespie calls the "American Five," a group of composers that also included Charles Ives, Carl Ruggles, Wallingford Riegger, and Cowell. He enjoyed an especially close association with Ives and Cowell and helped to promote their music in the Midwest. Active in Indiana, Minnesota, and Illinois, he was dubbed the "Midwestern Crusader" for his passionate devotion to modern music in an area of the country offering relatively few performance opportunities.[20] In addition to some twenty works for stage and screen, Becker composed symphonies, concertos, string quartets, and art songs.[21]

In his Stageworks, Becker sought to create a "combination of speaking, singing, dancing, pantomime, orchestral expression, and lighting, [and] to mould these into a natural logical art form, thus creating a new type of music drama, a Polytechnic Drama, doing away entirely with the present obsolete forms and methods."[22] His interest in integrated forms of theatrical performance was inspired by his teaching in humanities and performing arts departments. Gillespie notes that Becker's aim while teaching at the University of Notre Dame was to "bring music in closer contact with the total academic life of the school, making it an integral part of a liberal education."[23] Becker hoped to integrate the study of music performance with the study of other performing arts and in 1947 drafted a proposal for "an integrated course for the writer, composer, choreographer, producer, director, scenic designer, lighting artist, actor, dancer, singer, and theatre con-

ductor; presenting the problems in the creation and production of new mu-
sico-dramatic works."[24]

Becker's conception of music theater was influenced by Terrence Gray's
Dance Drama: Experiments in the Art of the Theatre (1926).[25] Gray was a
British theater producer and writer who cofounded the experimental Cambridge Festival Theatre.[26] His primary innovations included bringing performance closer to the audience by abolishing the proscenium arch and by
creating a forestage. Gray has been considered a mere imitator of Edward
Gordon Craig, but his work with the Cambridge Festival Theatre and his
writings were significant for their promotion of avant-garde production
techniques. In addition to suggesting various innovations in sets and staging, Gray called for a return to religion-based plays. He argued that Greek
drama and the medieval mysteries were successful and popular primarily
because they were religious. "If those persons who bewail the indifference
and obtuseness of the people of any district, where drama is concerned, will
produce there a religious play, I am entirely certain that they will meet with
an instantaneous and overwhelming public response save only that the puritan prejudice against the dramatic use of biblical personages have not too
powerfully survived."[27] Becker was particularly influenced by Gray's opinion that mime, movement, and dance are often the most natural and powerful means of dramatic expression.[28] Gray's influence is most pronounced
in Becker's third Stagework, *A Marriage with Space* (1935).[29]

This work, calling for dance, pantomime, speaking chorus, and a symbolic use of lighting intimately related to the text (a setting of Mark
Turbyfill's poem of the same title) is Becker's most complete realization of
"Polytechnic Theatre."[30] Turbyfill, who collaborated with Becker in creating the work, was a Chicago-based poet, dancer, and painter, whose poetry
was influenced by that of Pound and H. D. He was interested in unifying
the performing arts and had an active career in ballet and in modern dance.
(His 1951 poem-dance *The Words Beneath Us* was performed as a recitation accompanying choreographed dance.) *A Marriage with Space*, which
filled the entire May 1926 issue of the modernist journal *Poetry*, was
Turbyfill's most successful work. An extended Imagist poem, it centered on
the visions of a mystical figure, a divine architect named Emanuel Savoir,
who imagines a perfect city of the future, its reception by the people, and
its imperfect realization mocking the initial vision. Emanuel Savoir and the
fallen city were only thinly veiled metaphors for the Biblical Creation myth.
A Christian interpretation of Emanuel Savoir is suggested not only by the
character's name but by such passages as the following: "Terrible and wonderful, Emanuel Savoir, / Oh, wonderful and terrible / Was the hour when

you knew; / And the knowing / Was immortal reverberation / Of thunder in your soul, / Which rent the flesh of your very entity. / O ambrosial flesh / Framed by the word, / Immaculate speech of that ultimate body, / You groaned in knowing / What is conceived has birth."[31] In her comments accompanying the first publication of *A Marriage with Space*, Harriet Monroe, editor of *Poetry*, wrote: "The poem seems to us an effort to interpret the universal scheme, the overwhelming infinite cosmogony, in terms of a modern and unorthodox religious ecstasy—an ecstasy essentially religious, although free of the trammels of any historic creed."[32] In his introduction to the scenario, Becker described Emanuel Savoir as "the Builder, Architect, (Christ), Destiny, or what you will, symbol of the Ideal." The parenthetical "Christ" is as significant for understanding Becker's intentions as are the elements suggestive of social criticism: "City, City / Mocking hive, / Hollow, honeyless, / The sterile swarm / Works the walls / Of bitter wax / Between us!"[33] Becker notes that "the entire chorus thunders with bitter sarcasm" while reciting these lines.

Becker's sobriquet, "Midwestern crusader" for modern music, attested not only to his fierce promotion of the 1920s musical avant-garde, but also, obliquely, to his social criticism and devout Catholicism. Gillespie has suggested that "From the beginning of his modern period, Becker began to channel this nervous tension into social and political protest, into concealed extramusical programs reflecting his humanitarian concerns."[34] On the title page of his *Symphonia Brevis*, Becker expounded: "This symphony was written with an outraged spirit. It was not intended to be beautiful in the sentimental sense. It is a protest against intolerance, prejudice, pretense and sham. A protest against would-be humanitarians who talk much and do nothing. A protest against a world civilization which starves its millions in peacetime and murders those same millions in wartime."[35] Becker reused much of the music for this programmatic symphony in *A Marriage with Space*, suggesting that he also considered this later work to be a statement of social criticism. (Becker's fifth Stagework, *Privilege and Privation*, is another example in this vein.)

In addition to creating statements of political protest, Becker also expressed his religious convictions in his compositions and writings. He composed a significant amount of devotional choral music throughout his career and in 1950 served as the American musical delegate to the First International Congress of Catholic Artists in Rome. Gillespie relates that Becker's speeches in favor of modern music for the liturgy played a significant role in the official resolution in favor of modernist styles and earned him a papal medal in 1956.[36] In a speech delivered at the congress in September 1950, Becker lamented the current state of church music and condemned the indiscriminate use of nineteenth-century art music in the service. He argued that "we should ban the romantic philosophy that all art is feeling and emotion" and called for a "contemporary, forward looking, restrained music that will lend dignity and reverence to our church service."[37]

Although Becker's experiments in "total theater" owed more to his social conscience than to an interest in exotic models, he did collaborate on one work that combined both medievalist and Orientalist traits. In 1958, Becker composed incidental music for Raymond-Léopold Bruckberger's religious play *Madeleine et Judas: Tragédie en Trois Mystères*.[38] Bruckberger was a Dominican monk, an author, and a filmmaker who led an extraordinary life and became a celebrated figure in the press. He fought with the French Resistance during World War II, served with the French Foreign Legion, and spent a considerable amount of time in America during the 1950s. In the preface to *Madeleine et Judas*, Bruckberger discusses the importance of the medieval mystery play for modern theater and defends his decision to revive it. He compares the religious function of the mystery play to the drama of ancient Greece and remarks that, as with political theater, the audience members at a religious play are never neutral but are predisposed to approve or disapprove of the work depending upon their beliefs.

Madeleine et Judas presents the Passion story as seen through the eyes of the two title characters. Its most striking feature is a demonic character referred to as "the Musician," whom Bruckberger described as "un grand nègre, bizarrement et somptueusement habillé." Becker cast this character as a clarinetist, thereby creating one of the largest stage roles for that instrument. The Musician never speaks but communicates and seduces through his playing, tempting Madeleine and leading Judas to betrayal. Thus the exotic and evil other—in a true primitivist mode—is presented as a nonverbal, ominous black male. The Musician appears and disappears in sinister fashion at various critical points in the work. On Easter morning, he approaches the tomb furtively and finds his way blocked by an angel. In act I, scene ii, Madeleine and the Musician engage in a "strange dialogue" that climaxes in an "oriental dance tempo" that Becker realized with a sinuous, hypnotic solo line for the Musician accompanied by a constant drum tattoo. Clearly, the traditional acoustic signs for the Primitive were alive and well in 1958.

Although Becker's multimedia ambitions prefigure later developments, he had little direct influence. *A Marriage with Space* has yet to receive a premiere, and his contribution to *Madeleine et Judas* was incidental. (It is possible that Becker might have produced more works of religious music theater had he encountered Bruckberger earlier.)[39] We will discover that the conjunction of religious expression and social criticism in music theater recurred in numerous American works composed later in the twentieth century. Becker's crusade for an integrated form of music theater, and the interest in Asian music theater exhibited by Griffes and Hovhaness, represented elements that remained constant in twentieth-century American music and that found their most pronounced theatrical realization in the works of Harry Partch.

12　Partch's Vision of "Integrated Corporeal Theater" and "Latter-Day Rituals"

Corporeal Ritual

More than any other figure considered here, Harry Partch consistently and rigorously explored the possibilities of a genuine *Gesamtkunstwerk*. Moreover, his entire musical and theatrical outlook was profoundly influenced by both ancient Greek and East Asian models, and by primitivist and Orientalist fantasies. Finally, his ritualistic works were intended to have a direct spiritual effect on their audiences and to render social change. Despite Partch's warning that it "is not only difficult to define my theater concepts as a whole—it is impossible,"[1] I will venture to provide a sketch of these concepts, relying heavily on his own attempts to describe them, for Partch's writings and correspondence provide a rich source of information documenting an evolving vision of totally integrated theater.[2]

The fundamental impulse that animated Partch's desire to create a new form of music theater was his belief that the modern age was one of sterile specialization in which the various performing arts were ruthlessly segregated. He felt that an ideal of "purity" was rampant and that this ideal was an especially limiting factor in the contemporary performing arts.[3] "The age of specialization has given us an art of sound that denies sound, and a science of sound that denies art. The age of specialization has given us a music drama that denies drama, and a drama that—contrary to the practices of all other peoples of the world—denies music."[4] In another context Partch wrote: "This specialized trend toward a specialized product involving specialized talents is, in my opinion, a form of unconscious starvation. The theater is starved for music and doesn't know it. The opera is starved for drama, even though drama is right in front of them. And ballet all too often is starved for both, not because both are not present, but because they must be subordinated to incidental roles."[5] To counter the narrow, limited approach of mainstream theater and opera, Partch called upon performers to transcend their conventional, specialized roles and to sing, speak, dance, and play instruments. "My musical concepts are invariably involved with theater, or with dramatic ideas dramatically presented, and many years have been given to provoking musicians into becoming actors, and singers into making occasional ugly and frightening (but dramatic) sounds, appealing to them through heavy layers of Puritan inhibitions and academic intimidations."[6] By integrating the visual, aural, and verbal dimensions of theater, Partch hoped to reach performers and audience members alike as whole persons.

At the heart of this theatrical conception lay Partch's vision of ritual theater and his philosophy of corporeal music. "I use the word *ritual,* and I also use the word *corporeal,* to describe music that is neither on the concert stage nor relegated to a pit. In ritual the musicians are *seen;* their meaningful movements are part of the act, and collaboration is automatic with everything else that goes on."[7] Although Partch's music theater was modeled primarily on the theater of Japan and ancient Greece, his image of ritual performance also derived from African music and from his primitivist imaginings:

> The direction in which I have been going the last forty-four years
> has much in common with the activities and actions of primitive man
> as I imagine him. Primitive man found magical sounds in the materials
> around him—in a reed, a piece of bamboo, a particular piece of wood
> held in a certain way, or a skin stretched over a gourd or tortoise shell
> (some resonating body). He then proceeded to make the object, the
> vehicle, the instrument, as visually beautiful as he could. His last step
> was almost automatic: the metamorphosis of the magical sounds and
> visual beauty into something spiritual. They become fused with his
> everyday words and experiences—his ritual, drama, religion—thus
> lending greater meaning to his life. These acts of primitive man become
> the trinity of this work: magical sounds, visual form and beauty,
> experience-ritual.[8]

Partch admired the ritual functions of music and theater in African cultures and hoped that his own music theater could serve a vital reformative function for modern society. A basic compositional aim for Partch was to create works relevant to the present age.[9] Referring to his dance-drama *The Bewitched* as "a latter-day ritual designed to castrate the machine age,"[10] he proclaimed the power of integrated theater and celebrated art's "incalculable influence on the direction of our civilization. . . . Its influence may be minute, or it may carry a force beyond that of armies."[11] Rather than sitting passively and clapping politely to the well-worn warhorses, the audience was to be engaged in the performance and changed by it. Although Partch's music theater may be understood as ritual performance for the performers and as spiritual transformation for the audience, he never attempted to achieve the radical inclusiveness of the African rituals that he admired; he transformed the role of the individual performer but maintained the distinction between performer and audience.

For Partch, "corporeality" entailed the fundamental belief that music and life should be experienced physically; it demanded an inclusive approach to life and, by extension, to performance. Ben Johnston has written: "Corporealism was a theory that Partch lived. It is a vehement protest against what he considered the negation of the body and the bodily in our society. It resulted specifically in an attack on *abstraction.*"[12] In his broadest use of the term, Partch referred to the lack of corporeal engagement with life and the natural world in modern society. He decried the "labor-saver, the miracle button" and felt that "labor is saved, and a value is lost in the process."[13] In terms of musical aesthetics, he described corporeal music as "emotionally 'tactile.' It does not grow from the root of 'pure form.' It cannot be characterized as either mental or spiritual."[14] Each element of Partch's music theater formed part of his multifaceted corporeal ideal.

Partch's earliest corporeal objective concerned the fundamental organization of sound in his music. He argued that a corporeal music must be based on natural acoustical properties and therefore developed a system of microtonal just intonation and designed original instruments tuned in this system. These instruments produce an immense range of sounds, often including "fuzzy" sounds—extra noise that, as in many African musical cultures, was valued by Partch rather than disguised or refined away. His instruments were constructed from natural materials and incorporated found objects, further celebrating the inherent musical possibilities of the physical world.[15] Each instrument was handcrafted in order to achieve a sculptural beauty and was to be visible on the stage as a primary or often sole form of set and scenery. These instruments are predominantly percussive and attest to Partch's primitivist notion that "on the theater stage, as in primitive ritual, percussion becomes part of the 'act.'"[16] In contrast to an earlier "machine age" conception of percussion music—evident in the music of the Futurists, George Antheil, and Edgard Varèse—Partch believed that percussion was a fundamental expression of humanity and of biological impulses. "Percussion as a human art goes back, at least—one would imagine—to the Old Stone Age. So well ensconced is it in the genes of some races that it might well antedate fire."[17] Partch envisioned a form of music theater that would be experienced bodily, by both audience and performer.

His conception of corporeal instrumental performance called for an athletic approach to playing his instruments. In addition to the energetic movements required for playing, the instrumentalists are frequently called upon to perform simple dance steps both while performing and during tacit sections. As an ultimate form of corporeality, each of Partch's major works of music theater includes a significant amount of choreographed dancing.

To Partch, an inclusive approach to the integration of the performing arts, in which no form of performance is excluded, proved fundamental. He wrote, "There is at least one factor which my various theater concepts have in common; they tend to *include*, not exclude, and therefore to encompass a fairly wide latitude of human experience. They do not exclude—for example—'bad' material, simply because it is thought to be 'bad.' "[18] This "bad material" could include juggling, hobo characters, commonplace tunes, tonal harmonies, and slang text. In a 1952 article entitled "No Barriers," Partch called for works that would "not exclude any area of response—visual, aural, verbal— in any combination, in order to engage the whole person, either as performer or as observer."[19] The exclusion of certain forms of performance, he argued, was a self-impoverishment that limited the work's potential for reaching its audience. "If [the creative person] wants a whole-experience reaction from his audience, he employs or stipulates every possible stimulus at his command, singly or simultaneously; including music of any imaginable bastardy; dance and drama in any historical or antihistorical form; noise, light, shadow, substance, or perhaps only the semblance of substance; and sounds from the mouth that communicate only as emotion."[20] Partch turned to exotic traditions of music theater for models of such thoroughly integrated performance.

Back to Ancient Greece via Japan

Partch's vision of a corporeal, ritualistic music theater reflects his understanding of Japanese, Chinese, and ancient Greek theater. Ancient Greece provided an initial framework for his basic aesthetic and theoretical conceptions of music. His system of just intonation was inspired, in part, by readings in Greek music theory. In addition, Greek drama and mythology provided source material throughout his career, and he frequently cited Greek theater as an archetype of integrated corporeal performance.[21] In a 1955 letter, Partch wrote: "The Greek—and Roman—idea of music as an agent to ennoble, to maintain dignity and stature, and for transport into the realm of magic, was abandoned, and the consequences could have been predicted. . . . "[22] Partch acknowledged that our understanding of ancient Greek theatrical performance is limited, especially in its musical dimension, but he believed that something like an ancient corporeal approach to theater had survived in modern East Asia.

In *Genesis of a Music,* Partch argued that some suggestion of the ancient values of Greek theater was still to be found in modern Cantonese opera as heard in San Francisco and New York.[23] Although Partch had greater direct contact with Chinese theater and music, he often cited Japanese theater as a more perfect model. He asserted that "music occupied approximately the same place among the Japanese of this period as it had in ancient Greece two thousand years before. It was the expression of a fundamentally similar concept of musical values."[24] It is not certain whether Partch ever saw a performance of Japanese Noh or Kabuki. His knowledge of Japanese theater appears to have been based on the writings of Frank Lombard, Arthur Waley, and William Malm; he constructed an image of Noh and Kabuki performance styles from books and recordings and by extrapolating from his experience of Chinese opera. Thus, his encounter with Noh may not have been entirely different from that of early American Orientalists such as Griffes.

In *Genesis of a Music,* Partch cited Lombard's *An Outline History of the Japanese Drama*[25] and noted Lombard's discussion of Noh as an amalgam and refinement of several performance forms. Partch stated that the music of Noh created "an emotional tension quite unlike anything ever produced by Western music."[26] Of Noh and Kabuki, the latter was actually closer to his theatrical aesthetic. He admired Kabuki as a more inclusive form of theatrical performance and referred to it in several contexts. On Kabuki's relation to ancient Greek theater, Partch wrote:

> There was a time in the history of so-called Western man when music was so vital a part of ritual and ceremony as to have no pure and separate function. The integration of music with every important ceremonial in ancient Greece was so complete that, for example, the sounds of spoken words used in ceremonies were a basis for creating the sounds of music. But we do not have to theorize about ancient Greece. We can see contemporary cultures of our own world where the same kind of integration is taken for granted. The kabuki theater of Japan is an example. And here we have fact—not merely theory.[27]

One of the clearest and most provocative of Partch's presentations of his music theater ideal is found in a statement of proposed activity for a Fulbright grant application:

> I am drawn to the Oriental attitudes because, in the Orient, there has never been any great separation of the theater-music arts, therefore no need to conceive of integration. I am also drawn because of my studies into, and my appropriation of, the ancient Greek musical philosophies.

Despite our direct inheritance of Greek culture, despite the prevalence of Greek roots in our music-theater technical terms, the ancient spirit of integration has long since disappeared in the West. Through many centuries of Western specialization the forms of "theater" and "concert" have become separate and divorced entities. Probing beyond what I consider superficial differences, I see the ancient spirit, in virtually unadulterated form, in the Orient.[28]

Partch concluded this application by positioning his work in terms of a modern Western realization of the Asian theatrical spirit: "I should like to demonstrate to Orientals, . . . that at least one Occidental has been thinking and producing *in their terms* throughout the better part of his life." As a son of Whitman and an American, Partch felt fully capable of uniting East and West in his works. Of course, given his limited knowledge of his exotic models, it is no coincidence that "their terms" proved to be his own.

Back to Ancient Greece via the "Older Ears" of Yeats

In his earliest references to "corporeality," Partch was often concerned with issues of text setting. A corporeal setting of text is one that remains close to the natural inflections of speech and that supports a clear conveyance of verbal meaning. In this use of the term, "corporeal" was reserved for "the essentially vocal and verbal music of the individual—a Monophonic concept."[29] Partch found little evidence of corporeal vocal music and integrated theater in the recent history of Western music. As should be expected, he rejected most nineteenth-century opera for its nonintegration of the performing arts and for its treatment of text: "As auditors [of opera] we pretend to be listening to drama in words and music and by implication that we hear understandable words."[30] Partch felt that this pretense, this hypocritical neglect of the words, occurred whether opera was sung in English or in the original language. (Presumably, the literal separation between singer and presentation of verbal meaning made explicit by the recent use of supertitles would have seemed to Partch the ultimate act of cowardice.) For Partch, Wagner's professed intentions of creating "music-drama" and a form of *Gesamtkunstwerk* were laudable. However, he felt that the intentions of Wagner the theatrical theorist were never realized by Wagner the symphonist. Partch quipped: "In the wrestling match between Wagner's music drama and his symphony orchestra, Wagner's symphony orchestra (with yeoman help from his arias) gets both shoulders of Wagner's music drama on the floor within five minutes after the curtain rises and for the following two or three hours jumps up and down on the unconscious form."[31]

A few figures had approximated Partch's music theater ideals: "On the theater stage, with Bertolt Brecht, and occasionally with others, there is something like a ritualistic approach—a corporeal approach to music as an integrated part of theater."[32] In another context, Partch noted that "there have been breakthroughs away from specialization. I feel that Carl Orff with *Carmina Burana*, for example, was a breakthrough away from specialization. My own theater work was also. . . . I feel that the recent musical *Hair* was a breakthrough."[33] The one figure with whom he felt most in accord was W. B. Yeats. In his short history of text setting presented in *Genesis of a Music*, Partch presents Yeats as the "Voice in the Wilderness"—a voice plaintively calling for a musical realization of a corporeal theatrical vision. Partch introduced Yeats as "a poet who had great respect for the inherent musical beauty of spoken words"[34] and included a lengthy quotation from Yeats's discussion of drama's requirements from music. Yeats had called for a musical setting in which, as had been the case in "ancient times," "no word shall have an intonation or accentuation it could not have in passionate speech."[35] The poet claimed to "hear with older ears than the musician."[36] Partch conceived of his own music as a direct answer to Yeats's musical quest, and felt that they both thought in the same "terms." In setting Yeats's *King Oedipus*, Partch followed the poet's dictums for text setting and in doing so hoped to recreate the imagined music heard by the poet's older ears.[37]

Partch became interested in setting Yeats's version of Sophocles' *Oedipus Rex* in 1933.[38] During a 1934 research trip to England, he took a rough musical plan for the work to Yeats and demonstrated his musical style with pieces for intoning voice and adapted viola.[39] In writing about his encounters with the poet, Partch reported that Yeats was very enthusiastic and that his permission to set *King Oedipus* was easily won.[40] This encounter is also documented in collections of Yeats's correspondence.[41] In a 17 November 1934 letter, Yeats mentions that a "Californian composer" would be visiting him the next day. At this point, Yeats felt that Partch's ideas were immature and that the composer was "young, and very simple." After meeting Partch, Yeats wrote in a more approving tone and expressed the opinion that Partch's vocal style approximated that of ancient ballads. Yeats sent Partch to meet Edmund Dulac, the composer and designer of *At the Hawk's Well*. Partch met with Yeats several times in his approximately ten-day stay in Dublin, and at some point, Yeats intoned the chorus sections of *King Oedipus* while Partch made diagrams of the poet's vocal inflections.[42] This trip to Dublin was of mythical importance to Partch. In several articles, he quoted the last words Yeats spoke to him: "You are one of those young men with ideas, the development of which it is impossible to foretell, just as I was thirty years ago."[43] This blessing from Yeats, however, did not bring good fortune. He was not able to compose music for *King Oedipus* for some seventeen years. A first version, completed in 1951, set Yeats's text and was first performed at Mills College in 1952. However, Partch was denied permission by Yeats's literary agents to release a recording of the work after the poet's death. He therefore revised the work as *Oedipus* in 1952, employing his own text adapted from several translations. This version was produced twice in 1954 and a recording was then released.[44]

In addition to realizing Yeats's ideal for text setting in *Oedipus*, Partch was participating in the time-honored attempt to revive the theatrical experience of ancient Greece, to achieve its legendary power and ritual purpose. In "The Ancient Magic," Partch wrote: "In my version of Sophocles' *Oedipus the King*, I tried to rediscover some of the stature that the Western theater has lost in its long divorce from integrated music."[45] His purpose in composing *Oedipus* was to "bring together more of the elements that belong to theater with the purpose of increasing its power—its power of communication, its power to give meaning to our existence."[46] At this point in his career, Partch was particularly concerned with creating a form of text setting approximating that of the ancient Greeks. "For the Greeks the noblest purpose of music was to enhance the drama. Dramatists were frequently the composers of the music for their words. This music took the form of recitative in some of the dialogue, accompanied note for note by aulos or kithara or both. In this economy of accompaniment the words were perfectly understood by the audience."[47] Partch accepted as "a historical fact that the Greeks used some kind of 'tone declamation' in their dramatic works, and that it was common practice among them to present language, music, and dance as a dramatic unity. In this conception of *King Oedipus*, I am striving for such a synthesis, not because it might lead me to the 'Greek spirit,' but because I believe in it."[48] Partch, like Duncan and Craig before him, exhibited some anxiety lest the reader assume that he had hoped simply to recreate authentic Greek theatrical practice, rather than create a new form of music theater for the modern world. "I have not consciously linked the ancient Greek of Sophocles and this conception of his drama—twenty-four hundred years later. The work is presented as a human value, necessarily pinned to a time and place, necessarily involving the oracular gods and Greek proper and place-names, but, nevertheless, not necessarily Greek."[49] In several such statements Partch attempted to distance his work from its exotic model.

In contrast to Partch's subsequent works of music theater, *Oedipus* was somewhat constrained, rather than liberated, by its exotic model and by his theatrical theories. The work represents either the most perfect realization of Partch's text-setting ideal or the most academic demonstration of it. Though not as arid as Orff's *Oedipus der Tyrann*, Partch's *Oedipus* has long stretches of minimally accompanied or unaccompanied speech. *Oedipus* was composed according to Partch's conception of a corporeal, "natural" vocal style—an intoning rather than singing style—and has far more text, treated more reverently, than any of his later works of music theater. Partch described his intent as to "present the drama expressed by language, not to obscure it, either by operatic aria or symphonic instrumentation. Hence, in critical dialogue, music enters almost insidiously, as tensions enter. The words of the players continue as before, spoken, not sung, but are a *harmonic part* of the music. In these settings the inflected words are little or no different from ordinary speech, except as emotional tensions make them different. Assertive words and assertive music do not collide. Tone of spoken word and tone of instrument are intended to combine in a compact emotional or dramatic expression, each providing its singular ingredient."[50] The following guidelines were provided for the intoned dialogue: "The written notes are not to be adhered to religiously. They are not sung, and generally speaking only accents need to be intoned accurately, in order to integrate the voices with prevailing harmony and rhythm. . . . In performance it is better to hit any tone than to wait until the right tone asserts itself in the brain, since any delay arrests the dramatic continuity."[51] *Oedipus* was Partch's first music theater composition and marked a basic shift in his career from monophonic, bardic musical performance to an integrated theatrical ideal.[52]

Although Partch's other works of music theater differ greatly from this early example, two aspects of *Oedipus* indicate the direction his music theater would take. Oedipus's tragic exit scene is set as a "dance-pantomime." This decision to allow dance and pantomime, rather than dialogue, to express the drama of this final scene anticipates a major feature of Partch's later works. Second, in accordance with his monophonic ideal, Partch assigned the lines of the chorus to a male character—the Spokesman—accompanied by a female chorus singing nonsense text. The use of nonsense vocal sounds as a primary musical device predominates in his subsequent theatrical pieces. Both mimetic dance and nonsense vocalisms are prominent components of Partch's final work, *Delusion of the Fury: A Ritual of Dream and Delusion*— a work based more on that other (alleged) descendent of ancient Greek theater, Japanese Noh, than on the dramas of Yeats.

"On a Japanese Theme"

Partch cited Japanese Noh as important for his conception of music theater in writings from the early 1940s onward, but it was not until *Delusion of the Fury* (1966) that the influence of Noh became directly apparent in his composition. This work was produced at the University of California, Los Angeles, in 1969 and was submitted by Partch to satisfy an honorary commission from the Koussevitzky Foundation in 1974. *Delusion* was the culmination of Partch's theatrical career. It includes the largest array of his own instruments, several of which were created specifically for it, and calls for an integrated approach to performance. The instrumentalists "become actors and dancers, moving from instruments to acting areas as the impetus of the drama requires."[53] A variety of small hand-instruments allows this chorus also to perform simultaneously as instrumentalists and dancers. Partch reluctantly recognized that the demands placed upon the soloists in *Delusion* outstripped the practical possibilities of contemporary production: "Ideally, the singers would be skilled also in the arts of dancing, acting, miming, as they are in Noh and Kabuki. But in our specialist culture, singers are generally only singers, actors only actors, and dancers only dancers. Just one solution seems possible: put the singers in the pit, while the actor-dancers on stage mouth the words, the gibberish, or whatever."[54] In his introductory remarks to the score, Partch reasserted his music theater ideal: "The concept of this work inheres in the *presence* of the instruments on stage, the *movements* of musicians and chorus, the *sounds* they produce, the *actuality* of actors, of singers, of mimes, of lights; in fine, the *actuality* of truly integrated theater."[55]

Delusion consists of two acts with an extended instrumental introduction, the Exordium, and a connecting instrumental interlude entitled "Sanctus"—titles suggestive of ritual music. The Exordium is described as "an overture, an invocation, the beginning of a ritualistic web."[56] Act I, "On a Japanese Theme," is based on Arthur Waley's translations of two Noh plays: *Atsumori* by Zeami, the central writer and theoretician of Noh, and *Ikuta* by Zembo Motoyasu. Both plays are concerned with the legend of Atsumori, a prince killed in a famous battle by a young warrior. After many years, the young warrior, now a religious pilgrim, seeks forgiveness from the spirit of Atsumori. Act I of *Delusion* opens "with a pilgrim in search of a particular shrine, where he may do penance for murder. The murdered man appears as a ghost, sees first the assassin, then his young son, looking for a vision of his father's face. Spurred to resentment by his son's presence, he lives again through the ordeal of death, but at the end—with the supplication, "Pray for me!"—he finds reconciliation."[57] Partch merged elements from *Atsumori* and *Ikuta* in this act. For instance, the son is not present in the *Atsumori* version of the tale but is the central figure in *Ikuta*. Act II of *Delusion* is based on an Ethiopian story entitled "Justice," taken from an anthology of African writing.[58] While act I is "intensely serious," act II is farcical: a young Hobo prepares his meal over a simple fire. An Old Goat Woman enters and asks the Hobo if he has seen her lost goat. He is deaf and seeks to be rid of her by gesturing for her to go away. She exits in the direction of his gesture, finds the goat, and tries to thank the Hobo for his help. The Hobo assumes that she is accusing him of a wrong and a fight ensues. The Villagers arrive and force the couple to appear before the Justice of the Peace, who is himself deaf and nearsighted and misunderstands the situation entirely. He delivers a ridiculous verdict under the assumption that the Hobo and Goat Woman are married, the goat being their child, and that a domestic quarrel has occurred. The Chorus of Villagers ironically celebrates the importance of justice.

As noted above, Partch was careful to disavow any attempt at imitating ancient Greek theater in *Oedipus*. He exhibited a similar anxiety when discussing *Delusion* and its exotic models: "In Act I, I am not trying to write a Noh play. Noh is already a fine art, one of the most sophisticated that the world has known, and it would be senseless for me to follow a path of superficial duplication. The instrumental sounds (excepting my *koto*) are not Japanese, the scales I use are not Japanese, the voice usage is different, costumes are different. Act I is actually a development of my own style in dramatic music, particularly as evidenced in *Oedipus* and *Revelation*. If for no other reason than the music, its daimon is American."[59] Without disputing Partch's account of his intentions, nor attempting to create a detailed catalogue of exotic influence, it is possible to explore the relationship between *Delusion* and Japanese Noh (in particular) beyond his declarations of distance.

"On a Japanese Theme" is not a setting of the two Noh plays but is instead a transformation that results in a new work in the spirit of Noh performance. Whereas in *Curlew River*, Britten and Plomer transferred the Buddhist tale and the Japanese setting to a medieval Christian play set in England, Partch created a work without cultural reference or location.[60] Most of the text was jettisoned and replaced with vocal sounds rather than with words. Noh is a distilled form of drama, but Partch simplified the form even further, to the point that there is little suggestion of the original plot—only a basic emotional situation is evident. Partch extracted the essential elements of an archetypal tale from these Japanese plays. The only indications of the original story appear in programmatic headings printed in the scenario for each section of the act. Partch was interested in the underlying tensions of the basic dramatic situation rather than in specific elements of the historical legend. These dramatic tensions are suggested on stage through stylized movement, costume, and makeup and through the emotive quality of the vocal utterances and instrumental music.

Elements of Noh performance style are found throughout *Delusion* and in Partch's general aesthetic of music theater. The decision to place his instruments on stage without attempting to hide the players stems in part from his readings on Noh, as does his use of minimal sets and scenery. Partch's emphasis on the physicality of instrumental performance also has a parallel in Noh. (He is likely to have noted with approval William Malm's comment that "stage manners are equally important as playing technique in the study of noh drumming.")[61] Although Partch's conception of the role of the chorus derived primarily from ancient Greek theater, it included features that are particular to Noh. Arthur Waley had noted in 1921 that the Noh chorus often delivers "an actor's words for him when his dance-movements prevent him from singing comfortably."[62] This polyvocal approach to the delivery of a single protagonist's lines occurs throughout *Delusion* and, less obviously, in Partch's other music theater works.[63] His settings of nonsense text occasionally resemble the *kakegoe* calls of Noh drummers; in both cases, instrumentalists are producing vocal sounds.

Some detailed musical correspondence with Noh is also evident in this work. The Exordium section of *Delusion* is performed in darkness and functions similarly to the introductory piece performed backstage before every Noh performance. The unexpected drum strokes, particularly in the first section of act I, and the use of the Bolivian flute create an aural approximation of *nohgaku*. Partch's use of exotic instruments, however, is rather more Orientalist than "Oriental." Partch's orchestration employs a mélange that includes an imitation Zulu ugumbo, his Greek-inspired kitharas, a Bolivian double flute, an mbira from Zimbabwe, a Fijian "rhythm boat," several exotic hand drums, and an imitation koto (a Japanese instrument not employed in Noh). Although Partch seems to have reached a bit recklessly into the world music grab bag for *Delusion*, the following statement does indicate an appreciation for each instrument's cultural context: "The Japanese *koto* and the Chinese *kin* represent unspoken philosophies in the cultures in which they grew, and in the headlong plunge of the Orient to 'catch up' with the West, these old instruments and the values behind them are being threatened."[64] When Partch employed an exotic instrument for this "Ritual of Dream and Delusion," he hoped to incorporate not only its timbral value but its spiritual power as well.

Partch provided several indications for the dancing in act I and appears to have had the general styles of Noh and Kabuki in mind. The Pilgrim enters "slowly, solemnly" and at the end of his scene becomes a statuesque dark silhouette, remaining immobile for some ten minutes. His motionless period allows for the insertion of the *Ikuta* narrative, the entrance of the son, into the basic *Atsumori* plot. A Noh play normally has one climactic dance. Having combined two Noh plays in *Delusion*, Partch includes two climactic dances: a poignant dance between the Ghost and his Son, and a reenactment of the battle between the Pilgrim and the Ghost. Partch describes the Father-Son dance as follows: "It is slow, tender, even though the tempo of the music is very fast. They must never touch. Their bodies must be inviolate."[65] In his introduction to *The Bewitched*, Partch had listed features of "Oriental dancing" that he most admired, one of which was the avoidance of contact: "In a serious love duet or a fight duet, a dancer never touches another dancer, in a gesture of endearment or anger. I noted, long before I ever saw oriental dancing, how tension was likely to drop the moment two such characters became physically embroiled. . . . In dance aesthetics, the human body has a sacred, mysterious identity which can be easily and shockingly damaged, and the body's preserved sacredness tends to illumine the terrible fact of every person's aloneness."[66]

Partch's insistence that the Ghost and Son never touch in their dance is not a direct realization of the dramatic action as described in Waley's translation of *Ikuta*. The chorus in *Ikuta* says that the child "plucked at the warrior's sleeve" and that, before preparing to return to the realm of the dead, Atsumori "dropped the child's hand."[67] Partch's setting of this parent-child dance at the boundary between life and death is similar to Britten's in *Curlew River*. In *Delusion* the living son is searching for the spirit of his father, while in *Curlew River* the Madwoman is searching for her son. In discussing the Madwoman's encounter with the spirit of her son, I noted that Britten departed from the stage directions in the Noh play translation by not having the mother chase after her son in the attempt to hold him in the world of the living. Instead, Britten called for the spirit of the boy to circle his mother slowly while she remained transfixed and still. Clearly, these staged encounters between a man and an adolescent boy were particularly charged and sensitive moments for these two homosexual composers. (We will discover below that Bernstein's *Mass* also ends with the union of a boy and a man to the accompaniment of a flute.) Partch's Father-Son dance ends as the Pilgrim slowly rises. The Pilgrim takes thirty-six beats to stand up and, doing so, brings back the *Atsumori* narrative and prepares for *its* climactic dance—the reenactment of the battle (see Fig. 10). This final dance ends with Kabuki-like poses (*mei*) as the Pilgrim drops his stick and holds his hands up in a

Figure 10. The Ghost and the Pilgrim in *Delusion of the Fury*. Photograph by Cecil Charles. (Reproduced with the permission of Eileen Charles Spiller)

plea for forgiveness, while the Ghost maintains his own pose of attack. (The mimetic, comic dance style of act II, "On an African Theme," has more in common with Japanese folk dancing than with either Noh or Kabuki.)

In his study of Partch's exoticism in *Delusion*, Will Salmon argues that the most significant indication of Japanese influence is found in the dramatic structure of the work. Salmon writes: "The influence of Noh goes beyond just the story; Partch weaves the Noh art form into his works by a unique combination of scholarship and intuition."[68] Salmon deduces that Partch relied upon William Malm's outline of the Noh form for his merging of the two Noh plays in act I. He also argues that the work as a whole fits a specific type of Noh form: the *mugen-no*. In *mugen-no*, the principal characters discuss a story from the past in the first half of the play and then return to reenact that very story in the second half. Salmon's reading of *Delusion* as a *mugen-no* depends on the notion that act II is a retelling of act I—that the same figures return in different guise to relive the story—and that both acts are motivated by the delusions of the principal characters. In this interpretation, the Pilgrim returns as the Hobo, the Son as the Goat Woman, and the Ghost as the Justice of the Peace. Partch made these pairings explicit by calling for the same performer to perform each of the paired roles. In addition, his discussions of the work emphasized the complementary relationship between the two acts. For example, act I was intended to represent a reconciliation with death, while act II involved a reconciliation with life. The acts are connected musically by the "Sanctus" section and textually by the repetition of the final line of act I, "Pray for me again," heard from an off-stage voice at the end of act II.

Salmon compares the structures of *Delusion* and *mugen-no* in detail, suggesting that Partch arrived at an approximation of the larger *mugen-no* form by first following Malm's outline of Noh for act I, and then by adapting the Ethiopian tale to fit the same mold for act II. Salmon rightly notes how carefully Partch structured *Delusion* as a coherent whole. However, to argue that Partch intuitively arrived at the larger form, Salmon must dismiss the "Time of Fun Together" section in act II, in which the Villagers sing and dance in a celebratory call and response, as being outside the structure and of less importance. The section is significant in that it makes clear Partch's interest in African ritual. Concerning act II, Partch wrote: "There is probably no art form in Ethiopia comparable to Noh in Japan, but—generally—I am not trying to depict African ritual, although African ritual, as I have heard it on records, has obviously influenced my writing, in this and several other works. . . . Despite the use of much percussion, the tone is American. The furious irony is deeply and certainly American."[69] By subsuming the

Ethiopian act within a larger Japanese dramatic form, Salmon disregards Partch's interest in African ritual and neglects the substantial act II communal section. As is often the case in modernist music theater, multiple exotic models are at play in *Delusion*.

One final suggestion of exotic inspiration should be noted here. Although Partch cites only *Atsumori* and *Ikuta* as models for act I of *Delusion*, his work may also have been shaped by a third Noh play. A translation of *Tsunemasa* by Zeami immediately follows *Atsumori* and *Ikuta* in Waley's book, and it is based on the same primary legend. *Tsunemasa* deals with the death of Atsumori's brother at the same famous battle of Ichi-no-Tani. No specific character or element of plot from this play is evident in *Delusion*. Instead, Partch may have been intrigued by the theme of music's incantatory power in *Tsunemasa*. The ghost of Tsunemasa, a talented musician to whom the Emperor had given a special lute, is especially susceptible to music's power. In this play the priests perform on flutes and strings to benefit Tsunemasa's spirit and to dedicate the lute to his memory. The power of their performance summons his ghost; "while they played the dead man stole up behind them. Though he could not be seen by the light of the candle, they felt him pluck the lute-strings . . . "[70] The recognition of music's incantatory power is present to a lesser degree in *Atsumori*, whose hero was also musical: he had a bamboo-flute with him when he died in battle. *Atsumori* begins with a Young Reaper, who will be revealed as the ghost of Atsumori, playing a flute. Partch, a musician who had experienced the life of a transient worker, must have been drawn to the following passage:

> Priest: Was it one of you who was playing on the flute just now?
>
> Young Reaper: Yes, it was we who were playing.
>
> Priest: It was a pleasant sound, and all the pleasanter because one does not look for such music from men of your condition.
>
> Young Reaper: Unlooked for from men of our condition, you say! / Have you not read:—"Do not envy what is above you / Nor despise what is below you"? / Moreover the songs of woodmen and the flute-playing of herdsmen, / Flute-playing even of reapers and songs of wood-fellers / Through poets' verses are known to all the world. / Wonder not to hear among us / The sound of a bamboo-flute.
>
> Priest: You are right. Indeed it is as you have told me.[71]

After the Young Reaper vanishes, the Priest, Atsumori's slayer, begins a vigil for the dead man's soul. The chant and gong-playing of the Priest calls forth Atsumori's spirit. As the spirit retells his tragic story, the memory of Atsumori's flute heard on the eve of the tragic battle deeply moves the attentive Priest.[72]

Several sections of *Delusion* suggest that Partch attempted to realize this theme of music's power in his composition. The Exordium and the Chorus of the Shadows, the first section of act I, seem musically to invoke the old story. As noted above, the drum strokes and flute line in the Chorus of the Shadows suggest *nohgaku*.[73] In addition, the sustained chords of the chromelodeon (Partch's adapted reed organ) sound somewhat like the *sho*, a Japanese mouth organ used in *gagaku* but not in Noh. This music succeeds in calling forth the Pilgrim and then the Ghost as if both were departed spirits and as if the power of Japanese Noh—its drama and music—were being retrieved from the past. In addition to a lifelong interest in the legendary influence of ancient Greek music over its audience, Partch must also have been intrigued by the power accorded to music in these stories from Japan.

"Extraverbal Magic"

There are few words in *Delusion*. Not counting repetitions, there are ten words in act I and forty-four in act II. Instead of words, the chorus and principals produce a variety of nonverbal vocalisms throughout the work. As Partch noted in the scenario, "Dialogue as such is never present. I feel that the mysterious, perverse qualities of these story ideas can be conveyed through music, mime, lights, with more sureness of impact than with spoken or sung lines, and spoken and sung lines in reply."[74] This rejection of the spoken word appears to reverse Partch's early views of text setting. In *Oedipus*, Partch was devoted to articulating the spoken word. His "Monophonic" conception required that one voice deliver the text at a time in order to ensure clarity. In *Genesis of a Music*, he noted "An important distinction, then, as regards the Corporeal and the Abstract, is between an individual's vocalized words, intended to convey meaning, and musicalized words that convey no meaning."[75] As discussed above, Partch was working within a Yeatsian aesthetic of words and music in his composition of *Oedipus* and his vocal idiom in this period was very close to speech. In "Bitter Music," a prose-music journal predating *Oedipus*, Partch indicated that the passages of notated music should be read at the piano and that the "words should be spoken quickly, on the tones indicated. They should never be sung."[76] In stating that "words *are* music. Spoken words," he implied that words did not require much musical setting, but could stand on their own in a simple recitation style.[77] *Oedipus,* as noted, can be seen as a culmination of Partch's early style of text setting. However, *Oedipus* and a few earlier works also included a radically different type of vocal production that had nothing to do with enunciating English texts.

Partch's preoccupation with the spoken word transmuted into a broader interest in human vocal sounds. An early indication of this alternative approach to vocal music appears in *U. S. Highball,* particularly in the distorted and stretched pronunciation of city names. In *Oedipus,* the wordless chorus vocalized on "ohs," "ahs," and various other sounds. In his article "No Barriers," written the year of the revised version of *Oedipus,* Partch referred to these vocalisms as "sounds from the mouth that communicate only as emotion."[78] *The Bewitched* (1955) has no words at all; instead an astonishing range of vocalisms are heard from the chorus and the Witch, the principal vocalist. Significantly, Partch often asserted that the "nonsense text" in his music theater works was intended to convey meaning, and that nonverbal vocalisms were more effective in doing so than words. Of course, this notion of the transcendent expressivity of musical sounds has long Romantic roots. However, in the twentieth century, composers such as Partch acted on this concept in a literal fashion by employing extreme nonverbal vocalisms. In his introduction to *Delusion,* Partch described the sung text as consisting of "sounds from the throat, meaningless in English verbal communication but not meaningless in this music."[79] Partch's use of nonverbal vocalisms at first seems to conflict with the Yeatsian ideal, but it had Yeats's approval. In a letter dated 23 October 1934, Yeats noted his own use of nonsense words in the poem "Crazy Jane Reproved" and suggested that the old ballads were sung to a melody in the same manner that "Partch the Californian musician I told you of sings his 'meaningless words.' He uses them to break the monotony of monotone."[80] In his works of music theater following *Oedipus,* Partch found multiple uses for "meaningless words."

The masking of semantic meaning in the treatment of text by Stravinsky, Thomson, and Glass was mentioned in chapter 4, as were the stylized vocal effects in ritual music theater as a form of musical masking. Partch's use of nonsense syllables differs from these approaches in that his "meaningless words" were intended to carry definite and powerful meanings. As one might expect, Partch was attempting to tap into a more ancient conception of the power of vocal sounds—the belief that the sound of a word or vocalism infused it with power and energy. This belief is expressed in many cultures, even in those that forbid music and singing and that insist upon the primacy of the divine spoken word. Officially, Qur'anic recitation is not considered a form of singing, and the text is emphatically verbal. However, the style in which it is delivered, Tajwīd, "is believed to be the codification of the sound of the revelation as it was revealed to the Prophet Muhammad, and as he subsequently rehearsed it with the Angel Gabriel. Thus, the sound itself has a divine source and significance, and, according to Muslim tradition, is significant to the meaning."[81] In other cultures, ancient and contemporary, nonsense syllables and the sound of certain phrases are believed to contain magical power. In Hindu cosmology, one such powerful syllable, *om,* is associated with the creation of the universe. In Japanese Noh, a ritualistic sound environment is generated by the explosive *kakegoe* calls of the drummers and through the intense singing style of both chorus and soloist, which employ an ancient pronunciation not understood by modern audiences. Concerning the incomprehensible text delivery in Noh, William Malm notes that "what is lost in the immediacy of comprehension is gained in the transcendental euphony of words as sound."[82] In other ritual vocal music traditions, such as some Sufi *dhikr* ceremonies, words are broken down into syllables and fragmented to such an extent that the resultant sound resembles the chanting of nonsense syllables. Some forms of religious recitation, perhaps the recitation of the Catholic rosary, become so repetitive as to transcend meaning and to create a generalized spiritual sound. It is at the point when words are no longer heard for their meaning, but only for their hypnotic sound patterns, that the moment of most intense devotion and of highest religious vocal expression is reached.[83] In his post-*Oedipus* music theater, Partch moved beyond the semantic limitations of words to the expressive meanings of vocal sounds.

The idea that extraverbal vocal sounds contain specific expressive significance involves a peculiar form of onomatopoeia. The vocal sounds must somehow signal their general expressive meanings. In some cases, Partch took this view a step further toward explicit meaning. In act II of *Delusion,* and throughout *The Bewitched,* Partch "translated" his vocalisms into specific verbal phrases in his scores and scenarios. In the second act of *Delusion* several lines of text for the principals are not intended to be spoken or sung aloud, even though they are occasionally marked with such stage directions as "speaking plaintively." Instead, their meaning is conveyed through mime, by the nonsense vocalisms of the principal or of the chorus singing for the principal, or by the semantic text intoned by the chorus in its role of delivering lines for the principal characters. This complex method of text delivery is further complicated by the Hobo's deafness. When the Old Goat Woman reenters with her goat at the beginning of "The Misunderstanding" section, we *do* hear her happy vocalisms: "Mi O—ma mi—ah! O mi

O ma mi—," etc. However, when she turns to thank the Hobo we see her mouth move but hear no sound, whether from her mouth or from the Chorus. We are instead (not) hearing through the deaf ears of the Hobo. The "misunderstanding" itself is set with silent movements of the mouth by the two principals, who literally do not hear each other's meaning. For the "Trial" section, Partch notes in the score that "unlike preceding scenes, there is no imitation of speech here. The 'dialogue'—the testimony, the Justice's questions, the ejaculations of the Villagers—is accomplished through music, miming, singing."[84] The sung component consists of vocalizing on such syllables as: "Ee-oh!," "O—wee—o," and "Ee yah."

A similar use of vocalisms is found in Partch's *The Bewitched*, composed some five years after *Oedipus* and ten years prior to *Delusion*. In *The Bewitched*, Partch frequently translates the nonsense syllables emanating from the Chorus of Lost Musicians and from the Witch into specific words in his scenarios and in the score. These vocal sounds are not only conceived as meaningful but are intended to express meaning in a manner more forceful than words. In reference to one of the Witch's vocalisms, Partch relates that "because she communicates so eloquently without words her meaning is abundantly clear."[85] For instance, he "translates" the Witch's "Ee—Yow-oo-wuh!" as "You shallow idiots!" Partch's notes and textual clarifications for *The Bewitched* are so detailed that they turn the work into a micromanaged pantomime. The dancers' movements are described by Partch as though they were another form of text delivery, equivalent to the vocalisms. By rejecting verbal text, Partch was aiming for a more mystical form of communication, suitable for his rituals of music theater. Partch felt that in a performance of *The Bewitched* "the possessed dancers would speak with their bodies."[86] In another context, he wrote: "Communication, if it functions at all, comes in many disguises: in plain words, or in artfully inflected words, or perhaps no words at all; perhaps telepathically or, according to some, as the result of transmigratory souls recognizing each other from former lives. In any case, there *is* such a thing as extraverbal magic. And extraverbal magic is something I now wish to invoke."[87] In *The Bewitched*, the magical powers of the extraverbal were employed by Partch for the "unwitching" of modern society.

The Bewitched: A Satiric Ritual "Designed to Castrate the Machine Age"

After completing work in the high tragic mode of *Oedipus*, Partch expressed a desire to compose a work of comedy: "I understood the attitude of the ancient Greeks in producing a satyr play after a presentation of tragedy."[88]

Immediately following *Oedipus*, Partch composed a comic work entitled *Plectra and Percussion Dances*. His next major theater work was a "dance-satire," *The Bewitched* (1955). In a letter concerning casting for the first production of *The Bewitched*, Partch noted that Martha Graham would be an ideal choice for the Witch. However, Partch wrote that "I'm inclined to think that she only likes me in my Oedipus moods. The Bewitched is what I want to do, and it is no Oedipus."[89] Partch was interested in balancing the tragic and the comic throughout his career. (Act II of *Delusion*, as we have seen, releases tension and balances the serious first act in the manner of a Japanese *Kyogen* or a Greek satyr play.) He believed that satire was a powerful mode of theatrical expression, writing that theater "need be no less effective or significant . . . if its vehicle is satire rather than tragedy,"[90] and stressed the importance of a society's ability to laugh at itself intelligently: "One might be justified in saying that, in such a time as this, satire is in fact exactly what the doctor ordered."[91] Each of Partch's music theater works after *Oedipus* has a significant comic and satiric component. *The Bewitched* and *Water! Water!* are farcical burlesques. The shape of his career as a whole suggests that he may have been drawn more strongly to satire and parody than to tragic drama.

The *Bewitched* consists of a prologue, ten scenes, and an epilogue. It is not based on a specific plot but is instead a string of stylized scenes or situations parodying modern life. The instrumentalists function as a chorus, realizing Partch's ideal for multiple-role performers. The main figure is the Witch, who "belongs to the ancient, pre-Christian school. . . . is an omniscient soul, all-perceptive, with that wonderful power to make other people see also, when she feels so inclined. . . . [she] is a different Greek oracle, and the Chorus—like the choruses of ancient tragedy—is her instrument, always under the oracular power of suggestion."[92] The "Bewitched" are the individual dancers, who represent stereotypes from modern American society. In each scene, one or more of these characters enter and, through dance, display their particular form of bewitchedness, their prejudices and general ignorance.

Although *The Bewitched* contains no verbal text, Partch described each scene in versions of the printed scenario and provided detailed directions for the choreography in the score. Scene i, entitled "Three Undergrads Become Transfigured in a Hong Kong Music Hall," can serve as an example of his programmatic ideas for this work. In this scene, the bewitched consist of three undergraduates, represented by three dancers, whose particular form of bewitchedness consists of a confirmed xenophobia, a distaste for anything strange and exotic, such as the music of the Cantonese theater. The undergraduates are "charming and exuberant children, with plump bodies, shining teeth and eyes—exuding from a thousand pores a soap-scrubbed pinkish gleam."[93] They dance in mocking imitation of Chinese theater. The Witch slowly rises over thirty-five beats and, upon reaching her full height, employs a wild vocalism to unwitch the undergraduates. The Chorus emphatically stamps—perhaps in imitation of Noh foot stamps. The lesson learnt by these undergraduates and presented for the audience is that "the exotic—East or West—does not hold more mystery than it ought."[94]

The Bewitched relies on choreography rather than on verbal expression for its satire. The premiere was marred by a controversy between Partch and Alwin Nikolais, the choreographer, concerning Partch's detailed notes in the score. Nikolais and Partch had fundamentally different opinions on the role of dance and on the appropriate style for this work. Nikolais rejected Partch's satiric program and created choreography that was far more abstract than Partch had envisioned. As Bob Gilmore suggests of Partch in his study of the controversy, "having prepared such an imaginative and detailed scenario, all he really needed was someone to translate his rather clear ideas into choreographic reality."[95] Nikolais was not willing to realize Partch's integrated vision but instead approached the project as he would any other music. Partch's fear that his ideas were being undermined was well founded. It is clear from letters between Nikolais and Ben Johnston (and others involved in organizing the production) that Nikolais never intended to follow Partch's scenario and had little regard for Partch's mimetic approach to dance. Johnston was impressed by Nikolais's fame and wanted to allow him free reign. He wrote to Nikolais that Partch should not be involved in the theatrical and choreographic side of the work. (In later articles and interviews, Johnston consistently criticized Partch's abilities as a choreographer and librettist.) Partch would bitterly recall how he had conceived *The Bewitched* as an integrated whole "and then in the course of getting it performed . . . my conception simply didn't get across. No matter how hard I tried, the idea of purity was overwhelming in the minds of the persons that I employed."[96]

In a letter to the choreographer Eleanor King, Partch delineated those aspects of Nikolais's choreography that had disappointed him: "Do you hate satire? Do you hate humor? Do you reject—automatically—the idea of telling a story in dance? Do you oppose all situations that are recognizable as human in dance? Do you reject the idea of American situations, commonplace enough but unusual simply because they are not used, as dance themes? Well, Alwin Nikolais does all these things."[97] Partch wrote that he had conceived *The Bewitched* "as a kind of American Kabuki, telling a series of satirical stories throughout, all with a common motivation, which is the burden of the *Prologue*. I had hoped—no, expected—to find a choreographer who would *extend* the satiric idea in dance. The freedom and latitude for choreographic creativity is tremendous within that framework."[98] Several of Partch's statements concerning *The Bewitched* indicate that Japanese Kabuki and its dance had occupied his thoughts during this period:

> The value that we have lost—temporarily, I hope—is evident when we see a performance of the Japanese kabuki. It is not to be explained merely as a difference between widely separated cultures. The Japanese theater, which at the time of its revolutionary advent included all the skills of popular entertainment, such as juggling and tumbling, represents a quality in an integrated art, and however we may use music in conjunction with drama and dance, our value lies in 'purity.' . . . Yet it is a fact that we *do* respond, and magnificently—as in the case of kabuki—when we are somehow exposed to an ancient art that takes integration for granted. In ancient Greece, and to some extent in medieval Europe, the value *was* taken for granted.[99]

Partch's ideas for the dancing in *The Bewitched* were based on various exotic styles. The Witch was to dance in "Kabuki style" throughout. Stage directions for one scene refer to "Near East" dance; "East Indian" dance and tumbling are designated for another. As usual, Partch made a clear distinction between the influence of exotic styles and the attempt to imitate them. "Where oriental styles are stated, the dancing would only *suggest*. The result would *not* be oriental, of course, any more than my music is oriental, even though most Americans hearing it for the first time say so."[100]

Nikolais did not share Partch's interest in using exotic styles any more than he was willing to create imitations of modern "American situations." Most importantly, Nikolais did not share Partch's peculiar sense of humor. For Partch, the value of *The Bewitched*, its fundamental purpose, resided in its satiric program and its social criticism of contemporary America. In praise of theatrical satire, Partch wrote: "Satire need not be heavy-handed. It can descend lightly and with love, and imbue the listener and the viewer with a shaft of momentary recognition and delight. It can bring reevaluation and self-perception, because it precipitates momentary people and momentary scenes in a fresh-angle vision. And without seeming labor, finally, it can bring a spontaneous feeling for humanity through art, a feeling that lies within our bones and is precedent to all recorded history, and invokes the oldest of traditions."[101] During the first production of *The Bewitched*, Partch's collaborators clearly considered the composer's satire a bit heavy-handed. Undeterred, he would again employ satire for purposes of social criticism in *Revelation in the Courthouse Park* (1960) and *Water! Water!* (1961).

Despite their eccentricity, Partch's works fit within a larger trend in twentieth-century American music and prefigure works composed in subsequent decades. American music theater has often functioned as a form of staged social criticism and has thrived on stylistic eclecticism. This is evident in pieces from the period of the Great Depression, such as Becker's "Polytechnic Drama" *A Marriage with Space* (1935), as well as in numerous works from the Vietnam era. It is to the latter, American works embodying the conjunction of ritualized performance and religious subject matter for music theater of political protest in the turbulent 1960s and early '70s, that we now direct our attention.

13   Bitter Rituals for a Lost Nation: Partch and Bernstein

An Odd Juxtaposition

At the Metropolitan Opera gift shop at Lincoln Center one may purchase the "Chimes of Partch," one in a series of wind chimes that includes the "Chimes of Kyoto," the "Chimes of Olympus," and the "Chimes of Bali." I quote from the booklet accompanying this New Age tribute to Partch: "This happy chime is tuned to an uplifting major scale and named after American composer Harry Partch, who taught us that science and magic can harmonize in music. Its scale is common in the music of many ancient civilizations and is still heard today in non-Western countries of the world."[1] The occasional tinkling of these chimes is perhaps the closest the Met will ever come to hearing Partch's music or witnessing his corporeal theater. Also available in this shop are several recordings of Leonard Bernstein's *Mass*, recordings of his other compositions, videos of him conducting and lecturing, and books by and about him. Of course, Partch and Bernstein are divergent in many more dimensions than just their marketability. Yet through a juxtaposition of works by these apparent musical antipodes, it is possible to illumine the pervasiveness of certain basic issues in American music theater and to suggest how both Partch's *Revelation in the Courthouse Park* and Bernstein's *Mass* reflect several developments in the social history of the 1960s.

Although a great chasm exists between these works, numerous similarities affirm their common genre. Both *Mass* and *Revelation* are examples of music theater based on ritual models. They share a similar dramatic structure: beginning in satire, leading to a central ritual performance, and, through this ritual, ending with a psychological catastrophe for an individual. The text of both works alternates between a more refined idiom and the use of slang and nonsense syllables. Both Bernstein and Partch experiment with the performance space by placing instrumentalists onstage and, coincidentally, calling for a marching band to enter through the auditorium. These are works of multimedia and total theater designed to criticize and transform political, musical, and religious life.

In this chapter, I will consider three primary topics raised by these two works and will concentrate on cultural contextualization rather than on detailed comparison. (Borrowing the device of juxtaposition that structures both *Revelation* and *Mass,* the focus of this chapter will alternate between Partch and Bernstein without pause.) First, they are concerned with ritual and religious expression—with a critique of established American social and religious rituals and with the creation of a new work of ritualistic or didactic status. Second, this critique and transformation is achieved musically through the use, or perhaps abuse, of American popular music and through radical musical juxtaposition. Finally, Partch and Bernstein employ ritual expression and popular music references for the purposes of parody and social criticism, focusing on the relationship of the individual to society. Created at opposite ends of a turbulent decade, but yoked together by violence, *Revelation* and *Mass* arrive at somewhat different conclusions.

Ritual Models, Ritual Criticism, Ritual Aspiration

PARTCH

a. An Ancient Model

Partch's *Revelation in the Courthouse Park,* based on *The Bacchae* of Euripides, was first performed at the University of Illinois, Urbana-Champaign, on 11 April 1961. By the late 1950s, Partch had fully developed his concept of totally integrated theater. He planned every aspect of the performance of *Revelation* in detailed notes printed in the score.[2] He envisioned the set and costumes, choreographed the dancing and gymnastic tumbling, wrote the scenario and text, and even blocked the curtain calls and composed incidental music for them. However, in the course of the actual production, his ideas were modified in accordance with financial and temporal constraints.[3] The minimalist set was intended to serve a primarily symbolic function. In the score, for instance, Partch attributed special significance to the park fountain, which was to represent "stability, respectability, tenderness, gentleness within the human community, protection from an unpredictable Mother Nature, the national red-white-and-blue." *Revelation* is a true multimedia event, employing a filmed fireworks display, taped music, elaborate masks, and a detailed lighting scheme. It was billed as an "extravaganza" at the premiere and was described by Nicholas Temperley as an "orgy of the arts."[4] A performance of *Revelation* involves clog dancers, a marching band, baton twirlers, and tumblers.[5] Partch also maintained an inclusive approach to textual sources. In *Revelation*, he called for shouts, screams, whistles, and nasty and belligerent pronunciations of nonsense text. In short, *Revelation in the Courthouse Park* is an apotheosis of total theater.

Revelation is not a simple setting of Euripides' *The Bacchae*. As Partch mentioned in a letter to the work's future director: "I am sure I would outrage Greek scholars in what I intend to do with it."[6] In *The Bacchae*, the god Dionysus, born from the male womb of Zeus's thigh and a recent addition to the pantheon, arrives in Thebes with his Bacchae, or female devotees. As a punishment on this community for failing to observe his rites, Dionysus sets a craze on the women of Thebes, who then run wild in the mountains, wearing skins, eating raw flesh, and engaging in orgiastic rituals in his honor. Pentheus, the young king, is determined to put an end to this new cult; his own mother, Agave, leads the female revelers. Dionysus arrives in human form at the palace of Thebes and is imprisoned by Pentheus. He soon breaks free and convinces Pentheus to dress in women's clothing in order to witness the orgiastic activities. Pentheus, hiding in a tree, is recognized by the crazed women and then dismembered by his own mother. Agave, believing she has killed a lion with her bare hands, returns to the city with her trophy—the head of her son (represented by the mask of Pentheus in Partch's version.) She is made to realize her monstrous actions by Cadmus, her father, and regaining her sanity, reacts with horror. Dionysus returns, bringing doom to Thebes and painful banishment for Agave and Cadmus. A lengthy discussion of the justness of this punishment ensues.

On his decision to employ this particular ancient model, Partch wrote:

> Many years ago I was struck by a strong and strange similarity between the basic situation in the Euripides play and at least two phenomena of present-day America. Religious rituals with a strong sexual element are not unknown to our culture, nor are sex rituals with a strong religious element. (I assume that the mobbing of young male singers by semihysterical women is recognizable as a sex ritual for a godhead.) And these separate phenomena, after years of observing them, have become synthesized as a single kind of ritual, with religion and sex in equal parts, and with deep roots in an earlier period of human evolution—all of which sounds delightfully innocent.[7]

Partch, however, was not delighted with popular culture in 1969 when this retrospective statement was written, nor had he viewed these religio-sexual phenomena as purely innocent in the mid-1950s when he first envisioned this work.

Partch valued his ancient Greek model for its holistic approach to theatrical performance and for its ritual function, and he endeavored to revive this form of theater for modern America.[8] Partch alternates his setting of Euripides' play with sections set in a contemporary American courthouse park. (An abbreviated version of Partch's outline for *Revelation* with references to the primary action is contained in the appendix.) In the "Scenes" of *Revelation*, Partch remains close to the original text, omitting the lengthy denouement by ending with the moment of Agave's horrible realization. These Theban scenes contain passages of spoken dialogue with minimal musical accompaniment and with the major characters appearing masked (see Fig. 11).[9] The appearance of the large masks facilitates the transformation between the American Choruses and the Greek scenes. The choral passages of Euripides' play are transformed by Partch into "Hymns to Dionysus" within these scenes. Their texts and vocal style reflect Partch's experiences of American revivalist meetings and are only loosely related to the original Bacchic texts. The sections marked "Chorus" in the scenario occur in a small-town American park on the day when a rock-and-roll star, Dion, arrives and is ecstatically welcomed by his female fans. Partch creates parallel characters, each pairing performed by the same performer. The Greek Dionysus becomes the American Dion, "a symbol of dominant mediocrity" and Hollywood King of Ishbu Kubu, the cult of commercial success. Agave is represented by Mom, "a symbol of blind matriarchal power" and the leader of the local Dion fan club. Pentheus becomes Sonny in the American Choruses, "a symbol of nothing so much as a lost soul, one who does not or cannot conform to the world he was born to."[10]

The American Choruses are symbolic and psychological and contain only fragments of comprehensible text. Choruses one and three are extravagant ritual celebrations—modern approximations of Dionysian revels. Choruses two and four are psychological foretellings of the tragedy to come—the destruction of an individual at the hands of society. In these two sections Partch stresses the psychosexual and gender reversal dimensions of the play. In his dream-state section, Chorus two, Sonny expresses feelings of utter abandonment and loss of direction. Sonny sees a vision of his end, and sings "I see two moons above me, I see two arms around me." These moons represent his mother's breasts viewed from the perspective of a held babe, or of a carried, disembodied head. When he desperately asks for direction from the night, shouting "where, where," he is answered by high male voices, "Your mother's arms." Of course, Pentheus does end up in his mother's

Figure 11. Greek masks in *Revelation in the Courthouse Park*. Photographer unknown. (Reproduced with the permission of Danlee Mitchell, musical executor of the Partch estate)

arms—decapitated. The offstage male falsetto voices are but one musical re-inforcement of the basic gender reversals at the heart of the Euripidean drama and of *Revelation*. Pentheus, the masculine king, falls prey to the se-ductive influence of the effeminate god Dionysus and then cross-dresses as a woman, becoming the very image of his mother. The women of Thebes, normally confined to a limited and virtually invisible position in society, are roaming freely, cavorting in the hills.

Evidence suggests that Partch identified himself with the Sonny/Pentheus character. Much of the music and text of Choruses two and four appear in Partch's musical journal, "Bitter Music," written over twenty years before *Revelation* during Partch's transient period. At one point in "Bitter Mu-sic," Partch wrote that his "own efforts to bring beauty into the world have come to aimless wandering."[11] He then immediately set the following lines from Lao-tzu to music: "I am drifted about as on the sea / I am carried by the wind / As if I had nowhere to rest." Both the text and the musical set-ting of this excerpt appear in altered form throughout Chorus two of *Revela-*

tion, where they express Sonny's psychological turmoil, as they had expressed Partch's own feelings of "aimless wandering" in "Bitter Music." (This material also appears in Partch's "The Wind" in *Eleven Intrusions* from 1949–50.) In an entry dated 22 October 1935 in "Bitter Music," Partch recorded how, while in Sacramento, he looked up at the night sky and imagined he heard the stars singing: "Why wander? Why tire yourself uselessly? Stop and reflect. Rest. There is nothing but eternity infinity."[12] This is the same text and music that, in a slightly altered form, the offstage chorus of four male voices sings to Sonny in Chorus two. In yet another diary entry in "Bitter Music," Partch records an experience of remembering the cottonwood trees of his childhood home: "My friends and loved ones burst upon my consciousness like the cottonwoods' whitenesses."[13] He then set a few of his memories to music, including these images of falling cotton bolls: "ever so softly, as they fall. They hardly stop at all, and in the briefest moment they are away."[14] After a brief unset prose passage, the following lines are intoned: "How can I imagine that they [the cotton bolls] are here when with these eyes I have seen them taken before a hundred winds beyond my power to control?" These excerpted lines and music are sung by Mom in Chorus four as she intuits the fate of her own loved one, Sonny. The discovery that Partch borrowed from "Bitter Music" not only supplies a textual context allowing us to understand some of the more obscure fragmented lines in the second and fourth Choruses of *Revelation;* it also directly supports a reading of *Revelation* that emphasizes Partch's emotional involvement in the story and his deep identification with the Sonny/ Pentheus character.

b. Revivalists and Elvis

Why did Partch decide to update the Euripidean play so radically? And what models from popular culture might have served for the creation of the Dion character? By the late 1950s, Partch had come to view his 1951 setting of *Oedipus* as less than completely successful: "It seemed that the drama of Oedipus, however compelling, was deposited by the mind in an ancient category called *classical*—that it was not brought home to the audience as a here-and-now work."[15] Partch also commented, "I've seen many performances of Greek lyric tragedy, and I've always felt that the audiences could *admire,* in a distant sort of way, but *never,* absolutely *never,* relate. Well, this time, in contemplating *The Bacchae* of Euripides, this time—by golly— I decided that the audience *will* relate."[16] Partch believed that it was essential for the audience to be able to "relate" to a performance in order to have its outlook and behavior transformed by that performance. With each new music theater project Partch first developed the basic idea in detail by writing a scenario. In his initial concept of *Revelation,* Partch planned to transfer the entire play to a Californian setting rather than to alternate with scenes set in ancient Thebes. In a 1955 letter to Ben Johnston, Partch mentioned that during the previous year he had considered creating a modern Californian setting of *The Bacchae,* a work chosen because it "lends itself to dancing and percussion," but that he had "bogged down completely in the matter of dialogue" and had therefore decided to drop the project.[17]

In this early "Californian" version of the scenario, Pentheus is the district attorney of Alameda county; Cadmus, from a family of forty-niners, is a former governor of California; Tiresias is an elderly general and retired justice of the California supreme court; and Agave, portrayed as a fiercely matriarchal and dominating figure, is the president of the county discussion club. "Dion Isus" is said to have been "fathered by a vacuum, born prematurely of radio antennae."[18] The action is set specifically in the San Francisco Bay area. In this version, the work begins as Pentheus returns from a Republican rally in Chicago to discover a crisis at home: "The feminine air is electric, and his own mother, Agave, president of the Alameda County Discussion Club, is on the froth of the new frenzy," as Dion Isus "dances his way north from Hollywood on the air waves." Partch discusses at length the susceptibility of women to the Dionysian contagion in this draft scenario. Pentheus is said to have not yet learned that women "must have something more than education, suffrage, and children to believe in, in order to remain politically healthy." Pentheus had been aware that the women were "growing increasingly restive, not so much for political change as for something worthwhile to believe in. He has seen their wild forays into juvenile-delinquency roundtables, art festivals, little theaters, PTA sessions, camellia shows, and their rapt expressions while watching TV." In a later draft of the scenario, Dion is described as "the god of hysterical female delight," possessing a handsome body and voice. Clearly, Partch viewed the position of women in the 1950s as less than ideal, although I am not at all convinced that his portrayal of women in *Revelation* qualifies him for the honorific label "proto-feminist," as the *New Grove Dictionary of Opera* would have us believe.[19] He relishes his satire far too much.

The Dion character is a complicated figure developed from several models. Partch describes him in the draft scenario as "a synthesis of contemporary-art-in-our-time, revivalist, and consummate politician." Whether politician, preacher, or pop singer, Dion's appeal is clearly sexual at root: "In the prime of youth he has achieved the ultimate in American success. Test: the devotion of women—millions of them." Partch, in his discussions of this work, placed equal emphasis on Dion as revivalist preacher and as rock-and-roll star. The elements of parody and social criticism directed at forms of popular religious expression appear primarily in the "Hymns to Dionysus." Concerning these choruses within the Theban scenes, Partch wrote: "They are more in the nature of street corner revival meetings on East Fifth St. in Los Angeles, and many other places. That Dionysos' [*sic*] women attained a frenzy of religious fervor I have no doubt. But I have seen religious frenzy here also, and these choruses really come out of my experience."[20] Similar remarks appear in a letter dated 17 June 1960 to Rodney H. Mill: "I've written them as straight copies of Christian evangelistic services—same harmonies, same types of singing. I can hear any of those groups of evangels on East Fifth St. in Los Angeles singing—In holy joy, blessed by the gods, to get religion in holy joy—Or—Glory, glory, glory————to the male womb! And I even have a small Handelian figure in the male-womb bit. Just change Jesus Christ to Dionysus, and Blood of Lamb to Male Womb, and there's not a particle of difference."[21]

There was no shortage in the 1950s of revivalist models for Partch's creation of Dion.[22] American revivalism, having declined in the 1930s and early 1940s, was reborn in the years immediately following World War II. The years 1947 to 1958 have been referred to as the period of the "Healing Revival." Such Pentecostal figures as Oral Roberts, Asa Alonzo Allen, William Branham, and Jack Coe were hugely successful in the popular art of faith healing. During this period, revivalist meetings would climax in a miraculous moment of healing, a revelation of God's grace. According to Patsy Sims, A. A. Allen, in particular, was something of an entertainer, "singing, strutting, and performing one-man Bible extravaganzas."[23] David Harrell informs us that Allen's revival meetings were criticized for their carnivalesque atmosphere in the mid-1950s.[24] Oral Roberts and Billy Graham were already national figures by the time Partch drafted his early scenario and they owed some portion of their success to their physical appeal and television appearances. In October 1949, Billy Graham held a tent revival in Los Angeles that received national attention and lasted an astonishing eight weeks. Partch had been living in Gualala, north of San Francisco, for several months but would likely have been aware of the event. McLoughlin notes that Graham's revival attracted one hundred thousand visitors, including repeaters, and that the conversion of a few celebrities drew the attention of the press.[25] No one revivalist may have served as a model for Dion. Instead, American revivalism offered a general target for Partch's satire in this work.

Sims has written that, in the second half of the 1950s, the emphasis of revivalist meetings shifted more toward entertainment, "with musical skills as important to the ambitious revivalist as knowing how to preach."[26] Near the end of the decade, the revivalist audience and its financial offerings began to dwindle. This corresponds to the period during which Elvis Presley became a national figure. Partch's label "Hollywood singer" fits Elvis perfectly—he had made musical movies since 1956. In 1960, the very year Partch composed *Revelation*, the Tony Award for best Broadway musical went to *Bye Bye Birdie,* a spoof on the current Elvis-mania.[27] In Dion, Partch created a parody of both the rock-and-roll idol and the revivalist preacher. The moment of revelation referred to in the title occurs late at night in the courthouse park (in Chorus three, subsection three, entitled: "Ishbu Kubu— Revelation of the Mystic Power.") The chorus members vocalize with "sh's" and "k's," gradually forming the cultic words "Ishbu Kubu." Dion enters "as an exotic priest at an altar [whose] revolving ass is not a lustful and transitory whim, but a divine right." This satiric portrayal of American social rituals and religious expression climaxes in a fantastic section of gymnastic tumbling.

c. Revealing the Ritual

Partch intended his music theater works to effect change in contemporary society. With *Revelation*, Partch set out to expose the patterns of "mediocrity and conformity" he had observed in American society and to warn of the dangers to the individual. "I am endeavoring, while preserving the stark outlines of the ancient play, to bridge a gap of 2400 years, in the Courthouse Park, with the same profound and ancient purpose."[28] He believed that Euripides' ancient purpose was cathartic—namely, to counter the Dionysian menace of his time. Partch anticipated the reactions of the audience in a note to the score: "The audience will consider several of these 'numbers' as parodies of popular religious singing styles and lyrics if it chooses to. But it must *never* be led to feel that the *actors* are thinking of them as parodies. . . . The actors applaud and shout for themselves as though the audience did not exist." Thus, the audience members are forced to recognize their characteristic behavior and social rituals portrayed on the stage. The audience is intended to observe, rather than to participate or respond, and to consider the menace of mindless group behavior. From the performer's viewpoint, the work appears to be more of a participatory ritual. *Revelation* was specifically designed as a didactic ritual for performance by students.

BERNSTEIN

a. Transforming the Mass

Bernstein's *Mass: A Theatre Piece for Singers, Players, and Dancers,* was commissioned for the opening of the Kennedy Center for the Performing Arts in Washington, D. C., on 8 September 1971. As the original venue and subtitle suggest, *Mass* is a large-scale work of music theater involving multiple forms of performance by an enormous cast. Although Bernstein maintained artistic control over the work, he was assisted by several collaborators. Alvin Ailey served as choreographer and Stephen Schwartz assisted with the writing of the text. *Mass* was said to have been created "because the composer believes that the crisis of faith is the principal crisis of our century; because he has long been intrigued with the idea of writing a comprehensive religious service; because of his fascination with Roman Catholicism, especially since the memorable papacy of John XXIII; and, finally, because of his love for the man whose name the Center celebrates."[29] Each of these justifications for the composition entails a fascinating set of critical and historical ramifications.

There is indeed a Mass within Bernstein's massive *Mass:* nearly the entire text of the Ordinary is set, and the basic structure and ritual action of the Catholic service is presented. The work, however, was not intended for church performance. Interspersed between and within sections of the Latin text is contemporary commentary in English. This linguistic division is echoed in the division of the performance space into an upper area and a lower area. A continuous, symbolic path rises from the orchestra pit onto the stage apron, on which a square of earth suggests a small consecrated spot. The path continues to a central playing area that, in turn, leads to a raised circular altar space and then goes on as stairs ascending to a distant summit. This upstage area contains choir pews divided into right and left stage sections. The cast itself is divided into two basic vocal groups: the robed Church Choir, which remains in the upstage elevated pew area for most of the performance and sings primarily in Latin, and the Street Chorus, wearing everyday clothes, which moves within the downstage performance space. From the Street Chorus emerge several solo voices that together create an English subtext reflecting "the reactions, doubts, protests, and questionings—positive and negative—of all of us who are attending and perceiving this ritual."[30] A Boys' Choir assumes the role of altar boys assisting in the celebration. The central figure in this work is the Celebrant, who first appears as a jeans-clad, guitar-playing young adult answering a call to sing God's praise. He is invested with a simple robe by the boys and then functions as

Figure 12. The Celebrant interrupts bacchic revels in Bernstein's *Mass*. Photograph by Fletcher Drake. (Reproduced with the permission of Nancy Drake)

a spiritual leader for the entire cast, although his leadership will eventually be rejected.

The work is cyclically structured in sections of increasing tension broken off by the Celebrant's sudden call to prayer or reappearance and followed by sections of relative peace. (See the appendix for an annotated outline of *Mass*.) Each successive period of crisis reaches a higher level of intensity, ultimately resulting in cataclysm (see Fig. 12). Throughout the work, the ceremonial service and songs of praise to God are interrupted by the commentary and complaint of the Street Chorus and its soloists. This alternation between crying for God's mercy and singing God's praise is central to the Latin liturgy and is especially evident in the Gloria of the Mass Ordinary. Bernstein viewed the Catholic Mass as a dramatic form and thought that "it even suggests a theater work."[31] The dramatic structure of his *Mass* is propelled by the energy resulting from the conflict of various opposing elements. These include a conflict and alternation in language between Latin and English, an opposition between a complex and a more simple musical idiom, between taped and live music, and between an increasing formality and symbolism versus the Chorus's more irreverent demands. The Celebrant's initial guitar chord halts the taped, cacophonous Kyrie Eleison, and marks the onset of a pattern of alternation between opposing linguistic and musical styles. *Mass* is built on radical juxtapositions and sudden interruptions.

b. Religious Reception and Ritual Criticism

Although the Second Vatican Council had concluded its meetings in 1965, the debates over liturgical music continued into the next decade. These arguments focused on the proper interpretation and realization of the guidelines for church music as determined by Vatican II.[32] The two opposing sides in this debate, representing incompatible positions, have been referred to as the "pastoral" and the "sacred music" views. The pastoral ideal was one of complete inclusivity, in which the entire congregation would sing together for as much of the service as possible. For this ideal to be achieved, the pastoralists argued that the music would have to be simple and popular, so that the congregation would want to sing it. Any style of music was possible in theory, so long as it served this ultimate purpose. But the pastoralists held that Gregorian chant, particularly when sung in Latin, was incapable of inspiring group singing and was therefore inimical to the new, inclusive ideal. Those writers representing the "sacred music" view, argued that the pastoralist program was a willful misinterpretation of the spirit of Vatican II and constituted a direct attack on the musical heritage of the Catholic church. At the 1966 Fifth International Church Music Congress, held in Chicago and Milwaukee, the sacred music camp reaffirmed their commitment to chant and to sacred art music, as opposed to the recent innovations in church music performance. The sacred music viewpoint dominated the conference (as can be seen clearly in the published proceedings), and this meeting appears to mark the decisive break between the two sides.[33] Experimentation in Catholic church music occurred throughout the 1960s. These musical innovations resulted in the widespread celebration of "Folk Masses" and "Youth Masses" in which new devotional songs were featured, often accompanied by a guitar in the style of 1960s popular "folk" music.[34] By the early 1970s the dominance of the pastoral position in American Catholic churches resulted in a seemingly irreconcilable division in the Church music community that persists to this day.

Bernstein's *Mass* was received by the religious community within this contentious context. Bernstein was highly concerned with the Catholic reception of his work and consistently mentioned in interviews that he had received copies of numerous sermons interpreting the work positively. In one such interview he said, "I'm touched by the reaction of the religious community—the *whole* religious community."[35] A positive review in the Catholic publication *Commonweal* described the work as "the ultimate 'People's Mass,'" adding that "it is rather a show *about* the Mass, about the meaning or lack of meaning of the Mass."[36] This review stressed the work's relevance to contemporary American Catholicism and half-seriously envisioned Bernstein's imminent conversion. The extreme negative faction condemned the work as nothing short of blasphemy and viewed it as a direct attack on the traditional service and its music. The archbishop of Cincinnati, for instance, forbade Catholics to attend the production when it was performed in his city. The negative reactions of Catholics to this work are perhaps less surprising than the positive. From Bernstein's perspective, the Roman Catholic Mass, as a religious rather than purely musical form, was an exotic model of ritual theater. For many of those who considered the Mass a native form of religious expression, Bernstein's work was an act of aggressive appropriation, an especially egregious event occurring within a painful period when the basic features of Catholic worship, particularly musical, were in flux.

A survey of the religious response to Bernstein's *Mass* reveals a greater diversity of opinion than suggested up to now. A striking example of such variety can be witnessed in two opposing reviews published within the journal *Sacred Music*, the primary publication representing the traditional church music position. Both reviewers position themselves within the sacred music camp but, nevertheless, arrive at starkly different interpretations of this work. The first, negative, reviewer portrayed *Mass* as the ultimate desecration, as a work of ritual criticism directed against the traditional holy service. This reviewer accused Bernstein of appealing "to the hedonistic instincts of the masses, soothing their bad conscience with a covering of religious phraseology."[37] He concluded that *Mass* was a work of mere religious pretensions, a work of "cultural schizophrenia" attempting to be both deep and intellectual while popular and simple. Commercial music, having exhausted its traditional themes of "drug glorification" and "countercultural attitudes," was seen to be turning desperately to the exploitation of religious sentiment.

The second, rather eccentrically positive discussion of *Mass* in *Sacred Music* appeared in a column entitled "Open Forum" and was written in response to the earlier negative article. This writer understood Bernstein's *Mass* to be a work of ritual criticism directed explicitly against the new Folk Mass style.[38] In an unexpected interpretation of Bernstein's purpose, this reviewer wrote: "Perhaps we could accuse the composer of being a bit *too* realistic in portraying what he sees is happening to our sacred service, but maybe he sees it as an outsider, and gets a more realistic view of the situation, than those who belong to our faith and attend Sunday Masses merely out of routine, not caring what is happening either musically or liturgically."[39] This writer makes his own antipastoralist views explicit and argues that musical beauty has been replaced in the contemporary church by "the shallow, the vain, the sentimental, the vulgar, the worldly, and the mediocre of the circus and marching bands, the wild and brutal sounds of cave-men and the primitive, quasi-fetishistic songs and trivial rhythms, pleasing a sentimental minority to whom religion and especially certain para-liturgical devotions have become an emotional escape rather than the profession of a deep and living faith!"[40] In short, the music and drama of Bernstein's *Mass* are interpreted as a direct critique and "true picture of things happening in our churches these days."[41]

On a basic level, *Mass* functions as a work of ritual criticism directed against the traditional Catholic service. The Street Chorus explicitly criticizes the Mass as a ritual ceremony and disdains the merely symbolic comfort offered by the Celebrant and his Church. As Bernstein wrote, the Celebrant's "increasingly ornate robes and symbols . . . connote both an increase in the superficial formalism of his obligation and of the burden that he bears. There is a parallel increase in the resistance of the Congregants—in the sharpness and bitterness of their reactions—and in the deterioration of his own faith."[42] The diversity of critical interpretation inspired by *Mass* arose, in part, because Bernstein was also critical of these sharp and bitter sounds of protest.

c. The "Miracle" of Mass

Bernstein's *Mass* makes explicit use of a ritual model, but to what extent does it function as a work of ritual? Bernstein offered one answer to this question: "I consider both *Kaddish* [Symphony No. 3] and *Mass* as essentially religious statements, but not as works to be performed in the context of organized religion—that is, within a house of worship or on religious occasions."[43] While denying the work's potential for liturgical use, Bernstein did emphasize its religious motivations: "I have not written a Mass. I have written a theater piece about a Mass. It cannot be performed in church as a Mass. Yet it is still a deeply religious work. The Communion we give is the kiss of peace, which was a feature of the early Christian Mass. Catholics who heard it have told me it was one of the deepest experiences they ever had."[44] In another context, Bernstein discussed the performance as if it were a ritual experience for the performers: "At the climax of Communion, all ceremony breaks down and the Mass is shattered. It then remains for each individual on the stage to find a new seed of faith within himself through painful meditation, enabling each individual to pass on the embrace of peace (Pax) to his neighbor. This chain of embrace grows and spreads through the entire stage, ultimately into the audience and hopefully into the world outside."[45] The audience was to experience the work as a ritual performance and to be profoundly affected by it. According to one report of the opening night, when the Celebrant called for prayer "a handful of the spectators rose and bowed their heads. Everyone else remained seated, not sure how serious or how literal a consecration of the Kennedy Center was intended."[46] At the end of the work, the Boys' Choir spreads the touch of peace to the audience members, who in turn are asked to participate in the performance and to "pass it on." According to another report, at the premiere these handclasps "appeared to peter out fairly quickly along most rows."[47] Bernstein, however, clearly felt that the ritual performance succeeded in achieving its intended effect on both performers and audience: "And this is the miracle I saw take place: the waves of tenderness, these waves of touching and embracing, began to spread from the stage to the house, until they passed through the whole audience and then even out into the street. I saw people embracing strangers on the street—cops, just ordinary people."[48] This miraculous vision is indicative of Bernstein's supreme confidence in his ability to transform or manipulate his audience's feelings and social and political perspectives through music theater. *Mass* was also designed to serve a didactic function for the audience. It offered a translation of the Latin liturgy into contemporary language and articulated a contemporary relevance. The numerous translation passages are frequently musically underlined by a continuation of the same melody for both the Latin and the English texts. Bernstein "translated" the spiritual drama of the Catholic Mass in terms of the social drama of his time.[49]

Finally, the numerous public performances of *Mass* that Bernstein attended seem to have served a cathartic function for the composer himself.[50] Reviews of these productions rarely fail to discuss Bernstein's behavior at the end of the performance. Bernstein, profoundly affected by the performance and frequently in tears, would make every effort during the curtain calls to come into physical contact with each member of the production in a gesture of gratitude and love. The general "crisis of faith" Bernstein intended to address and to solve through the performance of this work was equally a personal crisis requiring relief and reassurance through ritual.

Representations of Popular Music

BERNSTEIN

A major criticism leveled against *Mass* concerned its "hodgepodge" and "wild mélange" of musical styles.[51] In the *New York Times,* Harold Schonberg was especially critical of Bernstein's musical juxtapositions. Robert

Craft, in a particularly cruel and scathing review entitled "Non Credo," described the work as "too insubstantial to wreak any harm more lasting than embarrassment" and concluded that Bernstein's "resources as a composer are meager. At any rate, he has not so far shown a very large command of a creative musical language."[52] More favorable discussions have compared Bernstein's musical eclecticism with the example of Mahler and with the trend in 1960s art music toward collage and quotation, and have argued that Bernstein, with his broad musical and cultural background, was uniquely qualified to produce such a syncretic work.[53] In a discussion of the multiple musical styles of *Mass*, Bernstein said "I knew that that was the essence of the work, the eclecticism of it; it *had* to be," and that "it's a work I've been writing all my life."[54] Why, however, was eclecticism a necessity for the composer? Those willing to give him the benefit of the doubt have assumed that the universality at which Bernstein aimed in his ritual statement demanded an equally all-encompassing musical approach.[55]

The use of radical juxtaposition and collage in Euro-American music of the 1960s has received consistent attention in the standard texts on twentieth-century music. In a chapter entitled "The New Pluralism," Robert P. Morgan discusses various examples and aspects of this topic in the period of the 1960s and early '70s:

> The most distinctive new feature of musical quotations in the 1960s is that they are normally treated as 'foreign objects'—as things drawn from other times and places, with stylistic conventions anachronous to their immediate contexts. . . . A second difference is that quoted material is no longer confined to an isolated moment and a dramatic purpose, but often appears consistently throughout a composition— some works even consist entirely of quotations and distortions thereof. . . . Finally, the range of borrowings is unprecedented. . . . the most unlikely partners are intimately juxtaposed.[56]

In exemplification of the wide range of musical pluralism, Morgan mentions works by such figures as Bernd Alois Zimmermann, Luciano Berio, Lukas Foss, Karlheinz Stockhausen, Mauricio Kagel, Peter Maxwell Davies, and Alfred Schnittke. Morgan also cites the prominent pluralistic developments in 1960s jazz, as evidenced by the music of Fusion and Free Jazz. In *Pyramids at the Louvre: Music, Culture, and Collage from Stravinsky to the Postmodernists*, Glenn Watkins views much of this century's musical history in terms of the radical juxtaposition of divergent styles, aesthetics, and materials.[57] Watkins cites the pluralistic techniques of composers in the 1960s as forming the basis for a musical postmodernism. As a composer and conductor active in diverse musical realms, Bernstein was clearly emblematic of this pluralistic period. In turn, *Mass* is the most emphatic statement of Bernstein's own musical and ideological eclecticism.

Creating style checklists for *Mass* became something of a contest for the critics. These analytic style and quotation catalogues could include: Stravinsky, Orff, blues, rock, Beethoven, cliché Exoticism, spirituals, twelve-tone music, Protestant hymns, Mahler, jazz, Broadway, and Copland. However, Bernstein's critics failed to hear elements of satire and parody in his use of these musical styles, several of which are to be sung "crudely," as marked in the score.[58] Bernstein did not present the Street Chorus's aggressive musical idioms in a positive light—rock and blues do not appear in the service of worship, but of protest. The Celebrant ultimately labels this music a "parody of God." In the penultimate section, entitled "Fraction," the Celebrant refers to the "braying and shouting" of the Street Chorus. Throughout the course of this solo scene, the Celebrant parodies all the major styles and melodies that have been heard in the work. This is a traditional mad scene, of course, but the popular musical styles have been directly implicated in his psychological disintegration.

PARTCH

In the American Choruses of *Revelation*, Partch does not quote directly from popular styles but instead creates music that is reminiscent of the Broadway show tune, 1950s rock rhythms and text manipulation, the music of clog dancing, and the chants of the college fight song.[59] Partch's parody of the rock concert ritual occurs in Chorus one. Dion enters through the auditorium with a marching band and baton twirlers while the onstage women swoon and call his name ecstatically (see Fig. 13). Dion and Mom then lead up a snake dance that includes prominent pelvic thrusts. In the fifth subsection, entitled "Wunnantu Anda—Primitive Percussion Ritual," Dion calls for a group dance and the chorus shouts "yeah yeah yeah." Partch's choreography is simplistic throughout and in this dance includes a rhythmic twist of the hip. Much of the dancing in *Revelation* is a parody of American social dance. The texts of both the first and third American Choruses have little syntactical meaning yet manage to express a boundless optimism and blind enthusiasm. In the collection of preliminary drafts, a scribbled list includes short phrases that Partch had heard in his daily life. These include: "Heavenly Days and a million years; right or wrong; from shore to shore; the happy way; forever ever more"—bits of Americanist hyperbole and patriotic tripe that, when set to satiric music in these Choruses, amply make their sardonic point. The line "Deep inside, way way down I am—" in Cho-

Figure 13.   Celebrating Dion in *Revelation in the Courthouse Park*. Photographer unknown. (Reproduced with the permission of the University of Illinois Music Library)

rus one is extremely ironic. These small-town citizens are shown to have little inner self, no core being that cannot be manipulated through the rituals of the commercial and religious world represented by Dion.

Partch's opinions of popular music are found in his writings throughout the 1950s. In the early years of the decade, Partch had admired the "strength" of popular music and its connection to contemporary society and admitted that it often contained corporeal elements. However, he disparaged the means that this music employed. In a 1952 article, Partch found many of the elements of popular music very disappointing: boring harmonies, average subject matter, and unimaginative, incessant rhythms.[60] By 1955 his views were a bit more scathing: "Is there a despairing soul who, after some forty years of it, has not consciously yearned for some counter-irritant to so-called popular music?" He referred to it as comic book music, music produced commercially for teenagers, "the most maudlin conformists."[61]

In *Revelation*, popular culture is portrayed as a device of the commercial world designed to destroy the individual and to create an undifferentiated, mindless mass of consumers. Through dramatic portrayal and written description, Partch presented a negative interpretation of the Dionysus/ Dion character and of popular culture. It appears that when Partch observed the physical reactions of young American women to rock and roll in the mid-1950s, he saw bloodthirsty Bacchae demanding "Join us or die!" From what was said earlier concerning Partch's devotion to corporeal music, one might imagine that he would have embraced the bodily power of rock and roll and the Dionysian spirit. To complicate matters, Partch himself once described his compositions as "Dionysian and dithyrambic."[62] The very performance of his music theater demanded something of a group mentality and fervent devotion to his corporeal vision. Did Partch see himself solely aligned with Sonny/Pentheus, the outsider and nonconformist or did he recognize a bit of himself in the Dionysian which Nietzsche argued exists in us all? Partch appears torn between embracing the Dionysian celebration of the body and condemning the group mentality and mediocrity that it so often entails.[63]

Social Criticism: The Individual and Society

PARTCH

For Partch, ultimately, the integrity of the individual was paramount, and *The Bacchae* represented the tragic sacrifice of an individual. As he remarked in a note to the score, "Nearly everyone onstage speaks or sings, 'I am!' before Sonny/Pentheus does so. Yet it is Sonny/Pentheus, finally, who sings these words . . . desperately, in the effort to imbue a life-death significance into them." He clearly believed that Euripides intended to criticize the group mentality of the Dionysian rites. George Talbot, the set designer for the first production, has told me that it was evident in Partch's rehearsals with the soloists that he most strongly identified with the Sonny/Pentheus character. In creating Sonny, Partch avoided any suggestion of the tyrannical, negative aspects of Euripides' Pentheus. In the American Choruses, Sonny is a completely innocent and silent observer. He undergoes psychological torture while watching the sexual flirtations between his mother and the charismatic Dion and we are meant to sympathize with the pain of this outsider. Partch's homosexuality clearly played some part in his own intense feelings of social alienation.

Partch struggled throughout his life to maintain his brand of radical individualism and the integrity of his unique musical vision. His massive, elaborate instruments and system of microtonal just intonation, while essential to his composition and entire concept of theatrical performance, were always, and continue to be, a great impediment to the dissemination of his music. He proved ill suited for collaboration and was only satisfied with a performance when he had designed every element himself. Much of his life was lived alone, and many of his important friendships ended in bitter dispute. A fundamental opposition between an individual versus a communal ideal of music making is evident in the basic division of Partch's oeuvre. As noted above, the first half of Partch's career was devoted primarily to a monophonic ideal and, by extension, to music for an individual bardic voice. In the 1950s and '60s the performance of his music theater works increasingly demanded a large performance group and production team. Ben Johnston has remarked that the performance of these works depended on a group of performers' cultlike devotion to Partch.[64] Johnston has also noted that Partch "talked a lot about Dionysus, the quintessential corporealist."[65] Although Partch remained an outsider and nonconformist, in the Sonny/ Pentheus mode, he necessarily assumed something of the role of a Dionysian leader of the revels for the realization of his music theater visions.

This ambiguous relation to the Dionysian is not unique to Partch and *Revelation*. What were Euripides' own views of Dionysus? Some have interpreted Euripides' intentions and the character of Pentheus and Dionysus quite differently from Partch. Nietzsche believed that Euripides had undergone a conversion near the end of a rather repressed life and had allowed himself to celebrate the Dionysian within him—*The Bacchae* being a product of that deathbed conversion.[66] Martha Nussbaum has written that "Nietzsche welcomed *The Bacchae* as a triumphant affirmation of the power of the irrational in human life" and that Nietzsche believed his own age required the Dionysian spirit in order to overcome the hatred of the body espoused by Christianity.[67] Nietzsche's nineteenth-century critics argued that Euripides remained a rationalist to the end of his life and that *The Bacchae* was intended as a warning against the Dionysian cult. This interpretive conundrum, the so-called riddle of *The Bacchae*, has continued to be debated by classicists throughout this century.[68] For example, in the introduction to his 1970 translation of *The Bacchae*, Geoffrey S. Kirk argued that there is no evidence for the assumption that Euripides intended to criticize Dionysus and to defend Pentheus. Kirk characterized the Pentheus character as a harsh and dictatorial figure incapable of sympathizing with his subjects.[69]

Nussbaum notes that *The Bacchae* has often been performed at moments of sudden upheaval. As one example, she discusses Richard Schechner's decision to produce *The Bacchae* for the first performances of his New York-based Performance Group. Schechner's *Dionysus in '69*, "in which nudity, ritual, and audience participation were explored with famous and controversial effect," became linked with the sexual revolution and with the opposition to the Vietnam War.[70] The work became emblematic of this period in American social history in which the "demand for peace and freedom was accompanied, frequently, with violence and disorder; in which compassion was sometimes strangely mingled with a lack of sensitivity to one's own excess and cruelty."[71] In his written discussion of *The Bacchae*, Schechner presented a negative interpretation of Dionysus as an insatiable figure who incites others to violence and offers nothing more than a hollow "politics of ecstasy."[72] And yet, as Christopher Innes argues, the orgiastic emphasis on nudity and nude audience participation in acts of communal ritual occurring in this production suggested for many audience members a positive portrayal of Dionysian behavior that ran counter to Schechner's early discussions of the play.[73] This type of paradox was central to the age of love-ins and protests.

Revelation, prophetic of developments to come, appeared at the beginning of a decade that could be described as emphatically Dionysian. As Ben Johnston has stated, "There isn't any question that what [Partch] was talking about symbolically in *Revelation in the Courthouse Park* actually happened all over the country, especially on campuses, but not only on campuses. The whole business blew up, and it came partly out of that salted spirit of independence that was typified by the young people's declaration of independence in the pop world. And this whole perception he made the subject of one of his major works."[74] Many aspects of the 1960s would seem to represent a triumph of the Bacchae and of group mentality in America with Woodstock as the ultimate Revelation in the Park. By the end of the decade, demands for peace and freedom were often accompanied by violence and disorder and delivered in a Bacchic tone. How did Partch view this turbulent decade? Partch was in his sixties during the 1960s and had begun to receive attention as an important figure in American music. Having come to prominence at this time, he is considered by many to be a product of the 1960s spirit, when, in fact, his viewpoint had changed little over several decades. Partch's stubborn individualism frequently collided head-on with the age of communal consciousness. The criticisms of American society in *Revelation* proved as relevant for him in the late 1960s as they had at the start of that decade. Although to some degree encouraged and excited by the corporeal energy of this period, Partch's extreme individualism, both musical and psychological, often left him isolated within a private realm of bitter music.

BERNSTEIN

Several commentators have assumed that, in writing *Mass*, Bernstein was siding with those demonstrators and rioters attempting to take power into their own hands at the end of the 1960s.[75] This interpretation stems, in part, from a recognition of Bernstein's political activities at the time, such as his January 1970 "radical chic" defense-fund party for the Black Panthers. Fund raising, speeches, and peaceful marches were, however, the extent of Bernstein's active social protest. His talks to students during the period advocated working within the system for social justice rather than dropping out or turning to violence. Bernstein was aware of the complex developments in Catholic social protest in the 1960s. In a retrospective statement, Bernstein stated that he had become "particularly interested in Catholicism during the Papacy of John XXIII, when it really seemed that the Catholic Church was taking the lead in certain movements: towards justice, equality, and all the things we dream about and try to work for but never quite know how to achieve. That was altogether too brief a Papacy, but it left a mark that began to be carried forward in many ways by other Catholic groups—one got the feeling that a new vitality was stirring among Catholic clergy."[76] For Bernstein, the most prominent examples of such "new vitality" in the American clergy and in Catholic social protest were Daniel and Philip Berrigan, whose influence (in some form) is present in *Mass*.

The Berrigans, brothers and priests, became prominent figures in the antiwar movement primarily through two major protest events.[77] On 17 May 1968 the Berrigans led a raid on a draft-board office in Catonsville, Maryland. They emptied files of draft records into garbage pails and then set them on fire using napalm. In an earlier event, Philip Berrigan invaded a draft-board office and poured blood into the files of draft documents. In addition to these dramatic acts of protest, both brothers wrote and spoke extensively against the war in Vietnam. Daniel Berrigan, in addition to his roles of priest and protester, produced a large body of poetry that received national recognition throughout his career. One lead in connecting the Berrigans to the composition of Bernstein's *Mass* was provided by J. Edgar Hoover, director of the FBI, in a memo to the Nixon White House. As reported by the journalist Jack Anderson, Hoover wrote warning of "proposed plans of antiwar elements to embarrass the United States government" with this new work.[78] Having received reports that Bernstein had asked Daniel Berrigan to write the Latin text for *Mass*, Hoover was concerned that the president would applaud the performance without understanding the subversive text. (As noted previously, the Latin text used in the work is borrowed directly from the Catholic Mass; any subversive "antigovernment" text is presented in standard American English.) Hoover's source reported that "the newspapers would be given the story the following day that the President and other high-ranking government officials applauded an anti-government song."[79] Bernstein had publicly expressed his support for the Berrigans by holding a benefit party for their defense fund on 12 May 1971. Because of this open display of support, *Mass* was viewed by several reviewers as a work dedicated to these radical priests.

Hoover's warning that the text of Bernstein's new work had been created in collaboration with Daniel Berrigan would suggest that a textual influence might be discovered by comparing Daniel Berrigan's poetry to the libretto of *Mass*. First, it is important to note that there is some disagreement among the standard biographies of Bernstein as to which of the Berrigan brothers might have provided assistance. In his recent biography, Humphrey Burton states that Bernstein met with Philip Berrigan to discuss *Mass* on 25 May 1971 at the Danbury Federal Correction Institute but that the visit was too short for any significant collaboration to have occurred.[80] In his published prison diaries, Philip Berrigan makes no mention of having met with Bernstein. In addition, it appears that Philip would not have been available for such a discussion on 25 May. He was transported from Danbury the previous day to be arraigned in Harrisburg and was returned only several days later.[81] Joan Peyser, following Hoover's lead, reports that Bernstein met with Daniel Berrigan.[82] If so, this meeting does not seem likely to have taken place on 25 May, for Daniel was recovering from an ulcer in the prison hospital at this time. I have found no reference to Bernstein in the writings of either Daniel or Philip.[83] Furthermore, having read through much of his work, I do not find Daniel Berrigan's poetry stylistically similar to the lyrics of Bernstein and Schwartz. However, the emphasis in the text of *Mass* on social injustice and antiwar protest in conjunction with Catholic imagery is certainly congruent with Berrigan's poetry. Daniel Berrigan's poem "Prayer from a Back Pew" is one example that does appear similar to the interpolated commentary on liturgical text in *Mass*. In this poem, we hear the priest's prayer to the congregation, set in capital letters, through the mind of a poor parishioner whose thoughts appear in italics. I quote the first two stanza pairs:

O GOD YOU HAVE DECLARED TO ALL THE
CHILDREN OF YOUR CHURCH BY THE
VOICE OF YOUR HOLY PROPHETS

> *Well I don't know, at least I wonder. One kid dead,*
> *the old man out of work, the girl on the town not*
> *coming home at all. You get to wonder. If the check*
> *doesn't come I*

THAT THROUGH THE WHOLE EXTENT OF
YOUR DOMINION YOU ARE THE SOWER OF
GOOD SEED AND THE GROWER OF

> *stand in line all afternoon; ache, varicose, dread.*
> *"Good seed and chosen vines!" I haven't seen*
> *anything green in years, the drought kills*[84]

Although I have been unable to find any published reference to *Mass* by the Berrigans, a poem by Daniel Berrigan entitled "Off Off Off Way Off Broadway" seems to refer to the premiere of this work. It begins:

> Sorrowfully helplessly after the cultural event
>   the decent faced people tears on their faces
>   in a pall of silence conscience honed
>   by words by music
>   music and words
>   depart[85]

Preaching peace was certainly within the bounds of the activity of a priest, but vandalism and running from the FBI were extraordinary behavior. Concern about the paradoxical conjunction in the late 1960s of demands for peace accompanied by violence, discussed above in relation to the social critiques of Partch and Schechner, is also pertinent to the reception of the protest activities of the Berrigans. This tension is expressed poignantly in an article on the Berrigans by Gordon C. Zahn, a Catholic peace activist of an earlier generation. Zahn, although not critical of the specific activities of the Berrigans, wrote of being "increasingly troubled by the failure of Catholic peace radicals of this generation to avoid violence."[86] He observed that "[t]oday's Catholic antiwar agitators are apparently gravitating more and more in the direction of the New Left and forming alliances with groups like the Black Panthers, condoning if not actually endorsing the often senselessly disruptive and destructive acts and rhetoric such groups tend to promote."[87] While believing that the Berrigan raids had been successful in garnering attention and public support from those who might not otherwise have actively opposed the war, he felt that these dramatic events may also have turned some individuals away from peace activities. Zahn labeled the protests of the late 1960s as an "antiwar" rather than a peace movement, since violence and vandalism had become prevalent tools of protest. He warned that it was becoming difficult to distinguish the strident slogans of the New Left demanding peace from the war cries of the "ultra-hawks." The aggressive voice of peace activism is heard in an astonishingly violent musical form in the Agnus Dei of Bernstein's *Mass*.

It is at the moment of highest ceremony in *Mass* as the Celebrant, richly vested, begins to consecrate the sacramental objects, that the congregation rebels. The Street Chorus and Church Choir join forces in a ferocious demand for peace. The Celebrant struggles to continue the communion, but his path to the altar is blocked as the stage becomes disorganized and the performing groups intermixed. The entire ensemble rejects the Celebrant's final plea to accept the symbolic *panem* by continuing to call for *pacem*. The music modulates into a heavy blues style and the tone of the text is as crude as its threats: "We're fed up with your heavenly silence, / And we only get action with violence, / So if we can't have the world we desire, / Lord, we'll have to set this one on fire!" Tension and volume build incessantly to a cacophony of improvisation, abruptly broken off when the Celebrant screams "*Pacem*," hurling the chalice and monstrance to the floor. The entire cast falls immediately to the stage as if dead. What follows, entitled "Fraction: Things Get Broken," is a mad scene for the Celebrant. In a catatonic state, he first studies the broken glass and spilt wine, in awe of the violent act he has committed. He then turns on the ensemble, accusing them of having enjoyed this destruction. He veers between an aggressive, mocking tone— at one point ripping off his vestments, violently attacking the altar, and then wildly dancing on it—and passages of quiet, sorrowful introspection. As he demands to know why they have stopped their complaining and shouting, he mocks the music of the preceding Agnus Dei. At the end of this section he abandons them, slowly descending into the pit.

The final section of *Mass*, the Communion of peace, serves as an affirmation of the work's implied meanings and offers an optimistic message. After a sustained silence, it begins with a reprise of the music from the earlier section entitled "Epiphany." Whereas a taped oboe was heard in the Epiphany, at this later point in the work the twelve-tone, fragmented melody is performed by an onstage solo flutist. This reprise has dramatic and symbolic significance, for an epiphany is an individual revelation and this moment is intended as a lesson on the importance of the individual. The earlier oboe statement of this music led directly to the aggressive sounds of the Confiteor, but here the flute line leads to a boy soloist's reprise of the "Simple Song." The boy soloist, representing the Choir, passes the melody to a solo bass from the Street Chorus, thus uniting the two groups in peace instead of in musical violence as occurred in the Agnus Dei. The boy and bass then sing a phrase in unison. The incessant, staccato high Fs in the flute, which have been heard as the boy crossed the stage to reach the bass and then throughout the bass solo, stop only at this moment, when the two performers embrace and begin to sing together. This simple musical gesture, this release of tension at the moment of embrace, reflects a much larger message. For Bernstein, the value of individualism resided in its potential for outward gestures of inclusion—overcoming difference and achieving community were his ultimate goals. Peace is shown to be achieved by individuals coming together in a simple song. At the opening of the work, the Celebrant entered by singing "Sing God a *simple* song." When the boy soloist sings this line near the end of the work, the word "simple" has been changed to "secret." In addition to a possible reference to the Secret of the Mass, this textual change encapsulates the tension between a communal music comprehensible to all, and an individual song of private devotion. Rather than dissolving into a violent musical protest of individual improvisation, as occurred in the Agnus Dei, this section gradually builds from a solo boy's voice to the entire ensemble. The choral hymn and final unison Amen seem to receive the long sought heavenly response when they are answered by a taped voice, "The Mass is ended; go in peace."

A Justified Juxtaposition

The vision expressed in *Revelation* in 1961 of American youth committing acts of violence with religious fervor and united by a group mentality and shared devotion to popular culture had become reality by the late 1960s. Partch's idealization of the individual does not appear to have allowed for the more positive possibilities of group consciousness valued by Bernstein a decade later. *Mass,* though transparent in its political sympathies, is less specific than *Revelation* in its criticism and parody. Bernstein both chastises the aggressive tones of group protest and mocks the official modes of mass religious expression while pointing toward an equally communal ideal. Although their rituals point to divergent moral messages, as conditioned by their separate cultural and compositional contexts, Partch and Bernstein employed similar techniques and responded to similar aspects of American society in these works of music theater.

In the composition of *Revelation* and *Mass,* Partch and Bernstein, each in his own highly eccentric manner, attempted to redirect the course of a nation that to them appeared to be lost. These works are but two examples of the broader tendency in American music theater, opera, and musicals to create ritual performances for the political and spiritual enlightenment of the modern world. Bernstein's *Mass,* in particular, is akin to several contemporaneous works, including Stephen Schwartz's *Godspell* and Andrew Lloyd Webber's *Jesus Christ Superstar.* It is to these "popular" works that we now turn.

14 God in Popular Music(al) Theater

Two Passion Plays, Off and On Broadway

Bernstein's presence in any discussion inevitably raises issues of high versus low in the performing arts. Throughout his career, Bernstein's music posed taxonomical questions and caused considerable consternation for those who felt secure with and within the boundaries of "serious" or "popular" music. Is *Mass* to be considered a work of music theater or of musical theater? Is the Broadway musical a subgenre of a larger category to be labeled "music theater" or is it a separate genre of similar status as "opera?" Ultimately, is much of twentieth-century American opera and music theater to be found on Broadway? Reading the reviews of *Mass* indicates that many critics received the work as a product of Bernstein's career in musical theater. Bernstein's combination of religious themes and imagery with popular music in *Mass* raises other examples from the popular sphere in the later 1960s and early '70s exhibiting similar features and intended for similar purposes.[1] As with *Mass*, these examples were often designed to function as music of both moral renewal and social criticism. In part, this trend was an ecumenical and commercial response to the post-Vatican II employment of popular idioms in the church. It was also an extension of the use of "folk" music by such figures as Joan Baez and Bob Dylan to communicate political and social critiques. The step from politically engaged popular music and popular music in the service of official religious ritual to *Godspell* and *Jesus Christ Superstar* turned out to be rather small.

The musical *Godspell* is particularly relevant to a discussion of Bernstein's *Mass*.[2] As noted above, Stephen Schwartz, the principal composer and lyricist for *Godspell*, assisted Bernstein in writing the English text of *Mass*. Bernstein had attended a performance of *Godspell* in July of 1971 before approaching Schwartz. Whether through Schwartz's direct influence or by coincidence, *Mass* has much in common with *Godspell*, not only in lyrics but in elements of musical design, including the eclectic use of various popular styles. One such element is evident from the musical and dramatic parallels of their openings. In both works, a complex and elevated musical and linguistic style is interrupted and conquered by a simpler form of expression with an obvious theological and critical implication. Unlike *Mass*, *Godspell* arose from a modest and unpromising inception. A drama student named John-Michael Tebelak visualized the work after experiencing spiritual dissatisfaction while attending an Anglican service. *Godspell* was intended to serve as a substitute form of worship for the official religious ritual—as a revitalization of the traditional service. In describing his motivation for creating the work, Tebelak said "The Church has become so down and pessimistic; it has to reclaim its joy and hope. I see *Godspell* as a celebration of life." When asked why he had chosen the title *Godspell*, Tebelak responded "The word godspell is the Old English for gospel and is reminiscent of the medieval morality plays."[3] Spiritual renewal and modernization in *Godspell* were to be achieved through the use of popular musical styles rather than through the creation of new texts. The spoken dialogue is taken primarily from the Gospel of Matthew and the song texts were adapted from the Episcopal hymnal and from lines of the Matthew Gospel. While the music consists of an amalgam of contemporary popular styles, the text retains some of the archaisms of the King James Bible. Schwartz was brought into the project at a late stage to compose the music and to provide additional lyrics.

Writing on *Godspell*, Joseph Swain states that true dramatization of religious experience on the stage requires "that the audience be taken along in the progressive action that is analogous to the experience itself."[4] Swain argues that *Godspell* succeeds in creating a religious experience through its performance by allowing the audience to witness in act I the effects of religious conversion on the lives of individual performers. These performers retain their real names and spiritual identities rather than assume the role of characters and thus maintain a connection with the world of the audience. Every effort is made to bridge the space between the performers and the audience, including the invitation of the audience onto the stage for a "wine break" during the intermission. The popular musical idiom itself serves to bring the audience into the work. In my experience of *Godspell* productions, audiences are addressed directly by the performers and encouraged to join in the singing and choreographed hand gestures (particularly during the number "Day by Day"). Much of the work is structured loosely as a series of prayerful songs and vignettes based on parables. The second act, however, becomes a more formal passion play as the story of the last days of Christ is reenacted. Swain finds this shift to the historical mode and to linear narrative unsatisfying in dramatic terms. He argues that "the subtle anonymity of stage people about whom nothing is known except their first names makes no sense in a traditional narrative that must depend on clearly drawn characters who motivate the action."[5] Perhaps the point of including a reenactment of the Passion was to universalize the story by calling for the performers, constructed as present-day individuals, to participate in the sacrifice of God on stage. In this reading, *Godspell* serves to reenact, as a ritual of moral instruction and spiritual catharsis, the Passion story before a modern audience.

Godspell was one of the most successful products of the movement in American religious life seeking to combine spiritual expression with the energy and festivity experienced through popular music.[6] The show enjoyed a generally positive reception from the religious community, particularly when compared to the response incited by *Jesus Christ Superstar*. Robert P. Ellis, writing in the Catholic journal *America*, saw the creation and tremendous success of *Godspell* as a clear sign of "religious awakening" and "spiritual invigoration."[7] Ellis drew a parallel between *Godspell*'s relation to its audience and the medieval mystery play, especially in its social function. "The medieval drama at its best and *Godspell* both do more than obliterate temporal and spatial distance and reorder our perspective on their subject matter. They foster an intimacy, a sense of community with the audience."[8] The intimate and festive religious spirit of *Godspell* was recreated and experienced in the 1970s, '80s, and '90s by performers and audience members in community theaters, churches, and high school and college auditoriums throughout America.

Another musical theater reenactment of the Passion, *Jesus Christ Superstar*, had been created in England by composer Andrew Lloyd Webber and lyricist Tim Rice in 1970. Prior to writing this "rock opera," a major commercial success in America both in its original recorded form and in its later realization on the musical stage, Webber and Rice had written *Joseph and the Amazing Technicolor Dreamcoat*. In its initial version, *Joseph* was a small-scale work commissioned for a performance at a boys' school by a boys' choir with adult soloists. It was a simple setting of the biblical story and was sung throughout with music consisting of a comical mix of styles. Composed in 1968, the same year as Britten's Church Parable *The Prodigal Son*, *Joseph* can be seen as an outgrowth of the British mystery play revival discussed in chapter 8. Early versions of this work were designed for performance in churches. At the 1972 Edinburgh Festival it was presented on a double bill with a performance of excerpts from the medieval Wakefield miracle plays. *Joseph* was expanded over several years until it grew into a show on the scale and in the style of a Broadway musical. Like *Godspell, Joseph* was performed in numerous church and school productions throughout the United States. It was not so much a work of ritual expression as one of religious entertainment, suitable, at least in its early versions, for Sunday school performance. The relationship between religious expression and *Jesus Christ Superstar* was a bit more complex and far more controversial.

Jesus Christ Superstar was initially conceived as a New Testament complement to *Joseph.* Michael Walsh notes that the new project had the endorsement of the liberal Father Martin Sullivan, who planned to have the first production staged at Saint Paul's Cathedral.[9] However, the new work proved to be a critical reinterpretation of the Passion story rather than a respectful reenactment. In addition, its predominant musical style was more in line with hard rock than with the lighter lyricism that prevailed in *Joseph.* In *Jesus Christ Superstar* the Passion story is presented from the critical perspective of Judas. Webber and Rice's Christ character is a more explicit version of Partch's Dion—an amalgam of the religious leader and the rock superstar. Judas suggests that Christ was just a man and that his death was brought upon him by his excessive fame. Judas speaks an even greater sacrilege by accusing Christ of choosing to die, implying that Christ's hubris led him to choose a course of action that would ensure his fame for all time. "Superstar," the most famous and bombastic hit song from *Jesus Christ Superstar,* issued before the rest of the opera had been written, explicitly questions Christ's divinity, the central theme of the work:

> Jesus Christ. Jesus Christ.
> Who are you? What have you sacrificed?
> Jesus Christ Superstar
> Do you think you're what they say you are?

Rice and Webber created a work that was not limited to a criticism of Christian ritual performance. It challenged, instead, the central story upon which Christianity is based.

Although of British origin, *Jesus Christ Superstar* was a major event in American musical theater and inspired a complex American reception. As might be expected, it was regarded as blasphemous by many, and both the recording and the stage production were met with protest and condemnation. Several writers who had responded positively to *Godspell* felt that the portrayal of Christ in *Jesus Christ Superstar* was purely negative rather than spiritually uplifting. Perhaps surprisingly, the work was received positively by other members of the religious community and was used for church-group performances in the hope of reaching American youth. Clearly, many American Christians thought that Judas's viewpoint did not disqualify the work for religious performance and that the questions it raised regarding Christ's divinity could be answered through supervised, and often heavily edited, productions. As Walsh relates, America was not willing to wait for an official stage version to cross the Atlantic. Pirated stagings of the work appeared in major cities throughout the country, and Webber and Rice and their agent were forced to engage in a legal battle to suppress these unauthorized performances.[10] Following the enormous success in the United States of the recording of "Superstar," a concert version of the entire work was presented on tour. Only after this intensive preview period did the work receive its first official stage performance on Broadway. The long-term influence of this work—as a recording, staged musical, and film—can be discerned throughout the decade after its first performance. *Godspell, Joseph,* and *Jesus Christ Superstar*—along with other examples of religious popular music from the 1970s—provided a foundation for what became the peculiarly American phenomenon of "Christian rock" in the 1980s. Other, more ambiguous manifestations of religious expression in recent popular music are also evident.

Madonna's Morality Play: Lingerie and a Crucifix

The above examples of Broadway musicals and rock operas differ from works of music theater and modern opera mainly in terms of their performance venue and their popular reception rather than in details of their form. How might a music video, perhaps the most commercially successful form of musical entertainment in the past decade and a half, be related to the examples of music theater discussed here? A music video is clearly an extreme form of "total theater" in its combination of music, lyrics, dance, lighting, sets, and film. Although many music videos represent little more than a filmed concert performance of a song, and others present a series of seemingly disconnected images related only tangentially to the lyrics, some videos do present a narrative. These minidramas are either visual realizations of a plot explicit in the lyrics or are newly created plots inspired by the song. The characters in these dramas may or may not be presented as the sources of vocal production. Of course, music videos are generally short performances and, as works of film, lie somewhat outside the genre of music theater. However, as will be seen in the conclusion, recent music theater has frequently employed both video and film on the stage. Moreover, one example participates so extensively in several of the themes with which we have been dealing that concluding this chapter with a music video example seems appropriate.

Madonna's music-video version of her song "Like a Prayer" first aired on 3 March 1989 and inspired a great deal of protest, mainly from American Protestant fundamentalists.[11] The simple narrative situation is suggested by brief shots that are not presented in strictly linear sequence. In the video, Madonna portrays a woman who has witnessed a violent assault committed by several white men and the subsequent wrongful arrest of an African-American male who had attempted to help the injured female victim. The female witness leaves the crime scene after receiving a threatening glance from one of the white male assaulters and enters a church, presumably seeking comfort and moral direction. She approaches the shrine of a black saint and falls to her knees. The statue, resembling the arrested black male, weeps and moves slightly. She then reclines on a pew and enters a dream state. In her dream she falls through the sky and is caught by an African-American woman who tosses her heavenward. Continuing her dream, she opens the cage enclosing the statue of the saint, which then comes to life, kisses her on the forehead, and leaves the church. As she sings "let the choir sing," she turns to see a gospel choir singing at the front of the church. At this point in the dream sequence—assuming that we are still seeing her dreams—she reenvisions the assault and the arrest, shown here at greater length than at the opening of the video. There follows an extended section of psychological crisis during which she sings and dances before a field of burning crosses. The choir then beckons her, and she dances with it while it assumes musical control. She then imagines the arrested man kissing her as she sleeps on the pew. This kiss sequence is interspersed with images of a burning cross, the statue crying tears of blood, and finally of the statue reentering the cage and the cage doors closing. She awakens as the choir begins to exit through the central aisle. After a shot of the statue in the cage, the camera cuts to the jailhouse and the woman mouthing the words "He didn't do it" to a police officer who then goes to unlock the cell of the innocent African-American male. With the support of the black gospel church and choir, and the miracle of the Catholic saint, she has been led to the moral action of telling the truth and defying racism. The video ends with a curtain call and bows, underlying the notion that we have witnessed a staged lesson designed to instruct its audience.

This music video has attracted a remarkable range of critical interpretation. The religious imagery, of both lyrics and visuals, has led several commentators to refer to the video as a morality play. In addition, several writers have discussed Madonna's conjoining of religious and erotic ecstasy. Carla Freccero has pointed to elements of Catholicism throughout the *Like a Prayer* album and has referred aptly to the title song's video as a political and spiritual "melodramatic medieval morality play."[12] Susan McClary has discussed the elements of Catholicism and black Gospel in the video as being "two very different semiotic codes."[13] McClary suggests that Madonna successfully connects the Catholic tradition of religious sexual ecstasy, as represented by Saint Teresa, with the more pronounced sexuality and physicality of worship in the black church. First, McClary argues that, although in the experience of a music video the visual elements may seem to predominate, the music "in music videos is largely responsible for the narrative continuity and the affective quality in the resultant work."[14] Writing from this premise, McClary attempts to demonstrate that the religious and social themes of the video are audible in the music itself and that a clear musical distinction is made between Catholicism and the black gospel church. For McClary, Catholicism is represented by the initial musical "halo" of the wordless chorus with pipe organ, and by the key of D minor. The black church is represented diegetically by the gospel choir and by F major. McClary hears something sinister in the return of the D-minor Catholic music, while the "funky, Gospel-flavored dance music" in F sounds consistently celebratory to her.[15] A reconciliation of these two worlds is achieved for McClary in the coda section, in which D minor alternates with F major. This is a musical illustration of the video's moral: "Within the security of the church, difference can be overcome and the boundless joy of the music can become reality."[16]

While McClary and others have discussed the conjunction of issues of race and religion in "Like a Prayer," two writers have interpreted the video and its reception more univocally, in racial or religious terms. Ronald B. Scott reads the video as a work of social criticism directed against racism: "Despite the fact that much of the direct criticism of this video focused on its so-called sacrilegious imagery and themes, I contend that the real problems posed by the video lie in the manner in which Madonna exposes America's negative and unresolved attitudes about race and racial interaction."[17] Scott argues that the controversy provoked by the video was as much a result of the inherent racism in American society as it was a religiously motivated response. He commends Madonna for using her talent and harnessing the inherent potential of television "to place before the public both the socially relevant issue of racial attitudes and an alternative form of black culture that many would choose to exclude from their consciousness."[18] He discusses Madonna's use of religious imagery in terms of its meaning within the black church, arguing that those who see Madonna's behavior in the video as blasphemous do not understand the style of worship that she is celebrating. "Though the [religious] images presented in *Like a Prayer* can justifiably be considered blasphemous from a strict Eurocentric perspective of religion, they can also be interpreted as a positive and accurate parable of the black experience in America."[19] Scott also considers Madonna, although white, to be within the tradition of African-American divas and to have successfully "tapped into images and aspects of black culture that speak to some of the social and political concerns that have long existed in the black community."[20] One of Scott's primary concerns is to argue against a reading of the video that emphasizes the erotic aspects of Madonna's performance and that suggests a sexual rather than spiritual and moral attraction between Madonna and the black male.[21] Scott argues that what may seem blasphemous and erotic from a white perspective is actually a legitimate form of religious expression in the black community and represents a statement of social rather than religious criticism by Madonna.

One strikingly different although equally positive reading of this video has emphasized Madonna's eroticism and has interpreted her message as one of religious criticism directed against the Catholic Church. This interpretation has been voiced from within the church, albeit from a unique position, by the sociologist, science fiction author, and Catholic priest Andrew M. Greeley. (Radical priests have formed something of a subtopic here: the discussion of John J. Becker's works introduced Father Raymond Bruckberger; Bernstein's *Mass* was connected to Philip and Daniel Berrigan.) Father Greeley has attempted to reclaim Madonna for Catholicism. He declares that "she is one of us—still identifies as Catholic, still praises the strength and backbone Catholicism provides, still carries a rosary even if she doesn't say it much."[22] In his introduction to *God in Popular Culture,* Greeley argues that popular culture is a realm in which one may experience God. He declares that the distinction between serious and popular art is anti-Catholic: "The very comprehensiveness and catholicity of the Catholic imagination ought to find that distinction abhorrent."[23] He concludes that "the Catholic sensibility requires that we keep an open mind about the possibility that experiences, images, and stories of God are to be found in popular culture and indeed that these experiences, images, and stories provide a wealth of material of immediate practical use in catechetics and homiletics."[24]

Having reclaimed popular culture for Catholic teaching and expression, Greeley thereafter had to confront a specific aspect of Madonna's performance style and persona—her sexuality. Rather than downplay her eroticism, as Scott attempted to do, Greeley celebrates it and declares that sexuality should not be divorced from Catholicism.[25] Sexuality coupled with religion does not result in blasphemy. He describes the video as a charming and chaste "morality play," a prayer that issues a challenge to the Catholic Church.[26] Greeley hears Madonna preaching the "sacramentality of human eroticism."[27] He discusses the conceptual problems that Madonna's "resurrection of the fleshy" and her occasional "innocent, waif-like" aspect initially created for many feminists. For Greeley, Madonna represents a positive integration of womanly sexuality with modest virtue—the ideal Catholic woman who celebrates her sexuality as a divine gift. In Greeley's vision, the Catholic imagination "sees no contradiction in the presence of a crucifix between two shapely (and quite adequately covered) breasts."[28] He declares that, as was true for Saint Teresa, "sexual passion may be revelatory."[29]

However, as his parenthetical reassurance that the celebrated breasts are "adequately covered" suggests, Greeley is not completely at ease about Madonna's dress code. Greeley had instructed his readers that "To find grace in a popular artist does not oblige one to accept all the paraphernalia of the artist's style."[30] He had also suggested that "the paraphernalia of the Madonna persona has blinded [her critics] to the message behind the mask."[31] This "paraphernalia" is the lingerie that Madonna sports during her performances. Madonna's celebration of her sexuality is interpreted by Greeley as a mask or sign that can be removed or decoded for its spiritual significance. But is the lingerie the message or the mask? Greeley offers a double interpretation of Madonna's lingerie, as a brash sign to "hardcore" feminists but also as a transparent mask for Catholics. In Greeley's reading, feminists should interpret Madonna's lingerie as a political statement celebrating the power of the unashamedly erotic feminine. On the other hand, Catholics should ignore the lingerie and focus on Madonna's well-placed crucifix. The questions remain, however, whether Madonna presents an image that is only "like" a Catholic, and whether the video is ultimately only "like" a prayer? The crucifix in Madonna's cleavage continues to excite debate.

The issue of religious and ritual verisimilitude has created an unresolved tension throughout these pages. Greeley claims that behind Madonna's erotic mask lies a religious message. Less generous views would hold that behind the mask of religious imagery—in *Mass, Jesus Christ Superstar,* and above all in "Like a Prayer"—there lies little more than a shallow commercialism. Perhaps beneath their masks, Bernstein, Webber, and Madonna were only making faces and sticking out their tongues. From this perspective, the religious and critical themes of these popular works are not seriously intended but serve instead as opportunistic camouflage for baser aims. The masks presented and employed by several of the figures considered earlier are somewhat more enigmatic and raise more serious concerns. Part V will address the unanswered question: Can the exotic masks of ritual and religious expression employed in modernist music theater be taken at face value? Or are other, more pervasive motives and masked intentions in play?

Part V

CONCLUSION: REMOVING THE MASKS

15 Masking the Human and the Misogyny of Masks

We search back for the origin of things, not to copy them, but to learn by what method and in what material they were made.

For centuries they understood in the East that only the masculine mind was fitted for stage performances. The actor had learnt his lesson thoroughly, and was content to hide his person and personality under the mask and the robe, and had learnt to value the result. He was following in the footsteps of nature where the Creator is always hidden.

Edward Gordon Craig, "Sada Yacco,"
in *The Theatre Advancing* (1921)

"Does little master know this picture's story?"

"No, I don't."

"This looks like a man, but it's a woman. Honestly. Her name was Joan of Arc. The story is that she went to war wearing a man's clothes and served her country."

"A woman . . . ?"

I felt as though I had been knocked flat. The person I had thought a *he* was a *she*. If this beautiful knight was a woman and not a man, what was there left? (Even today I feel a repugnance, deep rooted and hard to explain, toward women in male attire.) This was the first "revenge by reality" that I had met in life, and it seemed a cruel one, particularly upon the sweet fantasies I had cherished concerning *his* death. From that day on I turned my back on that picture book.

Yukio Mishima, *Confessions of a Mask* (1949),
trans. Meredith Weatherby

Putting on a mask is a magical act, a charged moment in which a threshold is crossed and a connection or conflation made between mask and masker. In many performance traditions, the act of assuming a mask involves its own ritual. The masker salutes the mask or makes an offering to it before daring to place it on his face. Once masked, the performer may consult a mirror in order to contemplate and come to terms with the transformation that has been wrought. Performers throughout the world realize that masking is not to be taken lightly, that masks both confer and take away power and identity. The mask is commonly understood to retain its power, to embody its spiritual energy, whether in use on a human face or displayed upon a shelf. Clearly, a mask brings spiritual power to the performer, but does it leave any aura behind once it has been removed?

In most discussions of masked performance, little attention is paid to the act of removing the mask and to the human face after it emerges from behind the mask. If a mask were to fall during a ritual performance (an experience similar to that of breaking character) it might prove a shocking, possibly horrifying event. But the removal of the mask following a performance is normally a private act for the performer, one occurring backstage and accorded little significance. As the masker wipes the sweat from his brow, one might wonder: Has the masker's face been transformed or affected by the experience? Has the mask left its mark? Every performer has experienced the tremendous decompression, the shock of postperformance reality. Having sported the mask of a deity or ancestral hero in a ritual performance, the performer's rapid descent to earth and return to the quotidian present can trigger a case of spiritual bends. From this perspective, the human performer appears to function merely as the temporary vehicle of the mask, the disposable servant of the performance. At the end of a Japanese Noh play, for instance, the performers exchange conventional salutations and then return to daily life—magical and spiritual power remain embodied in the mask and in the sanctified performance space.[1] Having performed as Biblical figures, the artisans involved in the production of medieval mystery plays would return to work in their guilds, to their more mundane social functions. (The medieval carpenter playing Christ would not be hailed as the Messiah after his performance.) Without the mask and outside the ritual frame, the performer is often just a performer—the mask, character, and all spiritual power remain behind. Likewise, the audience in ritual theater is conceived of as a congregation or group of worthy initiates only within the framework of the actual performance. Ritual theater does, however, observe a fundamental law of conservation. Spiritual power and sacred status do not evaporate into thin air at the end of the performance; they return to the source from whence they came: the mask, the god, the author.

In this chapter, I will reconsider masked performance in music theater, addressing the possible implications of the mask for the performer. I will also look behind the modernist devotion to exotic models of ritualized, "total" performance in order to investigate what deeper motives—conscious or unconscious—may be at play in these works. Statements of authorial intent tend to offer appreciations of exotic models and reports of how these models served in the creation of the work and how they were transcended. In most of the examples considered here, the aspiration to create music theater serving a higher spiritual or political purpose was clear, however nebulous the specific function of the given work. One is repeatedly left wondering what these "rituals" were meant to bring about, and who or what was worshipped or transformed. I find that the exotic masks valued by the modernists were often adopted not only to encode the work as a ritual and to transform the performer, but to exclude certain performers and more forcefully to assert authorial control. As Craig indicates, the modernist investigation of exotic models sought to determine "by what method and in what material they were made," rather than to discover what social or religious purposes they served.

Craig's provocative and influential writings do not only provide an outline of the general modernist performance aesthetic; they also disclose some of the ulterior motives behind the modernist attraction to exotic models. The striking quotation heading this chapter reveals two such motivations. Exotic models "taught" the modernists that only male performers should appear on stage and that the performer should suppress his individuality beneath the mask in order to function as a devoted servant of the performance. This particular quotation was provoked by the appearance of the Japanese actress Sada Yacco on the stage. Craig argues that although some changes in Japanese society are necessary and are to be encouraged (such as the adoption of Western tools of warfare), the "innovation" of allowing a woman to appear in Japanese theater "was a pity."[2] "There can be no hesitation in saying that she is doing both the country and its theatre a grievous wrong," Craig declares. He offers three justifications for his assertion that only men are suitable as performers. First, he claims, all-male performance is a natural law, one the Japanese learned long ago "as children learn from Nature."[3] Second, the use of female performers results in economic catastrophe, for women are willing to perform for less pay and therefore tend to drive male performers into poverty and unemployment. And in a final "explanation," he states that "men take themselves very seriously as artists, and the mimic world becomes for them the real world. With women it is quite different."[4] Providing his own emphasis, Craig declares *"Before the art of the stage can revive women must have passed off its boards"*[5] and ends this article by calling for "a masculine theatre. And then the Masks—!"[6] Although misogynistic outbursts frequently occur in Craig's writings, it was the appearance of a Japanese woman on the stage that provoked his most vehement declaration. The exotic woman needed to be silenced and banished from the stage with special urgency, for if the "timeless" exotic model were ever to change, then a major argument supporting the modernist ideal of all-male ritual performance would be lost.

In these statements, Craig offers an extreme view concerning the importance of exotic models of masked performance. However, as I have claimed from the outset, extreme manifestations and examples from the margins tend to highlight features that are less overt but nevertheless present in the mainstream. Although others considered here may not have made such pointed statements, their works frequently imply concurrence. The incessant call for a form of theater that would transcend the mundane function of entertainment can be understood in part as a panicked reaction to the social rituals of public adulation for the opera diva, the prima ballerina, and the leading lady. Traces of this attitude have been evident in several of the examples discussed in earlier chapters. Ida Rubinstein, in particular, appears to have inspired resentment in her male collaborators. Both d'Annunzio and Claudel bound her to a stake—d'Annunzio seeming to take particular pleasure in the image of her body being shot full of arrows—and Stravinsky expressed a desire to restrict her performance role. Misogyny assumed multiple forms in modernist music theater. Brecht avoided acknowledging the role of his female collaborators, while Partch expressed his distaste for American women in his Bacchic allegory set in a contemporary courthouse park. Several modernists expressed admiration for the gender ambidexterity of the male exotic performer. Inspired by his experience of Noh and by his vision of medieval Christian theater, Britten leapt at the permission they gave him to employ all-male casts, to dress Peter Pears in drag, and to allow boys to sing the seductive temptations of prostitutes. More explicit misogynist views are not hard to find among earlier modernists. Cocteau offered the following aphorism: "The creative artist must always be partly man and partly woman, and the woman part is almost always unbearable."[7] The use of masks in modernist music theater is not necessarily indicative of a misogynist sensibility, nor does the desire for all-male performance inescapably imply antifeminist views. However, modernists did generally believe that the creation of new ritualistic music theater would be a masculine affair. They were determined to bring Euro-American performance in line with the "timeless" principles of their exotic models. Male-exclusive performance was not simply a trait carried over in the process of exotic influence, for modernists turn out to have been quite selective in their adoption of exotic features and were fairly consistent in their admiration for this particular performance principle.

When commenting on exotic theater, modernists tended to exaggerate the importance of ritual and religious expression and to remain blind to aspects of entertainment in their models.[8] Even those Euro-Americans who thought that a particular exotic tradition had fallen away from its ritual origins proclaimed their admiration for the extreme devotion exhibited by the exotic performer and his audience.[9] Ultimately, the modernists were drawn to the (perceived) self-effacement and anonymity of exotic performers, and to the regulated and highly determined form of their performance.[10] Euro-American performers were to be reformed through the development of new genres of ritualized performance inspired by such exotic traditions. Craig suggested that when the masked performer is "content to hide his person and personality" he is then analogous to "the Creator" whose presence is likewise hidden in nature. Nevertheless, I believe that by masking the individual performer, the creator of ritual music theater (whether composer, choreographer, dramatist, or producer) intended to proclaim his own presence and power more forcefully.

The notion that the masks of modernism served as devices to conceal and suppress individuality rather than as tools to ennoble the performer has been suggested before. In her study of masks in modernist theater, Susan Valeria Harris Smith warned that "the mask can freeze, trapping the masker whose real self consequently will suffer arrested development or will waste away. . . . The mask can victimize the masker, reducing him to a fixed state of play."[11] Smith was considering the metaphorical implications of the mask for the character rather than for the actual performer. However, her observation that "it is one thing to assume a mask, another to be forced to wear one; the imposition of a mask by another or others in control denies the masker his identity and dignity" is suggestive of how masks may affect or afflict the individual on stage. In a discussion more specifically focused on the performer, Glenn Watkins has written that, in modernism, the mask may have "provided a scrim behind which the dramatist and composer could once again take command, control their message by means that prized directness and convention, and simultaneously recognize the force of a perennial authority."[12] Uncomfortable with this implication, Watkins offers a more benign interpretation: "In the depersonalization which attends use of the mask the potentially ominous consequences for the artist in the impersonation of self-effacement are typically avoided through their transfusion into a tension-bearing system that allows the playing out of the artist's innermost desires and secrets."[13] Yet Watkins's own quotations from modernist figures indicate that their intentions may have been less generous to the individual performer than he implies. Here, for example, is Fernand Léger on the importance of masks: "The mask dominated the ancient stage and the most primitive peoples use it in creating a spectacle. In spite of the feeble means at their disposal, they realized that the human likeness on the stage hindered the development of a lyrical state, of a state of astonishment . . . the individual must be made to disappear in order to utilize the human material properly."[14] Once again, the exotic and the primitive are cited as justification for making the performer's individuality "disappear" from the modernist stage.

The following description of masked acting in Noh by Kanze Hisao (1925–78), a Noh actor and scholar, would have resonated with the modernists' performance ideal: "The covering and hiding of the face is a denial of both normal acting and of the very existence of the actor as an individual as well. . . . His face is hidden, his movements are restricted, and the singing and dialogue are so set that he is not even allowed to breathe as he pleases. In other words, all normal desire to perform and express one's own individuality is closed off and denied to the Nō actor."[15] However, reading a bit further, the same modernists would have been brought up short by Hisao's perspective on masked performance: "the Nō mask does not obliterate the true individuality of the actor. Rather by sealing off the use of obvious expressive methods and natural physicality, the pure life essence of the humanity of the actor is brought to the fore."[16] Modernist inclinations aside, individual performers are generally more central to ritual performance than are invisible authors. The spiritual impact of ritual theater is achieved at a particular moment, at a specific location, and through the actions and voice of a particular human performer. Whether the performer is a mere receptacle for the visitation of a higher being and a tool of an authorial other, or whether the "life essence of the humanity of the actor" is made evident in the performance, the resultant magic occurs within or through the performer. In many forms of ritual performance the symbolic gestures and sacred chant are taken as a given. Interest is focused on the specific performance rather than on any postulated creator of the ritual (unless, of course, tradition specifies that the rite was created by a deity).

Whether the performer of modernist music theater proved "content to hide his person and personality under the mask," or whether individual performers succeeded in resisting or subverting modernist masking techniques, are questions requiring an ethno-historical approach to the performance of these works. In either case, the use of masks, the restricted and choreographed movement, and the extended vocal effects were employed so that the performer would function as the servant of the work, rather than the work function as the vehicle of the performer. By self-consciously developing their own forms of ritualized performance, by creating new genres and new conventions, modernists were drawing attention to themselves as rite-makers while simultaneously signaling that their work transcended theatrical entertainment and was thereby insulated from normal modes of criticism. Not that this conception of the art work and of the artist was a modernist invention. As Lydia Goehr has argued, the concept of the "musical work" was a product of romanticism. Goehr notes that romantic composers "enjoyed describing themselves and each other as divinely inspired creators—even as God-like—whose sole task was to objectify in music something unique and personal and to express something transcendent."[17] In what way did modernist conceptions, as exemplified in works of music theater, differ? Only in degree, the modernist understanding of the "work" being primarily an exaggeration or literal enactment of an inherently romantic vision. In their ritualistic and didactic works of music theater, the modernists joined the romantic claim for the transcendent importance of the creator and the autonomous work with the earlier paradigm of the artisan-composer whose products were intended to function in society, particularly in the service of worship. Modernist music theater often claimed the power both to transcend the everyday world and to transform its actual audience, even society at large.

Placing modernism within its historical context and reflecting on its bid to influence society at large can suggest some disturbing connections. The modernist interest in creating sacred and socially transformative art is often explained as a reaction to the cataclysms of world war and as a response to the impact of the "machine age" on the individual. Some ritologists have suggested that ritual performance, particularly that involving sacrifice, functions to sublimate violence in society and serves as a form of atonement. Although modernist music theater certainly failed to sublimate the violence of the twentieth century, ritual sacrifice was central to many of the works considered here, including *Le Martyre de Saint Sébastien, Der Jasager, Jeanne d'Arc au bûcher, Revelation in the Courthouse Park, Mass, The Martyrdom of St. Magnus, Naboth's Vineyard, Godspell, Jesus Christ Superstar,* and even *Perséphone* and *Oedipus Rex.*[18] Inventors of music theater were obviously not the only figures in the first half of the twentieth century bent on creating transcendent rituals of sacrifice derived from a heroic or mythic past, achieving total control over their events, and elevating their own status by techniques that suppress the individuality of others. Connections between the aesthetics of modernist music theater and those of "political aesthetes" are not difficult to draw. Most totalitarian regimes develop forms of integrated ritualized performance to transform and control their audiences. Individual dictators create their own rites and cults of control through the development of new systems of symbolic gesture, costume, and salutations. The Nazis, in particular, staged political rallies that were elaborately choreographed and synaesthetic ritual performances—the *Gesamtkunstwerk* manifested in society. (The Nazis even turned to the ancient Greeks for ideals of corporeal power and for models of colossal architecture for the building of the new Reich.)[19] The correspondences suggested between modernism and totalitarianism may appear primarily to inhabit the harmless realm of zeitgeist study. However, a few examples discussed here did have a more direct relationship with modern political propaganda movements.

Modernist interest in creating didactic works for children has parallels in the methods and aims of fascist and communist youth groups. As I noted in my discussion of Brecht and Weill's *Lehrstücke*, the flexible meaning and didactic form of *Der Jasager* allowed the work to be embraced (briefly) by both political extremes. In Russia, Duncan offered her dance for the purposes of revolution. In an article from 1921, Duncan wrote of her encounters with Nikolai Ilyich Podvoisky, the leader of "all the Red Armies," whom she compared to Prometheus, Christ, and Nietzsche. Podvoisky explained that her dance would be of great use: "We are building a great stadium for fifty thousand people. . . . We are preparing great festivals, dancing, songs, music. . . . we are preparing a house for two thousand children, who will be raised according to the ideals of the new world. You must stay and help us with all this."[20] Duncan responded enthusiastically to the call of duty, and averred: "I will teach them [the children of the Revolution] great heroic movements. Your girls will dance, and your boys will dance like Sophocles before the armies, and inspire them to new deeds of heroism."[21] In Italy, performances of *Le Martyre de Saint Sébastien* became celebratory occasions in honor of the Fascist hero d'Annunzio. The attractions of totalitarianism for Yeats and Pound are well known, while Stravinsky's fascist tendencies and anti-Semitism have been recently documented and discussed in relationship to his artistic productions.[22]

To be sure, in the decades following World War II, works of ritualistic music theater (including examples by Peter Maxwell Davies and Alexander Goehr discussed earlier) were also created in direct opposition to authoritarian politics. As is true of the misogynist implications of the modernist use of masks, not every attempt to achieve authorial control in music theater represents an expression of totalitarian political sympathies. Not every mask of modernism conceals something horrendous. The removal of masks does not always disclose secret meanings and intentions.

In the context of modernism, the most perplexing works have been those that employ the features of transformative and ritualistic art but that ultimately seem not to contain any direct message. The apparent vacuum of meaning in these works has frequently inspired their interpreters to fill the charged void. To take an extreme case, Theodor Adorno (in)famously argued that Stravinsky's ritualistic music, in particular, was devoid of meaning and was therefore sinister: "[Stravinsky] is attracted to that sphere in which meaning has become so ritualized that it cannot be experienced as the specific meaning of the musical act."[23] Adorno declared that Stravinsky's music was guilty of "arousing only bodily animation instead of offering meaning,"[24] a criticism that Adorno viciously applied to jazz and one that he might have used for the corporeal music of Partch, had he encountered it. For Adorno, this lack of referential meaning aligns Stravinsky with mental illness and worse. The rituals of totalitarian politics may also appear to be empty of external significance, pointing primarily to their own glorification (and, perhaps, prejudices). Methods of performative control and displays of power may aim at nothing beyond the perpetuation of control and power. In his final (psycho)analysis of Stravinsky, Adorno imagines that "his work plays the fool, thus offering its own grimace for practical purposes. It bows mischievously before the audience, removes the mask, and shows that there is no face under it, but only an amorphous knob."[25] The masks of modernist music theater—the trappings of exotic ritualization that seem to promise such profound meanings and transformative experiences—may often conceal little more than an inflated authorial ego.

Adorno's "amorphous knobs" of modernism continue to entice us to interpret these blank slates and to draw connections to their cultural context. But as is true whenever we "make connections"—whether between cultures, between an author's life and works, or between academic disciplines—we should not draw them casually. Having recognized the unsettling correspondences between modernist art and political history, we must then make certain to observe the crucial differences that persist between the staged presentation of rituals of sacrifice and their enactment in the world, between strategies of control in theatrical performance and methods of domination in mass society. In making connections, we must honor difference as well as similarity, lest we risk slandering the merely suggestive and thus indirectly dilute the horror of the actual. Of course, such interpretive concerns transcend the study of modernism. In more recent ("postmodern") music theater and opera, the methods and materials of ritualized performance and expression have become increasingly diverse and complex, even as the meanings and moral messages have grown more transparent.

16   Music Theater Now

Music theater is often treated as something of a caretaker genre that flour-
ished in the 1960s and ended with opera's alleged return in the 1970s.[1] I believe that just as reports of opera's death were exaggerated, so have been
proclamations of its rebirth. Many "operas" composed in the past two
decades could be better described by the term "music theater." Distinctions
between opera and music theater continue to be measured against the ideals
of total theater. As Meredith Monk puts it, "I have always been very interested in a form that has the possibility of combining music, dance, and visual images, and so for many, many years I have been calling my works
'opera' even though they're not really opera within the European tradition.
They're much more attempts to integrate all human resources into one
form."[2] Several contemporary works that closely fit the operatic mold have
incorporated techniques first explored in experimental music theater. In addition to enriching opera, music theater has continued to diversify into myriad forms of multimedia and performance art and has encouraged the emer-
gence of theatrical elements in concert works.[3] Such extreme diversification
would suggest that in recent decades music theater was both everywhere
and nowhere. As avant-garde composers, dramatists, and theater directors
came to realize the dictums of Shakespeare and Cage—that theater knows
no bounds—music theater of staged performance and narrative structure
became less prominent. Several features of modernist music theater considered here have become so generalized that they can now no longer be interpreted as distinctive. For example, the concept of a composer "masking"
the individual human voice through the use of extended vocal techniques
loses some of its relevance when individual performers, such as Laurie Anderson, are celebrated and recognized for specializing in these experimental vocal styles. (In performance art, moreover, the creator and performer

are often one.) Rather than being reserved for staged theater works of ritualized performance, aspects of choreographed "performance ritual" have
appeared in musical compositions of all types.[4]

Within the myriad new forms that music theater has taken, recent examples do exist that more closely resemble those modernist works considered above. Some recent works demonstrate not only a continued interest
in music theater but the persistence of many of the same basic features and
concerns, including experimentation with forms of total theater, the influence of exotic music and performance models, an interest in ritual function,
and the use of music theater for social criticism.[5] Rather than survey such
works, I have chosen to conclude this study by considering three specific
examples completed within a year of one another in the United States and
associated with the annual Next Wave festivals at the Brooklyn Academy
of Music (BAM), a primary venue for new music theater. Each of these works
features a different subset of the themes considered in the modernist examples. In some dimensions, they are quite similar to modernist examples
and thus call into question the historical division implied by the label "postmodernist." Just as modernist music theater can be considered an extension and exaggeration of Wagnerian principles of music drama and Romantic
aesthetics, these more recent works exhibit connections to their modernist
predecessors.

Njinga the Queen King (1993), written by the African-American playwright Ione, with music by Pauline Oliveros, is a "play with music and
pageantry" that includes dance, martial arts, chanting, speech, electronic en-
vironmental music, African drumming, and masked performers. The work
was inspired by the legends surrounding Njinga Mbandi, the seventeenth-
century regent of what is now Angola. In order to serve as king of her people
after her father's death, Njinga assumed his robes and thus ruled as a cross-
dressed "queen king" who successfully resisted Portuguese subjugation. The
work is framed by the more recent past: a late twentieth-century African-
American female journalist searches for her heritage and encounters the
story of her ancestor, Njinga.[6] Various stages in Njinga's life are presented
in a series of scenes involving multiple representations of the heroine. Just
as the modern African-American journalist is inspired by her encounter with
her African heritage, Njinga is herself encouraged and led through her dramatic life by the voices of her ancestors, particularly her female ancestors
(see Fig. 14). References to the modern world—including CIA involvement
in the Angolan civil war—are interwoven throughout. Thus, the lessons of
Njinga's bravery and leadership are infused with a contemporary relevance.
Her story is reenacted to inspire and transform the modern audience.

Figure 14. Bringing the Ancestors forward in *Njinga*. Photograph by Beatriz Schiller. (Reproduced with the permission of the photographer)

The concept of "exotic influence" is complicated by this work, as it is by much recent intercultural and postmodern music. The flier for the BAM production announced "The music blends ancient African chants, Portuguese church music, and references to Brazilian traditions; the movement is based on Angolan ritual dance and Capoeira (a dance-like martial art, which was developed by Angolan slaves who were brought to Brazil in the 17th century.)" *Njinga the Queen King* makes a bid for ethnic "authenticity," and advertisements for its premiere stressed the inclusion of live musicians performing on "authentic instruments." The inclusion of the "authentic other" is often cited as a distinguishing element of postmodern cross-cultural interaction. However, we must ask whether the use of an Angolan historical narrative and Angolan and Brazilian forms of music and dance by an African-American writer in the late twentieth century is fundamentally different from the European modernist use of the medieval mystery play, or Japanese Noh for that matter? Are the musical and dramatic representations of the Portuguese in this work the primary form of exoticism? Or are African cultures equally exotic to an African-American in the late twentieth century?

Oliveros was initially reluctant to collaborate with Ione on the work, for she felt disqualified by not being of African descent nor a scholar of African music.[7] She overcame these reservations once she had decided to think of the music on three levels serving three functions: her own electronic composition would serve to enhance the dramatic mood; the traditional music performed by African and Brazilian musicians would provide the requisite "authenticity"; and the ambient sounds recorded in the Angolan savannah and in a subway station would create a literal sonic environment for the African and New York City settings. Oliveros is quoted in the flier as saying "In the sound design I want to be able to show the beauty and variety and diversity of the African landscape in sound. And how easily the music blends with it . . . because it's part and parcel of the village, the environment." Technology and cross-cultural collaboration are employed here to achieve a greater "authenticity," to bring the exotic and its assumed spiritual power directly to the work.

Njinga the Queen King is coded as a ritual performance by its dramatic structure (particularly the nonrealistic conflation of historical time), its use of direct narration, its musical style, its stage design (strikingly similar to the ramp stage and placement of instrumentalists found in Britten's *Curlew River*), and by its representation of ritual dance. This ritualization suggests that the spiritual power of Njinga and her story are brought to the present to address contemporary concerns. Ione has stated that she intended the play to be "a message of encouragement and support for Freedom Fighters of all cultures, particularly Africans and African Americans. This work is dedicated to all women." Music theater once again functions in the service of social criticism and spiritual enlightenment but now as a medium for feminist and Afrocentrist messages—concerns quite removed from those of the modernist figures considered earlier in this book (although Duncan would have appreciated the use of heroic dance in the service of feminism.) Audience response at the Lincoln Center Out-of-Doors performance in June 1995 indicated that the inspirational intent was realized for some. Ione's advertised statements resulted in an audience dominated by African-American women. At this production the performers made a celebratory entrance through the audience, dancing to the accompaniment of the drummers, and some audience members joined in the dancing at various points throughout the performance.

Ione and Oliveros drew upon their idealized impressions of Africa (past, present, and transcendent) and upon exotic performance traditions and aesthetics for the ritualized staging of their contemporary political message. In several statements concerning *Njinga the Queen King*, they have emphasized their extensive historical investigation of Njinga and their research trips to Brazil and the African quarter of Lisbon. In what ways can this artistic approach be considered to differ from modernist examples and to achieve a postmodern status? Jann Pasler has suggested that the work's postmodernism is exhibited by its willingness to incorporate "the participation of people from other cultures" and by its respect for cultural difference.[8] Pasler writes that "*Nzinga* [sic] is an aesthetic model for intercultural cooperation" and quotes the following statement from Oliveros: "It has to do with interdependence, meaning interaction. Not as someone who is controlling the way things are going to go, it is cooperating to make a story or make a presentation. Each performer or collaborator has a stake in it, is aware of one another in a way that it can develop, can happen. There is an enrichment process."[9] Postmodern music theater hopes to escape certain aspects of modernism—the imbalances of exotic appropriation, the limited knowledge of exotic cultures, and the obsessions with authorial control—by including the "other" in the creative process and by sharing authorial responsibility with the performer. However, the basic modernist quest continues for spiritual "enrichment" through the creation of art inspired by the exotic.

Steve Reich and the video artist Beryl Korot were less willing to claim an explicit political meaning or message for their multimedia music theater video work, *The Cave* (1993). Nevertheless, the subject raises specific and volatile issues. The cave of the title is the Cave of the Patriarchs in modern Hebron, where Abraham and Sarah are believed to be buried and where both Jews and Muslims pray. (This is also the cave where on 25 February 1994, more than a year after the completion of *The Cave*, a Jewish fundamentalist massacred Muslims at prayer.) This work has been hailed as "one of the most radical redefinitions of opera the waning century has witnessed" and described as being "part MTV, part documentary, part music theater."[10] The performance takes place on a three-level scaffolding containing five large video screens. The remaining cubicles are reserved for the instrumentalists and four vocalists (see Fig. 15). This conjoining of recorded sound and image with live performers is central to the work and to much recent music theater.

There is no conventional plot or dramatic narrative in *The Cave*. Instead, the text and video images were created by editing material from recorded interviews. We hear and see on the screens individual interviewees piecing together bits of the story of Abraham and his children. The speakers in each act include scholars, artists, writers, and religious figures. (The final spoken text is from an interview with Daniel Berrigan.) The work is structured in three acts in which the story is addressed from three different cultural perspectives. In each act, the speech- or sound-bites of the "talking heads" respond to questions concerning the identity of the principal Biblical figures

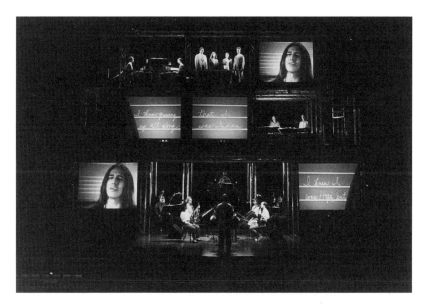

Figure 15.   Video as theater, *The Cave*. Photograph by Andrew Pothecary.
(Attempts to locate the photographer for permission were unsuccessful)

(Abraham, Sarah, Hagar, Ishmael, and Isaac) and provide commentary on
the stories of the casting out of Hagar, the near sacrifice of Isaac, and the
meaning of the cave. In act I, the interviewees are Israeli Jews. The relevant
texts from Genesis—sung by four soloists or heard and seen as "typing music" played on computer keyboards—are interspersed between the sections
of spoken response. In the second act, Palestinians answer such questions
as "Who is Ibrahim?" "Who is Hajar?" and provide their own commentary
on the story. Their speech is echoed in the music of the vocalists. In act III,
these questions are asked of people in New York City and Austin, Texas, and
sections of the Genesis text are sung by the vocal quartet.

Concerning the origins of *The Cave,* Reich has said that the initial motivation had nothing to do with the Cave of the Patriarchs nor with any particular content: "The true underpinnings were our interest in making a new
kind of musical theater based on videotaped documentary sources. The idea
was that you would be able to see and hear people as they spoke on the video-
tape and simultaneously you would see and hear on-stage musicians dou-
bling them—actually playing their speech melodies as they spoke."[11] Reich
has argued that contemporary subjects and themes require new theatrical
forms and contemporary vocal idioms. Both Reich and Korot acknowledge
the influence of popular music videos, which Reich has referred to as "a kind

of urban folk art."[12] Reich also acknowledges the influence of jazz on his musical style. His earlier interests in West African drumming are apparent in the "typing music" sections in this work. The most striking musical feature of *The Cave* is the relationship between the text and musical setting of the interviewee responses. In theory, there is no "relationship" or separation between text and music, for this vocal music consists of sampled speech from those interviewed in the documentary process and the instrumental accompaniment and live vocal parts are composed to mimic the speech melodies of the individual speakers. Korot has said that in this work, "the person speaking became embedded in a musical and visual portrait of him or herself," and Reich has insisted that "the speech melody of each person really is . . . *their* melody and I begin by writing it down as dictation. I have to find out the exact notes, rhythm, and tempo of what they say."[13] As was true of the use of African and Brazilian drumming and dance in *Njinga,* Reich sought something of a documentary authenticity in this work. In addition to his alleged fidelity to the spoken responses of the interviewees, we hear a taped Torah reading in act I, and in act II taped Qur'anic recitation. Acts I and II both conclude with a section consisting of the recorded ambient sound of people at prayer at the cave site. While in the mosque, Reich heard an "implied A minor sound" in this ambient noise, and so he supported this taped "authentic" sound with an instrumental A-minor drone.

Reich and Korot have emphasized that the entire work grew from the documentary material and thus from the interviewed people themselves.[14] All of the video material was derived from within the actual frame of the interviewee's image, just as the melodies were dictated by their speech. By employing recorded material, Reich and Korot succeeded in avoiding the need for live actors—the interviewees are simultaneously performers and characters. However, their attempts to distance themselves from the work's implications are less convincing. When asked about the work's political import, Korot replied "we attempted to steer away from the politics of the Middle East and the Arab/Israeli conflict. . . . However, insofar as the main actors of this work are the interviewees speaking today, politics inevitably seeps in around the edges."[15] Reich and Korot have denied that *The Cave* was intended as a statement on the Mideast peace process. In fact, following the massacre at Hebron, they wrote: "We do not think that 'The Cave' or any other art work can directly effect peace in the Middle East."[16] From their comments, one would assume that this work represents a radical departure from the modernist insistence on authorial control and intention. No longer are live performers manipulated by the composer and director—the performers appear to create the work themselves. Although Reich and Korot have implied that they are mere neutral observers and producers of a documentary-based work, their presence and intention is clear throughout and their exercise of authorial control was all that a modernist could wish.

Reich and Korot's emphasis on the authority of the documentary material—on the agency of the speakers (the others), rather than the authors—is misleading. Although every melodic shape and visual image derives from the taped material, voice and image have rarely been more firmly under a creator's command. From his descriptions of the vocal music, one might assume that Reich had realized the ideal of "words as music" proclaimed by such figures as Yeats and Partch. However, the speech of the interviewees was edited and "composed" through sampling. Not only is this speech fragmented and repeated by Reich, but what we are allowed to hear has been entirely preselected, as were the people to be interviewed. The composer chose what bits of speech would be used, in what order they would be heard, and how intelligible they would be. This vocal music is no mere "found object." The authors have engaged in the multi-dimensional masking and recomposing of their sources through the assistance of recording technology, and have thus exhibited full traditional control over their "performers."

Although *The Cave* may not be concerned with proclaiming a contemporary political message, it nevertheless seeks to bring about a transformation in its audience through the performance. In the first two acts, the importance of the cave and of Abraham/Ibrahim for the exotic Jewish and Muslim others is put on display. In contrast, the predominant response of the American voices in the third act is one of secular indifference. *The Cave* is aimed directly at such areligious American audiences. Korot has said: "In Act 3 the 'cave' comes home, and the audience, mostly Western, is asked to reflect on itself."[17] Reich has made clear, both in his statements and in his musical setting of the American responses (the vocalists' echoing of the interviewees' speech sounds mocking at certain points), that he views America's indifference to the cave as a spiritual failing: "They [Jews and Arabs in the Middle East] aren't looking for something; they *have* something. They know where they're from, and they're happy still being there and living that. Whereas for the Western Odyssean person, it's the searching that counts. In the American section of our piece you can see some people shedding the spiritual concern."[18] As in modernist works of exotic influence, the journey "out there" and the voices of the others, are intended to enlighten those back home. In its call to spirituality for an aimless America, the message of *The Cave* is not so different from certain earlier works of American music theater, such as Bernstein's *Mass* and Schwartz's *Godspell*. When asked what message the audience should take away, Reich answered that the cave and its spiritual power awaits all lost Americans: "Maybe you've dismissed it, or ignored it for a long time. But you're free to return to it. You came from here. Do you wish to keep your distance or do you want to reacquaint yourself?"[19] Underlying *The Cave* is the old assumption that there exists an ideal that can be returned to, that the author is in touch with the true path, and that music theater can lead an audience to it. Reich and Korot note that in Jewish mystical sources, the Cave of the Patriarchs is said to be a passageway back to the Garden of Eden. *The Cave* suggests that if all of Abraham's children were only willing to return to the source, to reenter the single monotheistic cave, paradise could be regained. One is reminded of Whitman's dream of cultural and spiritual unification, and of his salute and invitation to the world to follow his chant to the promised land.

Our final work, less clearly a form of music theater, may indicate one possible future for the genre. Richard Einhorn's *Voices of Light* (1994), "an opera/oratorio for voices and amplified instrumental ensemble in celebration of Joan of Arc," offers multiple points of contact with works considered earlier. It was inspired by Carl Dreyer's 1928 silent film *The Passion of Joan of Arc*, and was, in its original version, to be performed as a musical counterpart to the screening of the film.[20] At the BAM performance in October 1995, the singers and musicians were dressed in black and placed below the stage.[21] Einhorn's use of film differs from that found in Philip Glass's 1994 setting of Cocteau's film *La Belle et la bête*, in that Einhorn does not set the text of the film nor does he attempt exact synchronization.[22] *Voices of Light* resembles earlier medievalist examples of music theater (most obviously Claudel and Honegger's *Jeanne d'Arc au bûcher*), not only in its subject matter but in its reference to medieval music.

Einhorn's musical style in this work is a form of minimalism inspired by medieval European music—or rather, by modern recorded renditions of medieval musical performance. Some of the rhythmic character, the multilingual nature of the layered texts (sung in Latin, Old French, and Old Italian), and the general vocal quality were inspired by Einhorn's interest in the medieval motet. His composition can be viewed in light of the recent popular interest in medieval chant and polyphony and as a manifestation of what has become an international style of minimalist medievalism, led by the "Eastern European mystics" Henryk Górecki and Arvo Pärt.[23]

No single performer represents Joan or her voice in *Voices of Light*. Instead, excerpts from her dictated military correspondence are sung by four female voices. The performing group Anonymous 4 assumes this role on the recording, thus lending their particular authority to Einhorn's medievalist style. The multiple representation of the voice of Saint Joan accords with numerous settings of spiritual voices in modernist music theater. Einhorn's musical medievalism also involves the literal incorporation of exotic sounds, a form of "authenticity" encountered in *Njinga* and *The Cave*. In the spirit of Ida Rubinstein, Einhorn embarked on a "Joan of Arc pilgrimage" in preparation for this work. While at Joan's birthplace in Domremy, he employed a DAT recorder to capture the sound of the village church bells. Einhorn has said "I felt that Joan, who so loved churchbells, whose voices seemed to speak to her whenever they were ringing, would appreciate the effort."[24] In *Jeanne d'Arc*, Honegger employed the exotic electronic sound of the ondes Martenot for Joan's bells; in the 1990s, technology assists in achieving spiritual transcendence through a more literal "authenticity."

Whereas Claudel brought Joan to the stage to inspire French nationalism and spirituality, Einhorn presents her as a complex and universal feminist hero: "The piece explores the patchwork of emotions and thoughts that get stitched together into the notion of a female hero. Such a hero invariably transgresses the conventions and restrictions her society imposes. And Joan of Arc—the illiterate teenage peasant girl who led an army, the transvestite witch who became a saint—Joan of Arc transgressed them all."[25] For the text, Einhorn used the poetry of such medieval women as Christine de Pizan and Hildegard von Bingen. These protofeminist texts are to be understood as "the spiritual, political and metaphorical womb in which Joan was conceived,"[26] and as the voices that should inspire us today. *Voices of Light* rejects the image of Joan the "modest maid" suffering martyrdom for her nation at the stake, and presents her as the strong patron saint of contemporary feminism.

Einhorn's *Voices of Light*, Glass's setting of Cocteau's film, and the central role of video in *The Cave* are but three manifestations of the current interest in composing works of "music theater" that are primarily musically supported film screenings. Those live performers that remain visible on the stage in these works are essentially concert musicians rather than integrated "total" performers. In a sense, film allows for the avoidance of the living actor—certain masks and masking techniques are no longer necessary, for the author enjoys a greater control over both image and sound. (The illusory presence of living performers onscreen is undercut to some extent by the minimal theatrical frameworks of these pieces.) In statements issued with the recording of *Voices of Light*, Einhorn indicates that the film itself may not be necessary to the work—that the experience of the recording is sufficient. Perhaps this is an indication of music theater's future, for those works that resist being represented solely as recorded music are less marketable. As music theater itself arose in part from a frustration with the economic infeasibility of creating new operas, so now composers turn away from elements of live staged performance and the challenges of controlling performers to more transferable and marketable forms. Perhaps these works represent a form of "virtual" music theater.

In 1922, Cocteau predicted that "it is there, in this margin, that the future is being sketched. . . . This new genre, more consonant with the modern spirit, remains unexplored land, rich with possibility." While "the future" did not consist solely of music theater, this territory was intensely explored and was found to be "rich with possibility" throughout the twentieth century. I will not attempt any predictions myself. However, it seems clear that an interest in creating works belonging to unnamed genres, in forms of performance that incorporate "the fantastic, the dance, acrobatics, mime, drama, satire, music, and the spoken word," as well as media unknown to Cocteau, continues today. Likewise, a devotion to works of ritualized performance for the purposes of spiritual transformation and social criticism persists. We continue, even with the benefit of our postmodern heightened awareness, to "search back for the origin of things," seeking the spiritual authority of ancient and exotic voices in order to employ the methods and materials of others for the "expression and embodiment" of our own concerns.

Appendix

Annotated Scenario of Harry Partch's
Revelation in the Courthouse Park

Chorus One: Ritual of Welcome for Dion. (Late afternoon in the Courthouse Park.)
1. "Park Prologue": *primarily instrumental; Sonny hides behind tree*
2. "Fanfare and March": *entrance of band, majorettes, Dion and his eight female followers down aisle in auditorium; ecstatic reception from onstage women*
3. "Forever Ummorra"—First Ritual: *group snake dance with pelvic snap on each "Um"*
4. "Save My Soul and Bless My Heart"—Ritual for Strings and Clog Dancers: *flirtation between Dion and Mom; "Deep inside, way way down I am"*
5. "Wunnantu Anda"—Primitive Percussion Ritual: *entire cast in simple dance*
6. "Heavenly Daze and a Million Years"—Climax of Welcome: *entire cast*

Scene One: King Pentheus denounces the Bacchae. (Late afternoon at the entrance to the Palace of Thebes.)
- *Dionysus introduces himself, strikes Kabuki-style narcissistic poses in solo dance*
- Hymn to Dionysus: "Holy Joy and Get Religion," *leaping Bacchae*
- *Pentheus argues with Cadmus and Tiresias about Dionysus*

Chorus Two: Sonny, ghost-walking, sees himself in a dream vision, offered up as a sacrificial victim. (Early evening of the same day in the Courthouse Park)

> *Dreamlike state; female chorus giggles and flirts with male chorus; couples neck on park bench during the high point of Sonny's psychological crisis. He asks desperately where to turn and is answered by an offstage falsetto male chorus, "Your mother's arms!"*

Scene Two: Pentheus imprisons Dionysus, who then escapes. (Early evening of the same ancient day, at the entrance to the Palace of Thebes.)
- Hymn to Dionysus—"What the Majority Believes," *Bacchae sing*
- *Confrontation between Pentheus and Dionysus, Dionysus sent to jail*
- Hymn to Dionysus—"Glory to the Male Womb," *Bacchae sing*
- *Dionysus escapes*

Chorus Three: In Celebration of Dion. (Later that night in the Courthouse Park.)
1. "These Good Old-Fashioned Thrills"—Fireworks Ritual: *female chorus*
2. "Not So Young"—Ritual for Adolescent Girls and Brass: *female dance, majorettes*
3. "Ishbu Kubu"—Revelation of the Mystic Power: *vocal sounds, snake dance*
4. "Tumble On"—Climax of Welcome: *much tumbling*

Scene Three: Pentheus is tricked into transvestism. (Later in the ancient night, at the entrance to the Palace of Thebes.)
- *Pentheus questions Dionysus on his escape*
- *Herdsman enters with report of the wild attacks led by Agave*
- *Dionysus offers to guide Pentheus and allow him to see the revels*
- Hymn to Dionysus—"Oh, to Be Free Where No Man Is," *Bacchae sing and dance*
- *Dionysus has dressed Pentheus as a woman, leads him off*

Chorus Four: Mom, ghost-walking, witnesses an attack upon her son. (Midnight of the same evening in the Courthouse Park.)

[similar to Chorus Two, but with Mom as soloist]

Scene Four: Agave comes out of the night with a trophy of her power. (Early dawn of the next ancient day, at the entrance to the Palace of Thebes.)
- Hymn to Dionysus—"Hell-Hounds of Madness," *Bacchae sing*
- *Herdsman enters to report on Agave's brutal murder of Pentheus*
- *Agave enters holding mask of Pentheus, believing it to be a lion's head*
- *Cadmus forces her to realize what she has done, she regains sanity*
- *At the instant when she drops the mask in horror, the Coda begins*

Coda: Rays of the early morning sun strike horizontally across the Courthouse Park.

Tremendous musical explosion as mask hits floor; Agave walks slowly downstage with back to audience; Dion appears upstage; spotlights pick up the figure of Dion and the mask of Pentheus; lights fade to darkness

Annotated Scenario of Leonard Bernstein's *Mass*

I. Devotions before Mass

    1. Antiphon—Kyrie Eleison: *total darkness; taped voices in Latin; builds to cacophony*

    2. Hymn and Psalm—"A Simple Song": *Celebrant with guitar interrupts tape; simple musical style; he is invested by the altar boys with a simple robe*

    3. Responsory—Alleluia: *taped voices; light jazz style*

II. First Introit

    1. Prefatory Prayers: *Street Chorus entrance, march-style Latin Kyrie; marching band through auditorium; Boys' Choir entrance; boys play kazoos for one verse*

    2. Thrice-Triple Canon—Dominus Vobiscum

III. Second Introit

    1. In nomine Patris: *Celebrant speaking in English interrupted by taped voices in Latin singing in Orientalist style; Acolytes enter with ritual objects; Choir enters filing into the pews; Celebrant calls for prayer and all rise*

    2. Prayer for the Congregation (Chorale: "Almighty Father"): *traditional hymn style*

    3. Epiphany: *taped oboe solo, twelve tone; then Celebrant begins to speak the Confession in English*

IV. Confession

    1. Confiteor: *aggressive singing by Choir in Latin, interrupts the Celebrant*

    2. Trope—"I Don't Know": *onstage rock band; heavy blues style; rock tenor solo*

    3. Trope—"Easy": *alternation between blues and rock soloists; Acolytes dress Celebrant with ecclesiastical ornaments; section ends with Celebrant's call to prayer*

V. Meditation No. 1 (orchestral)

VI. Gloria

    1. Gloria Tibi: *Celebrant, playing bongos, and Boys' Choir; with joyous excitement*

    2. Gloria in Excelsis: *Choir in Latin interrupts; breathless rendition of the text*

    3. Trope—"Half of the People": *Street Chorus; Acolytes enrich Celebrant's robes*

    4. Trope—"Thank you": *plaintive ballad, soprano solo; Celebrant calls for prayer*

VII. Meditation No. 2 (orchestral): *on theme from Beethoven's Symphony no. 9*

VIII. Epistle—"The Word of the Lord": *altar boys enter with Bible; Celebrant and soloists "read" from Bible and from modern letters in English; suggesting connection between contemporary political demonstrators and the Apostles*

IX. Gospel-Sermon—"God Said": *led by Preacher; sarcastic text delivered in an increasingly nasty and arrogant tone; abrupt halt at Celebrant's entrance*

X. Credo

    1. Credo in Unum Deum: *Celebrant begins to recite in English; interrupted by taped voices in Latin; fast, rigid, twelve tone*

    2. Trope—Non Credo: *solo baritone with rock band; cut off by section of taped voices*

    3. Trope—"Hurry": *mezzo solo; interrupted by section of taped voices*

    4. Trope—"World Without End": *restless mezzo solo; interrupted by tape*

    5. Trope—"I Believe in God": *male rock singer solo; Celebrant demands prayer*

XI. Meditation No. 3 (De Profundis, part 1): *Choir sings in Latin; section of cacophony; altar boys bring communion vessels to Celebrant*

XII. Offertory (De Profundis, part 2): *Choir sings in Latin; Celebrant blesses sacred objects held by altar boys; Celebrant exits; the ensemble dances around holy vessels with fetishistic passion; Orientalist style; Celebrant reappears, the ensemble slowly backs off and exits*

XIII. The Lord's Prayer

1. Our Father: *Celebrant alone at piano, searching for the melody*
2. Trope—"I Go On": *Celebrant sings lyric solo; altar boys wash his hands*

XIV. Sanctus: *Celebrant rings Sanctus Bell; Boys' Choir enters singing joyfully; Celebrant sings with guitar; builds to "Kadosh"; the ensemble brings imaginary gifts to the Celebrant, completely encircling him; the Celebrant hurries to begin communion*

XV. Agnus Dei: *Street Chorus interrupts Celebrant in Latin; this music is aggressive and is punctuated by foot stamps; Celebrant finds it increasingly difficult to continue the service; he momentarily counters them by calling for prayer; stage becomes gradually disorganized, intermixing of performance groups; Choir sings in Latin in heavy blues style and Street Chorus sings aggressive threats to God in English; Celebrant is motionless and silent; music builds to a ffff chaos of improvisation*

XVI. Fraction—"Things get Broken": *Celebrant screams "Pacem!" and hurls sacraments to the floor; entire cast falls to stage floor and remains motionless throughout; Celebrant, in catatonic state, studies the shards of broken glass and the spilt wine; he aggressively addresses the cast, parodying their music and complaints as well as his own earlier songs of praise; he attacks the altar and dances upon it; he tears off his elaborate robes; he returns to catatonic state and descends into the pit; silence*

XVII. Pax: Communion ("Secret Songs"): *live flute solo, same as earlier oboe Epiphany; solo boy begins to sing; he stirs a bass soloist who joins him in song, they embrace; others awake and gradually two chains of embraces are formed singing "Lauda, Laudē"; eventually full tutti; Celebrant unobtrusively reenters, boy soloist sings to him and he answers and is reincorporated into the group; the work ends with full cast singing a hymn and with the boys entering into the audience, spreading the touch of peace; a taped voice says "The Mass is ended; go in peace."*

Notes

CHAPTER 1. DEFINING MUSIC THEATER

1. Jean Cocteau, "Preface: 1922" to *The Wedding on the Eiffel Tower*, in *Modern French Theatre*, ed. and trans. by Michael Benedikt and George E. Wellwarth (New York: E. P. Dutton, 1966), 98.

2. Of course, Cocteau's own stage works were major innovations in modernist music theater and exerted a profound influence. For an introduction to Cocteau's theater, see Frank W. D. Ries, *The Dance Theatre of Jean Cocteau* (Ann Arbor: UMI Research Press, 1986).

3. Andrew Clements, "Music theatre," *The New Grove Dictionary of Opera*, ed. Stanley Sadie (London: Macmillan, 1992), vol. 3, p. 529. I should note that the term has been employed in German musicology in studies of such works for some time. The term also appeared in the mid-1960s in international discussions of the genre. See, for example, Jack Bornoff, ed., *Music Theatre in a Changing Society: The Influence of the Technical Media* (Paris: UNESCO, 1968).

4. Robert P. Morgan, "Music theater," in *The New Harvard Dictionary of Music*, ed. Don Randel (Cambridge: Harvard University Press, Belknap Press, 1986), 522. See also Robert Morgan, *Twentieth-Century Music* (New York: W. W. Norton, 1991), 445–60.

5. Michael Bawtree, *The New Singing Theatre: A Charter for the Music Theatre Movement* (Bristol: The Bristol Press, 1990). Bawtree founded a company devoted to the production of music theater in Toronto in 1975 and established a training program for music theater performance at Banff in 1981. This book offers a brief overview of the development of music theater, but is primarily concerned with Bawtree's vision for the future of the genre and with the explication of his training program and its history.

6. See *Modern Times: From World War I to the Present*, ed. Robert P. Morgan, Music and Society (London: Macmillan, 1993), 452–53. As will be noted in chapter 14, some American musicals and music theater works did have a great deal in common during the 1960s and '70s.

7. Bawtree, *The New Singing Theatre*, 13.

8. See Eric Salzman, "Mixed Media," in *Dictionary of Contemporary Mu-*

sic, ed. John Vinton (New York: E. P. Dutton, 1974), 489. Salzman's emphasis on the term "mixed media" rather than "music theater" was perhaps influenced by the fact that this definition appeared in a volume devoted to more recent trends in twentieth-century music. Salzman has been very active in music theater as a composer, director, and critic. See also Salzman, *Twentieth-Century Music,* 3rd ed. (Englewood Cliffs, N. J.: Prentice Hall, 1988), 100–104.

9. Paul Griffiths, "Opera and Music Theatre, 1961–1975," in *The Oxford Illustrated History of Opera,* ed. Roger Parker (Oxford: Oxford University Press, 1994), 326.

10. Bawtree, *The New Singing Theatre,* 12.

11. For a useful anthology of writings on this topic, see *Total Theatre: A Critical Anthology,* ed. E. T. Kirby (New York: E. P. Dutton, 1969).

12. A convenient entry into the theatrical visions of Schoenberg and Kandinsky is offered by *Arnold Schoenberg—Wassily Kandinsky: Letters, Pictures and Documents,* ed. Jelena Hahl-Koch, trans. John C. Crawford (London: Faber and Faber, 1984), 104–7; 111–17; 148–52.

13. William James, *The Varieties of Religious Experience* (New York: Penguin Classics, 1985), 22.

14. See Mary Herron DuPree, "The Art Music of the United States during the 1920s: A Study of the Major Issues in Contemporary Periodical Sources" (Ph.D. diss., University of Colorado, 1980), chap. 5.

CHAPTER 2. THE MULTIPLICITY OF THE EXOTIC

1. Some have argued that Orientalism in modern music was untainted by motivations of cultural imperialism and was instead a purely positive transaction that allowed Euro-Americans to "extend the language of their art" and succeed in "revitalising their craft." See John M. MacKenzie, *Orientalism: History, Theory and the Arts* (Manchester: Manchester University Press, 1995), xv–xvi. (In his chapter "Orientalism in Music," MacKenzie offers a fairly inert survey of European musical exoticism.)

2. Wagner was himself criticized along these lines for his goals of unification. Adorno, building upon the critiques of Friedrich Nietzsche and Thomas Mann, noted Wagner's "amateurish" devotion to colossal formats. See Theodor Adorno, *In Search of Wagner,* trans. Rodney Livingstone (London: Verso, 1991), 28–30.

3. Penetrating studies of Orientalism in nineteenth-century opera include Ralph P. Locke, "Constructing the Oriental 'Other': Saint-Saëns's *Samson et Dalila,*" *Cambridge Opera Journal* 3, no. 3 (November 1991): 261–302; Michael Beckerman, "The Sword on the Wall: Japanese Elements and Their Significance in *The Mikado,*" *Musical Quarterly* 73, no. 3 (1989): 303–19; and James Parakilas, "The Soldier and the Exotic: Operatic Variations on a Theme of Racial Encounter, I and II," *Opera Quarterly* 10, nos. 2–3 (winter 1993–94; spring 1994): 33–56; 43–69.

4. The following is a sampling of the principal discussions of this topic: Chou

Wen-Chung, "Asian Concepts and Twentieth-Century Western Composers," *Musical Quarterly* 57 (1971): 211–29; Peter W. Schatt, *Exotik in der Musik des 20. Jahrhunderts* (Munich: Emil Katzbichler, 1986); Glenn Watkins, *Pyramids at the Louvre: Music, Culture, and Collage from Stravinsky to the Postmodernists* (Cambridge: Harvard University Press, Belknap Press, 1994), chaps. 1–8. For an introductory survey of the more recent globalization of world music, a process that calls into question the possibility of distinct cultural musics and of exoticism, see Michael Tenzer, "Western Music in the Context of World Music," in *Modern Times*, ed. Robert P. Morgan (London: Macmillan, 1993), 388–410. For a critical discussion of recent manifestations of musical exoticism, see Timothy Dean Taylor, "The Voracious Muse: Contemporary Cross-Cultural Musical Borrowings, Culture, and Postmodernism" (Ph.D. diss., University of Michigan, 1993). A broad historical survey of musical exoticism is offered in *The Exotic in Western Music*, ed. Jonathan Bellman (Boston: Northeastern University Press, 1998).

CHAPTER 3. RITUAL AND PERFORMANCE

1. Victor Turner, *From Ritual to Theatre* (New York: Performing Arts Journal Publications, 1982), 82.
2. Ibid., 81.
3. This diagram appears as figure 2 in Richard Schechner, "Victor Turner's Last Adventure," in Turner, *The Anthropology of Performance* (New York: Performing Arts Journal Publications, 1987), 11.
4. See Turner, *From Ritual to Theatre*, 121–22.
5. Ronald L. Grimes, *Reading, Writing, and Ritualizing* (Washington, D.C.: The Pastoral Press, 1993), 9.
6. For a discussion of Grotowski's ritualistic actor-training, see Ronald L. Grimes, *Beginnings in Ritual Studies* (Washington, D.C.: University Press of America, 1982), 168–74.
7. J. Ndukaku Amankulor, "The Condition of Ritual in Theatre, An Intercultural Perspective," *Performing Arts Journal* 33/34 (1989): 45–58.
8. Turner, *From Ritual to Theatre*, 112.
9. Martha Feldman, "Magic Mirrors and the *Seria* Stage: Thoughts Toward a Ritual View," *Journal of the American Musicological Society* 48, no. 3 (fall 1995): 423–84.
10. Tom F. Driver, *The Magic of Ritual* (San Francisco: Harper, 1991), 83.
11. Ibid., 91.

CHAPTER 4. THE MASKS OF MODERNISM

1. Susan Valeria Harris Smith, *Masks in Modern Drama* (Berkeley: University of California Press, 1984). Smith identifies four types of masks used in the modern theater: "satiric and grotesque; ritual, myth and spectacle; dream

images and psychological projections; and social roles assumed and imposed" (9). Anthropologists of ritual have also categorized the masks of the world by type. Thus, there are types of masks, as well as types that masks represent.

2. Jamie Shalleck, *Masks* (New York: Subsistence Press, 1973), ix–x.

3. On the use of makeup in Kathakali, see Sunil Kothari, "The Use of Masks in Indian Dances and Dance-Dramas," *World of Music* 22, no. 1 (1980): 89–106. For a discussion of the masklike makeup in Chinese opera traditions, see David Ming-Yüeh Ling, "The Artistic Symbolism of the Painted Faces in Chinese Opera: An Introduction," *World of Music* 22, no. 1 (1980): 72–88.

4. Mircea Eliade, "Masks: Mythical and Ritual Origins" (1964), reprinted in Eliade, *Symbolism, the Sacred, and the Arts*, ed. Diane Apostolos-Cappadona (New York: Crossroad, 1985), 71.

5. E. T. Kirby, "The Mask: Abstract Theatre, Primitive and Modern," *Drama Review* 16, no. 3 (September 1972): 9.

6. Ibid., 10.

7. Smith, *Masks in Modern Drama*, 51.

8. Eliade, "Masks," 64. It should be noted that at least one female modernist figure, the German modern dancer Mary Wigman, employed masks in the attempt to increase her "magico-religious" power in performance.

9. Colin McPhee, *A House in Bali* (Oxford: Oxford University Press, 1986), 32 (first published in 1947).

10. "Erick Hawkins on Masks," in *Mime, Mask and Marionette* 1, no. 2 (summer 1978): 109. Like so many other modernist figures, Hawkins acknowledges his model of masked performance as follows: "I learned from the Orient, where people know the premium is not the individual actor, but on the idea, the image" (112).

11. Eugene O'Neill, "Memoranda on Masks" (1932), in Oscar Cargill, N. Bryllion Fagin, and William J. Fisher, eds. *O'Neill and His Plays* (New York: New York University Press, 1961), 116.

12. Ibid., 117.

13. O'Neill, "Second Thoughts" (1932), in *O'Neill and His Plays*, 119.

14. Smith, *Masks in Modern Drama*, 6–8.

15. Glenn Watkins (*Pyramids at the Louvre: Music, Culture, and Collage from Stravinsky to the Postmodernists* [Cambridge: Harvard University Press, Belknap Press, 1994], 310–22) has discussed Oskar Schlemmer's production style and his collaborations with Paul Hindemith. Some producers considered masks to be highly effective training tools in preparation for nonmasked performance. The French producer and acting teacher Jacques Copeau was one of the first to employ masks in theatrical instruction. In addition, he used acting techniques borrowed from exotic models. In 1923 Copeau had his students produce a Noh play as part of their training program. For a discussion of Copeau's use of masks, see Sears Eldredge, "Jacques Copeau and the Mask in Actor Training," *Mime, Mask and Marionette* 2, nos. 3 and 4, (1979–80): 187–230; and Leonard Cabell Pronko, *Theater East and West: Perspectives Toward a Total Theater* (Berkeley: University of California Press, 1967), 89–92.

16. Craig's importance to modernist theater lies more with his written pronouncements of a new theatrical vision than with his somewhat sporadic attempts to realize these ideals. His use of luminous screens as an alternative to realistic stage scenery was, however, widely imitated.

17. Edward Gordon Craig, "A Note on Masks" (1910), in *The Theatre Advancing* (London: Constable, 1921), 120.

18. Craig, "On the Art of the Theatre," 13, quoted in Irène Eynat-Confino, *Beyond the Mask: Gordon Craig, Movement, and the Actor* (Carbondale: Southern Illinois University Press, 1987), 80.

19. Eynat-Confino, *Beyond the Mask*, 80.

20. Craig, "The Actor and the Über-marionette" (1907), in *Craig on Theatre*, ed. J. Michael Walton (London: Methuen, 1983), 82–83. Craig was not the first to express such views. For example, Maurice Maeterlinck had written in 1890: "One should perhaps eliminate the living being from the stage. It is not inconceivable that one would thus return to the art of distant centuries, whose last imprint may well be borne by the masks of Greek tragedians." Quoted in Henri Dorra, ed. *Symbolist Art Theories: A Critical Anthology* (Berkeley: University of California Press, 1994), 145.

21. Craig, "The Actor and the Über-marionette," 86. Presumably, Craig's term "Über-marionette" also referred to Heinrich von Kleist's 1810 essay "Über das Marionettentheater."

22. Eynat-Confino, *Beyond the Mask*, 83.

23. This ambiguity is common to many works of spoken and musical theater that appear to call for the use of puppets but, on closer examination, may actually be intended for puppetlike actors. The conceptualization of the human performer as a puppet was a very common modernist trope, particularly in association with the widespread interest in the *commedia dell' arte*. For a wide-ranging discussion of this topic, see Watkins, "Obsessions with Pierrot," in *Pyramids at the Louvre*, 277–309.

24. Christopher Innes, *Edward Gordon Craig* (Cambridge: Cambridge University Press, 1983), 122. Craig was also interested in the ritual theater of medieval Europe and was especially influenced by E. K. Chamber's *The Medieval Stage* (Oxford: Clarendon Press, 1903).

25. Innes, *Edward Gordon Craig*, 126.

26. Eynat-Confino, *Beyond the Mask*, 83.

27. Craig, "The Perishable Theatre" (1921), in *The Theatre Advancing*, 25–26.

28. Craig, "A Note on Masks," 122.

29. Craig, "A Durable Theatre," in *The Theatre Advancing*, 19.

30. Ibid., 20.

31. See Carolyn Abbate, *Unsung Voices: Opera and Musical Narrative in the Nineteenth Century* (Princeton: Princeton University Press, 1991), 13–14.

32. For a discussion of extended vocal techniques, see Istvan Anhalt, *Alternative Voices: Essays on Contemporary Vocal and Choral Composition* (Toronto: University of Toronto Press, 1984).

33. Quoted in Anhalt, *Alternative Voices*, 10.

34. For a discussion of *Sprechstimme* in terms of vocal masking see Watkins, *Pyramids at the Louvre*, 283–84.

35. A form of split subjectivity is a basic feature in Noh performance. The primary function of the Noh chorus is to assume the vocal part of the major character during periods in which the performer visibly representing that character is involved in the dance.

36. Physical separation and multiple representation are not features normally found in conventional European opera. Even in those special instances in which a singer may be momentarily replaced by a dancer, as used to be common in stagings of the "Dance of the Seven Veils" from Richard Strauss's *Salome*, the character is not intended to be heard as well as seen, and the audience is not supposed to perceive the multiple representation as such.

37. The magico-religious possibilities of the use of nonverbal text in music theater—vocal masking in the service of ritual marking—are noted in chapter 12.

38. Virgil Thomson, *Music with Words: A Composer's View* (New Haven: Yale University Press, 1989), 52.

39. Ibid., 52–53.

40. Antonin Artaud, *The Theater and Its Double*, trans. Mary Caroline Richards (New York: Grove Weidenfeld, 1958).

41. Ibid., 57–58.

42. Ibid., 59.

43. Claude Debussy, "The People's Theatre," in *Monsieur Croche the Dilettante Hater* (London: Noel Douglas, 1927), 98.

44. A. E. Haigh, *The Attic Theatre*, 3rd ed. revised by A. W. Pickard-Cambridge (Oxford: Clarendon Press, 1907) (1st ed., 1889); Roy C. Flickinger, *The Greek Theater and Its Drama*, 3rd ed. (Chicago: University of Chicago Press, 1926) (1st ed., 1918).

45. Haigh, *The Attic Theatre*, 1.

46. Ibid., 2.

47. Flickinger, *The Greek Theater*, 131–32.

48. Ibid., 123.

49. Haigh, *The Attic Theatre*, 242.

50. See Flickinger, *The Greek Theater*, 221–22.

51. Ibid., 223–24.

52. Ibid., 119; 123–24. Although classicists have tended to place a greater emphasis on the text of Greek tragedy, some have argued for a more contextual approach that emphasizes aspects of performance. Oliver Taplin stressed the visual components of Greek performance in his study *Greek Tragedy in Action* (Berkeley: University of California Press, 1978). Lillian B. Lawler has discussed the use of *cheironomia* in the stylized and strictly choreographed dances of the Greek chorus in *The Dance of the Ancient Greek Theatre* (Iowa City: University of Iowa Press, 1964). In his study *Public and Performance in the Greek Theater* (New York: Routledge, 1989), Peter Arnott emphasized the mimetic relationship between the deliverance of text and the gestural dance

and referred to Greek theater as a form of show-and-tell. See also J. Michael Walton, *Greek Theatre Practice* (Westport, Conn.: Greenwood Press, 1980), and David Wiles, *The Masks of Menander* (Cambridge: Cambridge University Press, 1991).

53. Noh masks represent basic character types, and many of the masks can be employed for different characters. For a succinct discussion of the Noh mask see Akira Tamba, "The Use of Masks in the Nō Theatre," *World of Music* 22, no. 1 (1980): 39–52.

54. Benito Ortolani, *The Japanese Theatre: From Shamanistic Ritual to Contemporary Pluralism*, rev. ed. (Princeton: Princeton University Press, 1990), 148. Donald Keene described the mask as the essence of Noh: "Nō begins with a mask, and within the mask the presence of a god." Keene, *Nō: The Classical Theatre of Japan* (Tokyo: Kodansha, 1966), 19.

55. *On the Art of the Nō Drama: The Major Treatises of Zeami*, trans. J. Thomas Rimer and Yamazaki Masakazu (Princeton: Princeton University Press, 1984), 12.

56. Ezra Pound and Ernest Fenollosa, *The Classic Noh Theatre of Japan* (New York: New Directions, 1959), 59 (first published in 1917 as *'Noh' or Accomplishment, A Study of the Classical Stage of Japan*). Pound himself drew parallels between the two forms on pages 12 and 37.

57. Basil Hall Chamberlain, *Things Japanese*, 5th ed. (London: Kegan Paul, Trench, Trubner and Co., 1905).

58. Ibid., 339; 340; and 342.

59. Ibid., 343.

60. Ibid.

61. Ibid., 463.

62. Ibid. Later scholars have continued on the well-worn path of Japanese-Greek comparisons. Peter Arnott was remarkable for having written on this topic from both perspectives. In both his *Greek Scenic Conventions* (Oxford: Clarendon Press, 1962) and his *The Theatres of Japan* (London: Macmillan, 1969), Arnott repeatedly compared the two theatrical forms and included references to the medieval mystery plays, emphasizing the nonrealistic and pure "presentational" performance styles of these three traditions. A more recent comparison of Noh and Greek theater, which focuses on textual style and structure rather than on performance, is Mae J. Smethhurst's *The Artistry of Aeschylus and Zeami: A Comparative Study of Greek Tragedy and Nō* (Princeton: Princeton University Press, 1989). Yet scholars have been careful to acknowledge the differences between the two forms as well. Donald Keene, for instance, compares the use of the chorus in both and notes that unlike the Greek chorus, the Noh chorus makes no comment on the action and "in fact, has no identity, but exists solely as another voice for the actors." See Keene, *Nō: The Classical Theatre of Japan*, 27.

63. Fletcher Collins Jr., *The Production of Medieval Church Music-Drama* (Charlottesville: University Press of Virginia, 1972), 17.

64. See Stanley J. Kahrl, "Medieval Staging and Performance," in Marianne

G. Briscoe and John C. Coldewey, eds., *Contexts for Early English Drama* (Bloomington: Indiana University Press, 1989), 219–37. John R. Elliott Jr. argues that acting in the mysteries was not amateur but of a high quality. See Elliott, "Medieval Acting," in *Contexts for Early English Drama,* 238–51.

65. Meg Twycross and Sarah Carpenter, "Masks in Medieval English Theatre: The Mystery Plays," *Medieval English Theatre* 3, no. 1 (1981): 29.

66. Ibid., 32–35.

67. Thomas Leims, "Japan and Christian Mystery Plays: Christian Kōwakamai Reconsidered," in Ian Nish, ed. *Contemporary European Writing on Japan* (Woodchurch: Paul Norbury Publications, 1988). Leims provides a list of performances of mysteries in Japan in his "Mysterienspiel und Schultheater in der japanischen Jesuitenmission des 16. Jahrhunderts," *Maske und Kothurn* 1 (1981): 57–71. All subsequent work on this topic is indebted to the original research of P. Joseph Schütte, S. J., at the Vatican Library.

68. Eta Harich-Schneider, *A History of Japanese Music* (London: Oxford University Press, 1973), 455–56.

69. Ortolani, *The Japanese Theatre,* 155–56. In addition to this interaction between Noh and the mystery play, several writers have discussed the possible European influence on the formation of the Kabuki theater. Others have written of the presence of Japanese characters and subjects in seventeenth-century European theater. It would be interesting to discover whether secondhand knowledge of Japanese and Chinese music theater in sixteenth-century Italy might have had any reciprocal impact, similar to the influence of writings on ancient Greek theater, on the early development of opera.

70. Fenollosa, *The Classic Noh Theatre of Japan,* 12.

71. Ibid., 62.

72. Copeau's remarks on Noh and the Mass are from a letter dated 9 August 1946 quoted by Leonard Cabell Pronko in *Theater East and West,* 89–90.

CHAPTER 5. HELLENISM IN MODERNIST PERFORMANCE

1. Isadora Duncan, "Childhood in San Francisco" (1903), in *Isadora Speaks,* ed. Franklin Rosemont (San Francisco: City Lights Books, 1981), 25.

2. Ibid.

3. "My Idea of Dancing" (1903), in *Isadora Speaks,* 36.

4. A reconstructed performance of *Bacchanale* by the Isadora Duncan Dance Ensemble under the direction of Andrea Mantell-Seidel and with the assistance of Julia Levien is available on the video *Isadora Duncan Dance: Technique and Repertory* (Pennington, N.J.: Dance Horizons Video, 1995).

5. Isadora Duncan, "The Dance of the Future" (1902–3), in *The Art of the Dance,* ed. Sheldon Cheney (New York: Theatre Arts, 1928), 58.

6. Ibid., 60.

7. Duncan, "The Dance of the Greeks," in *The Art of the Dance,* 96.

8. Ibid., 93.

9. In Duncan's opinion, Wagner had accorded the classical choral function

(detached commentary and critical reflection) to the major characters themselves, thus creating isolated individuals who function as "interpreters of the abstract" rather than as protagonists engaged in the drama. She cites examples from *Tristan und Isolde* in support of this view. (See ibid., 94.) For a discussion of Duncan's criticisms of Wagner, see also Ann Daly, *Done into Dance: Isadora Duncan in America* (Bloomington: Indiana University Press, 1995), 144–45.

10. Duncan, "The Dance of the Greeks," in *The Art of the Dance*, 94–95.

11. Duncan, "Fragments and Thoughts," in *The Art of the Dance*, 131.

12. Duncan employed Beethoven's Symphony no. 5 for her production of *Oedipus Rex*. (Her use of musical masterworks was both revolutionary and widely criticized.) The season also included productions entitled *Orpheus* and *Iphigenia*. On Duncan's "Dionysian Season," see Daly, *Done into Dance*, 150–53. Daly states that "with the Dionysian season, Duncan attempted nothing less than the fundamental re-creation of modern drama" (150).

13. Duncan, "The Dance of the Greeks," in *The Art of the Dance*, 96.

14. Duncan, "Short Statements" (1908), in *Isadora Speaks*, 51.

15. See Cynthia Splatt, *Isadora Duncan and Gordon Craig: The Prose and Poetry of Action* (San Francisco: The Book Club of California, 1988): 25–27.

16. Duncan worked on productions of *Iphigenia in Tauris, Iphigenia in Aulis,* and *Orpheus*—using Gluck's music—from 1900 to 1915. Daly notes that Duncan continued to work on *Orpheus* throughout much of her career and that the work "expanded in scope and in fullness of production, culminating in a drama-music-dancing version complete with chorus and vocal soloist." See Daly, *Done into Dance*, 148–49. The contemporary choreographer Mark Morris has followed Duncan's lead, particularly in his production with Christopher Hogwood of Gluck's *Orfeo ed Euridice*.

17. Duncan, "The Dance in Relation to Tragedy," in *The Art of the Dance*, 84.

18. Duncan, "Short Statements," in *Isadora Speaks*, 50.

19. Ibid.

20. Duncan's commitment to dance as ritual performance, and her devotion to Dionysus as her "eternal god," owed a great deal to her reading of Nietzsche. In a letter to her students in 1918–19, she reminded them that Nietzsche's *The Birth of Tragedy* was her "bible." See "A Letter to the Pupils," in *The Art of Dance*, 108.

21. Duncan, "Dancing in Relation to Religion and Love," in *The Art of the Dance*, 123.

22. Ibid., 123–24. The work referred to by Duncan appears to have been Scriabin's incomplete *Mysterium*. Duncan expressed her admiration for Scriabin in several writings and stated that he was a prophet of the Russian revolution, "with music, not words." See Duncan, "Notes on Scriabin," in *Isadora Speaks*, 79–80.

23. Duncan, "The Parthenon," in *The Art of the Dance*, 64.

24. Ibid., 65.

25. Ibid., 64–65.

26. Duncan, "Short Statements," in *Isadora Speaks*, 58.

27. Duncan, letter to A. V. Lunacharsky, spring 1921, in *Isadora Speaks*, 64.

28. Duncan, "A Great Step Forward" (1921), in *Isadora Speaks*, 66. For a discussion of Duncan's ties to Whitman, see Daly, *Done into Dance*, 10–11; 215–16.

29. Duncan, *Isadora Speaks*, 88. Duncan's *Dubinushka* of 1923 is a powerful example of her "Soviet"-style work. A reconstructed performance of this dance is available on the *Isadora Duncan Dance* video.

30. See Splatt, *Isadora Duncan and Gordon Craig*, 21. Daly has discussed the early twentieth-century craze for "classic dancing" among American women and has interpreted Duncan's use of ancient Greece as an attempt to legitimize dance in puritanical America and as part of a larger cultural program intended to instill high culture into the young nation. See Daly, *Done into Dance*, 100–116 passim.

31. Walter Terry, *Isadora Duncan: Her Life, Her Art, Her Legacy* (New York: Dodd, Mead, and Co., 1963), 101–2. Terry refers particularly to Shawn's dance *Death of Adonis*, in which Shawn appeared with a fig leaf and white body paint on a pedestal—a most literal attempt to represent a living classical statue. The works of Ruth St. Denis and Shawn were most often inspired by their enthusiasm for either Asia or ancient Greece.

32. Craig, "Belief and Make-Believe" (1915), in *The Theatre Advancing*, 66. Craig specifically cited the scholarship of Jane Harrison in support of his belief in the ritual function of Greek theater performance. Ibid., 57–58.

33. Craig, "The Open Air," in *The Theatre Advancing*, 52–53.

34. Ibid., 56. Also see Craig, "New Departures," in *The Theatre Advancing*, 275–76. This topic will be addressed more fully in the conclusion.

35. Duncan, "To Speak the Language of Humanity" (1917), in *Isadora Speaks*, 47.

36. Duncan, "Short Statements," in *Isadora Speaks*, 51.

37. Duncan, "The Dance of the Future," in *The Art of the Dance*, 62.

38. Duncan, "Short Statements," in *Isadora Speaks*, 52–53.

39. For an extended discussion of the importance of ancient Greece for Wagner, see Dieter Borchmeyer, *Richard Wagner: Theory and Theatre*, trans. Stewart Spencer (Oxford: Clarendon Press, 1991), 59–74; 75–86. Borchmeyer argues that Wagner's classical interests were directly connected to his interest in medieval culture (76).

40. *Wagner on Music and Drama*, ed. Albert Goldman and Evert Sprinchorn, trans. H. Ashton Ellis (New York: Da Capo Press, 1964), 62.

41. Ibid., 63.

42. Ibid., 81–82.

43. See Karen Dorn, *Players and Painted Stage: The Theatre of W. B. Yeats* (Sussex: The Harvester Press, 1984), 63–66. The German basis for this movement can be understood, in part, as a distant echo of the Weimar Classicism from a century prior. For an extensive discussion of German interest in ancient Greece,

see Suzanne L. Marchand, *Down from Olympus: Archeology and Philhellenism in Germany, 1750–1970* (Princeton: Princeton University Press, 1996).

44. Dorn, *Players and Painted Stage*, 63.

45. Ibid., 66.

46. Ibid.

47. Dorn suggests that Yeats studied the new classicist scholarship and that his "views of the effect of the stage image and his theory of drama in performance were strikingly similar to Jane Harrison's," particularly as expressed in her highly influential 1913 study entitled *Ancient Art and Ritual* (New York: Henry Holt and Co., 1913). Ibid., 64.

48. On this topic, see Elaine Waxgiser Newman, "Hero and Anti-Hero: The Oedipus Tyrannus of Sophocles in Twentieth-Century Music" (Ph.D. diss., Case Western Reserve University, 1973). See also Ruth Zinar, "Greek Tragedy in Theater Pieces of Stravinsky and Milhaud" (Ph.D. diss., New York University, 1968). George Antheil composed incidental music for *Oedipus* in 1928. Darius Milhaud wrote numerous works on Greek subjects, including settings of Paul Claudel's *L'Orestie* trilogy (1913–24), a short opera entitled *Les Malheurs d'Orphée* (1924), the three 1927 *opéra-minutes: L'Enlèvement d'Europe, L'Abandon d'Ariane,* and *La Délivrance de Thésée,* and the opera *Médée* (1938). In 1947 Martha Graham offered a unique interpretation of the Oedipus legend, presenting the story from the perspective of Jocasta, in her dance *Night Journey.*

49. See Glenn Watkins, *Pyramids at the Louvre: Music, Culture, and Collage from Stravinsky to the Postmodernists* (Cambridge: Harvard University Press, Belknap Press, 1994), 348–49.

50. Igor Stravinsky and Robert Craft, *Dialogues and A Diary* (Garden City, N.Y.: Doubleday, 1963), 4.

51. Andreas Liess, *Carl Orff,* trans. Adelheid and Herbert Parkin (London: Calder and Boyars, 1966), 63–64. Originally published in German in 1955.

52. Ibid., 63.

53. Perhaps to distance Orff from Germany's recent past, Liess emphasized the "universality" of Orff's stage works and argued that his music theater is culturally inclusive. See Liess, *Carl Orff,* 73. A slight suggestion of a more wide-ranging interest in the exotic is found in an early work entitled *Gisei, das Opfer* (1913), which was based on a play loosely adapted from a Japanese source. In other works, a provincial sensibility is evident, particularly when Orff's text is in his native Bavarian dialect.

54. Ferruccio Busoni had published a brief "Sketch for a Dramatic Performance of Bach's St. Matthew Passion," including a drawing of a possible stage design, in 1921. See Busoni, *The Essence of Music,* trans. Rosamond Ley (New York: Dover, 1965), 101–3.

55. The association of Adonis and Christ reflects a general association of Greek and Christian themes that was common in modernist theater. Adonis, Saint Sebastian, and Christ are brought together in d'Annunzio's *Le Martyre de Saint Sébastien,* while in Yeats's *The Resurrection,* Christ is associated with Diony-

sus. Stravinsky's Christianization of Greek mythology in *Perséphone* will be discussed below. An interest in renewing Christianity through classical infusion was expressed much earlier by Friedrich Hölderlin—Orff's textual source for *Antigonae* and *Oedipus Tyranus*—particularly in his poem *Brod und Wein* (1803).

56. Liess, *Carl Orff,* 53.

57. Ibid., 119.

58. Ibid.

59. *Antigonae* was composed in 1947–48 and had its first performance in 1949. The likelihood that this work was intended as a commentary on the recent defeat is nevertheless undermined to some extent by Liess's report that the work was first planned as early as 1940 and that Orff had completed a draft by 1943. See Liess, *Carl Orff,* 119.

60. Igor Stravinsky, *An Autobiography* (New York: Simon and Schuster, 1936), ix.

61. Richard Taruskin, building upon the critique of Theodor Adorno, has pursued this discussion within a broad cultural-historical framework. Of his numerous writings concerning Stravinsky's musical politics, see especially: "Stravinsky and the Subhuman," chap. in his *Defining Russia Musically* (Princeton: Princeton University Press, 1997) and "Back to Whom? Neoclassicism as Ideology," *19th-Century Music* 16, no. 3 (spring 1993): 286–302. In this article, Taruskin discusses Stravinsky's ideology in terms of an "Apollonian" distaste for "Dionysian" Expressionism in modern music (297–98). See also Adorno, *Philosophy of Modern Music* (New York: Seabury Press, 1973), 206–9. Adorno's critique will be taken up in the conclusion.

62. Wilfrid Mellers, "Stravinsky's Oedipus as 20th-Century Hero," *Musical Quarterly* 48 (1962): 300.

63. Ibid., 302.

64. Igor Stravinsky, *Stravinsky: Selected Correspondence,* vol. III, ed. and with commentaries by Robert Craft (New York: Alfred A. Knopf, 1985), 476.

65. Ibid., 475.

66. Igor Stravinsky and Robert Craft, *Memories and Commentaries* (Garden City, N.Y.: Doubleday, 1960), 138.

67. Michael de Cossart, *Ida Rubinstein: A Theatrical Life* (Liverpool: Liverpool University Press, 1987), 168.

68. Michael de Cossart reveals that Gide felt increasingly excluded during the planning of the first production. Jacques Copeau, who had just finished presenting a production of a mystery play in the cloisters of Santa Croce in Florence, was chosen to serve as the producer. Copeau emphasized the religious and ritual qualities of the work and set the performance in a Greek temple. During the production meetings, Stravinsky compared the work to the celebration of Mass and Copeau considered setting it in a cathedral. See Cossart, *Ida Rubinstein,* 169–70.

69. See Stravinsky, *Selected Correspondence,* vol. III, 475.

70. It is more than a bit ironic to consider this ceremonial opening in light

of Stravinsky's sarcastic description of his experience of *Parsifal* at Bayreuth, written not long after composing *Perséphone:* "The very atmosphere of the theatre, its design and its setting, seemed lugubrious. It was like a crematorium, and a very old-fashioned one at that, and one expected to see the gentleman in black who had been entrusted with the task of singing the praises of the departed. The order to devote oneself to contemplation was given by a blast of trumpets. I sat humble and motionless, but at the end of a quarter of an hour I could bear no more." Stravinsky goes on to criticize modern attempts to create mystery plays in "competition with the Church" and expresses his contempt for "putting a work of art on the same level as the sacred and symbolic ritual which constitutes a religious service." Stravinsky, *An Autobiography,* 59–62.

71. See particularly the Nymph chorus (nos. 7–16) and the chorus of Shades (nos. 74–93).

72. Igor Stravinsky and Robert Craft, *Dialogues and a Diary* (Garden City, N.Y.: Doubleday, 1963), 20–22.

73. Ibid., 21.

74. Ibid.

75. Stravinsky, *Selected Correspondence,* vol. III, p. 479.

76. Stravinsky and Craft, *Memories and Commentaries,* 140–41. In a footnote to this discussion Stravinsky wrote: "Since making these remarks I have witnessed an instance of word treatment similar to my own in the Kanjinchō play (Kabuki Theater). . . . a verse dialogue I did not have to understand to enjoy as music."

77. André Coeuroy, "'Oedipus' and Other Music Heard in Paris," *Modern Music* 5, no. 1 (Nov.–Dec. 1927): 39; reprinted in *Stravinsky in Modern Music (1924–1946),* compiled by Carol J. Oja (New York: Da Capo Press, 1982), 97.

78. André Schaeffner, "On Stravinsky, Early and Late," *Modern Music* 12, no. 1 (Nov.–Dec. 1934): 5; reprinted in Oja, comp., *Stravinsky in Modern Music,* 129.

79. See especially Daniel Albright, *Stravinsky: The Music Box and the Nightingale* (New York: Gordon and Breach, 1989), 28–41. See also Stephen Walsh, *Stravinsky: Oedipus Rex* (Cambridge: Cambridge University Press, 1993), 92–95; and Watkins, *Pyramids at the Louvre,* 353–54.

80. Vera Stravinsky and Robert Craft, *Stravinsky in Pictures and Documents* (New York: Simon and Schuster, 1978), 205, quoted in Albright, *Stravinsky,* 35. Albright has discussed Stravinsky's "violence" toward language and notes that Stravinsky seemed to regard all texts as nonsense (29). Richard Taruskin has argued that Stravinsky's text-setting style was influenced by both Russian folk music and his fanciful notion of Japanese declamation. See Taruskin, "Stravinsky's 'Rejoicing Discovery' and What It Meant: In Defense of His Notorious Text Setting," in *Stravinsky Retrospectives,* ed. Ethan Haimo and Paul Johnson (Lincoln: University of Nebraska Press, 1987), 162–99.

81. See Stravinsky and Craft, *Dialogues and a Diary,* 13.

82. Ibid., 5. This statement is strikingly similar to Paul Claudel's directions for the production of his *Choephori,* in which the chorus is to "hold in their

hands a paper on which their part is written, and they will be asked to raise their eyes from it as little as possible." In his comments on the production of his *Agamemnon,* Claudel writes that the chorus should function "as the precentors in our churches, and I would dress them in the same heavy robes, with cope and staff, each installed at his lectern, reading his part." Claudel believed that "the part of the chorus in classical drama is very like that of the choir in the liturgy as it is still sung in the old Roman churches." These quotations are from *Claudel on the Theatre,* ed. Jacques Petit and Jean-Pierre Kempf, trans. by Christine Trollope (Coral Gables: University of Miami Press, 1972), 24–25.

83. Stravinsky and Craft, *Dialogues and a Diary,* 12–13.

84. Ibid., 11.

85. Ibid., 9.

86. Ibid., 3–4.

87. Ibid., 9–10.

88. Ibid., 6–7.

89. See the opening statement in Stravinsky, *Oedipus Rex* (New York: Boosey & Hawkes, 1949).

90. Stravinsky referred to the possibility of performing the work with puppets but wrote that "I am also fond of masks, and while composing Oedipus' first aria, I already imagined him wearing a roseate, ogival one, like that of a Chinese sun-god." Stravinsky and Craft, *Dialogues and a Diary,* 7.

91. Walsh, *Stravinsky: Oedipus Rex,* 15.

92. Although this discussion has emphasized Stravinsky's dominating role in the creation of *Oedipus Rex,* Cocteau's theatrical style remained evident in the work. For a thorough study of the collaboration between Cocteau and Stravinsky, including an extensive survey of their performance aesthetics prior to *Oedipus,* see Dieter Möller, *Jean Cocteau und Igor Strawinsky: Untersuchungen zur Ästhetik und zu "Oedipus Rex"* (Hamburg: Karl Dieter Wagner, 1981). See also Frank W. D. Ries, *The Dance Theatre of Jean Cocteau* (Ann Arbor: UMI Research Press, 1986).

93. Jean Cocteau, "Preface to *The Wedding on the Eiffel Tower,*" in *Modern French Theatre: The Avant-Garde, Dada, and Surrealism,* ed. and trans. Michael Benedikt and George E. Wellwarth (New York: E. P. Dutton, 1966), 97.

94. Ries, *The Dance Theatre of Jean Cocteau,* 147.

95. This production actually disobeys Stravinsky's instructions not only by allowing the principal singers to move but also by leaving their faces uncovered—the "masks" are placed on extended headpieces rather than over the face.

CHAPTER 6. THE USES OF NOH

1. David Remnick, "Reading Japan," *New Yorker* (6 February 1995): 43. One prominent and provocative work that resonates strongly with Oe's remarks is Roland Barthes, *Empire of Signs,* trans. Richard Howard (New York: Hill and Wang, 1982).

2. Arthur Waley, *The Nō Plays of Japan* (Rutland, Vt.: Charles E. Tuttle, 1976), 17.

3. Several general studies have been written on the subject of Japanese influence. See particularly Earl Miner, *The Japanese Tradition in British and American Literature* (Princeton: Princeton University Press, 1958); Sang-Kyong Lee, *Nō und europäisches Theater* (Frankfurt am Main: Peter Lang, 1983); and Leonard Cabell Pronko, *Theater East and West: Perspectives Toward a Total Theater* (Berkeley: University of California Press, 1967).

4. For further discussions of Craig's influence on Yeats, see Liam Miller, *The Noble Drama of W. B. Yeats* (Dublin: The Dolmen Press, 1977), 49–52, 74–84, 147–87; Karen Dorn, *Players and Painted Stage* (Sussex: The Harvester Press, 1984), 13–33; and James W. Flannery, "W. B. Yeats, Gordon Craig and the Visual Arts of the Theatre," in Robert O'Driscoll and Lorna Reynolds, eds., *Yeats and the Theatre* (Niagara Falls: Maclean-Hunter Press, 1975), 82–108.

5. See Masaru Sekine and Christopher Murray, *Yeats and the Noh: A Comparative Study*, Irish Literary Studies 38 (Gerrards Cross, Buckinghamshire: Colin Smythe, 1990), 6–7.

6. Several monographs and numerous articles have been devoted to a detailed comparative study of Noh theater and Yeats's plays. In addition, the Pound-Fenollosa translations and descriptions of Noh, and Pound's own plays based on his impressions, have also received critical attention. See Nobuko Tsukui, *Ezra Pound and Japanese Noh Plays* (Washington, D.C.: University Press of America, 1963).

7. Yeats, introduction to Ezra Pound and Ernest Fenollosa, *Certain Noble Plays of Japan* (Churchtown [Ireland]: Cuala Press, 1916), 1.

8. Ibid., 2; 14.

9. These four plays were published jointly in 1921 as W. B. Yeats, *Four Plays for Dancers* (New York: Macmillan, 1921). A fifth play cited by Yeats as based on Japanese theater, *The Cat and the Moon* (1926), was intended to represent a *kyogen* play—a comic form performed in the interval between performances of Noh plays.

10. A detailed comparison between each play and its Noh model is offered in Sekine and Murray, *Yeats and the Noh: A Comparative Study*.

11. While *Nishikigi* inspired thoughts of Irish legend in the mind of Yeats, Pound imagined a correspondence to another famous pair of ill-fated lovers, as is evident in his 1916 play *Tristan*, which was based on *Nishikigi*. See Pound, *Plays Modelled on the Noh*, ed. Donald C. Gallup (Toledo: The Friends of the University of Toledo Libraries, 1987).

12. Yeats, introduction to *Certain Noble Plays of Japan*, 7.

13. Yeats, *Autobiographies* (London: Macmillan, 1955), 189.

14. Yeats, *Four Plays for Dancers*, vi.

15. Yeats wrote that *The Only Jealousy of Emer* was written "to find what dramatic effect one could get out of a mask, changed while the player remains upon the stage to suggest a change of personality." Ibid. Susan R. Gorsky has

suggested that in Yeats's dance plays, masks serve to enhance the archetypal roles of the legendary characters. Gorsky, "A Ritual Drama: Yeats's Plays for Dancers," *Modern Drama* 17, no. 2 (June 1974): 170–74.

16. Yeats, introduction to *Certain Noble Plays of Japan*, 1. Yeats is one of several modernist figures to have been interested in all three of the major forms of exotic influence considered here. As Richard Taylor has noted in *The Drama of W. B. Yeats: Irish Myth and the Japanese Nō* (New Haven: Yale University Press, 1976), "More often than not, his antique and exotic subject matter was realized within established historical forms; particularly the medieval [Christian] and classical Greek" (3).

17. Yeats to John Quinn, 2 April 1916, quoted in Miller, *The Noble Drama of W. B. Yeats*, 226.

18. Richard Taylor, *The Drama of W. B. Yeats: Irish Myth and the Japanese Nō*, 1.

19. Yeats, introduction to *Certain Noble Plays of Japan*, iv–v. For an extended discussion of dance in Yeats's theater, see Sylvia C. Ellis, *The Plays of W. B. Yeats: Yeats and the Dancer* (New York: St. Martin's Press, 1995).

20. For an outline of Ito's European years, see Helen Caldwell, *Michio Ito: The Dancer and His Dances* (Berkeley: University of California Press, 1977), 37–54.

21. Ibid., 20.

22. Ito's dances were composed of ten primary arm movements. For a pictorial representation of these "Ten Gestures" see Caldwell, *Michio Ito*, appendix four, 143–53.

23. Caldwell, *Michio Ito*, 69.

24. Yeats, introduction to *Certain Noble Plays of Japan*, xii–xiii.

25. Yeats, *Four Plays for Dancers*, v.

26. See Monica Bethe and Karen Brazell, "The Practice of Noh Theatre," in *By Means of Performance: Intercultural Studies of Theatre and Ritual*, eds. Richard Schechner and Willa Appel (Cambridge: Cambridge University Press, 1990), 190.

27. Yeats, introduction to *Certain Noble Plays of Japan*, iii.

28. Yeats, *Four Plays for Dancers*, 135.

29. Yeats, "Speaking to the Psaltery" (1902), in *Ideas of Good and Evil* (New York: Macmillan, 1903), 17.

30. Ibid., 16–17.

31. Florence Farr, *The Music of Speech* (London: Elkin Mathews, 1909).

32. Ibid., 17.

33. Ibid., 18.

34. Ibid., 21.

35. Yeats, *Four Plays for Dancers*, 90.

36. Rummel also collaborated with Isadora Duncan and was her lover for a time.

37. Yeats, *Four Plays for Dancers*, 108.

38. For a critical discussion of Dulac's and Rummel's music for these plays,

see Edward Malins, *Yeats and Music* (Dublin: Dolmen Press, 1968), or Peter Davidson, "Music in Translation: Yeats; Pound; Rummel; Dulac," in Sekine and Murray, *Yeats and the Noh.*

39. Yeats to T. Sturge Moore, 31 July 1929, in Ursula Bridge, ed., *W. B. Yeats and T. Sturge Moore: Their Correspondence 1901–1937* (London: Routledge and Kegan Paul, 1953), 156. Concerning this "lost faith," Gorsky has written: "Yeats laments the loss of real faith in the contemporary world which thus makes art nearly impossible. The 'lost faith,' then, is not only art itself but also the 'half-mythological, half-psychological folk-beliefs' which alone can instill symbolic power and relevance into that art." Gorsky, *A Ritual Drama: Yeats's Plays for Dancers,* 176.

40. W. B. Yeats, *Explorations,* selected by Mrs. W. B. Yeats (London: Macmillan, 1962), 129.

41. Yeats, "The Theatre," in *Ideas Good and Evil,* 258–59.

42. Ibid., 259.

43. Yeats, *Four Plays for Dancers,* 105.

44. I should acknowledge here that although critics continue to use the name "Brecht" to refer to the creative source of certain theatrical works and theories, authorship is not a simple matter with Brecht. It has been demonstrated that Brecht did not write some of the works appearing under his name and that, instead of implying an individual author, "Brecht" should be understood to indicate the contributions of one or more often uncredited individuals who worked within Bertolt Brecht's personal orbit. The issue of Brechtian authorship has been argued most fully by John Fuegi in *Brecht and Company: Sex, Politics, and the Making of the Modern Drama* (New York: Grove Press, 1994).

45. Bertolt Brecht, *Brecht on Theatre,* ed. and trans. John Willett (New York: Hill and Wang, 1964), 38.

46. Jürgen Engelhardt has linked the aesthetics of Brecht and Stravinsky in his *Gestus und Verfremdung: Studien zum Musiktheater bei Strawinsky und Brecht/Weill* (Munich and Salzburg: Emil Katzbichler, 1984). See also Ulrich Weisstein, "Cocteau, Stravinsky, Brecht and the Birth of Epic Opera," *Modern Drama* 5, no. 2 (September 1962): 142–53; and Vera Sonja Stegmann, *Das epische Musiktheater bei Strawinsky und Brecht* (New York: Peter Lang, 1991). Susan C. Cook has persuasively suggested that Stravinsky's use of a Greek-style male chorus in *Oedipus Rex* influenced Kurt Weill in his *Der Zar lässt sich photographieren* and that Weill's chorus "spoofed the Greek revivalism reflected in French and German art of the time." See Cook, "*Der Zar lässt sich photographieren:* Weill and Comic Opera," in *A New Orpheus: Essays on Kurt Weill,* ed. Kim H. Kowalke (New Haven: Yale University Press, 1986), 91–92.

47. This image of the performer holding the mask of the character away from his or her face is similar to Craig's conception of the use of multiple masks by the *Über-marionette.*

48. Brecht, *Brecht on Theatre,* 39.

49. For an extended study of this topic, see Renata Berg-Pan, *Bertolt Brecht and China* (Bonn: Herbert Grundmann, 1979).

50. Brecht, *Brecht on Theatre*, 92.

51. Ibid., 94.

52. Ibid., 95.

53. Ibid., 96.

54. Ibid.

55. These performances occurred too late to have influenced the first production of *Der Jasager* (*He Who Says Yes*), Brecht's most explicit and famous adaptation of a Noh play, but may have had some influence on the December 1930 premiere of *Die Maßnahme* (*The Measures Taken*). The performance styles of Noh and Kabuki, in any case, are quite different.

56. In a study devoted to Brecht and Noh, Masaharu Oba has argued that Brecht learned of Noh performance aesthetics through Arthur Waley's translations of passages from Zeami's treatises. Oba also argues that the concept of the *Lehrstück* was itself informed by Brecht's knowledge of Noh. See Oba, *Bertolt Brecht und das Nô-Theater* (Frankfurt am Main: Peter Lang, 1984), 11. Antony Tatlow has likewise emphasized the similarities between Brechtian aesthetics and Noh and has argued that Japanese theater and Zeami's writings modified Brecht's conception of *Verfremdung*. See Tatlow, *The Mask of Evil: Brecht's Response to the Poetry, Theatre and Thought of China and Japan* (Bern: Peter Lang, 1977), 228. Tatlow refers to an incomplete essay on Japanese theater written by Brecht, presumably after he had witnessed the 1930 performance of the traveling Japanese troupe in Berlin, and suggests that Japanese influence is apparent in the use of masks and isolated symbolic gesture in the first production of *Die Maßnahme* a few months after this performance (231, 233).

57. For extensive studies of the *Lehrstück* genre, see Klaus-Dieter Krabiel, *Brechts Lehrstücke: Entstehung und Entwicklung eines Spieltyps* (Stuttgart: J. B. Metzler, 1993); and Reiner Steinweg, *Das Lehrstück: Brechts Theorie einer politisch-ästhetischen Erziehung* (Stuttgart: J. B. Metzler, 1972). See also Stephen Hinton, "*Lehrstück:* An Aesthetics of Performance," in *Music and Performance during the Weimar Republic*, ed. Bryan Gilliam (Cambridge: Cambridge University Press, 1994), 59–73.

58. Brecht ridiculed Hindemith's emphasis on amateur participation and condemned *Gebrauchsmusik* as an empty innovation. See Brecht, *Brecht on Theatre*, 40.

59. Tatlow, *The Mask of Evil*, 201.

60. For Brecht's discussion of the educative potential of theatrical performance, see Brecht, *Brecht on Theatre*, 71–75.

61. For an extended review of Brecht's attitudes toward music, see Kim H. Kowalke, "Brecht and Music: Theory and Practice," in *The Cambridge Companion to Brecht*, ed. Peter Thomson and Glendyr Sacks (Cambridge: Cambridge University Press, 1994), 218–34.

62. Of course, Weill disputed Brecht's claims of ventriloquism. See Kowalke, "Brecht and Music," 225–26.

63. Brecht, *Brecht on Theatre*, 89. In these statements, Brecht prefigures Adorno's critique of the phantasmagoric aspects of Wagner's music drama. A

quite similar anti-Wagnerian sentiment had been offered by Cocteau: "this old sorcerer looked upon boredom as a useful drug for the stupefaction of the faithful." See Jean Cocteau, "Cock and Harlequin," in *A Call to Order* (1926), trans. Rollo H. Myers (New York: Haskell, 1974), 14.

64. Brecht, *Brecht on Theatre*, 35.

65. Ibid., 38.

66. Ibid.

67. Ibid., 90.

68. Ibid., 44–45.

69. Ibid., 203.

70. Ibid., 85. In addition, several of the numbers refer within themselves to the act of their singing.

71. Ibid., 105.

72. Ibid., 86. Kowalke has convincingly disputed this assertion. See Kowalke, "Brecht and Music," 223–24.

73. Weill, "New Opera," in Kim H. Kowalke, *Kurt Weill in Europe* (Ann Arbor: UMI Research Press, 1979), 465. On Weill's independent penchant for simplicity, see Susan Borwick, "Weill's and Brecht's Theories on Music in Drama," *Journal of Musicological Research* 4, nos. 1 and 2 (1982): 49–67.

74. Weill, "Opera—Where To?" in Kowalke, *Kurt Weill in Europe*, 506.

75. Weill, "A Note Concerning *Das Berliner Requiem*," in Kowalke, *Kurt Weill in Europe*, 504.

76. Weill, "Concerning the Gestic Character of Music," in Kowalke, *Kurt Weill in Europe*, 495. Regarding Brecht's own attempts at text setting, Weill wrote: "One sees that this is nothing more than an inventory of the speech-rhythm and cannot be used as music at all" (494).

77. Weill, "New Opera," in Kowalke, *Kurt Weill in Europe*, 465.

78. Weill, "Topical Theater," in Kowalke, *Kurt Weill in Europe*, 511 (emphasis in original).

79. Weill, "About My Didactic Opera *Der Jasager*," in Kowalke, *Kurt Weill in Europe*, 530. Weill's socially significant music theater included an experiment in Jewish religious drama. His "biblical drama" *Der Weg der Verheissung* was composed in 1934–35 and was first performed in New York City in 1937 as *The Eternal Road*.

80. Ibid., 531 (emphasis in original).

81. Ibid., 530.

82. See Fuegi, *Brecht and Company*, 219–22. Hauptmann and Weill, rather than Brecht, seem to have provided the major impetus for the adaptation of Japanese Noh in the *Lehrstücke*.

83. Gottfried Wagner, *Weill und Brecht: Das musikalische Zeittheater* (Munich: Kindler, 1977), 284.

84. Weill, "Topical Dialogue about *Schuloper* between Kurt Weill and Dr. Hans Fischer," in Kowalke, *Kurt Weill in Europe*, 524.

85. Ian Kemp, "Der Jasager: Weill's Composition Lesson," in *A Stranger Here Myself: Kurt Weill-Studien*, ed. Kim H. Kowalke and Horst Edler (Hildesheim:

Georg Olms, 1993), 155. (This passage appears on pages 38–40 of the piano-vocal score.)

86. Paul W. Humphreys, "Expressions of *Einverständnis:* Musical Structure and Affective Content in Kurt Weill's Score for *Der Jasager*" (Ph.D. diss., University of California, Los Angeles, 1988), 23.

87. Ibid.

88. John Fuegi, *Brecht and Company,* 245.

89. Roswitha Mueller, "Learning for a New Society: The *Lehrstück*," in *The Cambridge Companion to Brecht,* 79–95. Mueller argues that "the most far-reaching impact of the *Lehrstück* resides, not in its themes, but in its structural innovation, which aims at a total abolition of the division between performance and audience" (83).

90. Ibid., 90.

91. Andrzej Wirth, "Brecht and the Asiatic Model: The Secularization of Magical Rites," *Literature East and West* 15, no. 4 (December 1971): 601.

92. Ibid., 612–13.

93. See Kowalke, *Kurt Weill in Europe,* 78.

CHAPTER 7. MEDIEVALISM AND THE FRENCH
MODERNIST STAGE

1. Paul Claudel, *Claudel on the Theatre,* ed. Jacques Petit and Jean-Pierre Kempf, trans. Christine Trollope (Coral Gables: University of Miami Press, 1972), 104.

2. Ibid., 52.

3. Ibid., 102.

4. Ibid., 103.

5. Ibid., 53.

6. Ibid., 121.

7. Ibid., 55.

8. Ibid., 86. Claudel described Mei Lanfang as "neither a man nor a woman, but a sylph" (85).

9. On the impact of Noh in several of Claudel's plays, see Estelle Trepanier, "The Influence of the Noh on the Theatre of Paul Claudel," *Literature East and West* 15, no. 4 (December 1971): 616–31.

10. Claudel, *Claudel on the Theatre,* 105.

11. A third commissioned religious work, Claudel's *L'Histoire de Tobie et de Sara* (1938) based on an episode in the book of Tobit, was also abandoned by Rubinstein. Rubinstein had originally approached Stravinsky for the score of this work. Following Stravinsky's refusal, Claudel secured the interest of Milhaud. Claudel had envisioned a total theater production for this morality play—including music, film, and mime—but this goal was never realized and the play was eventually performed without music.

12. Claudel, *Claudel on the Theatre,* 110.

13. A detailed study of Rubinstein's career is offered in Michael de Cossart,

Ida Rubinstein (1885–1960): A Theatrical Life (Liverpool: Liverpool University Press, 1987).

14. See Cossart, *Ida Rubinstein (1885–1960)*, 27.

15. D'Annunzio based *Le Martyre* on his own 1883 *La Mort du dieu*, which was concerned with the death of the beautiful Grecian god, Adonis. He also charged the play with a particular energy by implying a homosexual desire on the part of Emperor Diocletian for Sebastian. Sebastian's dance of the Passion of Christ before the entranced Diocletian suggests a strong parallel with Wilde's *Salome*.

16. Gustave Cohen had published editions of *mystères* and *moralités* and had written on the performance aesthetics of medieval French theater. In his later *Études d'histoire du théâtre en France au Moyen âge et à la Renaissance* (Paris: Gallimard, 1956), Cohen devoted an entire section to the revival of French medieval theater during the first half of the twentieth century. Included in this section are two articles concerning d'Annunzio's *Le Martyre*, as well as an article describing Cohen's own attempts to revive the *mystères* at the Sorbonne in the 1930s. D'Annunzio was not the first writer interested in creating *mystères* for the modern stage. The trend in France dates at least from the series of mystery plays for marionettes written by Maurice Bouchor in the late 1880s. For a discussion of Bouchor's mysteries, see Harold B. Segel, *Pinocchio's Progeny: Puppets, Marionettes, Automatons, and Robots in Modernist and Avant-Garde Drama* (Baltimore: Johns Hopkins University Press, 1995), 79–86.

17. A good deal of sexual intrigue occurred during the creation of this work. Romaine Brooks, a bisexual painter who had been abandoned recently by d'Annunzio, began an affair with Rubinstein in revenge against the poet. A painting created by Brooks at this time provides an extremely provocative artifact for *Le Martyre*. As Cossart relates, "[Brooks's] *Masked Archer* (subtitled *The Persecuted Woman*) of summer 1911 depicts Ida [Rubinstein] as a Saint-Sebastian-like figure being shot through with arrows by a masked dwarf who, despite his obscured face, is clearly recognizable as d'Annunzio" (*Ida Rubinstein [1885–1960]*, 60). On the history of this love triangle, see ibid., 30–34.

18. Although there has been disagreement concerning how extensive André Caplet's role was in the creation of this score, it is generally accepted that Debussy at least sketched the sections discussed here. See Robert Orledge, "Debussy's Orchestral Collaborations, 1911–13. 1: *Le Martyre de Saint Sébastien*," *Musical Times* 115, no. 1582 (1974): 1030–35.

19. Quoted in Marcel Dietschy, *A Portrait of Claude Debussy*, ed. and trans. William Ashbrook and Margaret G. Cobb (Oxford: Clarendon Press, 1990), 166.

20. Robin Holloway, *Debussy and Wagner* (London: Eulenberg Books, 1979), 145–46.

21. See Debussy, *Debussy on Music*, ed. and trans. Richard Langham Smith (London: Secker and Warburg, 1977), 247.

22. Ibid.

23. Debussy, "Avant *Le Martyre de Saint Sébastien*," *Comoedia* (18 May

1911), reprinted in Debussy, *Monsieur Croche et autres écrits*, ed. François Lesure (Paris: Gallimard, 1971), 304–5.

24. Debussy and d'Annunzio's declaration is reproduced in Guy Tosi, *Claude Debussy et Gabriele d'Annunzio: Correspondance inédite* (Paris: Denoël, 1948), 32–33.

25. See Jacques Depaulis, *Paul Claudel et Ida Rubinstein: Une Collaboration difficile* (Paris: Annales Littéraires de l'Université de Besançon, 1994), 40.

26. Cossart, *Ida Rubinstein (1885–1960)*, 197.

27. Claudel, *Claudel on the Theatre*, 111.

28. See Geoffrey K. Spratt, *The Music of Arthur Honegger* (Cork: Cork University Press, 1987), 252.

29. Joan was repeatedly brought to the stage in the first half of the century. These diverse stagings—some produced in the style of the *mystères*, others presented in modern adaptations—include Charles Péguy's *Jeanne d'Arc* (1897) and *Le Mystère de la charité de Jeanne d'Arc* (1909), George Bernard Shaw's *Saint Joan* (1923), Brecht's *Joan of the Stockyards* (c. 1930), René Bruyez's *Jeanne et la vie des autres* (1938), Maxwell Anderson's *Joan of Lorraine* (1946), and Jean Anouilh's *L'Alouette* (1953). Anouilh's play was adapted for Broadway as *The Lark* by Lillian Hellman, with incidental music by Leonard Bernstein, in 1955. In 1948, Gustave Cohen offered a version of the fifteenth-century *Mystère du siège d'Orléans*. (See Cohen, *Sainte Jeanne d'Arc dans la poésie du XVème siècle* [Paris: Les Cours de Lettres, 1947–48].) Martha Graham created two dances on the story of Joan of Arc, both to a score by Norman Dello Joio. In *The Triumph of Saint Joan* (1951), Graham attempted to express Joan's inner life in a solo dance. In *Seraphic Dialogue* (1955), her final version, Graham employed three dancers to represent Saints Michael, Catherine, and Margaret, and three dancers to represent Joan the Maid, the Warrior, and the Martyr, in addition to a primary role for Joan the Saint. As in Claudel's *Jeanne d'Arc*, Graham's *Seraphic Dialogue* is set as an extended flashback at the moment of Joan's martyrdom.

30. Claudel, *Claudel on the Theatre*, 112–13. Claudel's discussion of his chorus reminds one of Stravinsky's vision of a "faceless chorus" for *Oedipus Rex*. The role of the chorus in *Jeanne* is similar to that found in Claudel and Milhaud's *Christophe Colomb* (1930). In this earlier work, the chorus serves as a surrogate for the audience. Claudel described this opera as being "like a Mass in which the congregation plays a constant part." Ibid., 77.

31. Ibid., 58.

32. Ibid., 232–33.

33. Ibid., 240.

34. For illustrations of Honegger's use of speech in his choral works, see Spratt, *The Music of Arthur Honegger*, 335–56.

35. Quoted in Spratt, *The Music of Arthur Honegger*, 233. Here Honegger echoes Florence Farr and Yeats.

36. Unfortunately for Joan, she has also been able to hear the chorus denouncing her as a heretic in its role as the Voices of the Earth.

37. The ondes Martenot and aspects of Japanese Noh music are also employed for celestial representation in Olivier Messiaen's medievalist opera *Saint François d'Assise* (1983).

38. Cossart, *Ida Rubinstein (1885–1960)*, 202.

39. The image of Saint Joan and performances of *Jeanne d'Arc* continued to serve French nationalism following the war. Until recently, Saint Joan was the primary symbol for the ultra-right-wing French National Front.

40. Spratt has referred to the prologue as being "quite simply a glorification of the Liberation." Spratt, *The Music of Arthur Honegger*, 254.

CHAPTER 8. THE AUDIENCE AS CONGREGATION

1. Wagner referred to *Parsifal* as a *Bühnenweihfestspiel*, a festival piece for the consecration of the stage. However, the festival audience is not invited to participate in the enactment of holy communion in the work—an extreme example of staged ritual performance.

2. Edward Gordon Craig, "A Note on Masks," in *The Theatre Advancing* (London: Constable, 1921), 127.

3. Quoted in Susan Valeria Harris Smith, *Masks in Modern Drama* (Berkeley: University of California Press, 1984), 62–63.

4. See Doug Adams and Diane Apostolos-Cappadona, "Changing Biblical Imagery and Artistic Identity in Twentieth-Century Dance," in *Dance as Religious Studies*, ed. Adams and Apostolos-Cappadona (New York: Crossroad, 1990), 3–14. See also Neil Douglas-Klotz, "Ruth St. Denis: Sacred Dance Explorations in America," 109–17, in the same collection.

5. Britten's Church Parables have more in common with ecclesiastical forms of medieval liturgical drama than with the inclusive and communal mystery plays that inspired *Noye's Fludde*.

6. Robin Holloway, "Church Parables (II): Limits and Renewals," in *The Britten Companion*, ed. Christopher Palmer (Cambridge: Cambridge University Press, 1984), 223.

7. As quoted in Michael Kennedy, *Britten* (London: J. M. Dent and Sons, 1981), 235.

8. Other European forms of liturgical drama included the medieval miracle play (celebrating the lives of the saints) and the isolated example of the Bavarian Oberammergau Passion play. The Oberammergau plays began with a 1634 performance of the Passion story as a religious offering by the town for having been delivered from the plague.

9. T. S. Eliot, "Religious Drama: Medieval and Modern," *Edinburgh University Journal* (autumn 1937): 8–17. The quotation is taken from John R. Elliott Jr., *Playing God: Medieval Mysteries on the Modern Stage* (Toronto: University of Toronto Press, 1989), 101.

10. Only the Oberammergau play was widely approved of—so long as one experienced it on holiday in the isolation of the Bavarian mountains.

11. My discussion of the twentieth-century British revival of the mystery

play is indebted to John R. Elliott Jr., *Playing God: Medieval Mysteries on the Modern Stage.* The most celebrated American equivalent to the British mystery play revival was Noah Greenberg's production of the thirteenth-century French *Play of Daniel* at The Cloisters in New York City in 1958. However, religious themes had formed part of the widespread performance of pageants in the United States during the first decades of the twentieth century. On these popular forms of mass theater, see Naima Prevots, *American Pageantry: A Movement for Art and Democracy* (Ann Arbor: UMI Research Press, 1990).

12. Elliott, *Playing God,* 76.

13. Elliott has speculated that medieval productions of the mystery plays "were acted more like Noh and Kabuki than we have suspected." Ibid., 131.

14. Ibid., 107. This combination of popular music and Christian ritual in new forms of music theater was to predominate in the United States and will be discussed in part IV.

15. The circumstances of this commission are given in Humphrey Carpenter, *Benjamin Britten: A Biography* (London: Faber & Faber, 1992), 381.

16. Britten had already turned to the Chester cycle for the text of his *Canticle II: Abraham and Isaac* (1952).

17. In 1961, Stravinsky composed his own setting of this Biblical episode. *The Flood* is based primarily on the same textual source as Britten's *Noye's Fludde* with additions from the Book of Genesis and from other mystery plays. The performance context of these two works is radically contrasting. Stravinsky's version was composed for a television production and was the result of a close collaboration with George Balanchine. It is a dance-drama and relies far less on the medieval text. While Britten employs preexistent hymns and a simple musical language, Stravinsky creates his own chantlike material and composes in a serial idiom. *The Flood* does retain several traits of ritualistic and stylized performance, including a rigid structure, musical framing device, and the use of masks for Noah and his family.

18. Britten had called for audience participation in his earlier children's opera *The Little Sweep* (1949) but only between acts, not as an integral and necessary part of the work itself.

19. Britten, *Noye's Fludde,* full score (London: Hawkes & Son, 1958).

20. It is thought that God's lines were always realized with a speaking, rather than singing, voice in the medieval performance of the mystery plays.

21. Britten was not the first British composer to create a new form of music theater while under an exotic influence. Gustav Holst's *Savitri* (1908), perhaps his most interesting work, is a chamber opera based on a Hindu legend. Britten conducted a performance of this work prior to his own experiments in music theater.

CHAPTER 9. BRITTEN'S PARABLES

1. This quotation of "A Note by the Composer" is taken from the liner notes for the 1965 recording of *Curlew River,* London OSA 1156/A 4156.

2. *Sumidagawa* is a Noh play attributed to Juro Motomasa (1395–1459), son of the seminal Noh theoretician and playwright, Zeami. It is a "mad woman" play consisting of a mother's search for her abducted son and ending with her discovery of the boy's grave upon crossing the Sumida River and with the brief appearance of the boy's spirit during her prayers. In addition to the role of the demented mother and the spirit of the boy, there is a ferryman and a traveler who, with the chorus, mock the woman and then come to sympathize with her upon discovering that she is the dead child's mother. The translation upon which Plomer based his libretto is found in *Japanese Noh Drama: Ten Plays*, ed. Japanese Classical Translation Committee (Tokyo: The Nippon Gakujutsu Shinkōkai, 1955), 145–59.

3. Peter F. Alexander, "A Study of the Origins of Britten's 'Curlew River,'" *Music and Letters* 69, no. 2 (April 1988): 229–43.

4. William Plomer (1903–73) was a South African poet and novelist of English descent who had lived in Japan from 1926 to 1929. Concerning Plomer's "Japanese" novels, Earl Miner wrote in 1958 that "Japan has been just another source of experience" for Plomer's work and that Plomer took whatever he found special about Japan and treated it in "techniques which are wholly of Western origin" (212). At another point in his discussion, Miner contradicts these criticisms by praising Plomer for writing "perhaps the only fiction which reads like a splendid translation of a modern Japanese novelist" (50). In general, Miner is critical of Plomer's attempt to deal with the "Japanese National character in terms of his own experiences." He quotes from Plomer's poem "Captain Maru" to demonstrate Plomer's tendency to generalize about the Japanese: "It is the challenge of his race, the short man scorned / Not satisfied with power, but mad for more" (205). Earl Miner, *The Japanese Tradition in British and American Literature* (Princeton: Princeton University Press, 1958).

5. The *Sinfonia da requiem* is charged with significance in the tale of Britten's relations with Japanese culture. Commissioned by the Japanese government in 1940 as part of the official celebration of the "2600th anniversary" of the nation, it was rejected as being unsuited for such a festive occasion and for its overtly Christian nature. In a letter to his publisher, Britten wrote that, "the publicity of having the work rejected by the Japanese Consulate for being Christian is a wow." At the time, the *Sinfonia* had caused a great deal of tension and misunderstanding, particularly in the context of the world political situation. The performance in 1956 must have been viewed as something of a reconciliation. It is noteworthy that Britten's first contact with Japan involved such a public clash between his Christianity and Japanese sensibilities. This episode is discussed in Humphrey Carpenter, *Benjamin Britten: A Biography* (London: Faber & Faber, 1992), 145.

6. From "Ausflug Ost 1956," in *Tribute to Benjamin Britten on His Fiftieth Birthday*, ed. Anthony Gishford (London: Faber & Faber, 1963), 60–61. This article is a translation of part of Prince Ludwig's travel diary from his 1956 trip with Britten and Pears.

7. Plomer to Britten, 17 April 1959, quoted in Alexander, "A Study of the Origins," 238.

8. This is also a much discussed and central feature of nineteenth-century Orientalist opera. The "mysterious exotic" was repeatedly referenced with great economy of means through the use of well-established musical signs that might or might not correspond to features present in the actual referent. The exotic setting and sounds, the *couleur locale,* often allowed for the playing out of specifically European concerns in a generic "Oriental" setting.

9. Miner, *The Japanese Tradition,* xi–xii.

10. The unabashed enthusiasm of a figure such as Henry Cowell, who wished to "live in the whole world of music" and who remained primarily in Miner's "imitation" stage, represents another form of relationship with the exotic.

11. Edward W. Said, *Culture and Imperialism* (New York: Knopf, 1993), 220–38.

12. Letter to Plomer of 15 April 1959, quoted in Alexander, "A Study of the Origins," 238. Britten's Christianization of Japanese Noh is similar to Stravinsky's approach to Greek myth as discussed in chapter 5.

13. This music is no different in kind from Camille Saint-Saëns's ceremonial music for the Philistines in *Samson et Dalila* (1877). Both composers supply their Israelite characters with Christian-style music. The music of the three young Israelites in Britten's work is closely derived from the opening chant and is often hymnlike as they sing together of their misfortune. In contrast, the Babylonian ritual procession music consists of typical Orientalist touches: tinkling percussion, ambiguous pitch in the glissandi vocal textures, loud dynamics, aggressive rhythms, and mystic "ah's."

14. White Southern Spiritual singing, particularly when involving the technique of "lining out," is another example of the freer treatment of rhythm and form in group religious singing.

15. Mervyn Cooke, "Britten and the shō," *Musical Times* 129 (1988): 231–33. Britten's use of accelerating drum rolls in this work is another musical feature likely borrowed from *gagaku.*

16. Malm's chapter ("The Noh Play *Sumidagawa* and Benjamin Britten's *Curlew River*—One Story in Two Musical Worlds") consists of a detailed musical and dramatic comparison of these two pieces. William Malm, *Six Hidden Views of Japanese Music* (Berkeley: University of California Press, 1986), 151–97.

17. Robin Holloway, "The Church Parables (II): Limits and Renewals," in *The Britten Companion,* ed. Christopher Palmer (Cambridge: Cambridge University Press, 1984), 217–18.

18. Britten also employed such glissandi in "Dance Song," the final movement in his 1957 *Songs from the Chinese.*

19. Perhaps Britten had Donizetti's Lucia and her mad scene in mind when creating this musical marker of madness.

20. Quoted in Arnold Whittall, *The Music of Britten and Tippett: Studies in Themes and Techniques* (Cambridge: Cambridge University Press, 1982), 113.

21. Britten and Graham had observed the ritual robing before Mass at a Venetian church and adopted some of these movements for the ceremonial cos-

tume change during the orchestral fantasy section of *Curlew River*. See Carpenter, *Benjamin Britten*, 426.

22. Colin Graham, "Production Notes and Remarks on the Style of Performing *Curlew River*," in Benjamin Britten, *Curlew River* (London: Faber & Faber, 1965), 143–60.

23. Eric Walter White, *Benjamin Britten: His Life and Operas* (Berkeley: University of California Press, 1970), 209.

24. Eric Roseberry, "Tonal Ambiguity in *Death in Venice:* A Symphonic View," in *Benjamin Britten: Death in Venice*, ed. Donald Mitchell (Cambridge: Cambridge University Press, 1987), 97. Further comparisons between the Church Parables and *Death in Venice* can be found in the reviews of the first performance quoted in the volume's final chapter.

25. For several of his stage works, particularly *Billy Budd*, Britten chose texts that would not require prominent female roles. In composing opera, it is difficult of course to avoid the female voice entirely. On the "oppressive" and "destructive" female characters in Britten's operas, see Ellen McDonald, "Women in Benjamin Britten's Operas," *Opera Quarterly* 4, no. 3 (autumn 1986): 83–101.

26. Knussen's comments are quoted in Carpenter, *Benjamin Britten*, 438. Carpenter also provides indications that members of the cast and production team were disturbed by this casting decision.

27. The cast list of the premiere performance indicates that the role of the Spirit of the Boy was divided between a silent visible performer and an offstage boy soprano voice.

28. Carpenter provides evidence for the possibility that Britten had experienced such intimidation from the government himself in late 1953. See Carpenter, *Benjamin Britten*, 335.

29. For comprehensive discussions of the legal history of homosexuality in England during Britten's career, see Jeffrey Weeks, *Coming Out: Homosexual Politics in Britain from the Nineteenth Century to the Present* (London: Quartet Books, 1977, rev. 1990), especially chaps. 14 and 15; Stephen Jeffery-Poulter, *Peers, Queers, & Commons: The Struggle for Gay Reform from 1950 to the Present* (London: Routledge, 1991); and H. Montgomery Hyde, *The Other Love: An Historical and Contemporary Survey of Homosexuality in Britain* (London: Heinemann, 1970). Articles by Philip Brett and Clifford Hindley, to be discussed below, have also relied on these important histories.

30. Philip Brett, "Britten and Grimes," *Musical Times* 118 (1977): 995–1000. This paper originally was delivered by Brett at the 1976 meeting of the American Musicological Society in Washington, D.C. Brett included a more nuanced postscript when this article was published in the Cambridge Opera Handbook for *Peter Grimes* in 1983.

31. Compare Whittall's discussions of the operas in his *The Music of Britten and Tippett: Studies in Themes and Techniques* (1982) with his "Twisted Relations: Method and Meaning in Britten's *Billy Budd*," *Cambridge Opera Journal* 2, no. 2 (1990): 145–71.

32. Clifford Hindley, "Why Does Miles Die?—Britten's *Turn of the Screw*," *Musical Quarterly* 74, no. 1 (1990): 1–17.

33. Clifford Hindley, "Contemplation and Reality: A Study of Britten's 'Death in Venice,'" *Music and Letters* 71, no. 4 (November 1990): 511–23.

34. Philip Brett, "Britten's Bad Boys: Male Relations in *The Turn of the Screw*," *repercussions* 1, no. 2 (fall 1992): 5–25.

35. Philip Brett, "Britten's Dream," in *Musicology and Difference: Gender and Sexuality in Music Scholarship*, ed. Ruth Solie (Berkeley: University of California Press, 1993); and Brett, "Musicality, Essentialism, and the Closet," and "Eros and Orientalism in Britten's Operas," in *Queering the Pitch: the New Gay and Lesbian Musicology*, ed. Philip Brett, Elizabeth Wood, and Gary C. Thomas (New York: Routledge, 1994).

36. Christopher Palmer, "The Colour of the Music," in *Benjamin Britten: The Turn of the Screw*, ed. Patricia Howard (Cambridge: Cambridge University Press, 1985), 101–25.

37. On the eve of World War II the tranquility of this island was disrupted, and McPhee left in 1938 just as Dutch officials began to arrest foreign homosexuals. For an account of McPhee's relations to Bali and its music see Carol J. Oja, *Colin McPhee: Composer in Two Worlds* (Washington, D.C.: Smithsonian Institution Press, 1990), and Richard Mueller, "Imitation and Stylization in the Balinese Music of Colin McPhee" (Ph.D. diss., University of Chicago, 1983).

38. Mervyn Cooke, "Britten and Bali," *Journal of Musicological Research* 7, no. 4 (1988): 307–39.

39. Ludwig of Hesse, "Ausflug Ost 1956," 63.

40. Quoted in Susan Valeria Harris Smith, *Masks in Modern Drama* (Berkeley: University of California Press, 1984), 157.

41. This term has received its most significant treatment in Eve Kosofsky Sedgwick, *Epistemology of the Closet* (Berkeley: University of California Press, 1990).

42. My use of the mask metaphor here resonates with Yukio Mishima's 1949 novel *Kamen no kokuhaku* (trans. *Confessions of a Mask*, 1958) in which a young Japanese male learns to disguise his homosexuality from society.

43. Clifford Hindley, "Homosexual Self-affirmation and Self-oppression in Two Britten Operas," *Musical Quarterly* 76, no. 2 (summer 1992): 143–68.

44. Ibid., 156.

45. Ibid., 163.

46. The association of the high male voice with evil or exoticism is common in the twentieth century. Stravinsky wickedly referred to his Lucifer, the original and eternal tempter of *The Flood*, as a "high, slightly pederastic tenor" and remarked that "at any rate, Satan is sexually less 'sure' than God." Igor Stravinsky with Robert Craft, *Expositions and Developments* (Garden City, N.Y.: Doubleday, 1962), 141.

47. Christopher Palmer, "The Colour of the Music," in *Benjamin Britten: The Turn of the Screw*, ed. Patricia Howard, 110.

48. Britten's *Death in Venice* contains several references to another opera partially composed in that famous city and likewise concerned with a forbidden

love: Wagner's *Tristan und Isolde*. A study of the presence of *Tristan und Isolde* in and behind the composition of *Death in Venice* would prove interesting.

49. These eleven measures pose the same sort of questions as the famous, and much interpreted, thirty-four "interview chords" in *Billy Budd*.

50. Holloway, "The Church Parables (II)," 223.

51. Quoted in Donald Mitchell, "An Introduction in the Shape of a Memoir," in *Benjamin Britten: Death in Venice*, ed. Donald Mitchell (Cambridge: Cambridge University Press, 1987), 21.

52. Brett, "Britten's Dream," in *Musicology and Difference*, 279. In general, Brett does not consider the Church Parables to be of much significance to Britten's oeuvre. In his view, they constituted the "narrow strait that had to be navigated successfully before Britten could turn back to opera in a more recognizable mold."

53. Brett, "Eros and Orientalism in Britten's Operas," in *Queering the Pitch*, 251.

54. Mark Levine, "The Outsider: Lou Harrison Comes in from the Fringe," *New Yorker* (26 August/2 September 1996): 157.

CHAPTER 10. LATER BRITISH MYSTERIES

1. Quoted from Pruslin's 1980 introduction to the opera as reprinted in the liner notes for the 1979 recording of *Punch and Judy*, Etcetera Records, KTC 2014, 1989. Michael Hall has noted the extreme stylization of this work, pointing to Baroque opera and to Bach's *St. Matthew Passion* as models, and referring to it as a "morality." See Hall, *Harrison Birtwistle* (London: Robson Books, 1984), 65.

2. Peter Maxwell Davies, "Pax Orcadiensis," *Tempo* 119 (1976): 20–22.

3. Peter Maxwell Davies, *The Martyrdom of St. Magnus: Libretto* (London: Boosey & Hawkes, 1977), 6–9.

4. Davies thus devised a musical equivalent for the linguistic temporal progression that occurs in Brown's chapter "The Killing." The chapter begins in the voice of a medieval bard, complete with archaic spellings and constructions, and ends in the modern voice of a Nazi concentration camp cook who is to serve as the reluctant executioner of a political prisoner, a Lutheran pastor "whose books were burned at the start of the war," a modern Magnus.

5. This was remarked upon in early reviews of the work, such as David Robert, "Maxwell Davies in Orkney: *The Martyrdom of St. Magnus*," *Musical Times* 118 (1977): 633.

6. Stanley Sadie, "Naboth's Vineyard: Alexander Goehr Talks to Stanley Sadie," *Musical Times* 109 (1968): 625–26.

7. Melanie Daiken, "Notes on Goehr's *Triptych*," in *The Music of Alexander Goehr*, ed. Bayan Northcott (London: Schott, 1980), 40. In a telephone conversation, Goehr informed me that his early interest in the films and theories of Eisenstein had aroused his interest in Japanese theater. (Eisenstein had repeatedly acknowledged the influence of Japanese theater on his work.) Follow-

ing the composition of *Naboth's Vineyard,* Goehr planned to set two of Yukio Mishima's modernized Noh plays and traveled to Japan to meet with the writer and to study Noh. Mishima committed ritual suicide before this meeting could occur. However, Goehr has recently composed music for these plays.

8. Sadie, "Naboth's Vineyard," 626.

9. See Don Harran, "Israel: Testimonium II, 1971," *Current Musicology* 15 (1973): 38–43. Luigi Dallapiccola, Lukas Foss, and George Rochberg were among the six other composers included in this event.

CHAPTER 11. ORIENTALISTS AND A CRUSADER

1. Walt Whitman, *Salut au Monde!,* in *Walt Whitman: The Complete Poems,* ed. Francis Murphy (New York: Penguin Classics, 1987), 271–74. Whitman describes Asia as the "Originatress . . . The nest of languages, the bequeather of poems, the race of eld" (ll. 26–27). In *Facing West from California's Shores* (p. 145, *The Complete Poems*) he more explicitly describes humans as having originated in Asia and having reached their destiny in America.

2. San Francisco's Chinese and Japanese populations made this city an ideal location for a composer interested in "exotic" musics. It is not surprising that many of the most enthusiastic intercultural composers, such as Henry Cowell, Harry Partch, Lou Harrison, John Cage, and Dane Rudhyar, have been associated with California and the West Coast.

3. Dane Rudhyar, "Oriental Influence on American Music," in *American Composers on American Music,* ed. Henry Cowell (Stanford: Stanford University Press, 1933), 184.

4. Ibid., 185.

5. Gauthier is an important figure in early twentieth-century musical Orientalism. She concertized throughout Asia and spent five years studying the music of Java. (She reportedly gave her collection of Japanese and Javanese melodic transcriptions to Maurice Ravel after Griffes's death.) My knowledge of Griffes's career is indebted to Donna K. Anderson's *The Works of Charles T. Griffes: A Descriptive Catalogue* (Ann Arbor: UMI Research Press, 1983), to Edward Maisel's *Charles T. Griffes: The Life of an American Composer* (New York: Alfred A. Knopf, 1984), and to Anderson's *Charles T. Griffes: A Life in Music* (Washington, D.C.: Smithsonian Institution Press, 1993).

6. Various forms of "Oriental" theater were being produced in New York City during the early 1910s. Griffes mentioned attending one further performance of an Oriental play during the same year as *The Yellow Jacket* and *Sumurun.* For documentation of Griffes's encounter with these productions, see Anderson, *The Works of Charles T. Griffes,* 24, 323–24.

7. See Maisel, *Charles T. Griffes,* 210.

8. Anderson, *The Works of Charles T. Griffes,* 322.

9. Helen Caldwell, *Michio Ito: The Dancer and His Dances* (Berkeley: University of California Press, 1977), 61.

10. Quoted in Maisel, *Charles T. Griffes,* 205–6.

11. For a history of the Neighborhood Playhouse written by one of its founders, see Alice Lewisohn Crowley, *The Neighborhood Playhouse: Leaves from a Theatre Scrapbook* (New York: Theatre Arts Books, 1959).

12. A letter written by Griffes indicates that he was present at a performance of a Noh play produced in "Japanese style" at the Playhouse in 1918 and that Ito was one of the two dancers. Griffes felt that "the whole thing gave a most strange and at the same time wonderful effect." See Maisel, *Charles T. Griffes*, 231.

13. The manuscripts for this work are in the Charles T. Griffes collection at the New York Public Library for the Performing Arts.

14. The producers especially emphasized Whitman's syncretic celebration of various world religions. Preparation for the production included a series of lectures by experts on comparative religion. See Crowley, *The Neighborhood Playhouse*, 124. The production itself was something of a religious experience for the performers: "Perhaps *Salut au Monde* more nearly achieved the atmosphere of festival than any offering before or after it at the Playhouse, though it was neither the first nor the last production to inspire in the company the fervor of a religious ritual" (Ibid., 126). In his lecture "The Religion of Healthy-Mindedness," William James noted that during the early years of the twentieth century, Walt Whitman was regarded by many Americans as the "restorer of the eternal natural religion" and that a religious cult had been established in his name. See James, *The Varieties of Religious Experience* (New York: Penguin Classics, 1985), 85.

15. Crowley, *The Neighborhood Playhouse*, 121. A much less optimistic view of the potential for cross-cultural understanding, particularly in terms of religion, was offered five years later with the publication of Eugene O'Neill's sardonic *Marco Millions*. This play, with a cast of Christians and heathens, is both a work critical of naive Western perceptions of exotic cultures and a work exhibiting such Orientalist perceptions.

16. Arnold Rosner, *The New Grove Dictionary of Opera*, ed. Stanley Sadie (London: Macmillan, 1992), vol. 2, p. 756.

17. The chanted chorus text in Hovhaness's 1962 dance-drama *Wind Drum* suggests the style of Japanese haiku: "Three hills dance on forest, winds sway branches of singing trees." In this work, the brief, imagist chorus sections alternate with danced instrumental sections. A dancer or group of dancers depicts the movements of the universe, ocean, mountains, and trees described in the text.

18. At the premiere of *The Burning House*, Vahaken and Death were represented by two stationary vocalists and two dancers. See Allen Hughes, "Tennessee Debut for Opera-Ballet," *New York Times*, 25 August 1964. My thanks to Don C. Gillespie of C. F. Peters Corporation and his assistant Susan Orzel for providing me with materials from the Peters file on Hovhaness.

19. The dance of the Mad Bird chasing the Mountain Climber in Hovhaness's *Spirit of the Avalanche* (1962) is also slow in tempo. This trait suggests the stylized dancing of Noh and other East Asian ritual dance forms. *Spirit of the Avalanche* contains many of the same Noh characteristics as observed in *The*

Burning House. These works resemble ritual performances based on sacred legend and are thus similar to Yeats's "plays for dancers."

20. Becker pursued a career as an educator and administrator at several Catholic universities and colleges and worked as a music and general art critic. A positive review of Ezra Pound's book on George Antheil initiated a correspondence with the poet and resulted in Becker's use of Pound's poem *Dance Figure for the Marriage in Cana of Galilee* for his *Stagework no. 1.* For a discussion of the Pound-Becker correspondence, see Don C. Gillespie, "John Becker's Correspondence with Ezra Pound: The Origins of a Musical Crusader," *Bulletin of Research in the Humanities* 83 (1980): 163.

21. Becker's compositional style represents a different direction in modernist music, one that shares little with the music of the "American Orientalists" mentioned earlier. His modernist musical style is characterized by a highly dissonant and contrapuntal texture. Becker's incomplete opera *The City of Shagpat* and his 1933 *Abongo, a Primitive Dance: Stagework no. 2* for dancers, wordless voices, and percussion, represent isolated examples of exoticism and primitivism in his works.

22. These comments appear on a typed sheet contained in the score of *The Life of Man: Stagework no. 4,* available in the John J. Becker Collection at the New York Public Library for the Performing Arts. All quotations from Becker's writings and works are with the permission of Don C. Gillespie, musical executor of the Becker estate.

23. Don C. Gillespie, "John Becker: Midwestern Musical Crusader" (Ph.D. diss., University of North Carolina, 1977), 39. Gillespie quotes the following from Becker's course description for his "Music and Appreciation" class: "the subject is not only discussed in its relation to musical history, but in its relation to art, philosophy, literature, history, and life." Becker taught at the University of Notre Dame between 1917 and 1927.

24. Becker, "Outline for Course in Experimental Theatre Production," in the John J. Becker collection at the New York Public Library for the Performing Arts.

25. My thanks to Eugene Becker for informing me of his father's interest in Gray's work.

26. For an illustrated introduction to Gray's production style see Richard Cave, *Terrence Gray and the Cambridge Festival Theatre* (Cambridge: Chadwyck-Healey, 1980).

27. Terrence Gray, *Dance-Drama: Experiments in the Art of the Theatre* (Cambridge: W. Heffer and Sons, 1926), 14.

28. In a section entitled "Tyranny of Words," Gray discussed the limitations of spoken theater. See Gray, *Dance-Drama,* 21–31.

29. The manuscript score of this work is found in the John J. Becker Collection at the New York Public Library for the Performing Arts.

30. Of course, Becker's vision of a "Polytechnic Theatre" was not the first projection of a multimedia conception. Kandinsky's *Der gelbe Klang,* Schoenberg's *Die glückliche Hand,* and Scriabin's inchoate *Mysterium* predate Becker's

Stageworks. The relationship between music and colored lighting is central in all these works. The text of *A Marriage with Space* contains many references to both music and light, and Becker calls for the stage lighting to correspond directly to these textual references. At one point in the scenario, Becker insists that the music itself suggests light. A line from Turbyfill's poem reads "Light becomes sound."

31. This passage is quoted from Becker's typescript scenario for the work (p. 4) in the John J. Becker Collection at the New York Public Library for the Performing Arts.

32. Harriet Monroe, "Comment: Mr Turbyfill's Poem," *Poetry* 28, no. 11 (May 1926): 92.

33. Becker's typescript scenario, 6.

34. Gillespie, "John Becker," 94. Gillespie also suggests that Becker's statements of moral outrage may have been inspired by his contact with Pound.

35. Becker's statement is reproduced in *Symphonia Brevis* (New York: C. F. Peters, 1972).

36. Gillespie, "John Becker," 175. Becker's success in championing the use of modernist music in the church proved short-lived; soon after Becker's death, Catholic church music was altered radically in favor of popular musical idioms following the reforms of Vatican II.

37. Becker, "Toward a New Church Music," unpublished manuscript, John J. Becker Collection, New York Public Library for the Performing Arts.

38. Raymond-Léopold Bruckberger, *Madeleine et Judas: Tragédie en Trois Mystères* (River Forest, Illinois: privately printed, 1956). Becker's score for this work is available at the New York Public Library for the Performing Arts. Becker also composed an incomplete score for Bruckberger's film *The Song of the Scaffold*.

39. Becker projected a work based on Thomas Mann's *Joseph and His Brethren*. The incomplete draft scenario employs a narrator and calls for Joseph both to perform in a "pantomime dance style" and to sing.

CHAPTER 12. PARTCH'S VISION

1. Partch, "Observations on *Water! Water!*" (1962), in Harry Partch, *Bitter Music: Collected Journals, Essays, Introductions, and Librettos,* ed. Thomas McGeary (Urbana: University of Illinois Press, 1991), 247.

2. I should note that Partch's vision of total theater, and even the language employed in his descriptions of it, is strikingly similar to that found in Antonin Artaud's writings. This is particularly apparent in Artaud's "Metaphysics and the Mise en Scène," "The Alchemical Theater," and in his discussion of musical instruments in "The Theater of Cruelty (First Manifesto)." However, these writings were not available in English until 1958, and Partch first encountered them the following year. Similarities between Partch's and Artaud's theatrical pronouncements are coincidental. See Artaud, *The Theater and Its Double,* trans. Mary Caroline Richards (New York: Grove Weidenfeld, 1958).

3. See Partch, "The University and the Creative Arts: Comment" (1963), in *Bitter Music*, 191.

4. Partch, "Show Horses in the Concert Ring" (1948), in *Bitter Music*, 179.

5. Partch, "Oedipus" (1954), in *Bitter Music*, 218. In another article, Partch provided a wry assessment of the relationship between theater and music: "They need each other so badly that they run to the edges of their specialities and shout to each other for help. They are both ambivalent up to the hilt. The theater gets its help from music—and then demonstrates its ambivalence by inventing the orchestra pit with the musicians operating in solitary confinement, excommunicated, stealing away through hidden secret passages to play cards or to shoot craps at every opportunity because they have no integrated part in the drama and are frankly bored. To show their ambivalence in turn, the musicians frequently drown out and render much onstage unintelligible." Partch, "A Soul Tormented by Contemporary Music Looks for a Humanizing Alchemy: *The Bewitched*" (1957), in *Bitter Music*, 241.

6. Partch, "The Ancient Magic" (1959), in *Bitter Music*, 186.

7. Partch, "Monoliths in Music" (1966), in *Bitter Music*, 194.

8. Partch, "A Quarter-Saw Section of Motivations and Intonations" (1967), in *Bitter Music*, 196.

9. This aim shares something with the *Gebrauchsmusik* of Hindemith and Weill as it does, paradoxically, with the Wagnerian theories that the modern Germans bitterly opposed; it is, moreover, consistent with Partch's criticism of the museum culture of the American concert hall and opera house.

10. Partch, "Some New and Old Thoughts after and before *The Bewitched*" (1955), in *Bitter Music*, 237.

11. Ibid., 238.

12. Ben Johnston, "The Corporealism of Harry Partch," *Perspectives of New Music* 13, no. 2 (1975): 85–97. For additional discussions of Partch's corporeality see Atesh Sonneborn, "Corporeality in the Music-Theatre of Harry Partch" (M.A. diss., University of California, San Diego, 1984), and Kenneth Gaburo, "In Search of Partch's *Bewitched*: Part One, Concerning Physicality," *Percussive Notes Research Edition* 23, no. 3 (March 1985): 54–84.

13. Partch, "Some New and Old Thoughts," in *Bitter Music*, 234–35.

14. Partch, *Genesis of a Music* (Madison: University of Wisconsin Press, 1949), 8. All quotations of *Genesis of a Music* are from this first edition, unless otherwise stated.

15. My thanks to Dean Drummond, composer and director of the New Band ensemble, for allowing me to study these instruments at the State University of New York, Purchase. Kenneth Gaburo noted Partch's heightened awareness of the detailed physical structure and the micro-maintenance of his instruments as an additional aspect of his ultra-corporeality. See Gaburo, "In Search of Partch's *Bewitched*," 78–79.

16. Partch, "The Ancient Magic," in *Bitter Music*, 186.

17. Partch, "Some New and Old Thoughts," in *Bitter Music*, 235.

18. Partch, "Observations on *Water! Water!*," in *Bitter Music*, 248. Here

Partch's inclusive approach to composition brings to mind that of Charles Ives or perhaps the sonic world of Erik Satie and Jean Cocteau's *Parade.*

19. Partch, "No Barriers" (1952), in *Bitter Music,* 181.

20. Ibid., 182.

21. Partch clearly admired the Greek emphasis on physicality in art. It is also likely that he was drawn to ancient Greece by its celebration of homoerotic love. A provocative entry from his musical journal "Bitter Music" suggests that Partch equated the musical exotic with male physical beauty. Having seen the beautiful face of an older man, a Whitmanesque face with "a luxurious beard with pagan curls," Partch remarked: "I know nothing about him—I don't want to—for the looks of him are complete. They are like exotic musics." The entry immediately preceding this one is explicitly concerned with homoerotic love. Partch, "Bitter Music," in *Bitter Music,* 20.

22. Letter from Partch to Emily Coleman of *Newsweek,* 10 December 1955. Collected in the Harry Partch Archive, Special Collections of the Music Library, University of Illinois. All quotations from unpublished Partch materials are with the permission of Danlee Mitchell, Partch's sole executor.

23. Partch, *Genesis of a Music,* 13. Partch also thought that Chinese and ancient Greek musics were similar. See *Genesis of a Music,* 244.

24. Ibid., 12. The modern Greek composer Iannis Xenakis made similar speculations: "Noh, coming as it does from Buddhist chant, it is not improbable that this resemblance comes from a historical relation lost in the centuries of Greco-Buddhism." Quoted in Nouritza Matossian, *Xenakis* (New York: Taplinger, 1986), 146. Xenakis's encounter with Noh influenced the settings of ancient Greek dramas that he completed in the 1960s.

25. Frank Alanson Lombard, *An Outline History of the Japanese Drama* (London: George Allen and Unwin, 1928).

26. Partch, *Genesis of a Music,* 13. Partch was dismissive of early attempts to incorporate exotic musical elements. "We confine our instruments and our repertoire to a few hundred years of Western Europe, and when we do have an oriental instrument, it becomes an idly twanged 'object of art,' or when we are intrigued by an oriental melody, we bring it home to crucify it: 'for violin and piano.'" Partch, "No Barriers," in *Bitter Music,* 182–83.

27. Partch, "A Soul Tormented by Contemporary Music Looks for a Humanizing Alchemy: *The Bewitched,*" in *Bitter Music,* 240.

28. Partch to Barnard Hewitt, 30 August 1959, collected in the Barnard Hewitt Collection, Harry Partch Archive.

29. Partch, *Genesis of a Music,* 8.

30. Ibid., 23.

31. Partch, "Oedipus," in *Bitter Music,* 219.

32. Partch, "Monoliths in Music," in *Bitter Music,* 195. Of course, it is ironic to find Brecht praised for the "integration" of music and drama.

33. From a transcript collected in the Harry Partch Archive of Partch's lecture on 9 July 1971 delivered at the Festival of the Arts of this Century, University of Hawaii, 38–39.

34. *Genesis of a Music,* 38.

35. Partch quoted this statement in *Genesis of a Music,* 39, and in "King Oedipus," in *Bitter Music,* 213. The quotation is from Yeats's *Plays and Controversies* (London: Macmillan, 1923), 183–85.

36. *Genesis of a Music,* 39.

37. Partch wrote in "Bitter Music": "Those are my words too. *I hear with older ears—." Bitter Music,* 33.

38. W. B. Yeats, *Sophocles' King Oedipus, A Version for the Modern Stage* (New York: Macmillan, 1928). For a discussion of the musical settings of Yeats's *King Oedipus* prior to Partch's, see Glenn Watkins, *Pyramids at the Louvre: Music, Culture, and Collage from Stravinsky to the Postmodernists* (Cambridge: Harvard University Press, Belknap Press, 1994), 348. Partch was not the only American composer to set Yeats's plays. Lou Harrison composed Noh-influenced incidental music for Yeats's *The Only Jealousy of Emer* in 1949. See Heidi Von Gunden, *The Music of Lou Harrison* (Metuchen, N.J.: Scarecrow Press, 1995), 98–99. Hugo Weisgall's 1961 opera *Purgatory* was based on Yeats's play of the same title.

39. During this trip Partch also met Katherine Schlesinger, a prominent historian of ancient Greek music and studied her reconstructed kithara. See Partch, "The Kithara" (1941), in *Bitter Music,* 169–73.

40. See both "Bitter Music," 26–27, and "W. B. Yeats" (1941), 165–68, in *Bitter Music.*

41. See Yeats's letters mentioning Partch in Roger McHugh, ed., *Ah, Sweet Dancer: W. B. Yeats, Margot Ruddock* (London: Macmillan, 1970), 26–31.

42. See Partch, "W. B. Yeats," in *Bitter Music,* 167. Actors at the Abbey Theatre recited the solo parts of *King Oedipus* to Partch.

43. Ibid., 167.

44. Partch completed a rescored version of *Oedipus* in 1967.

45. Partch, "The Ancient Magic," in *Bitter Music,* 186.

46. Partch, "Oedipus," in *Bitter Music,* 218.

47. Partch, *Genesis of a Music,* 10.

48. Partch, "King Oedipus," in *Bitter Music,* 214.

49. Partch, "King Oedipus," in *Bitter Music,* 214. When Partch was offered the prospect of having *Oedipus* performed in the ancient theaters of Greece—an opportunity that would have allowed him to follow in the footsteps of Isadora Duncan, whom he admired greatly—he resisted. In a letter to Barnard Hewitt dated 28 December 1965, Partch wrote: "Last week, also, I received a special delivery letter from Rallou Manou, from Athens. She is the head of Choredrame Hellenique, and wants to do Oedipus as a dance drama in the ancient theaters next summer, using tape, and large speakers. I immediately wrote an anguished letter to BMI in New York saying that *tape* is not the way to perform Oedipus in the ancient theaters. Manou wants the music without words, or with Greek words. Heaven give me strength!" Barnard Hewitt Collection, Harry Partch Archive.

50. Partch, "King Oedipus," in *Bitter Music,* 214.

51. From a note to the score, quoted in the libretto for *Oedipus* printed in *Bitter Music,* 270. Partch cited Schoenberg's *sprechstimme* and *Pierrot lunaire* in *Genesis of a Music,* 40–41.

52. In a preliminary description from the mid-1950s of a proposed work entitled "And I'll tell you my story," Partch acknowledged this basic division in his career and indicated that he intended to return to his earlier "intimate" musical conception for this one proposed work. The piece would have been designed to be heard alone as a communication from one male voice to an individual listener through the medium of the phonograph record. This preliminary draft is in the draft materials for *Revelation in the Courthouse Park* at the University of Illinois. (The title of this proposed work, "And I'll tell you my story," also appears in the text of "Bitter Music," in *Bitter Music,* 90.) Partch also noted this division in his career in the preface to the second edition of *Genesis of a Music* (New York: Da Capo Press, 1974): "the step from those somewhat less than epic presentations to the profound Sophocles drama, *Oedipus,* was to me most logical" (vi).

53. Partch, *Genesis of a Music,* 2nd ed., enl., 351.

54. Ibid. Also see note 63 below. Of course, Partch's reluctant solution of vocal separation had been employed earlier in several productions of the Ballets Russes.

55. Reprinted in *Bitter Music,* 445.

56. Ibid.

57. Ibid., 445–46.

58. "*Justice:* An Ethiopian Tale," in *African Voices: An Anthology of Native African Writing,* ed. Peggy Rutherford (New York: Vanguard Press, 1958), 67–68.

59. "Delusion of the Fury" (1965), in *Bitter Music,* 252.

60. However, Japanese culture was referenced to some extent in the act I makeup design created for the 1969 University of California, Los Angeles production. (The costumes employed in this production seem more Korean than Japanese.)

61. William P. Malm, *Japanese Music and Musical Instruments* (Rutland, Vt.: Charles E. Tuttle, 1959), 123.

62. Arthur Waley, *The Nō Plays of Japan* (Rutland, Vt.: Charles E. Tuttle, 1921), 18–19.

63. In the score of *Delusion,* Partch wrote, "it would be theatrically acceptable for a musician, or someone stationed among the instruments, to assume the rather slight singing roles of each principal, becoming a somewhat disembodied voice." See *Bitter Music,* 446.

64. Partch, "Some New and Old Thoughts," in *Bitter Music,* 232. It should be noted that several of these instruments were created by Partch and that, in the context of Partch's entire organological project, the notion of an "exotic instrument" is not entirely relevant.

65. Note in the score, reprinted in *Bitter Music,* 453.

66. Partch, "Introduction to *The Bewitched,*" in *Bitter Music,* 309. Partch may

have derived this characteristic of Noh dance from the following quotation (by Arthur Waley) of Zeami on child performers: "In plays where a lost child is found by its parents, the writer should not introduce a scene where they clutch and cling to one another, sobbing and weeping. . . . Plays in which child-characters occur, even if well done, are always apt to make the audience exclaim in disgust, 'Don't harrow our feelings in this way!'" Waley, *The Nō Plays of Japan,* 29.

67. Waley, *The Nō Plays of Japan,* 48, 50.

68. Will Salmon, "The Influence of Noh on Harry Partch's *Delusion of the Fury,*" *Perspectives of New Music* 22, nos. 1–2 (1983–84): 234.

69. Partch, "Delusion of the Fury," in *Bitter Music,* 252.

70. *Tsunemasa,* in Waley, *The Nō Plays of Japan,* 54.

71. *Atsumori,* in Waley, *The Nō Plays of Japan,* 37–38.

72. In the *Tale of the Heike* version of this story, which would be well known to Noh audiences, the presence of the flute on the dead body of Atsumori elicits a great deal of pathos.

73. Partch had created a similar musical affect with drums and flute in the prologue to *The Bewitched,* a section similarly intended to call forth a spiritual character—in this case, the Witch. Act II of *Delusion* also begins with flute and drums. However, instead of creating music reminiscent of Noh, the drums play more rhythmical patterns, vaguely suggestive of an African idiom.

74. Partch, "Delusion of the Fury," in *Bitter Music,* 252.

75. Partch, *Genesis of a Music,* 9.

76. Partch, "Bitter Music," in *Bitter Music,* 6.

77. Ibid., 12.

78. Partch, "No Barriers," in *Bitter Music,* 182.

79. Reprinted in *Bitter Music,* 446.

80. McHugh, ed., *Ah, Sweet Dancer,* 30.

81. Kristina Nelson, *The Art of Reciting the Qur'an* (Austin: University of Texas Press, 1985), 14.

82. Malm, *Japanese Music and Musical Instruments,* 128. Partch was not alone in his interest in this aspect of Noh. Pierre Boulez, for example, wrote in 1958: "The Greek theatre and the Japanese Noh also provide examples of a 'sacred' language in which archaisms gravely reduce, if they do not entirely abolish intelligibility." Pierre Boulez, *Orientations,* ed. Jean-Jacques Nattiez, trans. Martin Cooper (Cambridge: Harvard University Press, 1986), 181.

83. This may lead to the complete replacement of words with nonverbal vocalisms, a conceptual move that marks something of a full-circle return to the idealistic notion of an Ur-language of pure sound. The escape from verbal expression at moments of highest emotional or religious intensity is also evident in such African vocal performances as the Shona *mbira dzavadzimu* and Ewe laments.

84. Reprinted in *Bitter Music,* 461.

85. Quoted from Partch's description of the prologue on the first of two inserted pages found in *The Bewitched* score, ML1520.P27B5, Music Division, Library of Congress.

86. Partch, "Introduction to *The Bewitched*," in *Bitter Music*, 307.

87. Partch, "A Soul Tormented by Contemporary Music Looks for a Humanizing Alchemy," in *Bitter Music*, 239.

88. Partch, "Plectra and Percussion Dances" (1953), in *Bitter Music*, 228.

89. Partch to Ben Johnston, 13 April 1956, in the Lauriston C. Marshall Collection, folder no. 4, Harry Partch Archive.

90. Partch, "Some New and Old Thoughts," in *Bitter Music*, 238.

91. Ibid.

92. Partch, "Introduction to *The Bewitched*," in *Bitter Music*, 307.

93. Ibid., 311.

94. Ibid.

95. Bob Gilmore, "'A Soul Tormented': Alwin Nikolais and Harry Partch's *The Bewitched*," *Musical Quarterly* 79, no. 1 (spring 1995): 86.

96. This statement is from a circa 1966 recorded interview with Peter Yates preserved as duplicate cassette no. 3 in the Harry Partch Archive.

97. Partch to Eleanor King, 20 February 1957, in the Harry Partch Estate Archive, folder no. 6.

98. Ibid.

99. Partch, "Some New and Old Thoughts," in *Bitter Music*, 236.

100. Partch, "Introduction to *The Bewitched*," in *Bitter Music*, 309.

101. Partch, "Some New and Old Thoughts," in *Bitter Music*, 238.

CHAPTER 13. BITTER RITUALS FOR A LOST NATION

1. These chimes are available from Woodstock Chimes. This chapter appeared in a slightly different form as "Bitter Rituals for a Lost Nation: Partch's *Revelation in the Courthouse Park* and Bernstein's *Mass*," *Musical Quarterly* 80, no. 3 (fall 1996): 461–99.

2. Harry Partch, *Revelation in the Courthouse Park*, 1960, Music Library, University of Illinois, Urbana-Champaign. Partch's notations in the score and the complete text of *Revelation* appear in Harry Partch, *Bitter Music: Collected Journals, Essays, Introductions, and Librettos*, ed. Thomas McGeary (Urbana: University of Illinois Press, 1991), 321–75.

3. In an undated typed introduction to a film screening of *Revelation*, Partch mentioned that he had been pleased with the lighting, the American costumes, and the masks of the first production, but that the set and Greek costumes were "*bad* in terms of *my* concept." (This typescript is found in the Harry Partch Estate Archive, unnumbered folder series, University of California, San Diego folder, at the University of Illinois Music Library.) However, in the circa 1966 recorded interview with Peter Yates, Partch noted "Only once have I really gotten my staging, and that was in *Revelation in the Courthouse Park*." (Quoted from duplicate cassette no. 3 in the Harry Partch Archive.) George Talbot, the designer and technical supervisor for the first production, informed me in a conversation on 6 April 1995 that Partch was realistic concerning the capabilities and resources available at the University of Illinois and was easy to work with.

4. Quoted with permission from an unpublished review of the first performance found at the University of Illinois Music Library, Partch Archive, under "individual folders, Temperley, Nicholas." Temperley also described the work as "a triumph" and "a profound musical experience such as one rarely receives from contemporary music." He stated his strong conviction that he "was witnessing an event that will make musical history."

5. The inclusion of tumbling was inspired, in part, by the outstanding quality of the University of Illinois gymnastics team. Partch wrote *Rotate the Body in All Its Planes,* based on the "Climax of Celebration" music from *Revelation,* for the National Collegiate Gymnastics Championships held at the University on 8 April 1961.

6. Harry Partch to Barnard Hewitt, 30 August 1959. In this letter, Partch referred to *The Bacchae* as "one of the most topical of Greek tragedies." Partch based his libretto on the translations of Theodore Buckley and Gilbert Murray.

7. "Revelation in the Courthouse Park" (1969), in *Bitter Music,* 245. In these statements Partch was certainly prophetic of 1980s Christian rock and its peculiar juxtaposition of sexual appeal and religious devotion.

8. Partch's decision to update an ancient Greek play was not unique. Perhaps the most prominent example from the modernist spoken theater is Eugene O'Neill's 1931 trilogy *Mourning Becomes Electra.* Partch, however, placed more emphasis on the ritual and religious functions of his Greek model.

9. The musical style of these Theban scenes, compared to that heard in the American Choruses, is far more typical of Partch's other compositions and is scored chiefly for his own ensemble of unique instruments. The text setting in these scenes is similar to that found in Partch's *Oedipus.*

10. These descriptions of the three major characters are quoted from "Revelation in the Courthouse Park," in *Bitter Music,* 246. The correspondence between Dion and the name of the 1950s rock singer Dion DiMucci appears to be coincidental. Partch's intended pronunciation of "Dion" is different: Dy-on, rather than Dee-on. It is possible that Partch's choice of the name Dion owes something to O'Neill's Dionysian character, Dion Anthony, in *The Great God Brown* (1926).

11. Partch, "Bitter Music," in *Bitter Music,* 44–45.

12. Ibid., 81.

13. Ibid., 66.

14. Ibid., 66–67.

15. Partch, "Revelation in the Courthouse Park," in *Bitter Music,* 244.

16. Quoted from Partch's undated introduction to a screening of *Revelation,* Harry Partch Estate Archive, unnumbered folder series, University of California, San Diego folder, at the University of Illinois Music Library.

17. Harry Partch to Ben Johnston, 6 May 1955, in the Lauriston C. Marshall Collection, Harry Partch Archive, University of Illinois Music Library.

18. These descriptions are from the preliminary drafts of *Revelation* collected in the individual folder entitled "Partch, Harry/Revelation in the Courthouse Park," Music Library, University of Illinois, Urbana-Champaign. At various

stages in the creation of this work, Partch referred to it as "Revel and Revelation" or as "Dion Isus: A Dance-Fantasy, A Tragi-Comedy."

19. Andrew Stiller, *The New Grove Dictionary of Opera*, Stanley Sadie, ed.
(London: Macmillan, 1992), 896. I should note that Partch's parody is directed
solely against the reactions of women to rock music and that no more stridently
antifeminist plot could have been chosen than that of *The Bacchae*.

20. Quoted from Partch's undated introduction to a screening of *Revelation*,
Harry Partch Estate Archive, unnumbered folder series, University of California, San Diego folder, at the University of Illinois Music Library.

21. Harry Partch to Rodney H. Mill, 17 June 1960. Collected in the Miscella-
neous Manuscripts collection of the Music Division at the Library of Congress.

22. My discussion of mid-century American revivalism is indebted to the
following studies: David Edwin Harrell Jr., *All Things Are Possible: The Healing and Charismatic Revivals in Modern America* (Bloomington: Indiana University Press, 1975); William G. McLoughlin Jr., *Modern Revivalism: Charles
Grandison Finney to Billy Graham* (New York: Ronald Press Company, 1959);
and Patsy Sims, *Can Somebody Shout Amen!* (New York: St. Martin's Press,
1988).

23. Sims, *Can Somebody Shout Amen!*, xvii.

24. Harrell, *All Things Are Possible*, 69.

25. McLoughlin, *Modern Revivalism*, 489–91. One such figure, Stuart
Hamblen—a Los Angeles television personality who led a cowboy-style show—
turned to composing religious-western songs after his conversion in Graham's
tent. In *Revelation*, Partch employed cowboy-western style music for the clog-
dancing sections in this parody of revivalism. Partch's ears were always open to
the music of the western United States, whether that of southwestern Native
Americans or of cowboys. For a study of genuine revivalist songs in the cowboy idiom from the first half of the century see Austin and Alta Fife, *Heaven
on Horseback: Revivalist Songs and Verse in the Cowboy Idiom*, Western Texts
Society Series (Logan: Utah State University Press, 1970).

26. Sims, *Can Somebody Shout Amen!*, xviii.

27. While Elvis is indeed a likely model for Dion, I have found no evidence
to support Andrew Stiller's notion, as expressed in *The New Grove Dictionary
of Opera* (p. 1299) that Partch "greatly admired" Elvis. Elvis, of course, was to
become a cult figure in the Dion mold, particularly after his death.

28. Quoted from Partch's undated introduction to a screening of *Revelation*,
Harry Partch Estate Archive, unnumbered folder series, University of California, San Diego folder, at the University of Illinois Music Library.

29. Quoted from p. 27 of the liner notes to Leonard Bernstein, *Mass*, CBS
M2 31008.

30. "Notes by the Composer," in Leonard Bernstein, *Three Meditations from
"Mass"* (New York: Amberson/Schirmer, 1971).

31. "Leonard Bernstein Discusses His Mass with High Fidelity," *High Fidelity and Musical America* 22, no. 2 (February 1972): 68.

32. I am grateful to Peter Jeffery for guiding me through the extensive lit-

erature on both sides of this debate. I am especially indebted to his *Re-Envisioning Past Musical Cultures: Ethnomusicology in the Study of Gregorian Chant* (Chicago: University of Chicago Press, 1992), 76–86; and to an expanded study of this topic in his unpublished paper "Art Music vs. Folk Song, Myth vs. History: Catholics Debate Gregorian Chant."

33. Johannes Overath, ed., *Sacred Music and Liturgy Reform After Vatican II* (Saint Paul, Minn.: North Central Publishing Company, 1969). See especially the "Resolution on the Use of Profane Music in Worship," 182–84. A clear sign of dissent against the conservative character of the conference is evident in a protest statement circulated at the meeting and reproduced on p. 288 in *Sacred Music and Liturgy Reform After Vatican II*.

34. Innovations in church music had developed first in mission countries, particularly on the African continent. For a discussion of these developments, see Bruno Nettl, "New-Time Religion," in *The Western Impact on World Music: Change, Adaptation, and Survival* (New York: Schirmer, 1985), 100. Later developments in America have included the "Polka Mass" and the "Jazz Mass." For a discussion of the Polka Mass, see Robert Walser, "The Polka Mass: Music of Postmodern Ethnicity," *American Music* 10, no. 2 (summer 1992): 183–202. For discussion of jazz in Catholic worship, see Helmut Hucke, "Jazz and Folk Music in the Liturgy," in *The Crisis of Liturgical Reform*, trans. John Drury (New York: Concilium, 1969), 138–72.

35. "Leonard Bernstein Discusses His Mass with High Fidelity," 70.

36. Ralph Thibodeau, "The Media Is the Mass," *Commonweal* 1 (October 1971): 17–18.

37. Herman Berlinski, "Bernstein's Mass," *Sacred Music* 99, no. 1 (spring 1972): 3–8. Berlinski, a well-known organist and composer of reformed synagogue music, positions himself as a Jewish listener and asks whether Bernstein, as a Jew, had the right to compose a Mass. This article was originally printed in a magazine entitled *Midstream*.

38. Noel Goemanne, "The Controversial Bernstein Mass: Another Point of View," *Sacred Music* 100, no. 1 (spring 1973): 33–36. This issue marked the start of the hundredth year of continuous publication of *Sacred Music*. The column "From the Editor" celebrates this anniversary and refers to the "not so popular stand" that the journal had maintained in light of the "traumatic events that followed the Second Vatican Council in the field of church music." The editor declares: "Sensationalism, defiance of the law of the Church and lowering of musical standards may look attractive for awhile, but are, of necessity, barren detours and ultimately harmful for the spiritual interests of the entire worshipping community. They cannot bring forth good fruits and God's blessing will not be on them" (36).

39. Ibid., 34. As odd as this interpretation of Bernstein's intentions may seem, it is shared by at least one other writer. In his article "Liturgy on Stage: Bernstein's *Mass*," Paul Hume writes: "it is a clear mirror of much that was most disturbing in some parishes in those days." Hume, "Liturgy on Stage," in Steven

Ledbetter, ed., *Sennets and Tuckets: A Bernstein Celebration* (Boston: Boston Symphony Orchestra, Inc., 1988), 61.

40. Goemanne, "The Controversial Bernstein Mass," 35.

41. In a later issue of *Sacred Music* a brief response to this positive interpretation of Bernstein's work appeared in the column "Open Forum." This writer has clearly been offended that words of praise for *Mass* appeared within this conservative journal. He baldly states that with *Mass*, Bernstein committed "an act of desecration by using the most sacred words of our liturgy, the Ordinary of the Mass, as a crutch on which to lean and to give his 'jumble' a very dignified appearance." Frederick O. Beck, "You Cannot Make a Silk Purse Out of a Sow's Ear," *Sacred Music* 100, no. 4 (winter 1973): 32.

42. Bernstein, "Notes by the Composer," in *Three Meditations from "Mass."*

43. "Leonard Bernstein Discusses His Mass with High Fidelity," 68.

44. "Bernstein Talks about His Work," *Time* (20 September 1971): 42.

45. "Notes by the Composer," in *Three Meditations from "Mass."* See also Bernstein's discussion of this passage in "Leonard Bernstein Discusses His Mass with High Fidelity," 69. In another ritual performative gesture, immediately before the Offertory the Celebrant refers to the names of actual cast members in his prayer for the people.

46. William Bender, "A Mass for Everyone, Maybe," *Time* (20 September 1971): 42.

47. Kenneth Auchinclass, "Memorial on the Potomac," *Newsweek* (20 September 1971): 27. Auchinclass mentions that the audience had been more emotionally responsive at the two preview performances than at the formal premiere.

48. "Bernstein Talks About His Work," *Time* (20 September 1971): 42.

49. Paul S. Minear has discussed Bernstein's success in making the Mass modern and relevant for his audience. See Minear, "*Mass:* A Cry for Peace," in *Death Set to Music* (Atlanta: John Knox Press, 1987), 145–59.

50. Here I am in agreement with Joan Peyser's assertion that *Mass* was, in part, an autobiographical work. See Peyser, *Bernstein: A Biography* (New York: Beech Tree Books, 1987), 416–17. Although specific autobiographical clues are less prominent in *Mass* than in his later *A Quiet Place*, a few can be discovered. One possible musical example of such subtle self-reference is Bernstein's signal of sexual ambiguity in the number entitled "I Don't Know," where a high male descant voice sings "What I show isn't real."

51. For a detailed musical analysis of the entire work that attempts to refute the various critical attacks on the music of *Mass* by revealing an underlying organization, see Gary De Sesa, "A Comparison Between a Descriptive Analysis of Leonard Bernstein's *Mass* and the Musical Implications of the Critical Evaluations Thereof" (Ph.D. diss., New York University, 1984). For a study of Bernstein's use of symbolic motives within his religious works, see Jack Gottlieb, "Symbols of Faith in the Music of Leonard Bernstein," *Musical Quarterly* 66, no. 2 (1980): 287–95.

52. Robert Craft, "Non Credo," *New York Review of Books* (7 October 1971):

15–16. Craft also criticized the music for being both predictable and outdated *within* each musical style category represented in the work.

53. For a discussion of the presence of Mahler in Bernstein's *Mass*, see Clytus Gottwald, "Leonard Bernstein's Messe, oder die Konstruktion der Blasphemie," *Melos/NZ* 2 (1976): 281–84. Gottwald hears the final chorus of Mahler's Eighth Symphony in Bernstein's "Almighty Father." In this number, I hear Mahler filtered through the vocal style of Copland's *In the Beginning*.

54. "Leonard Bernstein Discusses His Mass with High Fidelity," 68–69.

55. This explanation has been suggested by Gottwald in "Leonard Bernsteins Messe, oder die Konstruktion der Blasphemie," 281. A similar discussion appears in Helmut Loos, "Leonard Bernsteins geistliche Musik: *Chichester Psalms* und *Mass*," in Reinhold Dusella and Helmut Loos, eds., *Leonard Bernstein: Der Komponist* (Bonn: Boosey & Hawkes, 1989), 105. One example of a contemporaneous work of similar pluralistic intent and compositional design is Dave Brubeck's 1969 *The Gates of Justice*. Although not a work of music theater, and concerned more directly with civil rights than with antiwar protest, *The Gates of Justice* shares a great deal with *Mass*. Both works employ a variety of musical and textual styles within a Catholic religious framework in an attempt to instruct and transform their audience in light of current social problems.

56. Robert P. Morgan, *Twentieth-Century Music* (New York and London: W. W. Norton, 1991), 411. See also chapter 13, "Collage and Quotation," in Elliott Schwartz and Daniel Godfrey, *Music Since 1945: Issues, Materials, and Literature* (New York: Schirmer Books, 1993), 242–62.

57. Glenn Watkins, *Pyramids at the Louvre: Music, Culture, and Collage from Stravinsky to the Postmodernists* (Cambridge: Harvard University Press, Belknap Press, 1994).

58. David Hamilton argued that the list-makers failed to understand the work. Hamilton wrote: "Hardly anyone writing on *Mass* seems to have considered the possibility that Bernstein was using stylistic variety for a conscious purpose, let alone that there is a careful stylistic structure in the work." Hamilton, "Mass and the Press," *High Fidelity and Musical America* 22, no. 2 (February 1972): 75. See also Humphrey Burton, *Leonard Bernstein* (New York: Doubleday, 1994), 407.

59. The setting of these Choruses received Partch's primary musical interest. In a letter to Rodney H. Mill dated 17 June 1960, the day after he completed the composition, Partch wrote: "In effect, the work was completed when I had finished the four Choruses and the Coda. That was the creative part of the job, and it is very good that you realize this. I spent three months on those, only three weeks on the Scenes."

60. Partch, "The Rhythmic Motivations of *Castor and Pollux* and *Even Wild Horses*," in *Bitter Music*, 222. In this article Partch discusses the connections between American popular music and "primitive" music and states that in his use of popular dance rhythms in these pieces he hopes to "*put back*, if I can, the nuance and subtlety" that were lost in the transformation from primitive to popular (223).

61. Partch, "Some New and Old Thoughts after and before *The Bewitched*," in *Bitter Music*, 233. In a section of *Genesis of a Music* entitled "Ennui over the Waves," Partch wrote that ninety-nine percent of radio music was "radio vibrations of frankfurters." He referred to popular music as "an industrialized development of something which small groups of musically leaderless people spontaneously cooked up a few generations ago" and asked whether the nation should stop this music from "turning us into a nation of amusiacs, or admit, frankly, that our kind of democracy means selling music short." Partch, *Genesis of a Music*, 58–59.

62. Partch, "A Soul Tormented by Contemporary Music Looks for a Humanizing Alchemy: *The Bewitched*," in *Bitter Music*, 242.

63. In his *New Grove Dictionary of Opera* entry on *Revelation*, Andrew Stiller also suggests that Partch identified with both Sonny/Pentheus and Dion/Dionysus and that "the irreconcilability of these roles constitutes the heart of the tragedy" (1299). Stiller has also written on *Revelation* in "Rethinking Harry Partch: a 'Revelation' for the '90s," *Musical America* 110, no. 5 (1990): 90–92.

64. Interview of Johnston by Walter Zimmermann in *Desert Plants: Conversations with 23 American Musicians* (Vancouver: ARC Publications, 1976), 355.

65. Johnston, "The Corporealism of Harry Partch," 90.

66. See Friedrich Nietzsche, *The Birth of Tragedy*, trans. Walter Kaufmann (New York: Random House, 1967), 81–82.

67. Martha Nussbaum, introduction to C. K. Williams, *The Bacchae of Euripides* (New York: Farrar, Straus, and Giroux, 1990), xxvi. This introduction is followed by a useful bibliography of works on both the play and on the interpretation of the figure of Dionysus.

68. An informative guide to the interpretive history of this riddle since Nietzsche is available in chapter two of Hans Oranje, *Euripides' Bacchae: The Play and Its Audience* (Leiden: E. J. Brill, 1984), 7–19. Oranje argues for a more generous interpretation of the Pentheus character and concludes that Euripides intended the work to be an ironical discussion of divinity.

69. Geoffrey S. Kirk, *The Bacchae by Euripides: A Translation with Commentary* (Englewood Cliffs, N.J.: Prentice Hall, 1970), 8.

70. Nussbaum, introduction to C. K. Williams, *The Bacchae of Euripides*, xxv. Music, the Dionysian spirit, and social protest are explicitly linked in E. Michael Jones, *Dionysus Rising: The Birth of Cultural Revolution Out of the Spirit of Music* (San Francisco: Ignatius Press, 1994). See particularly his chapter entitled "Sympathy for the Devil: Theodor Adorno, Aleister Crowley, Mick Jagger," 139–89, which includes a discussion of Schechner's *Dionysus in '69*. (Another setting of *The Bacchae*, completed five years after Partch's *Revelation*, was Hans Werner Henze's 1966 *The Bassarids*.)

71. Nussbaum, introduction to C. K. Williams, *The Bacchae of Euripides*, xxv.

72. See Richard Schechner, "In Warm Blood: The Bacchae," in *Public Domain: Essays on the Theatre* (Indianapolis: Bobbs-Merrill, 1969), 93–107.

73. Christopher Innes, *Avant Garde Theatre* (London: Routledge, 1993), 173. The spontaneous participation of audience members at various performances reveals that they were also of two minds about Pentheus and Dionysus. At some performances audience members attempted to block Pentheus from entering the performance space and stopping the orgiastic festivities, going so far as to drag the Pentheus performer out to the street at one performance. During other performances some expressions of sympathy for Pentheus and his tragic fate were evident. On one memorable evening, a female audience member volunteered to have sexual intercourse with Pentheus, signaling his triumph over Dionysus and bringing an end to that particular performance. A fully illustrated guide to the production, including commentary, production anecdotes, and a script containing text from multiple performances, is available in Richard Schechner, ed., *Dionysus in '69: The Performance Group* (New York: Farrar, Straus, and Giroux, 1970).

74. Ben Johnston quoted in Zimmermann, *Desert Plants,* 357. See also Peter Garland, *Americas: Essays on American Music and Culture 1973–1980* (Santa Fe: Soundings Press, 1982), 281; and Johnston, "The Corporealism of Harry Partch," 88.

75. For example, Joan Peyser: "In its most apparent meaning, Bernstein's *Mass* supported the demonstrators and rioters, telling them that they were right and should take matters into their own hands when the authorities were evil and didn't agree with what they thought." Peyser, *Leonard Bernstein: A Biography,* 413.

76. "Leonard Bernstein Discusses His Mass with High Fidelity," 68.

77. An interesting collection of articles on the Berrigans and the impact of their activities on the Catholic Church is found in William VanEtten Casey, ed., *The Berrigans* (New York: Avon Books, 1971).

78. Jack Anderson and George Clifford, *The Anderson Papers* (New York: Random House, 1973), 171–72.

79. Ibid., 172.

80. Burton, *Leonard Bernstein,* 403.

81. Philip Berrigan, *Widen the Prison Gates: Writings from Jails, April, 1970–December, 1972* (New York: Simon and Schuster, 1973), 126–30.

82. Peyser, *Leonard Bernstein: A Biography,* 414.

83. The Bernstein archival material that might possibly shed light on this question is not yet accessible at the Library of Congress.

84. Daniel Berrigan, "Prayer from a Back Pew," in *Love, Love at the End: Parables, Prayers and Meditations* (New York: Macmillan, 1968), 90–91.

85. Daniel Berrigan, "Off Off Off Way Off Broadway," in *Prison Poems* (Greensboro, N.C.: Unicorn Press, 1973), 108. I have been unable to ascertain the date of composition for this poem. However, it appears in this collection immediately before a poem dated 8 September 1971, the date of the premiere of *Mass*.

86. George Zahn, "The Berrigans: Radical Activism Personified," in William VanEtten Casey, ed., *The Berrigans,* 97.

87. Ibid., 97.

CHAPTER 14. GOD IN POPULAR MUSIC(AL) THEATER

1. A parallel trend is evident in jazz of the 1960s, with examples including Duke Ellington's *Sacred Concerts* and John Coltrane's *A Love Supreme*. Dave Brubeck created a series of such works in the 1970s and '80s, which includes his 1980 Mass, *To Hope! A Celebration*.

2. *Godspell*, *Mass*, and *Jesus Christ Superstar* had their first stage productions within months of each other and were consistently compared by their critics. In a 1972 article published in the Catholic journal *World*, Stephen Koch considered the religious significance of all three works. He argued that *Mass* and *Jesus Christ Superstar* were both shallow, flashy shows with little religious substance, but that *Godspell* had spiritual value and was "hands down the best theater the current wave had produced." See Koch, "God on Stage," *World* (12 September 1972): 58–61.

3. Both statements quoted in Joseph Barton, "The Godspell Story," *America* (11 December 1971): 517.

4. Joseph P. Swain, *The Broadway Musical: A Critical and Musical Survey* (Oxford: Oxford University Press, 1990), 277. Swain also notes that although Tebelak's discussions of the work make his religious intentions clear, Schwartz attempted to distance *Godspell* from its religious themes and text. In a personal communication to Swain, Schwartz stated that he considered *Godspell* to be concerned with the more general notion of the need for individuals to form a supportive community transcending religion. See Swain, *The Broadway Musical*, 292.

5. Swain, *The Broadway Musical*, 291. For a similar criticism of act II see Koch, "God on Stage," 61.

6. A contemporaneous theatrical production that had much in common with *Godspell* was the Bread and Puppet Theatre's 1972 *The Stations of the Cross*. This work was initially conceived as an Easter pageant and was performed in a church. The production included the use of masks and giant puppets and was structured musically by the singing of hymns from the *Sacred Heart* collection. This work was based on the group's earlier production entitled *Crucifixion* (1963). In December 1995, the Bread and Puppet Theatre offered a production entitled *Brother Marx Nativity*.

7. Robert P. Ellis, "'Godspell' as Medieval Drama," *America* (23 December 1972): 542–44.

8. Ibid., 544. At least one voice of dissent should be noted. H. Elliott Wright, although initially enthusiastic about the work, came to view it, along with *Jesus Christ Superstar*, as being as much a "searing lampoon" against Christianity as a show devoted to establishing Christianity's relevance to the 1970s. See Wright, "Jesus on Stage: A Reappraisal," *Christian Century* (19 July 1972): 785–86.

9. Michael Walsh, *Andrew Lloyd Webber: His Life and Works* (New York: Abrams, 1989), 61, 64.

10. Walsh notes that some of these performances used parts of the work in

combination with such other shows as *Godspell*. These performances often also included alterations resulting in a more unambiguous pro-Christian message. See Walsh, *Andrew Lloyd Webber,* 73–74.

11. "Like a Prayer," available on *Madonna: The Immaculate Collection,* Warner Reprise Video, 3-38195, videocassette. This video version of the song "Like a Prayer" is not to be confused with the Madonna Pepsi commercial "Make a Wish," which employed the same song and aired to great fanfare the previous day. The controversy stemming from the video "Like a Prayer" forced Pepsi to discontinue the presentation of their commercial, although there was nothing controversial about the commercial's visuals. For an extensive discussion of the commercial, see Nancy J. Vickers, "Maternalism and the Material Girl," in *Embodied Voices: Representing Female Vocality in Western Culture,* ed. Leslie C. Dunn and Nancy A. Jones (Cambridge: Cambridge University Press, 1994), 230–46.

12. Carla Freccero, "Our Lady of MTV: Madonna's 'Like a Prayer,'" *boundary 2* 19, no. 2 (1992): 169, 178.

13. Susan McClary, "Living to Tell: Madonna's Resurrection of the Fleshy," in *Feminine Endings: Music, Gender, and Sexuality* (Minneapolis: University of Minnesota Press, 1991), 163. This article first appeared in *Genders* 7 (spring 1990): 1–21.

14. McClary, "Living to Tell," 161.

15. Ibid., 164.

16. Ibid., 165. Carla Freccero has discussed the historical connections between the African-American and Italian-American communities in the United States as providing a foundation for this video. See Freccero, "Our Lady of MTV."

17. Ronald B. Scott, "Images of Race and Religion in Madonna's Video *Like a Prayer:* Prayer and Praise," in Cathy Schichtenberg, ed., *The Madonna Connection: Representational Politics, Subcultural Identities, and Cultural Theory* (Boulder, Colo.: Westview Press, 1993), 63. Although Scott does consider religious imagery in the video, he interprets it as social criticism—i.e., in terms of racial attitudes and relations rather than in terms of Madonna's religious criticism and expression.

18. Ibid., 62.

19. Ibid., 69–70.

20. Ibid., 62.

21. Scott responds here to what he feels is an overreaction to the interracial physical contact portrayed in the video and argues that this reaction stems from an inherently racist view which assumes that interactions between white females and black males are inescapably based on sexual attraction. Much of Scott's article consists of a detailed description of Madonna's dress, the interracial kiss, and the black statue designed to refute the "erotic" reading presented by Ramona Curry in "Madonna from Marilyn to Marlene—Pastiche and/or Parody?" *Journal of Film and Video* 42, no. 2 (1990): 15–30.

22. Andrew Greeley, *God in Popular Culture* (Chicago: Thomas More Press, 1988), 168. Although this book appeared a year before the release of *Like a*

Prayer, it is not clear whether it had any influence on Madonna's decision to treat her Catholicism as a major theme in that album and in the video of the title song.

23. Ibid., 14.

24. Ibid., 17–18.

25. In his interpretation of Madonna's "Like a Virgin," Greeley does argue against a simply erotic reading. He suggests that it is rather a celebration of "spiritual virginity," a celebration of a respectful and thus sacramental sexual encounter with a man that parallels the "sacrament of Divine passion." Ibid., 164.

26. Andrew M. Greeley, "Like a Catholic: Madonna's Challenge to Her Church," *America* (13 May 1989): 447.

27. Greeley, *God in Popular Culture,* 168.

28. Ibid., 165.

29. Greeley, "Like a Catholic," 449.

30. Greeley, *God in Popular Culture,* 162.

31. Ibid., 168.

CHAPTER 15. MASKING THE HUMAN AND THE MISOGYNY OF MASKS

1. For a discussion of the minimal post-performance conventions of Noh, see Monica Bethe and Karen Brazell, "The Practice of Noh Theatre," in *By Means of Performance: Intercultural Studies of Theatre and Ritual,* ed. Richard Schechner and Willa Appel (Cambridge: Cambridge University Press, 1990), 183–84.

2. Edward Gordon Craig, "Sada Yacco," in *The Theatre Advancing* (London: Constable, 1921), 262.

3. Ibid.

4. Ibid., 265.

5. Ibid., 264.

6. Ibid., 266.

7. Jean Cocteau, *A Call to Order,* trans. Rollo H. Myers (New York: Haskell, 1974), 12. Dreams of gender exclusivity work both ways. In many of Isadora Duncan's writings, it is clear that admission to her ideal artistic temple would be reserved for priestesses of dance.

8. For a discussion of how Euro-American modernists misread Noh and exaggerated the sacred function of the Noh mask, see Mark J. Nearman, "Behind the Mask of Nō," *Mime Journal* (1984): 20–64.

9. An example of this interpretation is found in a 1930 article on Javanese dance written by André Levinson, a Russian émigré who has been referred to as "the first real dance critic." Levinson reported that Javanese dance had once been a sacred form of performance but had become secular and courtly. He wrote: "But more than ever it is compact of duty and obligation; personality abdicates and is abolished," and declared that in modern Javanese dance, "a meticulous protocol supplants the fervor of a religious rite." Levinson did not explain why a religious rite should necessarily involve "fervor" rather than "protocol." For

several inventors of modernist music theater, "protocol" was deemed sufficient for the realization of ritualized performance. See Levinson, "Javanese Dancing: The Spirit and the Form," in *André Levinson on Dance: Writings from Paris in the Twenties,* ed. Joan Acocella and Lynn Garafola (Hanover, N.H.: Wesleyan University Press, 1991), 123.

10. Certain individual exotic performers, such as the Chinese opera celebrity Mei Lanfang, were known and admired by Euro-American modernists. The perceived modesty and self-control of these individuals contrasted favorably with the modernist perception of the self-indulgent diva.

11. Susan Valeria Harris Smith, *Masks in Modern Drama* (Berkeley: University of California Press, 1984),139.

12. Glenn Watkins, *Pyramids at the Louvre: Music, Culture, and Collage from Stravinsky to the Postmodernists* (Cambridge: Harvard University Press, Belknap Press, 1994), 360. In a chapter entitled "Obsessions with Pierrot" (277–309), Watkins discusses the significance—in relation to the human performer—of puppets and of the *commedia dell'arte* for modernism.

13. Ibid., 360–61. Watkins also writes that the modernists employed masks "not as escape mechanisms but as spiritual probes" (310). I would not deny that during the course of an actual performance the performer can circumvent the constraints imposed by the author and the plot. However, I believe that in much modernist music theater, the composer or dramatist actively attempted to circumscribe the agency of the performer and that such modernists were attracted to those exotic traditions in which the performer's personality appeared to be submerged rather than displayed as an object of audience adulation.

14. Quoted in Watkins, *Pyramids at the Louvre,* 119.

15. Kanze Hisao, "Life with the Nō Mask," trans. Don Kenny, *Mime Journal* (1984): 70–71.

16. Ibid., 71.

17. Lydia Goehr, *The Imaginary Museum of Musical Works* (Oxford: Clarendon Press, 1992), 208.

18. For a summary of the literature on the uses of ritual for purposes of social control and the role of ritual in power relationships, see Catherine Bell, *Ritual Theory, Ritual Practice* (Oxford: Oxford University Press, 1992), 171–223. For a very general study that juxtaposes the cultural and political history of this period with the aesthetics of modernist ritual, see Modris Eksteins, *Rites of Spring: The Great War and the Birth of the Modern Age* (London: Black Swan, 1990).

19. In Italy, fascists sought to establish a similar connection to the classical world through performances in the ancient theaters themselves. See Jeffrey T. Schnapp, *Staging Fascism: 18 BL and the Theater of Masses for Masses* (Stanford: Stanford University Press, 1996), 25–30. In the Soviet Union, a full calendar of social rituals and mass performances in celebration of the state and of the revolution was developed. See Christel Lane, *The Rites of Rulers: Ritual in Industrial Society—The Soviet Case* (Cambridge: Cambridge University Press, 1981).

20. Isadora Duncan, "A Meeting with Comrade Podvoisky," in *Isadora Speaks*, ed. Franklin Rosemont (San Francisco: City Lights Books, 1981), 73.

21. Ibid., 75. Duncan ends this article by quoting Podvoisky's challenge to her: "If you want results for your work, go, go alone amongst the people. . . . Teach the people the meaning of your dances. Teach the children. Don't ask for thanks!" (77). With Podvoisky's assistance, Duncan taught her dance to Russian children for several years. See "Come Children, Let's Dance" and "Dancing in the Red Stadium," in *Isadora Speaks*, 81–86.

22. See Richard Taruskin, *Defining Russia Musically* (Princeton: Princeton University Press, 1997), 451–60. For a more general overview of this topic, see Andrew Hewitt, *Fascist Modernism: Aesthetics, Politics, and the Avant-Garde* (Stanford: Stanford University Press, 1993).

23. Theodor W. Adorno, *Philosophy of Modern Music*, trans. Anne G. Mitchell and Wesley V. Blomster (New York: Seabury Press, 1973), 140.

24. Ibid.

25. Ibid., 172.

CHAPTER 16. MUSIC THEATER NOW

1. For one exposition of this view, see Paul Griffiths, "Opera and Music Theater, 1961–1975," in *The Oxford Illustrated History of Opera*, ed. Roger Parker (Oxford: Oxford University Press, 1994), 333–34. Griffiths suggests that the return to opera began around 1972.

2. "Remaking American Opera," in the newsletter of the Institute for Studies in American Music 24, no. 2 (spring 1995): 2. An example of Monk's large-scale operatic works is *Vessel: An Opera Epic* (1971) on the subject of Joan of Arc; the work involved seventy-five performers and required performance in three locations in New York City, including a parking lot.

3. These developments have received a good deal of attention in histories of twentieth-century music. For example, see Eric Salzman, *Twentieth-Century Music*, 3rd ed. (Englewood Cliffs, N.J.: Prentice Hall, 1988), 234–47. Salzman writes: "Performance art and music theater are crossover forms, hybrids descended from the experimental media and theater forms of modernism but incorporating traditional and popular elements within the framework of postmodernism" (238). The works that I have referred to as "music theater," are termed "mixed genre and chamber opera" by Salzman.

4. See Elliott Schwartz and Daniel Godfrey, *Music Since 1945* (New York: Schirmer, 1993), 289–314.

5. On exotic influence in recent music theater, see Mead Hunter, "Interculturalism and American Music," in *Performing Arts Journal* 33/34 (1989): 191–202.

6. I witnessed an abridged version of the work in June 1995 at the Lincoln Center Out-of-Doors Festival and have studied video excerpts of the complete work as performed at the Brooklyn Academy of Music, as well as excerpts contained in *Ancestral Voices*, a documentary film directed by Stephen Barnwell

on the making of *Njinga*. (These videos were made available to me by Pauline Oliveros, who generously discussed the work with me in October 1996.) For a review of the production presented at BAM, see Jon Pareles, "A Tale of Africa's Past That Haunts the Present," *New York Times* (3 December 1993): C 3.

7. See Pauline Oliveros, "Cues," *Musical Quarterly* 77, no. 3 (fall 1993): 379–82.

8. Jann Pasler, "Postmodernism, Narrativity, and the Art of Memory," *Contemporary Music Review* 7 (1993): 24. Of course W. B. Yeats might have imagined that he was involving the "participation of people from other cultures" in his collaboration with Michio Ito.

9. Ibid., 25. Ione and Oliveros view *Njinga* as a perpetual work-in-progress, one that ideally is reshaped through the participation of community members at each performance.

10. K. Robert Schwarz, "'The Cave' Walks, But Doesn't Quack, Like an Opera," *New York Times* (10 October 1993): sec. 2, pp. 31–32.

11. "Jonathan Cott Interviews Beryl Korot and Steve Reich on *The Cave*," notes to Nonesuch 79327-2, p. 11.

12. Ibid., 15.

13. Ibid., 13–14.

14. Reich has said: "*The Cave* really comes out of the documentary footage. Whenever there was a musical or visual question about the piece, the solution was to be found by a still more careful examination of the source material itself." Ibid., 14.

15. Ibid., 16.

16. Steve Reich and Beryl Korot, "Thoughts About the Madness in Abraham's Cave," *New York Times* (13 March 1994): sec. 2, p. 35.

17. "Interview" in notes to Nonesuch 79327-2, p. 17.

18. Ibid., 19.

19. Ibid., 21.

20. The text for this film is based on the actual transcripts from Joan's trial, as were many other dramatizations of Joan's life from this period immediately following her canonization. Similar to Claudel's version (and to *The Lark* of Jean Anouilh/Lillian Hellman), the film is set entirely during Joan's trial and burning. (Artaud appears in this film in the role of a sympathetic priest.)

21. See Amy Gamerman, "The Man Who Gave 'Joan of Arc' Her Voice," *Wall Street Journal* (23 January 1996): A 12.

22. Glass's setting of Cocteau's *La Belle et la bête* was also conceived as a work of music theater. In his interview with Glass reproduced in the liner notes to *La Belle et la bête*, Nonesuch 79347-2, Jonathan Cott states, "Your version of *La Belle et la Bête* seems like a perfect example of Wagnerian *Gesamtkunstwerk*" (19). Glass does not dispute this description: "this is a music-theater experience, not just a film" (20). For me, the use of the term "music theater" to describe this work is a bit of a stretch. Primarily, Glass is providing voice to a silent film—the "theater" aspect enters only in the visible presence of the vocalists and instrumentalists.

23. Although Einhorn's work represents a more innovative use of film in music theater, his music occasionally resembles the vocal style created by Glass in his Cocteau works. The score also contains suggestions of Orff's music, thus making the connection between Orff and minimalism explicit.

24. Notes to *Voices of Light*, Sony Classical 62006, p. 13. Another interesting setting of Joan's heavenly voices is discovered in Otto Preminger's 1957 film of Shaw's *Saint Joan*, with score by Mischa Spoliansky. I quote from the notes to the Capitol Records recording (W865) of the film score: "Spoliansky's score is modern in concept, and unusual in scope. For it combines medieval elements with music that underlines both the Shavian wit and stirring action of the story. The instruments used also make this score an unusual one. The haunting *Saint Joan* theme, which expresses the feelings of Joan when she hears the voices of Saints, features the pipes of Pan, an ancient folk instrument that suggests her peasant origins."

25. Notes to *Voices of Light*, Sony Classical 62006, p. 8. In light of Einhorn's use of Dreyer's film for this feminist opera/oratorio in celebration of Saint Joan, the modernist poet H. D.'s 1928 critique of this particular film will have an ironic ring. H. D. stated that *The Passion of Joan of Arc*, "caused me more unrest, more spiritual forebodings, more intellectual rackings, more emotional torment than any I have yet seen." She criticized Dreyer for his obsessively brutal presentation of Joan's end, for withholding any suggestion of Joan's angelic voices and spiritual triumph, and declared that the film left her "numb and beaten." H. D., "Joan of Arc," in *The Gender of Modernism: A Critical Anthology*, ed. Bonnie Kime Scott (Bloomington: Indiana University Press, 1990), 129–33. Perhaps Einhorn sought, through his music, to provide the spiritual comfort denied the silent Joan by Dreyer.

26. Notes to *Voices of Light*, Sony Classical 62006, p. 6.

Selected Bibliography

Abbate, Carolyn. *Unsung Voices: Opera and Musical Narrative in the Nineteenth Century.* Princeton: Princeton University Press, 1991.

———. "Opera; or, the Envoicing of Women." In *Musicology and Difference,* ed. Ruth Solie. Berkeley: University of California Press, 1993.

Adams, Doug, and Diane Apostolos-Cappadona. *Dance as Religious Studies.* New York: Crossroad, 1990.

Adorno, Theodor W. *Philosophie der Neuen Musik.* Tübingen: J. C. B. Mohr, 1949.

———. *Philosophy of Modern Music.* Translated by Anne G. Mitchell and Wesley V. Blomster. New York: Seabury Press, 1973.

———. *In Search of Wagner.* Translated by Rodney Livingstone. London: Verso, 1991.

Albright, Daniel. *Stravinsky: The Music Box and the Nightingale.* New York: Gordon and Breach, 1989.

Alexander, Peter F. "A Study of the Origins of Britten's 'Curlew River.'" *Music and Letters* 69, no. 2 (April 1988): 229–43.

Alter, Maria P. "Bertolt Brecht and the Noh Drama." *Modern Drama* 11 (September 1968): 122–31.

Amankulor, J. Ndukaku. "The Condition of Ritual in Theatre, An Intercultural Perspective." *Performing Arts Journal* 33/34 (1989): 45–58.

Anderson, Donna K. *The Works of Charles T. Griffes: A Descriptive Catalogue.* Ann Arbor: UMI Research Press, 1983.

———. *Charles T. Griffes: A Life in Music.* Washington, D.C.: Smithsonian Institution Press, 1993.

Anderson, Jack, and George Clifford. *The Anderson Papers.* New York: Random House, 1973.

Anhalt, Istvan. *Alternative Voices: Essays on Contemporary Vocal and Choral Composition.* Toronto: University of Toronto Press, 1984.

Arnott, Peter. *Greek Scenic Conventions.* Oxford: Clarendon Press, 1962.

———. *The Theatres of Japan.* London: Macmillan, 1969.

———. *Public and Performance in the Greek Theatre.* New York: Routledge, 1989.

Artaud, Antonin. *The Theater and Its Double.* Translated by Mary Caroline Richards. New York: Grove Weidenfeld, 1958.

Aslan, Odette, and Denis Bablet, eds. *Le Masque: Du Rite au théâtre*. Paris: Centre National de la Recherche Scientifique, 1985.

Barfoot, C. C., and Cobi Bordewijk, eds. *Theatre Intercontinental: Forms, Functions, Correspondences*. Amsterdam: Rodopi, 1993.

Barthes, Roland. *Empire of Signs*. Translated by Richard Howard. New York: Hill and Wang, 1982.

Bawtree, Michael. *The New Singing Theatre: A Charter for the Music Theatre Movement*. Bristol: The Bristol Press, 1990.

Beckerman, Michael. "The Sword on the Wall: Japanese Elements and Their Significance in *The Mikado*." *Musical Quarterly* 73, no. 3 (1989): 303–19.

Bell, Catherine. *Ritual Theory, Ritual Practice*. Oxford: Oxford University Press, 1992.

Bell, Michael. *Primitivism*. London: Methuen, 1972.

Bellman, Jonathan, ed. *The Exotic in Western Music*. Boston: Northeastern University Press, 1998.

Benedikt, Michael, and George E. Wellwarth, eds. *Modern French Theatre*. New York: E. P. Dutton, 1966.

Berg-Pan, Renata. *Bertolt Brecht and China*. Bonn: Herbert Grundmann, 1979.

Berlinski, Herman. "Bernstein's Mass." *Sacred Music* 99, no. 1 (spring 1972): 3–8.

Berrigan, Daniel. *Love, Love at the End: Parables, Prayers and Meditations*. New York: Macmillan, 1968.

———. *Prison Poems*. Greensboro: Unicorn Press, 1973.

Berrigan, Philip. *Widen the Prison Gates: Writings from Jails, April, 1970–December, 1972*. New York: Simon and Schuster, 1973.

Bethe, Monica, and Karen Brazell. *Dance in the Nō Theatre*. Cornell University East Asia Papers 29. Ithaca: China-Japan Program, 1982.

Blount, Gilbert L. "Britten's Curlew River: A Cultural Composite." *Literature East and West* 16, nos. 1–2 (1971–72): 632–46.

Borchmeyer, Dieter. *Richard Wagner: Theory and Theatre*. Translated by Stewart Spencer. Oxford: Clarendon Press, 1991.

Bornoff, Jack, ed. *Music Theatre in a Changing Society: The Influence of the Technical Media*. Paris: Unesco, 1968.

Borwick, Susan. "Weill's and Brecht's Theories on Music in Drama." *Journal of Musicological Research* 4, nos. 1–2 (1982): 49–67.

Boulez, Pierre. *Orientations*. Edited by Jean-Jacques Nattiez, translated by Martin Cooper. Cambridge: Harvard University Press, 1986.

Bradbury, Malcolm, and James McFarlane, eds. *Modernism: 1890–1930*. Sussex, N.J.: The Harvester Press, 1978.

Brecht, Bertolt. *Brecht on Theatre*. Edited and translated by John Willet. New York: Hill and Wang, 1964.

Brett, Philip. "Britten and Grimes." *Musical Times* 118 (1977): 995–1000.

———. "Britten's Bad Boys: Male Relations in *The Turn of the Screw*." *repercussions* 1, no. 2 (fall 1992): 5–25.

———. "Britten's Dream." In *Musicology and Difference: Gender and Sexu-*

ality in Music Scholarship, ed. Ruth Solie. Berkeley: University of California Press, 1993.

———. "Musicality, Essentialism, and the Closet," and "Eros and Orientalism in Britten's Operas." In *Queering the Pitch: the New Gay and Lesbian Musicology,* ed. Philip Brett, Elizabeth Wood, and Gary C. Thomas. New York: Routledge, 1994.

Bridge, Ursula, ed. *W. B. Yeats and T. Sturge Moore: Their Correspondence, 1901–1937.* London: Routledge and Kegan Paul, 1953.

Briscoe, Marianne G., and John C. Coldewey, eds. *Contexts for Early English Drama.* Bloomington: Indiana University Press, 1989.

Brody, Elaine. *Paris: The Musical Kaleidoscope 1870–1925.* New York: George Braziller, 1987.

Brown, George Mackay. *Magnus.* London: Hogarth Press, 1973.

Bruckberger, Raymond-Léopold. *Madeleine et Judas: Tragédie en Trois Mystères.* River Forest, Ill.: Privately printed, 1956.

Burton, Humphrey. *Leonard Bernstein.* New York: Doubleday, 1994.

Cage, John. "East in the West." *Modern Music* 23, no. 2 (spring 1946): 111–15.

Caldwell, Helen. *Michio Ito: The Dancer and His Dances.* Berkeley: University of California Press, 1977.

Cargill, Oscar, N. Bryllion Fagin, and William J. Fisher, eds. *O'Neill and His Plays.* New York: New York University Press, 1961.

Carpenter, Humphrey. *Benjamin Britten: A Biography.* London: Faber & Faber, 1992.

Casey, William VanEtten, ed. *The Berrigans.* New York: Avon Books, 1971.

Cave, Richard. *Terrence Gray and the Cambridge Festival Theatre.* Cambridge: Chadwyck-Healey, 1980.

Chamberlain, Basil Hall. *Things Japanese.* 5th ed. London: Kegan Paul, Trench, Trubner and Co., 1905.

Chambers, E. K. *The Medieval Stage.* Oxford: Clarendon Press, 1903.

Chase, Gilbert. "Toward a Total Musical Theatre." *Arts in Society* 6, no. 1 (1969): 26–37.

Chiari, Joseph. *Contemporary French Theater: The Flight from Naturalism.* London: Rocklift, 1958.

Cocteau, Jean. *A Call to Order.* Translated by Rollo H. Myers. New York: Haskell, 1974.

Cohen, Gustave. *Études d'histoire du théâtre en France au Moyen-âge et à la Renaissance.* Paris: Gallimard, 1956.

Collins, Fletcher. *The Production of Medieval Church Music-Drama.* Charlottesville: University Press of Virginia, 1972.

Cone, Edward T. *The Composer's Voice.* Berkeley: University of California Press, 1974.

Cook, Susan C. "*Der Zar lässt sich photographieren:* Weill and Comic Opera." In *A New Orpheus: Essays on Kurt Weill,* ed. Kim H. Kowalke. New Haven: Yale University Press, 1986.

———. *Opera for a New Republic: The Zeitopern of Krenek, Weill, and Hindemith.* Ann Arbor: UMI Research Press, 1988.

Cooke, Mervyn. "Britten and Bali." *Journal of Musicological Research* 7, no. 4 (1988): 307–39.

———. "Britten and the shō." *Musical Times* 129 (1988): 231–33.

Cowell, Henry. *New Musical Resources.* New York: Knopf, 1930.

———. *American Composers on American Music.* Stanford: Stanford University Press, 1933.

Craig, Edward Gordon. *The Theatre Advancing.* London: Constable, 1921.

Crowley, Alice Lewisohn. *The Neighborhood Playhouse: Leaves from a Theatre Scrapbook.* New York: Theatre Arts Books, 1959.

Crumrine, N. Ross, and Marjorie Halpin, eds. *The Power of Symbols: Masks and Masquerade in the Americas.* Vancouver: University of British Columbia Press, 1983.

Daly, Ann. *Done into Dance: Isadora Duncan in America.* Bloomington: Indiana University Press, 1995.

Davies, Peter Maxwell. "Pax Orcadiensis." *Tempo* 119 (1976): 20–22.

———. *The Martyrdom of St. Magnus: Libretto.* London: Boosey & Hawkes, 1977.

Debussy, Claude. *Monsieur Croche the Dilettante Hater.* London: Noel Douglas, 1927.

de Cossart, Michael. *Ida Rubinstein (1885–1960): A Theatrical Life.* Liverpool: Liverpool University Press, 1987.

Depaulis, Jacques. *Paul Claudel et Ida Rubinstein: Une collaboration difficile.* Paris: Annales Littéraires de l'Université de Besançon, 1994.

De Sesa, Gary. "A Comparison Between a Descriptive Analysis of Leonard Bernstein's *Mass* and the Musical Implications of the Critical Evaluations Thereof." Ph.D. diss., New York University, 1984.

Diamond, Elin, ed. *Performance and Cultural Politics.* London: Routledge, 1996.

Dietschy, Marcel. *A Portrait of Claude Debussy.* Edited and translated by William Ashbrook and Margaret G. Cobb. Oxford: Clarendon Press, 1990.

Dorn, Karen. *Players and Painted Stage: The Theatre of W. B. Yeats.* Sussex: The Harvester Press, 1984.

Driver, Tom F. *The Magic of Ritual.* San Francisco: Harper, 1991.

Duncan, Isadora. *The Art of the Dance.* Edited by Sheldon Cheney. New York: Theatre Arts, 1928.

———. *Isadora Speaks.* Edited by Franklin Rosemont. San Francisco: City Lights Books, 1981.

DuPree, Mary Herron. "The Art Music of the United States during the 1920s: A Study of the Major Issues in Contemporary Periodical Sources." Ph.D. diss., University of Colorado at Boulder, 1980.

Dusella, Reinhold, and Helmut Loos, eds. *Leonard Bernstein: Der Komponist.* Bonn: Boosey & Hawkes, 1989.

Earls, Paul. "Harry Partch: Verses in Preparation for *Delusion of the Fury.*" *Inter-American Institute for Musical Research Yearbook* 3 (1967): 1–32.

Eksteins, Modris. *Rites of Spring: The Great War and the Birth of the Modern Age.* London: Black Swan, 1990.

Eldredge, Sears. "Jacques Copeau and the Mask in Actor Training." *Mime, Mask, and Marionette* 2, nos. 3–4 (1979–80): 187–230.

Eliade, Mircea. Edited by Diane Apostolos-Cappadona. *Symbolism, the Sacred, and the Arts.* New York: Crossroad, 1985.

Elliott, John R., Jr. *Playing God: Medieval Mysteries on the Modern Stage.* Toronto: University of Toronto Press, 1989.

Ellis, Robert P. "'Godspell' as Medieval Drama." *America* (23 December 1972): 542–44.

Ellis, Sylvia C. *The Plays of W. B. Yeats: Yeats and the Dancer.* New York: St. Martin's Press, 1995.

Emigh, John. *Masked Performance: The Play of Self and Other in Ritual and Theatre.* Philadelphia: University of Pennsylvania Press, 1996.

Engelhardt, Jürgen. *Gestus und Verfremdung: Studien zum Musiktheater bei Strawinsky und Brecht/Weill.* Munich: Emil Katzbichler, 1984.

Evans, Peter. *The Music of Benjamin Britten.* Minneapolis: University of Minnesota Press, 1979.

Eynat-Confino, Irène. *Beyond the Mask: Gordon Craig, Movement, and the Actor.* Carbondale: Southern Illinois University Press, 1987.

Eysteinsson, Astradur. *The Concept of Modernism.* Ithaca: Cornell University Press, 1990.

Farr, Florence. *The Music of Speech.* London: Elkin Mathews, 1909.

Feldman, Martha. "Magic Mirrors and the *Seria* Stage: Thoughts Toward a Ritual View." *Journal of the American Musicological Society* 48, no. 3 (fall 1995): 423–84.

Flickinger, Roy C. *The Greek Theater and Its Drama.* 3rd ed. Chicago: University of Chicago Press, 1926.

Franko, Mark. *Dancing Modernism/Performing Politics.* Bloomington: Indiana University Press, 1995.

Freccero, Carla. "Our Lady of MTV: Madonna's 'Like a Prayer.'" *boundary 2* 19, no. 2 (1992): 163–83.

Fuegi, John. *Brecht and Company: Sex, Politics, and the Making of the Modern Drama.* New York: Grove Press, 1994.

Gaburo, Kenneth. "In Search of Partch's *Bewitched:* Part One, Concerning Physicality." *Percussive Notes Research Edition* 23, no. 3 (March 1985): 54–84.

Gamerman, Amy. "The Man Who Gave 'Joan of Arc' Her Voice." *Wall Street Journal* (23 January 1996): A12.

Garafola, Lynn. *Diaghilev's Ballets Russes.* Oxford: Oxford University Press, 1989.

Garland, Peter. *Americas: Essays on American Music and Culture 1973–1980.* Santa Fe: Soundings Press, 1982.

Gelineau, Joseph. *Voices and Instruments in Christian Worship.* Translated by Clifford Howell. Collegeville, Minn.: The Liturgical Press, 1964.

Gillespie, Don C. "John Becker: Midwestern Musical Crusader." Ph.D. diss., University of North Carolina, 1977.

Gilliam, Bryan, ed. *Music and Performance during the Weimar Republic.* Cambridge: Cambridge University Press, 1994.

Gilmore, Bob. "'A Soul Tormented': Alwin Nikolais and Harry Partch's *The Bewitched.*" *Musical Quarterly* 79, no. 1 (spring 1995): 80–107.

Gishford, Anthony, ed. *Tribute to Benjamin Britten on his Fiftieth Birthday.* London: Faber & Faber, 1963.

Goehr, Lydia. *The Imaginary Museum of Musical Works: An Essay in the Philosophy of Music.* Oxford: Clarendon Press, 1992.

Goemanne, Noel. "The Controversial Bernstein Mass: Another Point of View." *Sacred Music* 100, no. 1 (spring 1973): 33–36.

Gorsky, Susan R. "A Ritual Drama: Yeats's Plays for Dancers." *Modern Drama* 17, no. 2 (June 1974): 165–79.

Gottlieb, Jack. "Symbols of Faith in the Music of Leonard Bernstein." *Musical Quarterly* 66, no. 2 (1980): 287–95.

Gottwald, Clytus. "Leonard Bernstein's Messe oder die Konstruktion der Blasphemie." *Melos/NZ* 2 (1976): 281–84.

Gray, Terrence. *Dance-Drama: Experiments in the Art of the Theatre.* Cambridge: W. Heffer and Sons, 1926.

Greeley, Andrew M. *God in Popular Culture.* Chicago: Thomas More Press, 1988.

———. "Like a Catholic: Madonna's Challenge to Her Church." *America* (13 May 1989): 447–49.

Griffiths, Paul. *Modern Music: The Avant Garde Since 1945.* New York: Braziller, 1981.

———. *Peter Maxwell Davies.* London: Robson Books, 1982.

Grimes, Ronald L. *Beginnings in Ritual Studies.* Washington, D.C.: University Press of America, 1982.

———. *Reading, Writing, and Ritualizing.* Washington, D.C.: The Pastoral Press, 1993.

Hahl-Koch, Jelena, ed. Translated by John C. Crawford. *Arnold Schoenberg—Wassily Kandinsky: Letters, Pictures, Documents.* London: Faber & Faber, 1984.

Haigh, A. E. *The Attic Theatre.* 3rd ed. Revised by A. W. Pickard-Cambridge. Oxford: Clarendon Press, 1907.

Haimo, Ethan, and Paul Johnson, eds. *Stravinsky Retrospectives.* Lincoln: University of Nebraska Press, 1987.

Hall, Michael. *Harrison Birtwistle.* London: Robson Books, 1984.

Harding, James. *The Ox on the Roof: Scenes from Musical Life in Paris in the Twenties.* New York: St. Martin's Press, 1972.

Harich-Schneider, Eta. *A History of Japanese Music.* London: Oxford University Press, 1973.

Harrell, David Edwin, Jr. *All Things Are Possible: The Healing and Charismatic Revivals in Modern America.* Bloomington: Indiana University Press, 1975.

Harrison, Jane. *Ancient Art and Ritual.* New York: Henry Holt and Co., 1913.

Hawkins, Erick. "Erick Hawkins on Masks." *Mime, Mask and Marionette* 1, no. 2 (summer 1978): 107–13.

Hewitt, Andrew. *Fascist Modernism: Aesthetics, Politics, and the Avant-Garde.* Stanford: Stanford University Press, 1993.

Highwater, Jamake. *Dance: Rituals of Experience.* New York: Alfred van der Merck Editions, 1985.

Hindley, Clifford. "Contemplation and Reality: A Study of Britten's 'Death in Venice,'" *Music and Letters* 71, no. 4 (November 1990): 511–23.

———. "Why Does Miles Die?—Britten's *Turn of the Screw.*" *Musical Quarterly* 74, no. 1 (1990): 1–17.

———. "Homosexual Self-affirmation and Self-oppression in Two Britten Operas." *Musical Quarterly* 76, no. 2 (summer 1992): 143–68.

Hisao, Kanze. "Life with the Nō Mask." Translated by Don Kenny. *Mime Journal* (1984): 70–71.

Hoffman, Lawrence A., and Janet R. Walton, eds. *Sacred Sound and Social Change: Liturgical Music in Jewish and Christian Experience.* Notre Dame: University of Notre Dame Press, 1992.

Hoffman, Michael J., and Patrick D. Murphy, eds. *Critical Essays on American Modernism.* New York: G. K. Hall and Co., 1992.

Holloway, Robin. *Debussy and Wagner.* London: Eulenberg Books, 1979.

Howard, Patricia, ed. *Benjamin Britten: The Turn of the Screw.* Cambridge: Cambridge University Press, 1985.

Hume, Paul. "Liturgy on Stage: Bernstein's *Mass.*" In *Sennets and Tuckets: A Bernstein Celebration.* Edited by Steven Ledbetter. Boston: Boston Symphony Orchestra, 1988.

Humphreys, Paul W. "Expressions of *Einverständnis:* Musical Structure and Affective Content in Kurt Weill's Score for *Der Jasager.*" Ph.D. diss., University of California, Los Angeles, 1988.

Hunter, Mead. "Interculturalism and American Music." *Performing Arts Journal* 33/34 (1989): 191–202.

Hyde, H. Montgomery. *The Other Love: An Historical and Contemporary Survey of Homosexuality in Britain.* London: Heinemann, 1970.

Innes, Christopher. *Edward Gordon Craig.* Cambridge: Cambridge University Press, 1983.

———. *Avant Garde Theatre.* London: Routledge, 1993.

James, William. *The Varieties of Religious Experience.* New York: Penguin Classics, 1985.

Japanese Classical Translation Committee, ed. *Japanese Noh Drama: Ten Plays.* Tokyo: The Nippon Gakujutsu Shinkōkai, 1955.

Jeffery, Peter. *Re-Envisioning Past Musical Cultures: Ethnomusicology in the Study of Gregorian Chant.* Chicago: University of Chicago Press, 1992.

Jeffery-Poulter, Stephen. *Peers, Queers, & Commons: The Struggle for Gay Reform from 1950 to the Present.* London: Routledge, 1991.

Jelavich, Peter. *Munich and Theatrical Modernism.* Cambridge: Harvard University Press, 1985.

Johnston, Ben. "The Corporealism of Harry Partch." *Perspectives of New Music* 13, no. 2 (1975): 85–97.

———. "Beyond Harry Partch." *Perspectives of New Music* 22, nos. 1–2 (1983–84): 223–32.

Jones, E. Michael. *Dionysus Rising: The Birth of Cultural Revolution Out of the Spirit of Music.* San Francisco: Ignatius Press, 1994.

Josipovici, Gabriel. *The Lessons of Modernism.* 2nd ed. London: Macmillan, 1987.

Keene, Donald. *Nō: The Classical Theatre of Japan.* Tokyo: Kodansha, 1966.

Kemp, Ian. "Der Jasager: Weill's Composition Lesson." In *A Stranger Here Myself: Kurt Weill-Studien,* ed. Kim H. Kowalke. Hildesheim: Georg Olms, 1993.

Kennedy, Michael. *Britten.* London: J. M. Dent and Sons, 1981.

Kenner, Hugh. *The Pound Era.* Berkeley: University of California Press, 1971.

Kirby, E. T., ed. *Total Theatre: A Critical Anthology.* New York: E. P. Dutton, 1969.

———. "The Mask: Abstract Theatre, Primitive and Modern." *Drama Review* 16, no. 3 (September, 1972).

Kirk, Geoffrey S. *The Bacchae by Euripides: A Translation with Commentary.* Englewood Cliffs, N.J.: Prentice Hall, 1970.

Koch, Stephen. "God on Stage." *World* (12 September 1972): 58–61.

Koritz, Amy. *Gendering Bodies/Performing Art: Dance and Literature in Early Twentieth-Century British Culture.* Ann Arbor: University of Michigan Press, 1995.

Kothari, Sunil. "The Use of Masks in Indian Dances and Dance-Dramas." *World of Music* 22, no. 1 (1980): 89–106.

Kowalke, Kim H. *Kurt Weill in Europe.* Ann Arbor: UMI Research Press, 1979.

Krabiel, Klaus-Dieter. *Brechts Lehrstücke: Entstehung und Entwicklung eines Spieltyps.* Stuttgart: J. B. Metzler, 1993.

Lawler, Lillian B. *The Dance of the Ancient Greek Theatre.* Iowa City: University of Iowa Press, 1964.

Lee, Sang-Kyong. *Nô und europäisches Theater.* Frankfurt: Peter Lang, 1983.

Leims, Thomas. "Mysterienspiel und Schultheater in der japanischen Jesuitenmission des 16. Jahrhunderts." *Maske und Kothurn* 1 (1981): 57–71.

———. "Japan and Christian Mystery Plays: Christian Kōwakamai Reconsidered." In *Contemporary European Writing on Japan,* ed. Ian Nish. Woodchurch: Paul Norbury Publications, 1988.

"Leonard Bernstein Discusses His Mass with High Fidelity." *High Fidelity and Musical America* 22, no. 2 (February 1972): 68–70.

Levinson, André. *André Levinson on Dance: Writings from Paris in the Twenties.* Edited by Joan Acocella and Lynn Garafola. Hanover, N.H.: Wesleyan University Press, 1991.

Liess, Andreas. *Carl Orff.* Translated by Adelheid and Herbert Parkin. London: Calder and Boyars, 1966.

Ling, David Ming-Yüeh. "The Artistic Symbolism of the Painted Faces in Chinese Opera: An Introduction." *World of Music* 22, no. 1 (1980): 72–88.

Locke, Ralph P. "Constructing the Oriental 'Other': Saint-Saëns's *Samson et Dalila.*" *Cambridge Opera Journal* 3, no. 3 (November 1991): 261–302.

Lombard, Frank Alanson. *An Outline History of the Japanese Drama.* London: George Allen and Unwin, 1928.

Lommel, Andreas. *Masks: Their Meaning and Function.* Translated by Nadia Fowler. New York: McGraw-Hill, 1972.

MacKenzie, John M. *Orientalism: History, Theory and the Arts.* Manchester: Manchester University Press, 1995.

Maisel, Edward. *Charles T. Griffes.* New York: Knopf, 1984.

Malins, Edward. *Yeats and Music.* Dublin: Dolmen Press, 1968.

Malm, William P. *Japanese Music and Musical Instruments.* Rutland, Vt.: Charles E. Tuttle, 1959.

———. *Six Hidden Views of Japanese Music.* Berkeley: University of California Press, 1986.

Marchand, Suzanne L. *Down from Olympus: Archaeology and Philhellenism in Germany, 1750–1970.* Princeton: Princeton University Press, 1996.

Matossian, Nouritza. *Xenakis.* New York: Taplinger, 1986.

McClary, Susan. "Living to Tell: Madonna's Resurrection of the Fleshy." In *Feminine Endings: Music, Gender, and Sexuality.* Minneapolis: University of Minnesota Press, 1991.

McGeary, Thomas. *The Music of Harry Partch: A Descriptive Catalog.* Brooklyn: Institute for Studies in American Music, 1991.

McHugh, Roger, ed. *Ah, Sweet Dancer: W. B. Yeats, Margot Ruddock.* London: Macmillan, 1970.

McLaughlin, William G., Jr. *Modern Revivalism: Charles Grandison Finney to Billy Graham.* New York: The Ronald Press Company, 1959.

McPhee, Colin. *A House in Bali.* Oxford: Oxford University Press, 1986.

Mellers, Wilfrid. "Stravinsky's Oedipus as 20th-Century Hero." *Musical Quarterly* 48, no. 3 (1962): 300–312.

———. *Caliban Reborn: Renewal in Twentieth-Century Music.* New York: Harper and Row, 1967.

———. *The Masks of Orpheus.* Manchester: Manchester University Press, 1987.

Messing, Scott. *Neoclassicism in Music.* Ann Arbor: UMI Research Press, 1988.

Mester, Terri A. *Movement and Modernism.* Fayetteville: University of Arkansas Press, 1997.

Miller, Liam. *The Noble Drama of W. B. Yeats.* Dublin: The Dolmen Press, 1977.

Minear, Paul S. *Death Set to Music.* Atlanta: John Knox Press, 1987.

Miner, Earl. *The Japanese Tradition in British and American Literature.* Princeton: Princeton University Press, 1958.

Mishima, Yukio. *Kamen no Kokuhaku* (1949), trans. Meredith Weatherby, *Confessions of a Mask.* New York: New Directions, 1958.

Mitchell, Donald, ed. *Benjamin Britten: Death in Venice.* Cambridge: Cambridge University Press, 1987.

Möller, Dieter. *Jean Cocteau und Igor Strawinsky: Untersuchungen zur Ästhetik und zu "Oedipus Rex."* Hamburg: Karl Dieter Wagner, 1981.

Mordden, Ethan. *Opera in the Twentieth Century: Sacred, Profane, Godot.* New York: Oxford University Press, 1978.

———. *The American Theatre.* New York: Oxford University Press, 1981.

Morgan, Robert P. *Twentieth-Century Music.* New York: W. W. Norton, 1991.

———, ed. *Modern Times: From World War I to the Present.* Music and Society. London: Macmillan, 1993.

Mueller, Richard. "Imitation and Stylization in the Balinese Music of Colin McPhee." Ph.D. diss., University of Chicago, 1983.

Napier, A. David. *Masks, Transformation, and Paradox.* Berkeley: University of California Press, 1986.

Nassour, Ellis. *Rock Opera.* New York: Hawthorn Books, 1973.

Nearman, Mark J. "Behind the Mask of Nō." *Mime Journal* (1984): 20–64.

Nelson, Kristina. *The Art of Reciting the Qur'an.* Austin: University of Texas Press, 1985.

Newman, Elaine Waxgiser. "Hero and Anti-Hero: The Oedipus Tyrannus of Sophocles in Twentieth-Century Music." Ph.D. diss., Case Western Reserve University, 1973.

Nietzsche, Friedrich. *The Birth of Tragedy.* Translated by Walter Kaufmann. New York: Random House, 1967.

Northcott, Brian, ed. *The Music of Alexander Goehr.* London: Schott, 1980.

Nussbaum, Martha. Introduction to C. K. Williams, *The Bacchae of Euripides.* New York: Farrar, Straus, and Giroux, 1990.

Oba, Masaharu. *Bertolt Brecht und das Nô-Theater.* Frankfurt am Main: Peter Lang, 1984.

O'Driscoll, Robert, and Lorna Reynolds, eds. *Yeats and the Theatre.* Niagara Falls: Maclean-Hunter Press, 1975.

Oja, Carol J. *Colin McPhee.* Washington, D.C.: Smithsonian Institution Press, 1990.

———, ed. *Stravinsky in Modern Music (1924–1946).* New York: Da Capo Press, 1982.

Oliveros, Pauline. "Cues." *Musical Quarterly* 77, no. 3 (fall 1993): 373–82.

Oliveros, Pauline, and Fred Maus. "A Conversation about Feminism and Music." *Perspectives of New Music* 32, no. 2 (summer 1994): 174–93.

O'Neill, Eugene. *Marco Millions.* New York: Boni and Liveright, 1927.

———. *The Plays of Eugene O'Neill.* New York: Random House, 1954.

Oranje, Hans. *Euripides' Bacchae: The Play and Its Audience.* Leiden: E. J. Brill, 1984.

Orledge, Robert. *Debussy and the Theatre.* Cambridge: Cambridge University Press, 1982.

Ortolani, Benito. *The Japanese Theatre: From Shamanistic Ritual to Contemporary Pluralism.* Rev. ed. Princeton: Princeton University Press, 1990.

Oshima, Shotaro. *W. B. Yeats and Japan.* Tokyo: The Hokuseido Press, 1965.

Overath, Johannes, ed. *Sacred Music and Liturgy Reform After Vatican II.* St. Paul, Minn.: North Central Publishing Co., 1969.

Palmer, Christopher, ed. *The Britten Companion.* Cambridge: Cambridge University Press, 1984.

Parakilas, James. "The Soldier and the Exotic: Operatic Variations on a Theme of Racial Encounter, I and II." *Opera Quarterly* 10, nos. 2–3 (winter 1993–94; spring 1994): 33–56; 43–69.

Pareles, Jon. "A Tale of Africa's Past That Haunts the Present." *New York Times* (3 December 1993): C3.

Parker, Roger, ed. *The Oxford Illustrated History of Opera.* Oxford: Oxford University Press, 1994.

Partch, Harry. *Genesis of a Music.* New York: Da Capo Press, 1974.

———. *Bitter Music: Collected Journals, Essays, Introductions and Librettos.* Edited by Thomas McGeary. Chicago: University of Illinois Press, 1991.

Pasler, Jann. "Postmodernism, Narrativity, and the Art of Memory." *Contemporary Music Review* 7 (1993): 3–32.

———, ed. *Confronting Stravinsky.* Berkeley: University of California Press, 1986.

Payne, Harry C. "Modernizing the Ancients: The Reconstruction of Ritual Drama 1870–1920." *Proceedings of the American Philosophical Society* 122, no. 3 (June 1978): 182–92.

———. "Rituals of Balance and Silence: The Ideal Theatre of Gordon Craig." *Bulletin of Research in the Humanities* 82 (winter 1979): 424–49.

———. "The Ritual Question and Modernizing Society, 1800–1945—A Schema for a History." *Historical Reflections/Reflexions Historiques* 11, no. 3 (1984): 403–32.

Pernet, Henry. *Mirages du Masque.* Geneva: Éditions Labor et Fides, 1988.

Petit, Jacques, and Jean-Pierre Kempf, eds. *Claudel on the Theatre.* Translated by Christine Trollope. Coral Gables: University of Miami Press, 1972.

Peyser, Joan. *Bernstein: A Biography.* New York: Beech Tree Books, 1987.

Pollard, Alfred W. *English Miracle Plays, Moralities and Interludes.* Oxford: Clarendon Press, 1923.

Pound, Ezra. *Plays Modelled on the Noh.* Edited by Donald C. Gallup. Toledo: Friends of the University of Toledo Libraries, 1987.

Pound, Ezra, and Ernest Fenollosa. *Certain Noble Plays of Japan.* Churchtown: Cuala Press, 1916.

———. *The Classic Noh Theatre of Japan.* New York: New Directions, 1959.

Prevots, Naima. *American Pageantry: A Movement for Art and Democracy.* Ann Arbor: UMI Research Press, 1990.

Pronko, Leonard Cabell. *Theater East and West: Perspectives Toward a Total Theater.* Berkeley: University of California Press, 1967.

Randel, Don, ed. *The New Harvard Dictionary of Music.* Cambridge: Harvard University Press, Belknap Press, 1986.

Reich, Steve, and Beryl Korot. "Thoughts About the Madness in Abraham's Cave." *New York Times* (13 March 1994): sec. 2, p. 35.

Ries, Frank W. D. *The Dance Theatre of Jean Cocteau.* Ann Arbor: UMI Research Press, 1986.

Rimer, J. Thomas, and Yamazake Masakazu. *On the Art of the No Drama: The Major Treatises of Zeami.* Princeton: Princeton University Press, 1984.

Rousses, Jason. "Ancient Greek Tragedy and Noh." *Diotima* 13 (1985): 121–28.

Rubin, William, ed. *Primitivism in Twentieth Century Art: Affinity of the Tribal and the Modern.* New York: Museum of Modern Art, 1984.

Sadie, Stanley, ed. *The New Grove Dictionary of Opera.* London: Macmillan, 1992.

Said, Edward W. *Orientalism.* New York: Pantheon Books, 1978.

———. *Culture and Imperialism.* New York: Knopf, 1993.

Salmon, Will. "The Influence of Noh on Harry Partch's *Delusion of the Fury.*" *Perspectives of New Music* 22, nos. 1–2 (1983–84): 233–45.

Salzman, Eric. *Twentieth-Century Music.* 3rd ed. Englewood Cliffs, N.J.: Prentice Hall, 1988.

Schatt, Peter W. *Exotik in der Musik des 20. Jahrhunderts.* Munich: Musikverlag Emil Katzbichler, 1986.

Schechner, Richard. *Public Domain: Essays on the Theatre.* Indianapolis: Bobbs-Merrill Co., 1969.

———. *Between Theater and Anthropology.* Philadelphia: University of Pennsylvania Press, 1985.

Schechner, Richard ed. *Dionysus in '69: The Performance Group.* New York: Farrar, Straus, and Giroux, 1970.

Schechner, Richard, and Willa Appel, eds. *By Means of Performance: Intercultural Studies of Theatre and Ritual.* Cambridge: Cambridge University Press, 1990.

Schnapp, Jeffery T. *Staging Fascism: 18 BL and the Theater of Masses for Masses.* Stanford: Stanford University Press, 1996.

Schwartz, Elliott, and Daniel Godfrey. *Music Since 1945: Issues, Materials, and Literature.* New York: Schirmer Books, 1993.

Schwarz, K. Robert. "'The Cave' Walks, But Doesn't Quack, Like an Opera." *New York Times* (10 October 1993): sec. 2, pp. 31–32.

Scott, Bonnie Kime. *The Gender of Modernism: A Critical Anthology.* Bloomington: Indiana University Press, 1990.

Scott, Ronald B. "Images of Race and Religion in Madonna's Video *Like a Prayer:* Prayer and Praise." In *The Madonna Connection: Representational Politics, Subcultural Identities, and Cultural Theory.* Edited by Cathy Schichtenberg. Boulder: Westview Press, 1993.

Sedgwick, Eve Kosofsky. *Epistemology of the Closet.* Berkeley: University of California Press, 1990.

Segel, Harold B. *Pinocchio's Progeny: Puppets, Marionettes, Automatons, and Robots in Modernist and Avant-Garde Drama.* Baltimore: Johns Hopkins University Press, 1995.

Sekine, Masaru, and Christopher Murray. *Yeats and the Noh.* Irish Literary Studies 38. Gerrards Cross, Buckinghamshire: Colin Smythe, 1990.

Shalleck, Jamie. *Masks.* New York: Subsistence Press, 1973.

Shead, Richard. *Music in the 1920s.* London: Duckworth, 1976.

Sims, Patsy. *Can Somebody Shout Amen!* New York: St. Martin's Press, 1988.

Smethurst, Mae J. *The Artistry of Aeschylus and Zeami: A Comparative Study of Greek Tragedy and No.* Princeton: Princeton University Press, 1989.

Smith, Susan Valeria Harris. *Masks in Modern Drama.* Berkeley: University of California Press, 1984.

Sonneborn, Atesh. "Corporeality in the Music-Theatre of Harry Partch." M.A. diss., University of California, San Diego, 1984.

Sorell, Walter. *The Other Face: The Mask in the Arts.* London: Thames and Hudson, 1973.

Splatt, Cynthia. *Isadora Duncan and Gordon Craig: The Prose and Poetry of Action.* San Francisco: Book Club of California, 1988.

Spratt, Geoffrey K. *The Music of Arthur Honegger.* Cork: Cork University Press, 1987.

Stegmann, Vera Sonja. *Das epische Musiktheater bei Strawinsky und Brecht.* New York: Peter Lang, 1991.

Steinweg, Reiner. *Das Lehrstück: Brechts Theorie einer politisch-ästhetischen Erziehung.* Stuttgart: J. B. Metzler, 1972.

Stiller, Andrew. "Rethinking Harry Partch: a 'Revelation' for the '90s." *Musical America* 110, no. 5 (1990): 90–92.

Stodelle, Ernestine. *Deep Song: The Dance Story of Martha Graham.* New York: Schirmer Books, 1984.

Stravinsky, Igor. *An Autobiography.* New York: Simon and Schuster, 1936.

———. *Stravinsky: Selected Correspondence.* Edited and with commentaries by Robert Craft. New York: Alfred A. Knopf, 1985.

Stravinsky, Igor, and Robert Craft. *Memories and Commentaries.* Garden City, N.Y.: Doubleday, 1960.

———. *Expositions and Developments.* Garden City, N.Y: Doubleday, 1962.

———. *Dialogues and a Diary.* Garden City, N.Y.: Doubleday, 1963.

Stravinsky, Vera, and Robert Craft. *Stravinsky in Pictures and Documents.* New York: Simon and Schuster, 1978.

Struble, John Warthen. *The History of American Classical Music.* New York: Facts on File, 1995.

Stucki, Yasuko. "Yeats's Drama and the Nō: A Comparative Study in Dramatic Theories." *Modern Drama* 9, no. 1 (May 1966): 101–22.

Swain, Joseph P. *The Broadway Musical: A Critical and Musical Survey.* Oxford: Oxford University Press, 1990.

Tamba, Akira. "Symbolic Meaning of Cries in the Music of Noh." *World of Music* 20, no. 3 (1978): 107–19.

———. "The Use of Masks in the Nō Theatre." *World of Music* 22, no. 1 (1980): 39–52.

Taplin, Oliver. *Greek Tragedy in Action.* Berkeley: University of California Press, 1978.

Taruskin, Richard. "Back to Whom? Neoclassicism as Ideology." *19th-Century Music* 16, no. 3 (spring 1993): 286–302.

———. *Defining Russia Musically.* Princeton: Princeton University Press, 1997.

Tatlow, Antony. *The Mask of Evil: Brecht's Response to the Poetry, Theatre and Thought of China and Japan.* Bern: Peter Lang, 1977.

Taylor, Richard. *The Drama of W. B. Yeats: Irish Myth and the Japanese Nō.* New Haven: Yale University Press, 1976.

Taylor, Timothy Dean. "The Voracious Muse: Contemporary Cross-Cultural Musical Borrowings, Culture, and Postmodernism." Ph.D. diss., University of Michigan, 1993.

———. *Global Pop: World Music, World Markets.* New York: Routledge, 1997.

Terry, Walter. *Isadora Duncan: Her Life, Her Art, Her Legacy.* New York: Dodd, Mead, and Co., 1963.

Thibodeau, Ralph. "The Media Is the Mass." *Commonweal* 1 (October 1971): 17–18.

Thomson, Peter, and Glendyr Sacks, eds. *The Cambridge Companion to Brecht.* Cambridge: Cambridge University Press, 1994.

Thomson, Virgil. *Music with Words: A Composer's View.* New Haven: Yale University Press, 1989.

Torgovnick, Marianna. *Gone Primitive: Savage Intellects, Modern Lives.* Chicago: University of Chicago Press, 1990.

Tosi, Guy. *Claude Debussy et Gabriele d'Annunzio: Correspondance Inédite.* Paris: Denoël, 1948.

Trepanier, Estelle. "The Influence of the Noh on the Theatre of Paul Claudel." *Literature East and West* 15, no. 4 (December 1971): 616–31.

Tsukui, Nobuko. *Ezra Pound and Japanese Noh Plays.* Washington, D.C.: University Press of America, 1963.

Turner, Victor W. *The Ritual Process.* Chicago: Aldine, 1969.

———. *From Ritual to Theatre: The Human Seriousness of Play.* New York: Performing Arts Journal Press, 1982.

———. *The Anthropology of Performance.* New York: Performing Arts Journal Publications, 1987.

Twycross, Meg, and Sarah Carpenter. "Masks in Medieval English Theatre: The Mystery Plays." *Medieval English Theatre* 3, no. 1 (1981): 7–51.

Vickers, Nancy J. "Maternalism and the Material Girl." In *Embodied Voices: Representing Female Vocality in Western Culture,* ed. Leslie C. Dunn and Nancy A. Jones. Cambridge: Cambridge University Press, 1994, 230–46.

Vinton, John, ed. *Dictionary of Contemporary Music.* New York: E. P. Dutton, 1974.

Vogel, Martin. *Musiktheater 1.* Bonn: Verlag für systematische Musikwissenschaft, 1980.

Von Gunden, Heidi. *The Music of Lou Harrison.* Metuchen, N.J.: Scarecrow Press, 1995.

Wagner, Gottfried. *Weill und Brecht: Das musikalische Zeittheater.* Munich: Kindler, 1977.

Wagner, Richard. *Wagner on Music and Drama.* Edited by Albert Goldman and Evert Sprinchorn. Translated by H. Ashton Ellis. New York: Da Capo Press, 1964.

Waley, Arthur. *The Nō Plays of Japan.* Rutland, Vt.: Charles E. Tuttle, 1976.

Walsh, Michael. *Andrew Lloyd Webber: His Life and Works.* New York: Abrams, 1989.

Walsh, Stephen. *Stravinsky: Oedipus Rex.* Cambridge: Cambridge University Press, 1993.

Walton, J. Michael. *Greek Theatre Practice.* Westport, Conn.: Greenwood Press, 1980.

———, ed. *Craig on Theater.* London: Methuen, 1983.

Watkins, Glenn. *Soundings: Music in the Twentieth Century.* New York: Schirmer, 1988.

———. *Pyramids at the Louvre: Music, Culture, and Collage from Stravinsky to the Postmodernists.* Cambridge: Harvard University Press, Belknap Press, 1994.

Weeks, Jeffrey. *Coming Out: Homosexual Politics in Britain from the Nineteenth Century to the Present.* Rev. ed. London: Quartet Books, 1990.

Weisstein, Ulrich. "Cocteau, Stravinsky, Brecht and the Birth of Epic Opera." *Modern Drama* 5, no. 2 (September 1962): 142–53.

Wen-chung, Chou. "Asian Concepts and Twentieth Century Western Composers." *Musical Quarterly* 57, no. 2 (1971): 211–29.

White, Eric Walter. *Benjamin Britten: His Life and Operas.* Berkeley: University of California Press, 1970.

Whitman, Walt. *Walt Whitman: The Complete Poems.* Edited by Francis Murphy. New York: Penguin Classics, 1987.

Whittall, Arnold. *The Music of Britten and Tippett.* Cambridge: Cambridge University Press, 1982.

———. "Twisted Relations: Method and Meaning in Britten's *Billy Budd.*" *Cambridge Opera Journal* 2, no. 2 (1990): 145–71.

Wiles, David. *The Masks of Menander: Sign and Meaning in Greek and Roman Performance.* Cambridge: Cambridge University Press, 1991.

Williams, Simon. *Richard Wagner and Festival Theatre.* Westport, Conn.: Greenwood Press, 1994.

Wirth, Andrzej. "Brecht and the Asiatic Model: The Secularization of Magical Rites." *Literature East and West* 15, no. 4 (December 1971): 601–15.

Wright, H. Elliott. "Jesus on Stage: A Reappraisal." *Christian Century* 89 (19 July 1972): 785–86.

Yates, Peter. *Twentieth Century Music.* New York: Pantheon Books, 1967.

Yeats, W. B. *Ideas of Good and Evil.* New York: Macmillan, 1903.

———. *Four Plays for Dancers.* New York: Macmillan, 1921.

———. *Plays and Controversies.* London: Macmillan, 1923.

———. *Sophocles' King Oedipus: A Version for the Modern Stage.* New York: Macmillan, 1928.

———. *Autobiographies.* London: Macmillan, 1955.

Zimmermann, Walter. *Desert Plants: Conversation with 23 American Musicians.* Vancouver: ARC Publications, 1976.

Zinar, Ruth. "Greek Tragedy in Theater Pieces of Stravinsky and Milhaud." Ph.D. diss., New York University, 1968.

Zuguang, Wu, Huang Zuolin, and Mei Shaowu. *Peking Opera and Mei Lanfang: A Guide to China's Traditional Theatre and the Art of Its Great Master.* Beijing: New World Press, 1981.

Index

Text:	10/13 Aldus
Display:	Syntax Bold
Composition:	Integrated Composition Systems
Printing and binding:	Thomson-Shore